Believers Church Bible Commentary

Elmer A. Martens and Willard M. Swartley, Editors

BELIEVERS CHURCH BIBLE COMMENTARY

Believers Church
Bible Commentary

Ephesians

Thomas R. Yoder Neufeld

HERALD PRESS

Harrisonburg, Virginia

Herald Press
PO Box 866, Harrisonburg, Virginia 22803
www.HeraldPress.com

Canadian Cataloguing-in-Publication Data
Yoder Neufeld, Thomas R.
    Ephesians
(Believers church Bible commentary)
Includes bibliographical references and index.
ISBN 0-8361-9167-6
    1. Bible. N.T.—Ephesians—Commentaries. I. Title. II. Series.
BS2695.53.N48 2001   227'.5077   C2001-903038-X

The translation of Ephesians is by the author (see Schematic Trans. in an appendix), and other Bible text is from *New Revised Standard Version Bible*, copyright 1989 by the Division of Christian Education of the National Council of the Churches of Christ in the USA, and used by permission. Abbreviations identify other versions briefly compared.

BELIEVERS CHURCH BIBLE COMMENTARY: EPHESIANS
© 2002 by Herald Press, Harrisonburg, Virginia 22801. 800-245-7894.
All rights reserved
Library of Congress Control Number: 2001095570
Canadiana Entry Number: C2001-903038-X
International Standard Book Number: 978-0-8361-9167-7
Printed in the United States of America
Cover and charts by Merrill R. Miller

21 20 19 18   10 9 8 7 6 5

To my parents, Abe and Irene Neufeld—
always well dressed in the armor of God

Abbreviations

For other abbreviations in capital letters, see the Bibliography.

*	The Text in Biblical Context (as starred in Contents)
+	The Text in the Life of the Church (as in Contents)
//	parallel to
=	equal, parallel to
adj.	adjective
BAGD	See Bibliography
ca.	circa, about
cf.	compare
chap/s.	chapter/s
e.g.	for example(s)
esp.	especially
et al.	and other(s)
lit.	literally
n.	note
notes	Explanatory Notes in sequence of chapters/verses
GNB/TEV	Good News Bible/Today's English Version
HWB	Hymnal: A Worship Book
KJV	King James Version
LXX	Septuagint, Greek translation of OT
NAB	New American Bible
NASB	New American Standard Bible
NIV	New International Version
NJB	New Jerusalem Bible
NKJV	New King James Version
NRSV	New Revised Standard Version
NT	New Testament
OT	Old Testament
par.	parallel(s)
pl.	plural
[Powers]	typical reference to Essays in an appendix
REB	Revised English Bible
RSV	Revised Standard Version
Schematic Trans.	Author's Schematic Translation, in an appendix
TBC	The Text in Biblical Context
TLC	The Text in the Life of the Church
TRYN	Translation of biblical texts by Thomas R. Yoder Neufeld
v./vv.	verse/verses

Contents

Series Foreword

The Believers Church Bible Commentary Series makes available a new tool for basic Bible study. It is published for all who seek more fully to understand the original message of Scripture and its meaning for today—Sunday school teachers, members of Bible study groups, students, pastors, and others. The series is based on the conviction that God is still speaking to all who will listen, and that the Holy Spirit makes the Word a living and authoritative guide for all who want to know and do God's will.

The desire to help as wide a range of readers as possible has determined the approach of the writers. Since no blocks of biblical text are provided, readers may continue to use the translation with which they are most familiar. The writers of the series use the *New Revised Standard Version*, the *Revised Standard Version*, the *New International Version*, and the *New American Standard Bible* on a comparative basis. They indicate which text they follow most closely, and where they make their own translations. The writers have not worked alone, but in consultation with select counselors, the series' editors, and the Editorial Council.

Every volume illuminates the Scriptures; provides necessary theological, sociological, and ethical meanings; and, in general, makes "the rough places plain." Critical issues are not avoided, but neither are they moved into the foreground as debates among scholars. Each section offers explanatory notes, followed by focused articles, "The Text in Biblical Context" and "The Text in the Life of the Church."

The writers have done the basic work for each commentary, but

11

not operating alone, since "no . . . scripture is a matter of one's own interpretation" (2 Pet. 1:20; cf. 1 Cor. 14:29). They have consulted with select counselors during the writing process, worked with the editors for the series, and received feedback from another biblical scholar. In addition, the Editorial Council, representing six believers church denominations, reads the manuscripts carefully, gives churchly responses, and makes suggestions for changes. The writer considers all this counsel and processes it into the manuscript, which the Editorial Council finally approves for publication. Thus these commentaries combine the individual writers' own good work and the church's voice. As such, they represent a hermeneutical community's efforts in interpreting the biblical text, as led by the Spirit.

The term *believers church* has often been used in the history of the church. Since the sixteenth century, it has frequently been applied to the Anabaptists and later the Mennonites, as well as to the Church of the Brethren and similar groups. As a descriptive term, it includes more than Mennonites and Brethren. *Believers church* now represents specific theological understandings, such as believers baptism, commitment to the Rule of Christ in Matthew 18:15-20 as crucial for church membership, belief in the power of love in all relationships, and willingness to follow Christ in the way of the cross. The writers chosen for the series stand in this tradition.

Believers church people have always been known for their emphasis on obedience to the simple meaning of Scripture. Because of this, they do not have a long history of deep historical-critical biblical scholarship. This series attempts to be faithful to the Scriptures while also taking archaeology and current biblical studies seriously. Doing this means that at many points the writers will not differ greatly from interpretations that can be found in many other good commentaries. Yet these writers share basic convictions about Christ, the church and its mission, God and history, human nature, the Christian life, and other doctrines. These presuppositions do shape a writer's interpretation of Scripture. Thus this series, like all other commentaries, stands within a specific historical church tradition.

Many in this stream of the church have expressed a need for help in Bible study. This is justification enough for the Believers Church Bible Commentary. Nevertheless, the Holy Spirit is not bound to any tradition. May this series be an instrument in breaking down walls between Christians in North America and around the world, bringing new joy in obedience through a fuller understanding of the Word.

—The Editorial Council

Author's Preface

The letter to the Ephesians has been my almost constant companion over the past years of research, teaching, and preaching. My friendship with this document has not cooled. Indeed, I live with a sense of having had the immense privilege of being part of an inspired circle of the friends of Wisdom—a circle encompassing then and now—all listening intently for the Word, pondering it patiently and deeply, with a disposition to make it real in life, and always with worship in the heart and on the tongue.

As Ephesians stresses repeatedly, none of us live in isolation from others. More, our lives are given meaning in *the body* of Christ, who is its peaceable *head*. I'm grateful for the members of this great and diverse body who have accompanied me as I wrote this commentary. My students gave both encouragement and helpful advice. Anne Brubacher, Harold Bauman, and George Shillington, willingly read portions of the commentary and offered indispensable advice along the way. The ever-vigilant Editorial Council had suggestions and sometimes demands that enriched the commentary. The editor, Willard Swartley, consistently offered up a wonderful stew of great patience, insightful advice, and the kind of affirmation that reminded me of what a privilege such an undertaking surely is. Finally, David Garber of Herald Press saw this project to completion with great care.

Anyone who has labored long and hard at a task such as this knows what a debt is owed to one's family. To Rebecca, my companion on the road, and to my children, Miriam and David, I say thanks from the depths of my heart for their interest, patience, love, and support. I pray that some of what I have learned from Ephesians about truth, love, and peace has rubbed off on me as father and husband.

Most especially I thank God for a "burden" that has, for the most part, been "light" (Matt. 11:30).

I dedicate this commentary to my parents, Abe and Irene Neufeld, who home-schooled me in the way of Christ (Eph. 6:4). May this commentary be a small fruit of their faithfulness and diligence.

—Thomas R. Yoder Neufeld

Introduction

PREVIEW

The following commentary is the fruit of having lived with the letter to the Ephesians for many years—reflecting on it, analyzing it, discussing it, preaching it, teaching it, and writing about it. My deep appreciation for this letter has not waned. I am struck by the force of argumentation, by the beauty and power of expression, and by the comprehensiveness of vision. Most of all, I am convinced more than ever of how critically relevant it is to the life of the church today—urbane, cosmopolitan, generous, and at the same time radical and prophetic. I offer this commentary as one more attempt to make sure the church listens to the prompting of the Spirit as it speaks through Scripture.

The following introduction begins with a brief overview of the contents of Ephesians and a discussion of its structure. This is followed by a consideration of special issues and problems that emerge in a careful study of the letter.

OUTLINE

Content and Major Themes of Ephesians

Structure of Ephesians

Ephesians as Enigma

Address, Authorship, Date, and Historical Context

Pastoral and Hermeneutical Considerations

Translation

Other Commentaries

Content and Major Themes of Ephesians

After the initial address or greeting in 1:1-2, Ephesians opens with a eulogy or blessing of God in one sentence that is 12 verses long in Greek (1:3-14). It expresses the central conviction underlying the letter as a whole: the infinitely gracious God has blessed Jews and Gentiles alike in every conceivable way. He has chosen them, made them sons and daughters, and let them in on *the* secret, that in and through Christ, God is gathering up all things, especially all people, into a divine unity (1:10; 4:6).

Usually such telescoping and announcing of central features of a letter are performed by the thanksgiving section in a Pauline letter, which typically follows immediately after the address *[Pauline Letter Structure]* (see the Essays, in the back of the book). Among Pauline letters only 2 Corinthians contains a eulogy or blessing, where it replaces the thanksgiving, serving much the same purpose. But in Ephesians 1:15, we encounter also a thanksgiving section, which can be seen formally to extend to the end of chapter 3. However, the expression of gratitude gives way immediately to a prayer of intercession, or at least to a rehearsal of the content of that intercession, that readers be given wisdom to know what power is at work in them and on their behalf. This power is measured by the power that raised and exalted Christ to the right hand of God, above all powers in the cosmos (1:18-23).

Ephesians 2:1-10 provides a glimpse of what this power has already effected in believers. Those who were *once* dead in sin have *now* been brought to life together with Christ: they have been raised and seated together with him in the heavenly places. Believers have been saved by grace from the control of the evil ruler of the air in order to do *good works* (2:10). The full meaning of *good works* will become clear in the second half of Ephesians.

A lengthy hymnlike celebration of Christ's act of bringing peace follows in 2:11-22. Outcasts and enemies—the Gentiles—have been befriended. They have also been offered citizenship, inclusion in the family of God and more: they have been made building blocks of God's dwelling, his holy temple. Together with Jews, Gentiles have become an integral part of a new humanity reconstituted in the image of the God in whom all things cohere (cf. 1:10, 20-22). At the very center of this act of re-creation is the violent death of Christ. It is this act of ultimate self-giving that nevertheless deals the lethal blow to enmity (2:16).

In chapter 3, Paul appears as the expert guide into the secret of God, here defined as the inclusion of the Gentiles in the people of God. The task of the church, made up now of Jews and Gentiles, is in turn to lead the powers to knowledge of God's infinitely manifold wisdom (3:10). Quite fittingly, this is immediately followed in verses 14-19 by the apostolic prayer of intercession for power and knowledge (cf. 1:17-23), especially the unfathomable love of Christ. The goal is, as in 1:23, nothing less than the fullness of God (3:19). The recitation of the immeasurable blessings of God in the first three chapters concludes appropriately with a flourish of praise (3:20-21).

The second half of Ephesians is largely exhortation *[Pauline Letter Structure]*. The exhortation (paraenesis) begins in 4:1 with a *therefore*. As in Romans 11:33—12:2, the exhortation follows immediately on the heels of a doxology that celebrates the immeasurable grace of God. This is of critical importance: in all of Paul's letters; ethics is first and foremost a *response* to God's blessings. Because God's grace *always* precedes and prepares the ground for human faithfulness (see esp. 2:1-10), the recitation of God's blessings and benefactions *necessarily* calls for a response of active gratitude on the part of the recipients of God's blessings. Just as the first three chapters of Ephesians recite the blessings of God, the last three chapters indicate the response of those who have been blessed. They point to the *good works* (cf. 2:10) the saints are to perform in worshipful gratitude.

The exhortation begins in chapter 4 with a focus on the church. This is appropriate since the first half of the letter has indicated the central importance of the church as the place where God has begun the re-creation of humanity. So chapter four begins with a ringing call for unity in the church (4:1-6). This is followed in verses 7-16 by a clear reminder that the ministry of building up the body of Christ is not the special prerogative of leaders and teachers, but that of all members of Christ's body. Leaders are reminded that their task is first and last to equip the saints to practice this ministry—a ministry that must be seen in light of Christ's peacemaking (see 2:11-22).

No break is intended or even perceived when the author now moves from church to ethics. It becomes apparent that *good works* are what *the new human* does (2:10; 4:24, TRYN). The church is to live the new life, first in relationships within the church, but also in relation to the surrounding world. After all, the new human is being created in the midst of a world that is hostile to it. In Ephesians, ethics means honesty, integrity, and a loving attitude toward others (4:1—5:2). Ethics means turning away from greed and lust and idolatry (5:3-14) and turning toward empowered mutual servanthood (5:15—6:9). This is all finally summed up as the courageous struggle with the *powers* through the exercise of truth, justice, peace, the sharp word of God, and prayer (6:10-20).

The gulf between death and life depicted in chapter 2 is addressed in chapter 5 in the call to separation of light from darkness. However, that call is not a call to disengagement. The harsh dualism of darkness and light is to be overcome by the transformation of darkness into light; confrontation and exposure are intended to bring about transformation (5:11-14). So the dualistic language serves not to remove the children of light from the world of darkness, but rather to hone their sensitivities so that they might become and remain alert and faithful, aware of the transformative task before them. Their nonconformity is to serve the mending of *all things*. The children of light are to be the embodied Christ (cf. 1:23; 2:15), participating in God's work of unifying the world into a reconciled whole (1:10), even if that reconciling and transforming work brings confrontation and division.

It is in such a frame of reference that the Household Code is taken up in 5:21—6:9. In the first century, the household did not refer to a nuclear family nor was its meaning exhausted by the extended family that included servants and slaves. The household was a paradigm for the whole of society. The household instructions fall between the call to be filled with the Spirit (5:18) and the summons to wage war on the powers (6:10-13). This sequence tells us forcefully that in Ephesians the everyday world of human relations is an arena in which light and darkness, good and evil, God and the powers meet.

God's calling and empowerment of the saints *in Christ* (1:19-23; 2:1-10; 3:14-21) finds its full complement at the end of the letter, in an image rooted in the old biblical tradition of God as divine warrior (6:10-20). Only now it is the messianic community—the body of the Messiah—that dons God's armor and enters the fray of battle with the powers resisting God's reconciliation of the world. All knowledge, all power, and all resurrection life are required for such an enterprise (1:17-23; 2:4-8; 3:14-21; 6:10). In this way the final and perhaps most dramatic image of the letter combines the purposes of both parts of the letter. Readers are confronted at once with their elevated status as the elect sons and daughters of God, called to be the body of the Messiah, and with the breathtaking obligations that go with such status. Even as they exercise the often apparently modest virtues of humility, truth, justice, peace, and prayer in the ordinary arenas of everyday life, they are engaged in a cosmic battle *in the heavenlies* (TRYN).

No document in the New Testament puts as much stress on the church as does Ephesians, but it is not the *church* as such that is, finally, the center of the story. First, the church is *in Christ*. That means that it is a messianic phenomenon, inextricable from what *God* intends to do in and for the world. The church, or better "Christ-in-his-church" (R. Martin, 1991:4), is God's means of reclaiming the whole *world*. In the end, that daunting mission provides the larger framework for the repeated stress in this letter on power and empowerment, on Spirit, and on identification with the resurrected Christ.

The overall gist of Ephesians can be summarized as follows: The secret is out! In Christ, God is gathering up all things. God's mercy and grace not only extend forgiveness to sinners. The Creator has also taken the initiative to mend broken humanity by removing enmity and by re-creating humanity anew in Christ. This reclaimed human community is immediately drawn into the process of peacemaking: it has become a new home for insiders and outsiders, for humanity and God. But it is also summoned and empowered to take up the divine struggle against the powers of evil that still thwart the full realization of God's peace, and to do so in the trenches of everyday existence.

Structure of Ephesians

Attempts to categorize Ephesians in terms of known forms of communication in the first century have been frustrating (see, e.g., Best, 1998:59-62). Ephesians begins and ends like a letter, but beyond that, Ephesians conforms only loosely to the form of letters we have come to expect of Paul *[Pauline Letter Structure]*. So some prefer to think of Ephesians less as letter than as homily or sermon. Letters such as Ephesians served a public function. They were written, but they were read aloud and heard by an audience. It should come as no surprise, then, if Ephesians has a certain sermonic quality. Rhetorical and epistolary considerations quite naturally converge.

Ancient theories of public speech make a distinction between two kinds of speech: one, where the speaker tries to strengthen convictions the audience already holds (epideictic), and another, where the author or speaker intends to move the audience to a particular action (deliberative). The rhetorical character of Ephesians conforms to these categories. The first half of the letter, chapters 1–3, is mostly epideictic, rehearsing for the reader or audience the blessings of God. The second half, chapters 4–6, is largely deliberative, challenging readers and hearers to respond to the blessings of God.

Whatever the difficulties of analyzing Ephesians as a letter, we clearly observe that the structure and form of Ephesians conform to the basic line of thought we have outlined above. Holland Hendrix has suggested that Ephesians be considered an "honorific epistolary decree," a public proclamation in which a somber and weighty recital of a great benefactor's gifts are followed by a list of the obligations on the part of the beneficiaries (Hendrix: 9; but cf. Best, 1998:62). The first half of Ephesians thus focuses on the benefactions, the second on beneficiaries' response. Similarly, Ralph Martin proposes that we view Ephesians as "a diptych, a double-facing panel" (1991:46).

What we might call Panel A (chaps. 1–3) consists of an extended thanksgiving section that contains a worshipful celebration of what God has done in and through Christ for the church. Panel B (chaps. 4–6) is the exhortation that prods the church to act accordingly. Making much the same point, Raymond Brown refers to the first half of the letter as the *indicative* section, what *is* the case, given God's blessings; the second half then is the *imperative* section, what *should be* the case, given God's blessings (1997:621-3).

We see further evidence of literary artistry by observing the structure of the first half of Ephesians. Biblical writers frequently constructed passages, both small and large, with matching sets of phrases or sections, sometimes parallel, at other times contrasting. Frequently corresponding sentences or larger units of text were shaped to frame the central emphasis or feature of the text. We call this compositional and rhetorical device *chiasmus* or *chiasm* because it creates a pattern like the Greek letter *chi*, *X* (recent discussion in Breck: 15-70, 333-57; Thomson: 13-45; Geddert: 416-7).

As will be shown in the commentary, Ephesians 2:11-22 is an easily recognizable example of chiasm (Thomson: 84-115; I am less convinced from pages 46-83 that 1:3-10 is a chiasm, or that chapters 5–6 contain obvious chiasms, as claimed by Breck: 267-9, and Lund: 197-206). Indeed, 2:11-22 appears to be the very center of a chiasm, shaping the first half of the letter as a whole. Beginning and ending with praise, a rehearsal of God's making peace with humanity frames a great hymn to Christ as Peace (2:14-18).

The least obvious links in this chiasm are clearly *C-C¹*. Even so, while quite different, both celebrate what has happened for both Jews and Gentiles in Christ. They both reflect on the implications of 1:9-10, the great ingathering through and in Christ. Both do so with particular reference to Jews and Gentiles (in 2:1-10 this is done with *we* and *you*), thus brilliantly framing the central passage of the second half of chapter 2.

These various analytical tools lead to the conclusion that Ephesians is not haphazard in shape and form. Rather, in its two-part structure it expresses a fundamental Pauline, Jewish covenantal, and also Greco-Roman notion: blessings call for gratitude expressed in life, and benefactions demand an appropriate response.

But there is more to such a structure or pattern of exhortation. The benefactor enables the beneficiaries to respond. One of God's blessings is enablement. God makes people capable of performing the tasks to which God calls them. Those who were once dead, rebels under the sway of God's archenemy (2:1-2), have been blessed with adoption (1:4-5), divine citizenship (2:19-22), with a seat in the heavenlies (2:6), and finally, with the ability to perform the *good works* prepared for them (2:10; 4:24).

God has saved those rebels by re-creating them, and God also empowers them in an ongoing way through the abiding gift of divine energy, the Holy Spirit (1:13; 2:18; 3:16; 5:18; 6:18). Most striking, by identifying the beneficiaries with the Benefactor, by integrating them into the body of the Benefactor (e.g., 1:22-23; 2:5, 15; 3:17; 4:15-16; 5:1-2, 30-32), ordinary Jews and Gentiles are themselves drawn into the lofty role of benefactors. Is it any wonder that the first panel ends on a doxology, and the second on a call to take up the divine role of peaceable warrior?

Ephesians as Enigma

Ephesians evokes strong but quite different responses. On the one hand, it has been dubbed "the quintessence of Paulinism" (Bruce, 1984:229). Many appreciate the grand and majestic flow of the letter and the memorable phrases that capture the essence of Paul's formulation of the Christian message (among many, e.g., 2:8, *by grace you have been saved through faith*; 4:4-6, *one body, one Spirit, one hope, one Lord, one faith, one baptism, one God*). One scholar claims that "no part of the New Testament has a more contemporary relevance than the letter to the Ephesians" (R. Martin, 1991:1). It continues to enjoy a favored position in worship, with its imposing vision of the church as the united body of Christ.

Others miss the vibrancy and personal engagement usually found in Paul's letters (e.g., Beker: 109-11). Many experience the style and tone as ornate and ponderous, much like an overworked painting. In recent years, readers sensitive to issues of gender-based injustice have often been troubled by the identification of the relationship of Christ and the church with that of husband and wife in chapter 5, and still others by the militaristic nature of its imagery in chapter 6. Many have thus cooled to this letter, some to the point of antipathy.

At the same time, and with some irony, Christians engaged in peacemaking have found strong support for their work not only in the celebration of Christ as peacemaker in chapter 2, but also in the summons to do battle with the principalities and powers in chapter 6. In short, the reception Ephesians has received is mixed. Could it be that Ephesians is itself somewhat of an enigma?

Ephesians presents the reader with a number of puzzles. First, it is not clear to whom the letter was written (see 1:1, notes). Second, Ephesians conforms only loosely to the structure of Paul's letters; it contains both a blessing and a thanksgiving and then moves immediately to the exhortation *[Pauline Letter Structure]*. Is Ephesians then only apparently a letter? Given the unusually extensive use of hymns and prayers, is it more worship resource than letter? Third, what should one make of the unusual style of long "tapeworm-like sentences" (Lincoln: xlv), overloaded phrases, and overqualified and repetitive nouns? Fourth, there are striking echoes of all the letters in the Pauline collection, with the exception of 2 Thessalonians and the pastoral letters.

Ephesians and Colossians

It is perhaps most puzzling that more than one third of Colossians appears again in Ephesians, even if seldom in exact quotation. As apparent throughout this commentary, there is a very close affinity between Ephesians and Colossians. The vast majority of scholars think Colossians was written before Ephesians and view Ephesians as in some sense dependent on Colossians. (An important recent exception to this broadly held view is Ernest Best, 1998:20-40, who considers the "overlap" between the two instead to reflect common dependency on the shared traditions of a Pauline "school.") The treatment in Ephesians of Christ, church, and eschatology, and of the Household Code, appears to share more with Colossians than with any other letter in the Pauline collection. The relationship of the synoptic Gospels to each other provides a useful analogy for the relationship between these two letters.

However, just as in the case of the synoptic Gospels, similarities also draw attention to important differences. Colossians is seldom reproduced at any length in Ephesians, and shared material also usually receives a distinctive stamp. A few examples: the Christology in Ephesians owes much to that found in the famous hymn in Colossians 1:15-20, with its stress on the lordship and preeminence of Christ. At the same time, in Ephesians it is the *church* that moves to center stage, albeit as Christ's body (cf., e.g., Col. 1:19 and Eph. 1:23; 3:19).

Further, Colossians asserts that Christ created the powers (1:16), that, when rebellious, were defeated and paraded publicly in a victory procession (2:15). By contrast, in Ephesians the powers are still definitely present as hostile forces (2:1-3; 3:10; 6:10-13). In Ephesians the pastoral agenda is less to reassure believers, as in Colossians, than to empower them for conflict with the still-active powers (6:10-20).

As a final example, Ephesians takes the Household Code from Colossians and expands the wife-husband section into a compact meditation on the loving intimacy between Christ and the church (cf. Eph. 5:22-33 and Col. 3:18-19). We should notice, too, that in Ephesians the Household Code is wedged between the call to be filled with the Spirit (5:18-21) and the summons to cosmic battle (6:10-20).

At precisely the points, then, where motifs from Colossians are taken up in Ephesians, we find telling evidence of the special character of Ephesians (for full comparison, see Best, 1998:20-5; Lincoln: xlvii-lviii; Schnackenburg: 30-3; for another view of the relationship between Colossians and Ephesians, see *Colossians*, by Ernest Martin: 27, 284-5).

Ephesians and Paul's Teaching

Is Ephesians an attempt at a distillation or summary of Paul's teaching? Perhaps so. Even then, careful readers will notice some departures from Paul's usual way of addressing issues, even as they will likely disagree on what importance to give to these differences.

A few examples will suffice to illustrate these differences. First, while Paul normally speaks of the church as a local congregation, in Ephesians the church is always a catholic reality, a single universal whole. Has *the church* become the object of reflection in its own right?

Second, Paul usually refers to salvation as something expected in the near future (e.g., Rom. 13:11; 1 Thess. 1:10; 4:13—5:11). In Ephesians, however, salvation, and with it resurrection and exaltation together with Christ, is referred to in 2:4-8 as *already* having taken place. There are only few references to a future event of redemption (e.g., 1:14; 4:30; 5:5), and none explicitly to a return or future appearance of Christ.

Third, Ephesians does not make any mention of justification. Instead of justification by grace (Rom. 3:24), we read of salvation by grace (2:5, 8).

Fourth, in 1 Corinthians 15:20-28, Paul pictures Christ as the divine warrior locked in battle with the powers, but in Ephesians it is the church that is summoned to such a struggle (6:10-18).

Finally, in Galatians 3:28, Paul cites with approval a radical slogan: "There is no longer Jew or Greek, . . . slave or free, . . . male and female; for all of you are one in Christ Jesus." In Ephesians, as in Colossians, however, wives and husbands, children and fathers, slaves and masters are exhorted to live within what appear to be traditional roles of dominance and subordination. Each of these issues receives careful consideration in this commentary.

Address, Authorship, Date, and Historical Context

Considerations such as those listed above have raised some difficult questions for students of Ephesians, especially regarding address, authorship, date, and context. More fully discussed in an essay [Authorship], the questions center on whether we know to whom the letter was sent, when it was sent, and who wrote it.

If Paul was the author of this letter, we should imagine a date late in his missionary career (early 60s, during Roman imprisonment?) [Authorship]. Ephesus is then problematic as an address. Apart from the textual problems in 1:1 (see 1:1-2, notes), chapter 3 implies that Paul is only remotely familiar to his readers, unlikely for a congregation he would have known intimately, after spending several years in Ephesus. We should rather imagine a general letter sent to one or more churches in the area around Ephesus, some of which he would

have known, others perhaps less so. No specific issue emerges explicitly as the reason for writing this letter. Perhaps Paul felt the need
to prepare a final reflective treatise or sermonlike letter, celebrating
God's act of reconciling the world.

If, on the other hand, Ephesians was written after Paul's death
[Authorship; Pseudepigraphy], then the time of writing would fall
late enough to account for the theological and historical developments
it presupposes. But we would also need to place it early enough for
Ephesians to have achieved circulation and acceptance by the time
the bishop Ignatius of Antioch was writing in the first decades of the
second century (he appears to make reference to it in, e.g., the letter To Polycarp 5.1 [Holmes: 197]; Best, 1998:15-6, sifts possible
parallels). A date toward the end of the first century therefore seems
best, reflecting the majority opinion at present (full discussion in Best,
1998:6-20; Kitchen: 1-34; Lincoln: lxxii-lxxiii; Schnackenburg: 33-4).

The absence of an explicit address in the usually most reliable manuscripts still leaves the question of address unexplained (1:1-2, notes).
If Ephesus is unlikely to have been the address of the recipients, some
have suggested the letter's eventual association with Ephesus might
point to that location as the address of the author. Given how long
Paul had worked in Ephesus (Acts 20:31 says three years), that city
may have become a magnet for Pauline study and reflection, a center
for a Pauline "school" (cf. Acts 19:9-10; recently again Brown: 630;
cf. Best, 1998:36-40). This remains at best an educated guess. In the
end it is safest to think of Ephesians as emerging somewhere within
the environs of Paul's mission in Asia Minor and intended for a wide
readership in that orbit.

It has been notoriously difficult to pinpoint what prompted the
writing of Ephesians [Authorship]. Clinton Arnold has gone further
than anyone in proposing the place and the context. In his view of
Ephesians, the emphasis on power and the specific interest in "the
powers" suggests a context in which believers were struggling to come
to terms with magic and astrology. Ephesus was a major center of
such religious activity (1989:5-40; cf. Acts 19). Other scholars are
less sure. They suggest that, given the slender threads tying this letter
to Ephesus, we might look more broadly at the currents of thought
that were affecting Pauline communities throughout the area of his
mission toward the end of the first century (e.g., Best, 1998:63-75;
Lincoln: lxxiii-lxxxvii).

The second half of the first century was a time of great turbu-
lence and change in early Christian communities, not least in Pauline
churches. Christians found various ways of dealing with the ongoing

relevance of the Law, which played a major role in Jewish-Gentile relations in the church. Further, they struggled in diverse ways with the fact that Jesus did not return as soon as or in the way they initially expected. Some prized the salvation that enlightenment and spirituality bring *now;* others anticipated keenly what God would do in the *future.* These and other highly divisive issues left their mark on New Testament writings.

Those who believe Ephesians was written after Paul's death see the marks of these turbulent years clearly imprinted on its pages. First, the relationship of Jews and Gentiles, addressed in 2:11-22 and chapter 3, was a matter of ongoing concern in Pauline churches and thus also of the author of Ephesians. More than likely, most of the readers of Ephesians were Gentile. But Jews too were part of the church community, among whom were the author of Ephesians and no doubt many readers of this letter. It is quite possible that tensions would have been exacerbated by issues of holy living and also by conflicting views on salvation and eschatology (Koester, 1982a:269-70). The Jewish author of Ephesians struggles to help both fellow Jews and Gentiles see themselves as part of one new humanity.

Second, there are many features in Ephesians that appear to reflect what we might, at the risk of oversimplification, call gnostic concerns *[Gnosticism].* Few New Testament writings, with the possible exception of the Gospel of John, place as much value on *knowledge (gnōsis,* as in 1:15-23; 3:14-21). We note also the emphasis on having *already* been saved and raised to the heavenly realms with Christ (2:6). With its stress on awakening from sleep, the short hymn fragment in 5:14 could be sung with enthusiasm in gnostic circles. In the second century, motifs from Ephesians such as *fullness (plērōma,* 1:23; 3:19), *the heavenlies* (e.g., 1:3; 2:6), the descent and ascent of the Savior (4:8-10), *the perfect man* (4:13), and the holy marriage between Christ and believer (5:25-32)—all would find a ready home in gnostic writings.

But, third, there are features in Ephesians that would have been appreciated just as likely by those who held to Paul's apocalyptic teachings *[Apocalyptic].* Note the letter's depiction of the world in darkness and under control of evil powers (e.g., 2:1-3; 6:12), sinners awaiting the wrath of God (5:5-7), the battle against evil cosmic powers (6:10-20), and the anticipation of the day of redemption (4:30). A number of scholars believe they have identified the influence on Ephesians of the apocalyptic views associated with the Dead Sea community at Qumran (e.g., Kuhn; Perkins).

Interpreters of Ephesians often feel obliged to choose one line of interpretation over the other. However, as the following commentary will show repeatedly, to choose exclusively one alternative over another leads to ignoring or downplaying elements that are undeniably present in Ephesians. One should allow for the possibility that the mix of gnostic and apocalyptic elements reflects a melding of perspectives and traditions, both scriptural and Pauline. Emphases often perceived as in tension with each other are forged in Ephesians into a holistic unity in keeping with the peaceable vision underlying the letter as a whole. We should see the author's theology as itself an act of peacemaking—peacemaking as "ingathering" (1:10; Yoder Neufeld, 1993:211-32; but cf. Zerbe).

We thus find in Ephesians profound affirmation for the importance of knowledge and insight, spirit and freedom, resurrection and exaltation. At the same time, this euphoric rehearsal of what is *already* true is set inseparably alongside a sober stress on the corporate and ethical nature of Christian life. Christian existence takes place *in the heavenlies*, but these places evidently extend into the very earthly trenches of everyday social existence (e.g., the Household Code), where the cosmic battle against evil powers is waged. Those tempted to interpret Paul's eschatological teaching as a call to patient waiting in the meantime are confronted with their need to know not only God's *future* salvation. They also need to know and avail themselves of the resurrection power *presently* at work in them, a power that then pushes them into the thick of battle *now already*. There are no bystanders in Ephesians.

The oft-noticed absence in Ephesians of any explicit mention of a future appearing of the Lord should be viewed in the light of this emphasis. Without doubt the author believes in the future culmination of the process of salvation, as implied in the motif of the *gathering up of all things in Christ* (1:10). Further, it is unlikely that Ephesians was ever meant to be read apart from the letters of Paul already in circulation. Those letters unambiguously reflect Paul's expectation of the full coming of the Christ and his kingdom in the future (e.g., 1 Thess. 4:16—5:1; 1 Cor. 15:20-28; Rom. 8:18-25; 13:11-14; cf. also Col. 3:4). The absence of any mention of that arrival would have been quickly noticed in Pauline circles.

Could it be that the author of Ephesians intended to force readers to recognize fully the implications of being the body of the Christ who is *now* present in the world? To sum up, Ephesians would have confronted readers favoring an apocalyptic outlook with what it means *already* to be chosen, called, saved, and empowered, just as the letter would have nudged readers favoring the gnostic view to consider that God still has an *unfinished* agenda with *this* world.

Such issues preoccupied Pauline churches increasingly in the years after his death. Ephesians thus probably reflects an animated dialogue within the Pauline "school" over the implications of the apostolic deposit, to use the thought mode of 1 Timothy (e.g., 1:3; 4:6; 6:20-21), for churches at the close of the first century [Authorship]. In its general nature and reflective quality, as well as in its engagement with the prophetic legacy of the apostle Paul, a letter such as Ephesians is less prophecy than theological reflection on prophecy in a manner akin to the wisdom tradition of Israel [Wisdom]. Ephesians is, for all that, no less inspired. Its ground is *the foundation of the apostles and prophets*, its focal point the *headstone*, Christ, and its edifice the result of the collaborative ministry of the saints (2:20; 4:12-16).

Pastoral and Hermeneutical Considerations

Christians caught up in the warmth of first love or the passion of discipleship will read Ephesians like a charter, especially its image of a church *in Christ* caught up in the struggle with the powers, fully participating in the *gathering up of all things into Christ* (1:10). But most readers of this commentary will be in congregations far removed from such passion, having long ago made accommodation to the perceived needs of the long haul.

If, as proposed, Ephesians reflects Paul's views as transmitted by his follower(s) and also the experience of second- and third-generation believers, then congregations and denominations that show signs of wear should listen especially carefully to this letter. Its radicalism is intended to be a wake-up call to precisely such churches. To draw on the image of the marriage between Christ and the church in chapter 5, one might see Ephesians as an invitation to marriage *renewal*.

This commentary is written from within a particular tradition, the so-called believers church tradition, that has held that the Bible is a call to peace and servanthood. Its view of the church is that of a community of those who have made a conscious decision to follow Christ in life and have been baptized on confession of faith. All baptized members are called to minister in various ways. This commentary respects that tradition and its vision.

Ephesians offers both support and challenge to this tradition. On the one hand, the believers church tradition finds support in the high value placed on baptism as entry into a new life marked by *good works* (chaps. 2 and 4). The cherished emphasis on the costliness of discipleship will find an echo in the call to separation from darkness and the summons to do battle with evil (chap. 6). The central emphasis on Christ as peacemaker is of special interest (chap. 2). On the other hand, both the unalloyed stress on election and divine initiative (chap. 1) and the view of sin as bondage to evil powers (chap. 2) will rub hard against the strong belief in human freedom held widely in believers church circles.

Those uncomfortable with ecumenism may be troubled by the catholicism present in the pervasive emphasis on unity or oneness in Christ (e.g., chap. 4). The more politically and socially radical elements in believers church communities will be troubled by patriarchal and military imagery (chaps. 5 and 6).

Whatever the challenges this letter presents, the core commitment of the believers church tradition to listening to the Bible as the word of God must take precedence over maintaining its traditional interpretations of the Bible. It therefore cannot be the task of this commentary to provide a mirror or a soapbox for believers church perspectives, or to attempt to manage the text so as to make it palatable, or to have it serve a particular agenda, however radical. The task must be to provide access—first to open a way for the biblical text to address the community of faith listening for God's word, and second, to open a way for the community to bring its agenda to the scriptural text (e.g., Swartley, 1983:270-5).

One should not be naive, however. *Every* commentator and *every* reader comes to the text with senses and imagination shaped in and by a culture or community. Insofar as that culture is faithful and attentive to God's reconciling presence in the world, such pre-understanding is one for which one can be thankful. But many Bible students have their imagination and attentiveness conditioned by a culture that has learned to explain reality without God, to be more accepting than suspicious of sin and evil, and to lower its expectations of what it means to be church. Insofar as that has happened, such pre-understanding will be an obstacle to hearing God's word.

The tendency, most often unconscious, will be to tailor the text to already existing needs, desires, and expectations. As commentator and readers, we have no recourse other than to take the prayer of chapters 1 and 3 to be for us. It is a prayer for wisdom and a spirit of revelation so we can grasp the height and depth, the width and length, and most important the love of God in Christ Jesus for us and for the whole cosmos.

Translation

I am aware that the vast majority of the readers of this commentary will use either the NIV or the NRSV translation in their study of the Bible. I do not want to privilege either translation, nor do I want to marginalize those who use another excellent translation (e.g., KJV, NJB, or REB). I have thus furnished my own translation, offered in schematic form in an appendix (Schematic Trans.). I have frequently drawn attention to the NIV and NRSV. No one translation—including the one offered here—is by itself adequate to capture the range and shades of meaning of words and concepts. You will find this commentary most useful if you use your favorite translation alongside the one offered here.

Other Commentaries

Every commentary is in essence the fruit of collaboration between commentator, reader, and text, and also the vast community of students of the biblical text. I am thus deeply indebted to the work of others. The frequent references to other scholars are intended to witness to the communal nature of such an enterprise and to point the reader to other guides and sources of information. I especially commend the technically thorough and theologically insightful commentary by Andrew Lincoln (1990).

The most recent commentary by Ernest Best (1998) is exhaustive and indispensable for a serious engagement with both Ephesians and recent scholarship. His view that Ephesians is solely interested in inner-churchly reality is markedly different from the one taken in this commentary. Markus Barth's imposing two-volume work (1974) is a virtually inexhaustible mine of information and thoughtful reflection. Rudolf Schnackenburg's commentary (1982), translated in 1991, is masterful, not least for its study of the influence of Ephesians throughout Christian history.

Though less technical, the commentaries by Ralph Martin (1991) and Letty Russell (1984) are particularly engaging. Pheme Perkins's commentary (1997) is especially valuable in exploring the points of contact with the Dead Sea Scrolls. I have also gained much from German scholarship, in particular the work of Joachim Gnilka (1971) and Heinrich Schlier (1971; see previous comment on Schnackenburg), but have cited such scholars sparingly. The Bibliography and Selected Resources supply specific information about commentaries and other books and articles useful while studying Ephesians.

Ephesians 1:1–2

Address and Opening Greeting

PREVIEW

Ephesians opens like any other ancient letter: "Sender to Addressee, Greetings!" But, as is typical of Pauline letters, the opening becomes a vehicle for making key assertions about the sender and the addressees. The sender is a messenger of Jesus Christ, commissioned by God. He addresses a community of faithful saints *(holy ones)*. As a greeting, the writer invokes upon them the grace and peace of God the Father and the Lord Jesus.

These features are typical of letters bearing Paul's name. The only real surprise is the difficulty in the first sentence regarding the place name *Ephesus*.

OUTLINE

Greeting, 1:1-2

Addressees, 1:1

EXPLANATORY NOTES

Greeting 1:1-2

Sender and Addressees

From the beginning of his writing career, Paul adapted the typical letter form of his day and culture, including the opening, to suit his apostolic purposes [Pauline Letter Structure]. He intended his letters to be personal but also official communication at the behest of Christ, indeed of God. Ephesians 1:1 is typically Pauline. The author identifies himself as *Paul, an apostle (messenger) of Christ Jesus,* a commission he received *by the will of God.* What follows should therefore be read as carrying the authority of an important messenger—Paul, of the one who sent him—Christ Jesus, and finally of the one whose will it is that he carry that authority—God. So whether it is directly Paul or one of his followers who carries the message we know as the letter to the Ephesians (see Introduction and Essays) [Authorship] [Pseudepigraphy], the letter is to be given the full measure of respect accorded the ultimate sender, God.

Pauline letter openings often include terms or concepts that play an important role in the following letter. So also here. As in Ephesians generally, stock Pauline emphases are treated like windows through which the wondrous mystery of God's grace can be glimpsed.

This letter is addressed to *the holy and faithful ones* (TRYN). *Holy ones* is usually rendered *saints.* The term *holy ones* has taken on a range of meanings over biblical times. Sometimes it refers to members of the heavenly court (for possible allusion to heavenly beings, see 1:18, notes; cf. Deut. 33:2; Ps. 89:5-7; Dan. 7:21), at other times more generally to the people of God. Paul loves to call members of his congregations "holy ones." For Paul the Jew, this was an act of great generosity, given that his audience was predominantly, though not exclusively, Gentile.

After all, the term *holy ones* carries with it connotations of special status, but also of separation and difference: "You shall be holy to me; for I the LORD am holy, and I have separated you from the other peoples to be mine" (Lev. 20:26; cf. Deut. 7:6; 14:2). In chapters 2 and 3, the writer celebrates the Gentiles' inclusion *into* the realm of holiness, the inclusion of those who once defined the limits of holiness by being *outside* its sphere. Those who were once outside the wall now make up the walls of the new holy of holies, as it were (2:19-22).

Faithful (pistos) is a common but loaded term in Pauline usage. The Greek *pistos* can mean *faith-full* as in "believing" (e.g., Acts 10:45; 2 Cor. 6:15; Gal. 3:9; the noun *pistis* is most often translated "faith"). More frequently it means *faithful* as in "trustworthy" and "obedient" (e.g., 6:21; cf. Matt. 25:21; 1 Cor. 4:2; 2 Cor. 1:18; 3 John 1:5). So also the Greek noun *pistis* can mean "faithfulness" (as in, e.g., Rom. 3:3, 22; Gal. 2:16; 1 Tim. 6:11; cf. James 2:14-26). Given the letter's emphasis on *good works* in 2:10 (expanded upon in chaps. 4–6), we should read the phrase here not primarily as "believing in Christ" (as do Best, 1998:95; Lincoln: 6), as true as that is, but as *acting faithfully in and through Christ*.

Being *faithful in Christ Jesus* captures the heart of the vision of this letter. *In Christ* appears in one form or another more than twenty times in Ephesians (regarding *in Christ,* see 1:3-14, notes). Ephesians as a whole might well be seen as a wisdom treatise on the implications of being *in Christ.* This distinctive Pauline idiom expresses the conviction that the life of believers takes place *on the basis of* what God has done *through* Christ, that their actions are thus shaped and empowered *by* that identification, and that their *good works* are *participation in* what God is continuing to do *through* Christ to bring the world to wholeness *["In" (essay)].*

Greeting

In verse 2, instead of the conventional "Greetings!" *(chairein),* the letter pronounces a blessing on the readers: *Grace and Peace! [Pauline Letter Structure].* All of Paul's letters open with this blessing, a majority of them with identical wording. Recognizing it as a stock Pauline greeting does not at all diminish its significance (Mauser: 106-9). *Grace* and *peace* reemerge in the closing blessing as well (6:23-24), and these two blessings frame this letter's profound explorations of *grace* (e.g., 1:6; 2:8; 3:8; 4:7) and *peace* (e.g., 2:14-17; 4:3; 6:15).

The source of the blessing is *God our Father and the Lord Jesus Christ.* This familiar vocabulary again carries great freight. In Ephesians, the term *Father* comes to signify God's relation to creation, care, nurture, salvation, and the bestowal of identity (e.g., 1:3; 2:13; 3:14; 4:6; 5:20).

The divine parent bestows all this on creation and its inhabitants through *the Lord Jesus Christ.* Markus Barth translates *Christ Jesus* in 1:1 and elsewhere in Ephesians as *the Messiah Jesus,* drawing attention to the role of Jesus as the agent of God's reconciliation (Barth, 1974:65). Such a translation also correctly emphasizes that the appellation *Messiah* or *Christ* is fundamentally Jewish. It draws attention to the distinction between God as Father, as divine parent, and Jesus as God's Son, as God's Christ.

Even so, the remarkable degree of identification between God and Messiah in the minds of Paul and his students is indicated in the use of the term *Lord* to refer to the Messiah. *Lord*, the preferred Jewish way of referring to God, is here as elsewhere in the Pauline writings applied to Jesus in immediate proximity to God (in addition to opening and closing blessings/greetings, see 1:3, 17). In short, what is celebrated in the great christological hymns in Philippians 2:6-11 and Colossians 1:15-20 has taken root in the greetings and blessings of early Pauline communities.

Lord is an expression of respect and worship. To call Christ *Lord* also acknowledges fealty (intense fidelity) to him. In addition, to identify Christ as the source of grace and peace means pledging oneself to respond appropriately to that gift, to be faithful to and through that Lord.

Addressees 1:1

Ephesians 1:1 presents us with some difficulties. First, the usually most reliable manuscripts (codices Sinaiticus and Vaticanus, as well as Papyrus 46, the earliest known collection of Paul's letters) do not contain a place name at all. Did the letter originally not have a specific address? That would fit the popular hypothesis that this was not a letter to a specific place but an encyclical, a circular letter intended from the outset to present Pauline teaching to a wider circle of churches (Introduction).

The grammar, however, appears to demand a place name. In Paul's letters, the words *who are (tois ousin)* are always followed by an address: ". . . in [place name]" (e.g., Rom. 1:7; 2 Cor. 1:1; Phil. 1:1). Could it originally have been *in Ephesus*, as the majority of manuscripts read? The problem is that in this letter it appears that Paul's readers did not know him well (3:1-7; cf. 1:15). That hardly fits Ephesus, where he had spent three years (Acts 20:31; cf. 19:1-22). Of course, if the letter was written some decades *after* Paul's death, then it is possible that the Ephesians needed a reminder of their great apostle and his teaching.

Ephesus as address makes most sense, then, if the letter was written a considerable time after Paul's death. Even so, the place name may have been suggested by Paul's long association with Ephesus, or perhaps because Tychicus, the bearer of this letter, was identified with Ephesus (6:21-22; 2 Tim. 4:12; Perkins: 34).

An alternative suggestion, made already by Bishop Usher in 1654, is that the place name was left blank and that addresses were inserted as required, perhaps by Tychicus. In the mid-second century, for example, Marcion seems to have known the letter as addressed to Laodicea. A major difficulty with this otherwise attractive theory is that we have no other examples that encyclicals of the time were handled in such a way.

Even if we grant such a hypothesis, a puzzle remains regarding the verbal sequence *who are and* (see Schematic Trans.). One solution has been to translate *and* as meaning *also* (RSV: *to the saints **who are also** faithful*) But are not saints already faithful by virtue of being holy? Some translators simply do not bother with the conjunction (e.g., NIV: *to the saints in Ephesus, the faithful in Christ Jesus*).

Andrew Lincoln proposes that there was originally not one place name but two, in which case the conjunction *and (kai)* would combine two place names (Lincoln: 1-4, in some dependency on van Roon: 72-85). Taking into account the heavy dependency of Ephesians on Colossians, he suggests that Ephesians might have been sent originally to Laodicea and Hierapolis. (Colossians 4:13 says Epaphras worked in both places.) The original text of 1:1 would then have read, *To the holy ones who are [in Hierapolis] and [in Laodicea], faithful in Christ Jesus.* The place names would later have been deleted when apostolic letters were receiving wide circulation. (Some manuscripts delete "Rome" from Romans 1:7, 15, for example, suggesting that the same thing might have happened to that most general of Paul's undisputed letters.)

This is only one attempt among many to explain the peculiarities of the grammar and textual history of 1:1 (for critique of proposals from Lincoln and others, see Best, 1998:99-100; 1997:1-24). However we explain the data, they point to the fact that this letter was viewed from the beginning as having relevance well beyond any specific group of readers. Ephesians is a letter for the church.

Ephesians 1:3-14

Opening Worship: "Ever Blessing, Ever Bless'd"

PREVIEW

Imagine this letter being read again and again in the context of gathered worship. No sooner has the author introduced himself than the audience is swept up in an act of grateful worship. With the exception of the blessing which opens 2 Corinthians (1:3-7), Paul's letters typically begin with thanksgiving *[Pauline Letter Structure]*. Ephesians, however, contains both. It begins with an extended blessing, an act of corporate worship. A thanksgiving follows immediately in verse 15. This alone should alert us to the weight that the author gives to this opening blessing or eulogy, as it is sometimes called. God is blessed for blessing us, or as the hymn states so succinctly, "Thou art . . . ever blessing, ever bless'd" (Henry van Dyke, "Joyful, Joyful, We Adore Thee," *HWB*, 71).

The blessing is lengthy and comprehensive. God is blessed for having blessed the chosen through Jesus Christ. Chosen before creation, the elect have been granted redemption, forgiveness of sin, salvation, and an inheritance guaranteed by the Spirit of God. The purpose of their election is to live for the praise of God's glory. But the elect are only one part of God's comprehensive plan *to gather up all things* in the cosmos *in and through Christ*. The scope of God's saving pas-

36

sion reaches to the edges of space and time, and beyond. Verse 10 is without doubt the key to understanding the cosmic vision shaping this letter.

These verses are not easy to read in the original Greek. Lengthy cumbersome phrases, weighed down with chains of synonyms and nouns qualified by overloaded adjectives, are fused into one long sentence that carries the immense freight of most of the great themes of this letter. Ironically, one gets the distinct impression that the author is more than aware that language, even when pushed to its limits, is inadequate to do more than weakly express the wonder of God's love and care for the cosmos and its inhabitants. Understatement would be out of character for such a euphoric blessing.

Translators as well as the editors of the Greek text have broken the difficult sentence up into several shorter sentences so that we will not get lost in the maze. The NRSV, for example, renders the section in six sentences, the NIV in eight. A price is paid for this ease of reading, however. We lose the experience of reading or hearing the passage as one long, unbroken, deliberately exhausting recitation of how God has blessed us. The sentence breaks rob us of the experience of running out of breath as we bless God.

An outline of this section should reflect the grammatical character of this remarkable sentence. Three main participles—*having blessed* (or *who has blessed*, 1:3), *having predestined* (1:5), *having made known* (1:9)—are the subheadings under which God's many blessings are rehearsed. With recurring phrases referring to God's *pleasure*, attention is drawn to God's preeminence as first and last actor (1:5, 9, 11). Further, the frequent equivalent phrases *in Christ*, *in him*, and *in whom* help shape the passage by indicating that Christ is the one *through whom* God acts. Specific attention is drawn to Christ's blood as means of redemption (1:7). God's blessing is guaranteed by the Spirit (1:3, 13-14). The recurring *to* (or *for*) *the praise of his glory* (1:6, 12, 14) identifies the purpose of God's call—the worship of God expressed in holy living (1:4).

The following skeletal outline provides indentations that show recurring phrases and emphases as well as grammatical dependency.

Structure of 1:3-14

BLESSED BE GOD the Father,
 who blessed us . . .   *in Christ*
  just as he chose us . . . *in him,*
 who predestined us . . . *through Jesus Christ*
  for adoption (sonship) . . .
   according to the pleasure of his will,
    to the praise of his glorious grace,
   in whom we have redemption and forgiveness,
  who made known to us the mystery of his will,
   according to his good pleasure . . . ,
TO GATHER UP ALL THINGS IN CHRIST,
  in whom we have received an inheritance,
   according to the pleasure of his will,
    to exist for the praise of his glory,
  in whom you have been sealed with the Spirit,
   to the praise of his glory

This great blessing is a virtual inventory or table of contents of Ephesians. It functions as a primer or as an overture to the letter as a whole. I attempt to reflect this special overture quality in the notes. While there is a certain structure to this long sentence, many of the themes are repeated several times. It thus is difficult to follow the text rigidly. The discussion is organized around the opening blessing in verse 3, and then around the three main participles identified above.

OUTLINE

The Blessing: General Comments, 1:3-14
 1:3a Blessing God the Father of Our Lord Jesus Christ
 1:3b-4 Blessing the God Who Has Blessed Us in Christ
  Every Spiritual Blessing 1:3b
  In the Heavenlies   1:3b
  In Christ   1:3b
  Chosen for Holiness   1:4

Blessing the God Who Has Predestined Us Through Christ, 1:5-8
 1:5-6a Predestined for Adoption (Sonship)
 1:6b Graced Through (in) the Beloved
 1:7   The Wealth of Grace: Redemption and Forgiveness
 1:8   Wisdom and Insight

Blessing the God Who Has Revealed the Secret in Christ, 1:9-14
 1:9-10 The Mystery: Gathering Up All Things in and
     Through Christ

EXPLANATORY NOTES

The Blessing: General Comments 1:3-14

Verse 3 makes it clear that this long sentence is first and foremost an act of worshiping and blessing God. The subsequent rehearsal of God's blessing of us does not shift the focus; the way to bless God is to rehearse the blessings we have received at God's hand.

Blessing God is the core of all worship. It constitutes the most common form of Jewish prayer—the *berakah,* blessing. The Greek translation (LXX) of the Hebrew Bible often translates *baruk* (blessed) with *eulogētos,* the term we encounter in Ephesians 1:3—hence, the frequent designation of this passage as a *eulogy,* an English word directly borrowed from the Greek.

Perhaps an early Jewish Christian hymn or prayer has here been adapted and expanded (e.g., Barth, 1974:77; Best, 1998:105; Lincoln: 10). Some see a trinitarian structure in this blessing, focused on the Father in verses 3-6, the Son in 7-12, and the Spirit in 13-14 (e.g., Houlden, 1977:262-3; R. Martin, 1991:14). While the use of hymns is not uncommon in Pauline letters (e.g., Phil. 2:6-11; Col. 1:15-20), including Ephesians (2:14-16; 5:14), we cannot be certain in this case. We know of no hymns or liturgies from the early decades of the Christian church that are quite like this passage (for full discussion see, e.g., Best, 1998:107-9; Lincoln: 12-5).

It may well be that this blessing was composed for this letter, and that it deliberately emulates the tone of public adoration familiar to author and readers. In any case, the hymnic character of the passage places readers and hearers alike in a disposition of gratitude and worship at the outset of the letter. Further, many of the emphases of the letter as a whole are anticipated and announced in this introductory blessing, which suggests that the whole letter should be read with a worshipful disposition (cf. Penner: 11-22).

An analogy to such a blessing of God is the honorific decree, common in inscriptions and on monuments in the Gentile world. In long, laborious, and weighty sentences, benefactors were praised for their gifts. Beneficiaries would then be exhorted to respond with actions befitting such generosity, like much earlier the Hebrews were enjoined to be faithful to the law as a grateful *response* to their liberation by YHWH (e.g., Exod. 20). This opening sentence of Ephesians praises

God as benefactor and sets the stage for the response of the beneficiaries (Hendrix: 3-15; Perkins: 36).

1:3a Blessing God the Father of Our Lord Jesus Christ

Verse 3, as does the whole blessing, expresses the central conviction that God stands before all and at the end of all persons, times,
and things (cf. 4:6). God is acknowledged to be the principal actor in
the drama of creation and re-creation (*gathering up*, 1:10).

God is called *the Father of our Lord Jesus Christ*. While common in the NT as a way to refer to God, *Father* here enjoys special
importance and expresses several interrelated notions. First, God
is *origin* of all that is. As parent, God cares for, nurtures, and sustains—blesses!—every *person*, every *community*, and every *thing* in
creation (cf. 3:14-15; 4:6). Second, in keeping with ancient understandings of fatherhood, as *Father,* God is also *Lord*. Such comprehensiveness fits well with the theocentric (God-centered) perspective
that informs this letter.

Here God is specifically the Father of Jesus the Messiah. This
ascribes special status to Christ (cf. *the Beloved* in 1:6 with Ps. 2:7-9;
110:1). It clarifies that Christ does the will of his Father. It also indicates that he is the one through whom God exercises authority over
all creation. The unavoidable implication is that the nature and character of God come to expression in the Jesus we see. The lordship of
God is inextricable from the servanthood and passion of Christ—"like
father, like son."

It is precisely the inextricable relationship of the Father and the
Son that allows this Jewish author, along with other followers of
the man from Nazareth, to use the appellation *Lord* for Christ. This
should not be taken for granted. "Lord" was, after all, the usual way
a Jew would refer to YHWH. The Son becomes *our Lord* precisely
because in him we encounter *God's* saving presence and activity. To
illustrate, notice how the greeters at the beginning of the letter are
God our Father and the Lord Jesus Christ. In 4:17—5:2 the practice of truth, kindness, and love is the imitation of God (5:1) and of
Christ (4:20; 5:2). It is not difficult to see how later Christians came to
express this mysterious interchangeability in trinitarian terms.

As 1:2 has already made clear, God is *our* parent too. As we will
see, the Father of Jesus Christ has in, through, and with him also
blessed *us* with adoption; *we too* have been offered *sonship* (1:5).
What was granted God's *Beloved* (1:6) is granted also to those who
are *in him* (see esp. 2:4-7). Accordingly, *we* have also been granted
an *inheritance* befitting those who are by *God's* choice and adoption

offspring of God (1:11, 14). As sons and daughters, we are to live holy and blameless lives in keeping with the divine parent's will and pleasure (1:4).

1:3b-4 Blessing the God Who Has Blessed Us in Christ

If verse 3 is the opening exclamation of praise and blessing of God, then the three participles that follow give the reason for the blessing: God blessed us first! The fact that the term *bless* appears three times in one form or another in verse 3 is an indication of the air of generosity and gratitude that pervades this act of worship. Quite appropriately, the first major participle is that God *has blessed us with every spiritual blessing in the heavenlies in Christ.*

Every Spiritual Blessing 1:3b

While common in the Pauline writings, in Ephesians the adjective *spiritual* is somewhat enigmatic. On one hand, we read here of **spiritual** blessings in the heavenlies. On the other hand, there is the reference in 6:12 to the **spiritualities** of evil in the heavenlies. The word *spiritual* can thus have either positive or negative connotations. It carries overtones of divine or, in some cases, demonic *power*. In this passage, the connection of *spirit* to *promise* and *guarantee* in verses 13 and 14 suggests that *spiritual* in verse 3 implies that what will be realized more fully in the future (cf. 4:30) is experienced now already as the effective and powerful experience of God's generosity. Gordon Fee calls *spiritual blessings* "Spirit blessings, blessings that pertain to the Spirit" (Fee, 1994:666).

What are these *spiritual blessings*? Befitting its nature as one long worshipful blessing, this passage only names the various dimensions of God's *spiritual blessings* and does not elaborate upon them:

- chosen in Christ to be holy and blameless in the exercise of love (1:4)
- predestined from before creation to be God's offspring (1:5)
- liberated through Christ's offering of his life (1:7, 14, anticipating 2:13)
- forgiveness of transgressions (1:7; anticipating 2:4-5)
- revelation of God's secret plan of cosmic restoration (1:9-10, anticipating chap. 3)
- enabled to live for God's glory (1:12)
- sealed with the *Holy Spirit of promise* (1:13-14).

As much as these blessings are *spiritual*, they have great consequence for the everyday material life of believers (so also Fee, 1994:667). These *spiritual blessings* relate to both *status* (divine sonship and daughtership, intimate *knowledge* of God's designs for this world), and *task* (holiness, blamelessness, good works, love in action, and most important, participation in the gathering up of all things; 1:10). I will return to the *Holy Spirit of promise* below.

In the Heavenlies 1:3b

Are these blessings experienced at once on the human plane and *in the heavenlies*? Or do *the heavenlies* refer to a place and time awaited in the future? The use of the past tense *(has blessed us)* should put us on notice that this act of worship is in gratitude for what has *already* happened and for what happens *now* in the life of believers. Even so, questions remain.

The phrase *in the heavenlies*, unique in the NT but frequent in Ephesians (1:3, 20; 2:6; 3:10; 6:12), is mysterious. Grammatically, it is unclear whether here we are dealing with an absolute neuter plural *(the heavenly things* or *heavenly matters [ta epourania])* or with a masculine adjective implying *places* (*the heavenly places [hoi epouranioi]*, as in most versions). The adjective *heavenly (epouranios)* appears elsewhere in the Pauline literature but never in the absolute sense (e.g., 1 Cor. 15:40, 48-49; Phil. 2:10; 2 Tim. 4:18). In absolute form it appears in the NT only twice: in John 3:12 it can fairly be translated as "heavenly matters"; in Hebrews 9:23 it refers to aspects of heavenly worship.

Along with virtually all translations, the NRSV understands the phrase to refer to a locality and thus translates it as *heavenly places* (similarly NIV: *heavenly realms*). That would appear to be the best understanding at 2:6—literally, *in the heavenlies in Christ Jesus*. The matter is complicated, however, by the fact that *in the heavenlies* is also the place where the evil powers reside (3:10; 6:12). An understanding of the cosmology or worldview of Ephesians sheds light on this puzzle *[Cosmology of Ephesians]*. Here it is enough simply to note that the term is not precise; even when it is used positively, as here, it is not referring to a place away from where the saints presently find themselves nor to a time removed from the present. That does not preclude that there are more blessings to come in the future (cf. 1:11, 14, 18!).

In Christ 1:3b

As noted earlier, God elects, chooses, redeems, and re-creates in and through his beloved Son, Jesus the Christ. *In Christ* is a typically Pauline turn of phrase. *In* (Greek: *en*) is highly elastic, sometimes translated in a spatial sense as "in" and "with" Christ, at times instrumentally as "through" or "by means of" *["In"]*. Since the author chose to use this imprecise but richly suggestive preposition, we should respect the range of possible interpretations. Each of these meanings fits well the thought here. Christ is one *in whom* God's blessings have been and are being realized (1:3, 7, 11, 13). The image of *the body of Christ* that plays an important role in the rest of the letter is dependent on this remarkable understanding of Christ's expansive personhood (1:23; 2:16; 4:4, 12, 16; 5:30) *["In"]*. Believers are *in Christ* in the sense that Christ becomes the "space" where they meet God and experience *every spiritual blessing in the heavenlies* (1:3). The "size" of Christ is cosmic. As the sphere of redemption and re-creation grows through this great ingathering (1:10; cf. 4:12-13), Christ's body will finally extend to the very edges of creation, embracing *all things, . . . things in heaven and things on earth* (1:10, NRSV; cf. 1:23).

It is an understatement to say that such a conception bursts the boundaries of present-day views of what is a human person (e.g., Best, 1998:153-4; Lincoln: 21-2, and literature cited there). On one hand, Christ is *Jesus*, the one who died on the cross (1:7; cf. 2:16). More, Christ is the "preexistent" agent of God's creation (1:4; cf. 2:10). Through the agency of Christ, God *blesses* (1:3), offers *adoption* (1:4-5) and thus a share in the *inheritance* (1:11, 14), *redeems* (1:7, 14), *forgives* (1:7), and thereby *saves* (1:13). This is all summed up in the phrase *gathering up all things **in Christ*** (1:10).

Chosen for Holiness 1:4

It is often observed that in Ephesians the center of gravity has shifted from Christology to ecclesiology (Introduction). There is a large measure of truth in this, even if it would be better to observe the shift as being from Christ-as-distinct-from-the-church to "Christ-in-the-church," in Ralph Martin's words (1991:4). In keeping with this overall pattern in Ephesians, attention shifts in verse 4 to the *chosen*, providing both the first glimpse of the content of the blessings of God and anticipating the next major emphasis beginning in verse 5—*predestination*.

In several ways verse 4 recapitulates emphases already explored in relation to verse 3. First, it is *God* who has chosen *us*. This cannot be emphasized enough. God is the benevolent parent who chooses *first*; worship, here as an act of praise, is a *response* to God's first act.

Second, God has chosen *us in him*, that is, in Christ (see above). *In* should be understood as referring both to identification *with* Christ, and to Christ as the one *through whom* God's choice is realized *["In"]*.

Third, the phrase *before the foundation of the cosmos* serves to emphasize that it is *God* who has chosen us, not that we chose God. That choice rests in the wisdom of God that "predates" creation. Temporal language is here employed to make the point that God's choice is not a response to humanity's predicament, not to mention behavior; instead, it is an initiative that underlies the creation of humanity to begin with (cf. 2:10; 4:24). "God is not a chess player who makes his next move only after he has seen the last move of his opponent. He works to a plan" (Best, 1998:120).

The fact that this *pre*-creation choice is made *in Christ* also means that God's blessing of humanity *in Christ* goes beyond the cross and resurrection, as important as they are. Informing this line of thought is the Pauline connection between Christ and *wisdom* (1:8; cf. 3:10). Wisdom was there when creation took place (cf. Col. 1:16); and wisdom is engaged in the costly reconciliation of humanity to God (1 Cor. 1:17-25) *[Wisdom]*.

Fourth, to say that choice and election are God's initiative, taken *before* humanity came into existence, does not in any way diminish the importance of how humanity relates to God, with what quality of life and worship it stands *before him. Holiness* and *blamelessness* constitute the very purpose of being *chosen* (cf. 5:3-11). Recall that the blessings or benefactions of God call for an appropriate response on the part of the beneficiaries. First-century Jews, such as the author of Ephesians, would have understood the emphasis on holiness to reflect both the context of cult (temple and sacrifice) and ethics (worship as life). At the best of times, the distinction would not have been acknowledged (cf., e.g., Psalm 50; Isa. 58).

As we will discover in the next chapter, *holiness and blamelessness before God* are grateful responses to God's blessings and also essential aspects of God's blessing. God blesses us in that we are rendered capable of offering God a holy and blameless life. In 2:10, walking in *good works* is the reason believers have been saved and re-created; in addition, those works have themselves been prepared *beforehand* by a God who blesses (2:10, notes).

The placing of the qualifying phrase *in love* is grammatically ambiguous. It can be read in relation to either holiness (our love for God), as NRSV has it (also NJB), or in relation to predestination (God's love for us; NIV). In the first instance, it qualifies *holiness and blamelessness* as essentially relational. Worship and ethics finally are nothing other than loving God with heart, mind, soul, and body (cf. Deut. 6:5; 30:6, 16; Mark 12:30 and par.). Without love, on the other hand, worship and ethics betray the love of God expressed in election (cf. 1 Cor. 13). Most commentators lean toward associating *in love* with predestination, but it is best to allow both associations to affect the understanding of the text. As in so many cases, eliminating either option impoverishes us.

Blessing the God Who Has Predestined Us Through Christ 1:5-8

1:5-6a Predestined for Adoption (Sonship)

The second major participle—*having predestined*—has been anticipated in the reference to *being chosen* in verse 4. The chosen have been *predestined for adoption, sonship or daughtership.* NRSV's inclusive *adoption as his children* is entirely correct insofar as God adopts both sons *and daughters.* But one should not miss the overtones of royal status implied in being chosen and adopted to be a divine son (cf., e.g., Ps. 2:7; Matt. 3:17; cf. Best, 1998:125; also literature on adoption cited in Lincoln: 25; Schweizer, 1972:334-99). Strikingly, in 2 Corinthians 6:18, Paul explicitly extends God's adoption or coronation of his "son" as found in 2 Samuel 7:14 to include "daughters."

Again we notice the use of the temporal element to indicate how deeply predestination or foreordination is rooted in God's initiative. Just as God chose us *before* the foundation of the cosmos, so now God has **pre**destined *(proorisas)* us for adoption (cf. also 1:9, *established **before**hand, proetheto*). This is linguistic excess as we come to expect it in Ephesians. As always, however, we should be wary of dismissing such repetition as a matter of style. This is the vocabulary of gratitude and praise, befitting such a grand blessing or eulogy. The chief purpose of this choice of language is to celebrate the immeasurable extent of God's loving disposition toward the readers. In such contexts, overstatement is inherently understatement.

Small wonder that the phrase *in love* at the end of verse 4 is most often related to predestination. The love and benevolence of a blessing God pervade the eulogy from beginning to end. Nothing is said here about those *not* chosen, those *not* predestined for adoption. Nor is there any indication that the author has the remotest interest in the philosophical problems predestination might raise for the relationship between divine will and human freedom. This is the ecstasy of worship, the euphoria of gratitude. The passionate desire of the Sovereign of all time and space to enter into relationship with humanity—*the pleasure of his will* (cf. 1:9)—has existed from even *before* the onset of creation.

Although the chosen are blessed by God's benevolence, *God* himself is the ultimate beneficiary of this relationship. Sons and daughters are adopted *for himself* (these words are inexplicably not included in NIV or NRSV; I take the phrase to refer to God rather than to Christ). Moreover, God chooses and predestines *to the praise of his [own] glorious grace* (cf. the similar phrase that brings the sentence to a close in 1:14). One is reminded of Psalm 22:3: "You are holy, enthroned on the praises of Israel." The worship of the sons and daughters of God provides a home for God, a thought that shapes the great peace text in Ephesians 2:11-22. The reclamation of alienated humanity in Christ results in the "construction" of a home for God (2:19-22).

That both God and humanity are beneficiaries comes to expression in verse 6, where God's "amazing grace" is said to be praised by the predestination of the saints (on *grace* [Greek: *charis*], see also below). As the end of verse 4 made clear, it is holiness and blamelessness that most fittingly praise God's *glorious grace. Living to the praise of [God's] glorious grace* might thus well be the rubric under which ethics is treated in Ephesians 4–6.

The formal beginning of the exhortation section in 4:1 in fact sums up the ethical task of the saints as living up to their *calling,* echoing the stress on election and predestination in this opening blessing. This overture to the letter indicates that the *calling* consists of *living to the praise of God.* It is premised on assurance of the power of God at work within the saints (1:19; 3:20). Such assurance elicits doxology (3:21). The call to a holy and blameless life is a call to a living doxology (cf. Rom. 11:33—12:2; Isa. 58). In light of God's grace, ethics becomes worship; in light of God's grace, worship must never be severed from ethics.

1:6b Graced Through (in) the Beloved

Here as elsewhere, it is virtually impossible to capture the full allusive freight of the language in Ephesians. The term almost universally translated as *gave (charitoō)* means literally "to bestow on freely" and is related to the noun *grace (charis).* Even if it is difficult to capture in English, we should not miss the wordplay: God has *graced* us with *grace.*

The phrase *in the loved one,* or *Beloved,* restates what we have already explored in relation to *in Christ* in verse 3 *["In"].* Now, however, the messianic overtones have become more personal and relational. The agent of God's love is himself called the *Beloved.* On one hand, this expresses special favor. Christ is God's agent and also God's beloved Son. On the other hand, it is a measure of God's glorious grace that this special favor is granted also to those sons and daughters who are **in** the Beloved.

In Ephesians, Christ is never the object of reflection or worship apart from what has happened to humanity through him. This is true in the second half of chapter 1, where the resurrection and exaltation of Christ serve as a measure for the power of God active in and for believers (1:19-23). Identification of believers with the Messiah is made explicit in 2:5-6: we have been raised *with* Christ and seated *with* Christ in the heavenlies. The great peace hymn to Christ in 2:14-16 celebrates Christ as cosmic peacemaker and also his creation of a new humanity—*in himself!* In that sense, such grace has been received *in* and also *through the Beloved.*

1:7 The Wealth of Grace: Redemption and Forgiveness

Framed by references in verses 6 and 7 to the glorious riches of grace is the "work" of grace—the death of Christ. The central role of the cross in making peace between God and humanity seen in 2:16 is here anticipated with the reference to *blood* (cf. 2:13; Col. 1:20). There is little if any discussion in Ephesians of either the historical circumstances of Christ's life and ministry or the cross in the process of salvation. Nevertheless, grace's "manifestation in history" (Best, 1998:127; cf. Lincoln: 28) is made explicit here as in 2:13, 16, even if only tersely. It is treated as a given, as already understood by the readers. Even so, it serves no less than the resurrection as the measure of the immeasurable wealth of God's grace and power (1:19).

The Messiah's *blood* is related to redemption and the forgiveness of sins. The treatment is too brief for us to be sure of what all the author has in mind. The image evokes the experience of deliverance from Egypt, the payment of ransom as in freeing slaves or releasing prisoners, and also biblical sin offerings. We follow the lead of the author of Ephesians when we allow the evocation to be as rich as our understanding of redemption and liberation (so also Lincoln: 28; contra Best, 1998:130, and Schnackenburg: 56, who reject the notion of ransom here). What is central to the gospel, and a true measure of God's grace and love, is the identification of *God*, specifically his *Messiah*, whose blood is offered on the cross (cf. 2:14-16). The offended party pays the price of peace—his *own* life!

The thoroughly *theo*centric nature of this whole blessing in 1:3-14 makes it crystal clear that Christ's blood does not appease an angry God, but instead Christ's blood emerges from *God's own* treasury of grace (cf. Rom. 5 for a fuller treatment of the relationship between the crucified Messiah and an enemy-loving God). *By grace you have been saved!* exclaims the author twice in the next chapter (2:6, 8).

The reference to the *forgiveness of sins* or *trespasses* is meant to parallel redemption through Christ's blood. Forgiveness is implied in Paul's preaching and writing, but it is not nearly as prominent in the letters that we are sure he wrote. In those letters we read more about justification and reconciliation. Those doctrines imply forgiveness, of course (Lincoln: 28), but we must note that the language of Ephesians shifts from justification to forgiveness (cf. also Col. 1:13-14). *Sins* or *trespasses* represent the bondage of the walking dead in 2:1-3. There Easter comes to the fore as the drama of bringing to life (2:4-8). Here it is Good Friday that works the release.

1:8 Wisdom and Insight

Abundance continues to set the tone in verse 8—grace is said to have been *lavished on us.* As in the case of *in love* at the end of verse 4, there is some question about the next phrase, *in* (or *with) all wisdom and insight.* Should it accompany the lavishing of grace (NJB; Lincoln: 29) or should it go with verse 9 and define the mode by which God has divulged the secret to us (NRSV, NIV; Best, 1998:133)?

A good case can be made for both connections. Given how important wisdom, insight, and knowledge are in Ephesians (e.g., 1:17-18; 3:14-19; 4:17-24; 5:15-17), *wisdom and insight* can rightly be seen as *spiritual blessings* God graciously offers the elect (Paul explicitly connects grace and wisdom in 1 Cor. 1:17-31; cf. Wisd. of Sol. 10). It is just as true that divine wisdom is shown in God's act of disclosing the mystery (cf. 1 Cor. 1:18—2:16). The phrase *with all wisdom and insight* is thus cleverly placed to relate equally well to both grace and revelation.

The use of two virtual synonyms *(wisdom, sophia; insight, phronēsis)* fits the ornate style of Ephesians well. Proverbs 8:1, however, shows that this is not the first time these two terms have been placed next to each other. *Wisdom (sophia) and insight (phronēsis)* are essentially interchangeable ways of referring to the figure of Wisdom. In our text, the phrase *wisdom and insight* might therefore be more than a simple reference to insight into God's grace and how to live in light of it. It may well be a pointer to the biblical figure of Wisdom.

The more we are attuned to the tradition of personified Wisdom *[Wisdom],* the more we will hear in the phrase *in all wisdom* a variant of the frequent *in Christ, in him,* or *in whom* (1:3, 4, 6, 7, 9, 10,

11, 12, 13) *["In"]*. *In Wisdom* we come face to face with the immeasurable wealth of God's grace. We might take the reference to *all wisdom* as precluding the identification with Christ. But notice that in 3:10 Christ is referred to as the *multivaried wisdom of God*. As stated earlier, it is difficult if not impossible to set limits to the allusive and evocative power of the language of Ephesians, least of all in this great eulogy.

Blessing the God Who Has Revealed the Secret in Christ 1:9-14

1:9-10 The Mystery: Gathering Up All Things in and Through Christ

Verse 9 introduces the last of the three participles that shape this great eulogy—*having revealed* or *made known*. The secret or mystery is that God has had a plan from before the beginning to *gather up all things in heaven and on earth in Christ*.

Verses 9 and 10 are undoubtedly the apex of this recitation of God's blessings and the key to understanding the vision of Ephesians as a whole. It is important to explore the meaning of some of the key terms in these verses more closely (see Schematic Trans. for a literal version).

There are several words in this passage that allow for a considerable range of meaning. First, the majority of translations render *mystērion* as *mystery*. In English *mystery* often suggests something puzzling or remaining beyond full comprehension. Its use in 1 Corinthians 15:51, where Paul "explains" the mystery of the resurrection, comes closest to such usage. In the ancient world, most especially in the so-called mystery cults, *mystērion* came to be associated with rites of initiation into the divine "mysteries." The secret knowledge was imparted only to the initiated and kept secret from all others. Some have interpreted Christian beginnings as yet another form of such a mystery religion and have taken writings like Ephesians to be evidence for that (discussion of scholarship in Barth, 1974:123-7; Best, 1998:134-7; Lincoln: 30-1).

A focus on mystery was very much part of apocalyptic thought and writing (cf., e.g., Dan. 2:18-19, 27-30; 2 Esdras 14:5), and is a major theme in the writings of the Qumran community at the Dead Sea (e.g., 1QM 3.9; 1QpHab 7; 1QS 4.18-19; 1Q27; 4Q299-301). In apocalyptic literature the mystery was God's secret plan known only to those (few) to whom God chose to reveal it *[Apocalyptic]*. This notion of a divine secret comes close to the meaning of the term *mystērion* in Ephesians, even if it retains something of the sense of wonder and awe that defies full comprehension. (See 5:32, the *great mystery* of the relationship of Christ and church; for discussion of the literature, cf. Lincoln: 30; Perkins: 40; Schnackenburg: 57-8.)

Contrasting with apocalyptic, in Ephesians once-privileged information (the *secret*) is released to everyone (Best, 1998:135; R. Martin, 1991:17-8). This divulging of the secret lies at the heart of the early apostolic mission, especially as it relates to the inclusion of the Gentiles (see esp. 3:1-13; Col. 1:26-27). In these verses the *secret* is called the *word of truth* and also the *good **news** of liberation* (1:13)—gospel as public news. In 3:9-10 it is the task of the church to let even the powers in on the secret about the *multivaried wisdom of God*.

To be sure, this *secret* is not a puzzle that can be figured out by human ingenuity. It is *God's* secret, disclosed at *God's* initiative. Such revelation is an act of grace (1:7-9), since evil has clouded human minds and also rendered much of reality illegible with respect to God's lordship over creation and history (4:17-19). Revelation is but one of the spiritual blessings of God, a gracious intrusion into a world of alienation, sleep, and death (2:1-3; 4:17-19; 5:14; 6:15, 19).

Second, the *secret* relates to what the NRSV calls *the plan (oikonomia) for the fullness (plērōma) of time*. This leaves the impression that God's action in Christ has taken place according to a preordained plan. That may well be what the author intends to communicate (cf. Mark 1:7; Luke 21:24; John 7:8). But there are some possible meanings such a translation does not quite grasp. First, *oikonomia* (picked up in English as "economy") can be rendered literally as "the rule or law *(nomos)* of the household *(oikos)*." The term appears again in 3:2 and 9, where its meaning is better given as "administration," "management," or "commission" for a particular task (so also in 1 Cor. 9:17 and Col. 1:25). *Administration* suggests "active management of a household" (e.g., NJB: *to act upon*). This catches the *active* and *ongoing* nature of divine intervention in Christ. Both meanings together reflect the will and work of God.

Third, one might take *the fullness of times* to refer to history having come to the right and ripe moment for God to have acted in Christ (e.g., NJB; cf. Rom. 5:6). *Fullness* translates *plērōma*, a term that would come to play a large role in Gnostic thinking (on *fullness*, see notes on 1:23 and 3:19 *[Gnosticism]*. In this case it highlights the word for *time*, namely *kairos*. In contrast to *chronos,* which denotes linear time (Gal. 4:4), *kairos* implies "loaded" time. The exact wording here is *times* (plural! unlike NRSV, but correctly translated by NIV,

NJB, and NKJ). *Fullness* and *times* together are meant to express that the *times* of Christ's *administration* of the mystery are "full of fullness."

The *gathering up* of all things in Christ is not a onetime event in the future, let alone one already brought to completion, but a "filling up of times." The imagery implies that in the filling up of times, there is movement toward a climax when the times of ingathering will have been fulfilled (Schnackenburg: 139). There is no need to think of *times* in terms of the periods or dispensations of apocalyptic (contra Gnilka: 79).

To be sure, Ephesians also celebrates God's action in Christ as *completed*, nowhere more dramatically than in the way the resurrection of believers is celebrated as an accomplished fact in 2:4-7. Despite the presence of this tone of completion, one should remember that this is typical of hymnody, which clearly marks our passage. Worshipers celebrate as assured what they still anticipate, albeit with certainty, because they worship the one who is sovereign over past, present, and future.

This dynamic understanding of administration, fullness, and loaded time keeps us from looking too closely at only one moment in the history of salvation, either at the cross and resurrection in the past or at the return of Christ in the future. Ephesians wants readers to pay attention to the *present* time in which they are living, which was then and is now *full time* (5:16, notes, on *exploiting the time because the days are evil*). Such an understanding greatly enlarges our grasp of the work of Christ in and through the church. It also sensitizes us to the distinctive eschatology of Ephesians, which loads the present to overflowing while also seeing it as movement toward culminating the process of reconciling the cosmos in Christ, a process that began already before the beginning, so to speak.

The heart of the secret is salvation. And the central image of salvation and reconciliation in verse 10 is the *gathering up of all things* in the universe *in Christ*. *Gathering up* translates the rare term *anakephalaiōsasthai*. It is rooted in *kephalaion*, which means "summing up" or "heading," rather than "head" (*kephalē*; Lincoln: 32; Schnackenburg: 59), even if that term undoubtedly resonates in the background (e.g., NIV, NJB; cf. 1:22-23; 4:11-16; cf. Barth, 1974:89-92; Best, 1998:140; Kitchen: 36-42) *["Head"]*. A good translation would also be "to subsume" or "recapitulate." *All things* in the cosmos—*things on the heavens and things on the earth*—are "summed up in Christ" (Best, 1998:142-3), who is the final "focal point" of the process (Lincoln: 33; R. Martin, 1991:17).

With respect to *in Christ,* we recall that *in* can have spatial as well as instrumental meaning *["In"].* The instrumental meaning is clear: *through* Christ all things are being brought into unity (celebrated hymnically in relation to Jews and Gentiles in 2:11-22). If *in* is understood spatially, however, then the final result of the ingathering is that Christ encompasses *in himself* the whole of the reconciled cosmos. Christ becomes the "heading" for all things, and in that sense the head of his body, the whole world (cf. 4:12-16). Both process and goal are present in the phrase. The central role of Christ as both agent and endpoint is given added emphasis in the otherwise redundant *in him* at the end of verse 10.

It is impossible to plumb the depths of this image of universal ingathering. Comprehensive and embracing to the utmost, it reflects both the generosity and "worldliness" we find in the wisdom tradition of Israel *[Wisdom].* There is no part or feature of the cosmos beyond the loving and renewing reach of the Creator. Second, the image is also intensely eschatological, without being tied to any scheme or without emptying either the past or the present of the benevolent and saving attention of God. Growth as much as loaded times and filling as much as fullness inform the understanding of salvation.

1:11-12 The Lot of the Predestined

The focus now shifts from Christ *in whom* (cf. 1:7, 13 *["In"]*) the predestined have received redemption, to the beneficiaries of God's action in Christ, *us the predestined.* What follows is somewhat puzzling, illustrated by the various ways translators render the same Greek words:

- NAB   we were chosen
- NIV   we were also chosen
- NJB   we have received our heritage
- NKJV   we have obtained an inheritance
- NRSV   we have also obtained an inheritance
- REB   we have been given our share in the heritage
- TEV   God chose us to be his own people

Some translations view the predestined ones as God's chosen "lot" or "portion," whereas others understand the author to be speaking of the inheritance the predestined ones receive. The difficulty emerges from the Greek verb *klēroō,* which appears only here in the NT. In the active it means "to appoint by lot" *(BAGD).* In the passive, as here, it means "to be appointed by lot," meaning "in whom our lot was cast" *(BAGD).* In the OT it could refer to the land allotted to Israel as an inheritance (e.g., Num. 26:52-53; Josh. 12:7). But it could also refer to Israel as God's allotted portion (e.g., Deut. 9:29; Zech. 2:12). To think of the community as God's "lot" is also frequent in the literature of Qumran (e.g., 1QS 2.2; 1QM 1.5).

The very nature of this eulogy encourages us to see both meanings. The presence of the vocabulary of election, predestination, and adoption invites us to think of Christ as the one in whom God claims his lot. The predestined have been "chosen" or "appointed" (Lincoln: 25) to live to the praise of God's glory (1:12). In bringing into being a worshiping community, God has given *himself* a present!

It is also entirely in keeping with the gist of this rehearsal of God's blessing to interpret this as the "lot" or inheritance the predestined have received through Christ. This is given support by the reference to the *inheritance (klēronomia)* in verse 14 (cf. 1:18; 5:5). By blessing God through praise and worship, *we too* are blessed beyond measure.

However much God is the recipient of this *lot*, it is God the loving Creator who is first and last actor in the drama. This is driven home with two similar phrases:

- according to the plan (*oikonomia*, 1:10) of the one who energizes all things
- *according to the resoluteness of [God's] will*

The process of gathering up all things in Christ, the redemption of the chosen, and the creation of a people who praise God with their whole life (cf. 1:4; cf. 2:10; 5:15-21) are rooted in God's will and secured by God's sovereignty.

1:12-13 We and You

Verse 12 refers to those *who first hoped in the Christ* or *the Messiah*. Up to this point, in *every* verse *we* or *us* appears to refer to *all* believers in Christ. Verse 12 apparently places a restriction on *we*, referring to those who believed *first*. Then verse 13 surprises us with *you also*.

There are a number of possibilities. Many suggest that *you* in verse 13 is simply a way of addressing more directly the audience or readership (Best, 1998:144-5, 148; Bowe: 31; Lincoln: 38; Schnackenburg: 64-5; and others). After all, this "letter" was a public oral and aural event and thus marked by rhetorical features characteristic of public speech. *We* refers in verse 12 to the author(s), and elsewhere throughout the blessing to *all* who are *in Christ*.

Relatedly, *we* as distinct from *you* may refer more specifically to the apostle, highlighting Paul's status and authority (Houlden,

1977:265-6; Perkins: 43). True, Paul sometimes refers to himself in the plural when defending his calling and mission (cf. 2 Cor. 3–4 and 10–13, where singular and plural are interchangeable). Here the distinction between *we* and *you* would then highlight Paul's authority as the apostle who has divulged the divine secret to the readers (cf. 1:8-9 with 3:1-13).

Another possibility is that the switch from *we who first hoped in the Christ (Messiah)* in verse 12 to *also you* in verse 13 refers to those who have been part of the church for some time and those who have more recently become believers (e.g., Mitton: 57). This relates closely to taking *we* to refer to Jewish and *you* to Gentile believers in the Messiah (Barth, 1974:130-3; Patzia, 1990:156; cf. esp. 2:11-22). In the early decades "first believers" (if that is how *proēlpikotas* in 1:12 should be interpreted) would more often than not have been Jews convinced that Jesus Christ was the fulfillment of Jewish messianic hopes. Such Jews would have offered hospitality to Gentiles as newcomers to the extended family of God. In that sense, *we* and *you* could easily refer at one and the same time to Jews and Gentiles as well as to mature and new believers.

Such an interpretation suggests that when Ephesians was written, there was still a lively sense of pedigree among followers of Christ, and that Jewish believers were still experiencing the novelty of including Gentiles in the ranks of those who had hoped for centuries in the Messiah. I cannot agree with the many scholars who believe the Jew-Gentile issue no longer mattered for the author of Ephesians (Perkins: 29-32).

Perhaps a choice between these proposals is neither necessary nor possible. Different ears hear different things. When the language is ambiguous, the possibility of variation in hearing increases. Best is correct only in part when he says that the author "wrote Ephesians expecting it to be listened to, not worked over in the study!" (1998:144). A document as intentionally worked over as Ephesians was surely also intended to be studied and repeatedly reflected upon. So the identification of *we* and *you* with Jews and Gentiles in 2:11-22 (less directly in 2:1-3) makes it more than likely that that distinction is anticipated here and serves, as it does in chapter 2, to emphasize unity *in the Christ.*

The line *in [Christ] you also* reflects the scandal and the wonder of the mission of Paul and his heirs. Divine choice and election typically serve to mark off who is in and who is out. That sense is critically important here for us to catch the true measure of the wondrous blessing. God's embrace in Christ has selected also those hitherto deemed

rejected (see esp. 2:1-2, 11-12). The return in verse 14 to a clearly
inclusive *our* expresses the vision in Ephesians of God's people made
up of both *we* and *you*, the *near* and the *far*—Jews and Gentiles, old
and new, first and second (and third) generation believers. *We* and
you **together** constitute the community of *the chosen*.

Verse 13 provides a succinct sketch of this mission: *hearing,
believing the word of truth*, and *receiving the Spirit* (cf. Rom.
10:14-21 and Gal. 3:1-5!). Then as now, these words evoke the
evangelistic enterprise of the church. The *word of truth* might be
taken as an "objectification of the gospel" (Best, 1998:149), the truth
the church proclaims. This may be correct, especially since we find
such formulations also in other late writings in the NT (e.g., Col. 1:5;
2 Tim. 2:15; James 1:18). On the other hand, *truth* as both noun
and verb appears frequently in Ephesians (4:15, 21, 25; 5:9; 6:14),
and not in ways that are set or limited to specific content. The turn of
phrase here anticipates the evocative reference in 4:21 to the *truth
that is in Jesus* (4:21, notes).

1:13-14 Sealed with the Holy Spirit

In addition to God the Father and Christ the beloved Son, we also
encounter *the Holy Spirit of promise*, explicitly referred to in verses
13 and 14, but alluded to already in verse 3 with the adjective *spiritual*. To capitalize Spirit is a convention of the English language, not
of the Greek. I do so only for purposes of convenience in indicating
that the Spirit is the spirit of God.

The phrase *having been sealed in [with,* or *through] the holy
Spirit of promise* in verse 13 is frequently related to baptism (cf.
2 Cor. 1:22; e.g., Houlden: 270; Kirby: 153-4; Patzia, 1990:158-
9; Schnackenburg: 65; discussion in Barth, 1974:135-43; Best,
1998:150-2; Lincoln: 39-40). While one will want to be careful
about seeing this as the only meaning of the image (rejected by Fee,
1994:669-70), it is highly instructive to see baptism as the rite of
identification *with Christ* and empowerment *with the Spirit* for the
messianic task such identification implies.

The image of the seal might have been familiar to Jews of Paul's
day as a reference to circumcision (cf. Rom. 4:11), although other
Jewish uses of that term for circumcision are much later. Notice that
Colossians 2:11-12 explicitly relates circumcision to baptism. Were
this connection between seal, baptism, and circumcision to hold, then
baptism can be seen as a rite of inclusion in the community of saints,
one equally meaningful to both Jews and Gentiles. Regardless of the
connection between seal and baptism, the reception of the *Spirit* is

a gift of God to daughters and sons, a *guarantee* that they will never be abandoned in their life of faithfulness, in their participation in the messianic task of reconciling *all things.*

The phrase *Holy Spirit **of promise*** brings into view an essential if often-disputed dimension of this letter—its eschatology. On one hand, God *has* blessed the elect already *with every spiritual blessing in the heavenlies* (1:3), and God has revealed to them the mystery of his plan for the fullness of times *already* being realized *in Christ* (1:10). However, the presence and experience of the Spirit is a promise that the word about what God *has done* is true (1:13), and proof that the saints have *not yet* experienced the fullness of all those blessings. The "eschatological reservation," as it is sometimes called, is indicated by the fact that the Spirit is, first, a *spirit of promise* (1:13), and, second, a "security deposit" or "down payment," the *guarantee of our inheritance* and *redemption* (1:14; cf. Rom. 8, esp. 8:23).

At the same time, it is the *present* experience of the Spirit that constitutes the guarantee of what will be experienced in the future. This experience comes to clearest expression in a life lived as an act of worship. So quite fittingly, this great eulogy to God's blessings concludes with the phrase *to the praise of [God's] glory.*

Spirit, power, and *glory* are intimately related to each other (notice the close relationship of *power* and *glory* in 1:17 and 19; Arnold, 1989:76, 137-42). We might well think of the divine Spirit (*pneuma,* equally well translated as "wind") as divine energy (see Schematic Trans. of 1:11). By implication, when people live in such a way that they thereby praise the *glory* of God, they also give evidence of God's *power* and *energy* (1:11), of God's "wind" at work in their lives.

THE TEXT IN BIBLICAL CONTEXT

Blessing

In the biblical world, words—whether blessings or curses—were believed to have the power of action: words could wound, even kill, and words could heal (recall the warnings about the tongue in James 3:1-12, esp. 3:9-10; cf. Eph. 4:29). Spoken blessings (benedictions) were one form of blessing. Blessings could also be acts of benevolence (benefactions), most typically on the part of God: health, children, land, good crops, and security.

The much-debated question of whether the words of blessing had a kind of independent magical force does not really fit the context here (Richards; Urbrock). The focus on blessing is directed, on one hand, to *God's* benefactions and, on the other, to the *responsive* praise of the blessed. In other words, blessings function within the context of relationship.

In the Hebrew Bible, as in the NT, the foundation of divine blessing is God's relationship to humanity as Creator, King, Father, Lord or suzerain, and as sustainer and nurturer of life (Matt. 5:43-48 should be read in this light). Whatever power the blessings have is ultimately related to God and thus to God's relationship to the people blessed. The relationship factor is sharpened when blessings are related to the gifts of liberation, land, and nationhood, as in the case of Israel (cf. Deut. 27–30). Blessings thus come to be related to God's *special* favor and thus to *election* (see below). It is God's special concern for those who suffer that underlies the implied blessing in the Beatitudes, for example (Matt. 5:3-10; Luke 6:20-26).

In our text the whole of God's intervention in and through Christ is celebrated as blessings from God. Usually such blessings are related to the faithfulness of the people (cf., e.g., Pss. 119; 128). Remarkably, the vocabulary of special favor is applied in Ephesians to both old-time insiders and newcomers (*we* and *you*; cf. 1:3-14; chaps. 2–3).

The blessing of God can be invoked by means of human words of blessing. The opening (1:1-2) and closing (6:21-24) of Ephesians, offering peace and grace, are precisely such blessings, invoking God's peace and grace on the readers. Further, the brief hymnic fragment in 5:14 evokes the most famous of blessings, still current in both Jewish and Christian circles, Numbers 6:24-26:

> Arise, sleeper,
> and rise from the dead,
> and the Christ will shine on you! (5:14, TRYN)

> The LORD bless you and keep you;
> the LORD make his face to shine upon you, and be gracious to you;
> the LORD lift up his countenance upon you, and give you peace.

Notice the centrality of *peace (shalom)* in the blessing in Numbers 6. *Shalom* encapsulates the fullness of God's blessing. In 2:13-18 Christ is himself identified *with* peace and also *as* peace. As 5:14 reminds us, Christ is God's blessing of humanity with the fullness of his peace.

The blessed people bless in turn. The chief verbal form their blessing takes is one of praise and thanksgiving (cf., e.g., Pss. 9; 40:1-10; 47; 68; 89:1-18; 95–100; 103–105; 107; 113; 135–136; 144-150; cf. Eph. 5:19-20). But as we discover at a number of places in the

Bible, blessing God with words cannot be divorced from blessing God with concrete everyday material living—the practice of justice and peace. It is true that God takes pleasure in the praise of the beneficiaries of his largesse. Indeed, such praises provide God with a throne (Ps 22:3; cf. in Eph. 2:20-22 the way the reconciled community of erstwhile enemies provides God with a home in a place of worship). But worship apart from a *life* of worship is odious to God (Ps. 50: 1-15, 23; Isa. 58).

These two dimensions—praise and the practice of God's generous justice—are combined in Paul's "fundraising" argument in 2 Corinthians 9:6-15. Paul believed in a kind of circular economy of blessing, where God's liberal dispensing of gifts is intended via the generosity of the blessed to result in the worship of the gift giver— God. God's blessing results in God's being blessed (cf. Shillington: 194-7).

Election and Predestination

Election is a critically important biblical theme. I can do no more here than identify a number of features that bear on our text, either directly or by way of contrast. (For surveys of issues regarding election, see Bruce, 1976; Mendenhall, 1962, 1962b; Patrick; Quell; Schrenk, 1967; Shogren).

In the OT, especially in Deuteronomy, *election* and the closely related *adoption* imply special status and favor that set Israel apart from the nations. The Hebrew term *bḥr,* meaning to "choose" or "select," takes on great significance in contexts where YHWH is said to have "selected" or "chosen" Israel, or where Israelites are called to "choose life" in response to God's having chosen them (Deut. 30:19). Israel is God's specially selected possession (1:11, notes; Exod. 19:5; Deut. 7:6; 14:2). God chooses Israel not because of Israel's righteousness, but because of love for Israel (Deut. 7:7-8; 10:15), to keep the promise made to the patriarchs (Deut. 9:5, 25-29), and finally, as judgment on the "other" nations (e.g., Deut. 9:4-5).

Along with status and special favor comes obligation. Election is closely related to covenant. God chooses a people who subsequently live up to that calling by the quality of their service and their worship— they "choose life." Deuteronomy 10:20-21 expresses this in language that anticipates a number of themes in the great eulogy in Ephesians:

You shall fear the LORD your God; him alone you shall worship; to him you shall hold fast, and by his name you shall swear. He is your praise; he is your God, who has done for you these great and awesome things that your own eyes have seen.

Then as now, special status has often been wrongly understood to bring with it preferential treatment and indulgence of shortcomings. The prophets, in particular, take issue with this perverse reflex to God's generosity. Amos 3:1-2 indicates that election implies God's careful attention, yes, but therefore also judgment. Hosea's naming of his third child "Lo-ammi" (Not-my-people, 1:9) is an intentional message to those who mistake election for impunity. Holiness is appropriately related in the Bible to both blamelessness and "set-apart-ness."

There are two further features of election that bear on our text. One *concentrates* election in the Anointed One; the other *extends* it beyond the borders of Israel. The two are, in fact, interrelated. Through the election of Abraham, God chooses to bless "all nations" (e.g., Gen. 12:1-3; Gal. 3). So also God's relationship to the anointed king is one of election; the king is God's chosen son (e.g., Ps. 2:7; 1 Chron. 28:6). At the same time, the king is representative of God's people. Nowhere does this come to richer expression than in the prophecies collected in Isaiah 40–55, most notably in the Servant Songs.

Scholars still debate over whether YHWH's chosen servant (e.g., Isa. 41:8-9; 43:10; 44:1-2; 45:4) is a specific individual (king? prophet?) or a way of speaking corporately of God's people. To choose one over the other misses the point, however. As Isaiah 55:3-5 makes clear, the role of God's anointed king as witness to the nations is to be the royal mission of the whole people of God. He/they are to be "light to the nations" (42:1-12, esp. 42:6-7; the Greek *ethnoi* is equally well translated as "nations" or as "Gentiles").

It is this fusion of identity, so to speak, between the Anointed One (king/Messiah/Christ) and the people of God that becomes so fruitful for early believers in Jesus. They recognize Jesus to be the Christ, God's Son and Chosen Servant (some manuscripts in fact refer to Jesus as the "Chosen One" in John 1:34 and Luke 9:35; sarcastically on the lips of his tormentors in Luke 23:35). At the same time, they also believe *themselves* to be a "chosen race" (1 Pet. 2:9), even if drawn from the ranks of the foolish, weak, and those of low social standing (1 Cor. 1:26-29; cf. Matt. 11:25-27; James 2:5). Perhaps most mind-boggling for early believers, even if anticipated in Scriptures such as Isaiah (see above), is that God has *chosen* Gentiles!

It is of great importance that this motley crew of "the chosen" has been selected *in Christ*. Just as Deuteronomy makes clear to Israel that its calling emerges from the love of God, and not its own merit, so in the NT the elect are chosen in and through the Chosen One. As such they partake of the lot and task of the Elect One. That means, first, living holy lives in the presence of God. It also means being a witness to the nations. To be *in Christ* is to be in mission. Paul expresses this identification of the elect with Christ in Romans 8:28-30:

> We know that all things work together for good for those who love God, who are called according to his purpose. For those whom he foreknew he also predestined to be conformed to the image of his Son, in order that he might be the firstborn within a large family. And those whom he predestined he also called; and those whom he called he also justified; and those whom he justified he also glorified.

This text brings us to the issue of *predestination*. The concept is not prominent in the NT. The sovereignty of God together with the culpability of humanity is expressed well in Proverbs 16:4-5.

> The LORD has made everything for its purpose,
>   even the wicked for the day of trouble.
> All those who are arrogant are an abomination to the LORD;
>   be assured, they will not go unpunished.

Such a notion of "double predestination" found a ready echo among the covenanters at Qumran. They believed that God had put two spirits into human beings: the "spirit of truth" into the "sons of light," and the "spirit of deceit" into the far more numerous "sons of darkness" (e.g., 1QS 3.17—4.26; 1QM).

Though there are indications in the NT that the negative fate of some sinning individuals is determined by God's choice (e.g., Judas in Mark 14:21 par., and Pharaoh in Rom. 9:17), even that is intended to serve the overall designs of reconciliation and redemption. No attempt is made to resolve the mystery of human responsibility and freedom and God's sovereignty. The tough questions are simply turned aside with a pointed reminder that clay has no rights over the potter (Rom. 9:20-21). Paul's struggle to put together his belief in the absolute sovereignty of a loving and merciful God with the resistance of his own people to the gospel is resolved in favor of salvation (Rom. 11:11-33).

Even if Ephesians 1 shows no explicit interest in those who are *not* chosen or pays no attention to those who do *not* give God pleasure (R. Martin, 1991:14-6), Paul's final words in Romans 11 (vv. 32-33) capture well the disposition that also informs the opening eulogy of Ephesians:

For God has imprisoned all in disobedience so that he may be merciful to all.

O the depth of the riches and wisdom and knowledge of God! How unsearchable are his judgments and how inscrutable his ways!

Christ and Wisdom

In 1:3-14, as in the rest of the letter, Christ is understood to be a comprehensive reality, encompassing in his life and person the reclamation of all creation. That includes, most specifically, reconciled and re-created humanity. The roots of this Christology are found in the tradition of the representative king (see above), and especially in Jewish wisdom, particularly in those traditions that personify wisdom as Lady Wisdom [Wisdom].

The identification of Christ as Wisdom is expressed dramatically in the great christological hymn in Colossians 1:15-20 (E. Martin: 59-77). Christ is the firstborn of creation (1:15) through whom in turn all things in heaven and on earth were created, including all powers (1:16). In fact, in him *all things*, the whole cosmos, hold together (1:17). Christ is the head of the body—the church—holding first place in everything (1:18). He is the image of God, in whom the fullness of God dwells (1:15, 19). Finally, his cross is the means by which God makes peace with *all things* in heaven and on earth (1:20).

This rich mix of creation, re-creation, salvation, redemption, reconciliation, and comprehensiveness, is anticipated in the opening blessing of Ephesians 1:3-14 and explored with great perceptiveness in the rest of the letter, especially its first half (chaps. 1–3).

THE TEXT IN THE LIFE OF THE CHURCH

Worship

The worshipful character of this hymnic and poetic passage alerts us to a number of important insights. First, worship is always accompanied by our consciousness of the limits of human language. Worshipers are aware that language is at best only a pointer, especially when the subject is God. We should be careful not to ask such a passage to bear the weight that some theologians want to place on it.

For example, this passage is concerned to praise God for the blessing of being chosen daughters and sons, and it betrays no philosophical interest in what such a view might imply for those who are not chosen (see above). Further, the view of salvation as gathering up all and everything in Christ (1:10) moves in the direction of limitless generosity. As such, it is ill suited to give precise information on the limits of salvation, limits suggested elsewhere in Ephesians, for example, by the stark dualism of chapter 5. Again, hymnic language is not well suited for philosophical or theological precision; it serves best as a vehicle for gratitude and praise.

Having said that, the language of worship does have the ability to introduce us to worlds and realities beyond, to awaken in us a sense of awe and wonder, even to move us to change our lives. These verses move us to a disposition of gratitude to God for the gift of being chosen, adopted as daughters and sons, to a sense of awe at the scope of God's saving intervention, but also to a willingness to live life as an unbroken act of worship.

This is of great importance for Christian traditions that prize obedience to God's will as evidence of belonging to the people of God. Such an orientation, though correct, is always vulnerable to rendering the Christian life a matter of compliance with rules or conformity to certain church-cultural norms. Life in Christ is thereby impoverished, in that goodness, justice, peace, and love are emptied of freedom and joyful gratitude; they cease to be worship.

Reaction to arid obedience or discipleship is understandable. It often goes hand in hand with a yearning for liturgical renewal. However, rather than reinvesting ethics with the freedom and love of worship, the renewal of worship often focuses on what is done on a Sunday within the confines of gathered worship. Liturgical renewal is less the reinvigoration of service, as one might well recast that phrase (*liturgy [leitourgia]* means "service"), than chiefly a matter of the aesthetics of piety. Beauty is then in danger of becoming divorced from the *practice* of goodness, justice, and peace.

What confronts us in this introductory blessing, indeed in the whole of Ephesians, is a view of worship rooted in and expressed in a *life* of beauty—holiness, blamelessness, and love (1:4; cf. 2:10; 4:24; 5:2). Stated the other way around, holiness, blamelessness, and love are truly present only when they are art, when they are the joyful creative expression of gratitude to God and love for God.

Election and Predestination

In the major traditions of the Reformation, most notably in Calvinism, election and predestination have played a major theological role (on the history of these doctrines, from Augustine to the great Reformers and beyond, see Finger, 1989:129-32, 199-210; McClendon, 1994:180-5; and Schnackenburg: 312-5; among countless other resources). In the believers church tradition, the focus has typically fallen on conversion and the adult decision to follow Christ in discipleship in the context of Christian community. Doctrines such as *election* or *predestination* are viewed with uneasiness if they are seen to undermine the church's efforts at both evangelism and discipleship (Finger, 1985:86-7). Those who have spoken to the issue have done so gingerly, careful to stress the importance and gravity of human decision and to focus God's election solely in a positive light, as a demonstration of God's love as expressed in Christ.

James McClendon states this approach well:

> What is wanted is a doctrine that insists in regard to creation and salvation and last things . . . that God remains a God of electing love, whose choices are never made to set the creation or some part of it at naught, but who always chooses in wisdom for creation's good and (what is the same thing) for God's ultimate sharing of the divine glory with the creature. . . . [Here McClendon cites Ephesians 1:4-5, 9-10 as support.] Still, the old associations of the doctrine [of election and predestination] die so hard that (in my judgment) this part of Christian teaching is of little present service. We do well to emphasize the rule of God in every effective way, while exercising great reserve with regard to this Augustinian deposit. Above all, there must be *no gap* between what we know of God in the biblical narrative that climaxes in Jesus Christ and what we say of God's inclusive, electing love (1994:184-5; italics his).

Much earlier J. C. Wenger also expressed this perspective:

> In order to present the nature of God fairly to the race, it is necessary to emphasize the centrality of the love of God in the same way as does the NT, to place the responsibility for the rejection of Christ squarely on the shoulders of those who refuse to yield to the Savior, and to attribute the surrender of faith on the part of believers to the electing love and mercy of a gracious God. (270)

In short, election and predestination have to do with God lovingly choosing humanity for salvation. Human beings are quite capable of resisting such a divine initiative. Moreover, by means of the Spirit, God sovereignly enables humans freely to participate in the messianic project (e.g., Finger, 1989:136).

The view presented above certainly captures the essential gist of Ephesians 1, a text not well suited to solving these difficult theological and philosophical questions that have occupied Christian theology for centuries. This is because the language is intentionally unguarded. After all, this euphoric recitation of God's benevolence is an act of praise. The eulogy celebrates a love and mercy with taproots so deep they cannot possibly be measured—hence the *pre-* in *predestination*; hence God's selecting us *before* creation of the cosmos. Here is vocabulary better suited to expressing wonder, gratitude, and assurance than theological precision.

Even so, this text speaks to disciples who are apt to see Christian faith as a work ethic. It forcefully reminds them that their relationship to God is first and foremost a result of *God's* grace, not their effort. At the same time, the chosen are elected and predestined precisely for justice and peace, *holiness and blamelessness* (1:4). God has prepared *good works* for the elect so they might *walk in them* (2:10). Seeking justice and making peace are in the end not human achievements—*lest anyone boast* (2:9)—even if they require all the zeal and effort we can muster (4:3). We are *called, chosen, predestined* so as to live for the *pleasure* (1:5, 9) and *praise of God's glory* (1:5-6, 12, 14).

Gathering Up All Things

The expression *all things* in 1:10 signals that salvation is not a matter of saving people from a world that is written off, but a matter of saving, liberating, or restoring reality *in all its dimensions*, **gathering up** all its **things**. This stands in considerable tension with a view that God's care is restricted to humanity, let alone individuals.

As presented in Ephesians, salvation is a matter of the forgiveness and restoration of those who were once sinners, bringing them into the new humanity God has chosen as a dwelling place (chap. 2). But salvation also encompasses *groupings* that divide humanity (e.g., Jews and Gentiles in 2:11-22). This is an important foothold for Christians today who search for ways to address the tears and rifts that have brought oppression and bondage to individuals and also to groups, communities, and societies. Many are working at issues of racism, sexism, victim-offender reconciliation, social and military conflict, and economic inequity, to name only a few.

The comprehensiveness inherent in *all things* leaves nothing—no person and no thing—beyond the reach of God's saving interest. This notion of salvation as re-creation of the world—as recapitulation of *all things*—influenced the thinking of early church fathers, notably Irenaeus (e.g., *Against Heresies* 5.20.2), and has played a significant role up to the present (discussion and texts in Schnackenburg: 315-8; cf. Edwards: 116). The "wideness in God's mercy" implied in *all things* rekindles a sense of urgency for persons to be reconciled to God and enter a new life in Christ. It also invites us to see issues such as poverty, sexism, militarism, and ecological consciousness as on God's agenda of salvation.

For example, we need to be concerned about the destruction of nature, accelerated through industrialization and technology. The fact that the circumference of salvation encompasses *all things* alerts us to extend our understanding of salvation beyond the human community.

It means life also for trees and lakes, bugs and birds. They too are encompassed ultimately in Christ's cosmic body.

Father

Today the designation of God as *Father* has become deeply embroiled in the struggle for salvation within the realm of gender relations. The world in which Ephesians (and the other biblical writings) emerged was patriarchal. We should not be surprised to find God referred to as *Father*. But what is meant thereby, and who is this father?

In contrast to Judaism, Gentile religions were polytheistic, containing both male and female gods. Aside from whether this rendered them more friendly toward women, Gentiles could encompass both genders in their imagery for gods. The legacy in Judaism of believing in, and adhering to, one God made that impossible for Christians. Even so, Jewish wisdom in its early stages personified wisdom in the female figure of ḥokmah or *Sophia* (*Wisdom* in Hebrew and Greek), thus extending the degree to which both genders could model divine reality *[Wisdom]*. Followers of Jesus drank deep drafts from this well in developing their understanding of Jesus.

We cannot be sure how Paul and those who followed him would speak of God today. Whatever difficulties they would have had in referring to God as father or mother may not be ours. Today it might well be in keeping with God's work of *gathering up all things* and both *genders* to speak of God more inclusively as divine parent, reflecting characteristics of *both* father and mother. The use of *Father* as an appellation for God does not preclude that. Indeed, Jesus' frequent use of the term may well have had that as its intention.

As Willard Swartley has pointed out, most biblical texts that speak of God as Father stress divine love, nurture, and the sustaining relationship of paternal care (1992:12-4). Ephesians, in applying *Father* to God, intends to express God's authority and sovereignty, and especially his generativity, love, and care for all people(s) and *all things* (3:14-19). So, while Ephesians was clearly written in a patriarchal culture and has been used to undergird it (see 5:21—6:9, notes), its overall vision is not one that absorbs reality into *maleness*, but through Christ into the God who stands before and after all division (2:11-22; 4:6). That insight is neglected at too great a cost.

Today Christians find themselves in a world as religiously diverse as that of the first century, even *within* the Christian community. This is a context in which the meanings of words change and shift, often slipping beyond control. It is likely, therefore, that much debate and struggle will yet attend the question of the fatherhood of God (TLC for 3:14-21).

Ephesians 1:15-23

Thanksgiving and Intercession

PREVIEW

In Pauline letters it is customary to follow the introductory greeting with thanksgiving [Pauline Letter Structure]. There are only three exceptions. In 2 Corinthians 1, a blessing takes the place of the thanksgiving. In Galatians 1, Paul is so displeased with the Galatians that he offers neither blessing nor thanksgiving. In Ephesians, we find *both* a blessing and a thanksgiving. A tone of thanksgiving already pervades the blessing in 1:3-14 and also reaches to the end of chapter 3. The specific expression of thanks comes in 1:15-16, then quickly gives way to an "intercessory prayer-report" (Lincoln: 49; "thanksgiving prayer report," Perkins: 46). The thanksgiving congratulates the readers, while the report of intercession continues from the previous sentence (1:3-14) the recitation of God's loving initiative toward the readers on a more personal note.

Ephesians 1:15-23 recapitulates the recital of God's blessings in 1:3-14 in the context of a prayer that believers might come to know and appropriate these blessings. This prayer will be taken up again in 3:14-21 after further elaboration in chapters 2 and 3 of what God has done through Christ and his great apostle. A quick comparison shows how closely the two passages are related to each other:

Ephesians 1:15-23		**Ephesians 1:3-14**	
15	faith in Christ	13	believed in him
15	love for all saints	4	holy . . . in love
17	God of Lord Jesus Christ	3	God and Father of . . .
17	Father of glory	6, 12, 14	praise of glory
17	wisdom and revelation	8	with wisdom and insight
18	hope of his calling	4, 12	the called . . . hoped first in Christ
18	inheritance	11, 14	inheritance
20	raised Jesus according to his great might	11	accomplished all according to his will
20-23	Christ as head over all *(kephalē)*	10	all things gathered up in Christ *(anakephalaiōsasthai)*

Like 1:3-14, the Greek text of 1:15-23 is one long sentence. To ease the reading, editors and translators have broken the passage into several sentences (two in Nestle-Aland Greek text; five in NIV; four in NRSV). Following is a skeleton of the section, with indentations to show the structure and chief emphases (cf. Schematic Trans.).

Structure of 1:15-23

For this reason also I,
  since (or once) I heard of your faith and love,
do not cease to give thanks for you,
  remembering you in my prayers,
    that God might give you knowledge of
        [note synonyms for knowledge and insight in 1:17-18]
    the hope of his calling,
    the wealth of his inheritance,
    the greatness of his power for you,
        [note string of power synonyms in 1:19]
    measured by the power at work in Christ,
      raising him from the dead,
      seating him at the right hand of God,
        over all powers, *[note list of powers in 1:21]*
      putting all things under his feet,
      making him head over all
        with/for/through the church
        his body
        the fullness of him who fills all.

Grammatically, the main assertion of this sentence is the expression of thanksgiving. The bulk of the sentence is built, however, around the prayer that readers might receive knowledge (1:17-18) of hope, inheritance, and power (1:18-19)—power at work in Christ in, for, and through the church (1:20-23).

As in verses 3-14, the theocentric emphasis is immediately noticeable: God is *the Father of glory* (1:17). The *calling, inheritance,* and *power* are solely the result of God's initiative (1:19). Most dramatically, God's prime role in the drama shines forth in the *raising* and *exalting* of Christ (1:20-22). It is that resurrection and that exaltation that becomes the measure for what God is doing for the *church*—Christ's *body* (1:19, 22-23).

OUTLINE

Thanksgiving and Prayer of Intercession, 1:15-16

Content of Intercession, 1:17-19a
1:18b	Knowledge of Hope
1:18c	Knowledge of Inheritance
1:19a	Knowledge of Power

The Measure of Immeasurable Power, 1:19b-22a
1:20	The Raising and Enthronement of Christ
1:21-22a	The Subjection of All to Christ as Head

The Church, 1:22b-23
1:23a	The Body
1:23b	The Fullness

EXPLANATORY NOTES

Thanksgiving and Prayer of Intercession 1:15-16

Verse 15 begins, *For this reason also I*, and continues in verse 16 with *do not cease to give thanks for you*. Grammatically, the grounds for thanksgiving are related to the blessings of God just rehearsed in the lengthy blessing in verses 3-14. Most immediately, however, thanksgiving is precipitated by the report of the *faith* and *love* of the recipients. In thanking *God,* it is recognized that the faith and love of the addressees are part of God's manifold blessings toward them (1:13).

Faith *(pistis)* is identified as *in the Lord Jesus,* and *love (agapē)* as *for* (lit., *into) all the saints* or *holy ones.* We most naturally and not incorrectly read this as faith directed toward Jesus and love toward fellow believers. But *pistis* can be translated also as *faithfulness* (1:1, notes). To be *faithful in the Lord Jesus* is then virtually synonymous with *love toward all the saints.* In such a reading, *in Christ* indicates not so much the object of faith as it does the context or condition of faithfulness (so also Barth, 1974:146; Best, 1998:160; Lincoln: 55; Schnackenburg: 72).

Thanking God for the readers' fidelity and love serves pastorally to affirm believers. At the same time, in keeping with the theocentric perspective of this whole chapter, credit is thereby firmly lodged with God. In other words, the thanksgiving, however brief, serves to congratulate readers on their faith(fulness) and love, even as such faith and love are acknowledged to be *God's* blessings.

Content of Intercession 1:17-19a

The clause *remembering you in my prayers* in verse 16 is immediately dependent on *I give thanks constantly for you* (Structure of 1:15-23). However, the bulk of the lengthy sentence reports on the content of the intercession.

Though translations such as NIV and NRSV begin a new sentence at verse 17, the Greek moves into the content of the intercession with a purpose clause, *in order that God.* Such prayer is a request directed to God and also ceaseless labor on behalf of the readers for a specific purpose *(hina: in order that).* The outcome of this labor is guaranteed by *the God of our Lord Jesus Christ, the Father of glory* (cf. 1:3, notes on relationship between God and Jesus Christ).

The unique phrase *the Father of glory (doxa)* may be a Semitic way of saying "glorious father." But it also recognizes God as source and goal of all *glory* (cf. "Father of lights," James 1:17). Specifically, God is source, guarantor, and goal of what is offered to the saints— hope, inheritance, and power (in Pauline thought, glory and power are virtual synonyms; e.g., Rom. 6:4; Best, 1998:162; Lincoln: 56).

The prayerful concern for knowledge recalls wisdom and insight in 1:8. Here it reflects specific dependency on Colossians 1:9. The list of words for knowledge or wisdom has grown: *spirit of **wisdom** and **revelation** in the **knowledge** of God, having the eyes of the heart **enlightened** so as to **know**.* The discussion of wisdom in Colossians 1:9 has alerted us to the close connection between *wisdom and insight* on one hand (cf. Eph. 1:8), and *revelation* on the other hand *[Wisdom]*. Now the connection is made explicit (1:17). Alongside many synonyms for knowledge and wisdom, God is identified also in several ways as the source of such wisdom: *spirit, revelation,* and *opening of the eyes of the heart* (cf. 1 Cor. 2:6-16).

Little is to be gained from seeking precise differences in nuance between these various words for wisdom and revelation. It is typical of the style of Ephesians to heap up terms to emphasize their importance. The varied terminology is meant to spark the imagination of readers to the wonder of God's wisdom revealed to believers.

First, as we noted in the discussion of wisdom in 1:3-14, to understand that God is the *source* of wisdom in no way downplays the importance of the human exercise of that wisdom and vice versa (note how personified Wisdom relates to the faithful as companion and teacher in, e.g., Prov. 8–9, Wisd. of Sol. 6–9 *[Wisdom]*). This is expressed clearly in the phrase *spirit of wisdom*, echoing texts such as Isaiah 11:2 and Wisdom of Solomon 7:7; 9:17. In such texts the immense privilege of receiving such knowledge is indicated by the fact that the *spirit of wisdom* falls on royal representatives of God—on kings and messiahs. In Ephesians such special knowledge is being prayerfully requested for *all* "ordinary" sons and daughters of God.

The *spirit* in verse 17 is a *spirit of wisdom* and *revelation*, indicating that wisdom and revelation are intimately related; both have God as source. This suggests that *wisdom* is participatory and also that God and human beings meet as active participants in the event of *revelation*. Within the broader context of Paul's letters, we think, for example, of prophetic activity, described in 1 Corinthians 14:1 as the greatest gift the Spirit bestows on the church (cf. emphasis on *revelation* in 14:6, 26, 30). But, as 1 Thessalonians 5:19-21 reminds us, prophecy needs to be tested in the community. And that requires wisdom.

Spirit appears here without an article, leaving it ambiguous as to whether *spirit* refers here to God's Holy Spirit (NIV; so emphatically Fee, 1994:675-9; also Best, 1998:162-3; Lincoln: 56-7; Schnackenburg: 74) or more generally to the presence of a spirit of wisdom, divine and/or human (NRSV; so Barth, 1974:162). The phrase recalls Isaiah 11:2, where the Messiah of God exercises his rule with *the spirit of the Lord* upon him, *the spirit of wisdom and understanding*. With the presence of revelation in the phrase as adapted here, the connection to God as source of wisdom is only strengthened. With or without an article, *spirit* is God's Spirit enlightening believers who are called to a messianic vocation.

We encounter, further, the striking and unusual image of *the enlightened eyes of the heart*. The heart is commonly viewed in biblical literature as the seat of emotion, will, and understanding, much like the mind (e.g., Gen. 6:5; Ps. 77:6; Prov. 15:14; Jer. 31:33; Mark 12:30; Acts 4:32; Rom. 10:10). NJB thus freely translates the phrase as *the eyes of the mind*. Elsewhere in Ephesians we find related expressions. Thus 4:23 contains the phrase *the spirit of your minds* in a context like the present one. And Gentiles are noted for their ignorance and *hardness of heart* (4:18). With respect to *eyes*, note in Psalm 13:3 the image of eyes having light as a sign of life itself.

The combination of the two motifs into one image is as unusual as it is illuminating (it later finds an echo in, e.g., 1 Clem. 36.2; 59.3; Odes of Sol. 15). This image expresses the twin convictions that it is God who both opens the innermost organ of perception and conviction and, in the process, gives life to those who were dead (cf. 2:5-6; 4:22-24). It is quite possible that the event of baptism lurks in the background (cf. Rom. 6 and 13; Houlden: 275). Indeed, Ephesians 5:14 may well be a baptismal hymn or hymn fragment in which baptism is celebrated as the experience of illumination: *Sleeper, awake! Rise from the dead, and Christ will shine on you* (Perkins: 48).

1:18b Knowledge of Hope

The content of this knowledge relates to hope, inheritance, and power. The first object of knowledge is *the hope to which [God] has called you* (lit., *the hope of his calling*). Without recourse to the other Pauline letters, it is difficult to give precise content to this hope. We should be somewhat cautious about filling in the blanks that way, however, even if Ephesians was likely intended to be read alongside them from the beginning.

Ephesians has some clues as to the content of *hope*. Those who *hoped first* are mentioned in 1:12, and *hope* is again referred to in 4:4. In Ephesians, however, there is no explicit mention of Christ's appearing, little of final judgment (beyond a reference to *wrath,* 5:6), and little of future salvation (except *the day of redemption* in 4:30 [cf. 1:14] and possibly *the kingdom of Christ and of God* in 5:5). Even so, in the opening blessing, we noted the movement toward unity in Christ, captured in the image of *gathering up all things in Christ* (1:10). In light of a present reality so marked by evil (e.g., 2:1-2; 5:3-16; 6:10-13), the image of gathering up all things in Christ is an inherently eschatological—*hope-full*—image. A further clue is found in the next item on the list of "must-knows."

1:18c Knowledge of Inheritance

Verse 18 ends with the phrase, literally translated, *the wealth of the glory of his inheritance in the holy ones*. As the chart comparing this section with 1:3-14 shows (Preview), *inheritance* is a recurring emphasis in this chapter (1:11, 14). It relates to what sons and daughters of God have coming to them, participation in *the kingdom of Christ and of God* (5:5; cf. Gal. 3:23—4:7). To speak of the wealth and glory of the inheritance does not tell us much about the inheritance, but it does reflect the sense of awe with which we are to contemplate what God has in store for *the holy ones*. To be given certain knowledge of this is not to have received information so much as confidence to look with enlightened eyes of the heart and thus to live now in light of that future.

The phrase *in the holy ones* (lit.) is more puzzling. *In (en)* can certainly mean *among*, as the NRSV translates it. The difficulty rests chiefly with the identity of *the holy ones (hagioi)*. On one hand, *hagioi* translated as *saints* is one of the most common ways of referring to believers in Pauline letters, as also in Ephesians (1:1, notes; 2:19; 3:8; 4:12; 5:3; 6:18). To identify *saints* as believers suggests that the *inheritance* will be experienced with all other believers.

In the OT, on the other hand, *holy ones* often refers to heavenly beings surrounding God's throne. They are variously portrayed as angels or even as a community of divine beings surrounding the throne of God, the so-called divine council (e.g., Ps. 89:3-18). In this case the phrase is derived most immediately from Colossians 1:12, where *sharing the inheritance of the holy ones in light* is even more suggestive of heavenly beings than is the wording in Ephesians. The implication of such an interpretation is that believers share an inheritance with heavenly divine beings in the heavenlies (2:5-6). The writings of the Dead Sea covenanters at Qumran provide numerous passages in which the faithful enjoy close interaction with angelic beings (e.g., 1QS 11.7; 1QM 12.1-2; 1QH 11.21-22; cf. Wisd. of Sol. 5:5).

Such an interpretation goes against many translations of this verse (*saints*, NRSV, NIV; *holy people*, NJB; *members of the church*, NAB; *his people*, NEB, REB, GNB/TEV). Nevertheless, we must reckon with the biblical and more broadly Jewish understanding of *holy ones*, and with the tendency of Ephesians to emphasize the lofty status of believers. Hence, we should hear in *the holy ones* more than a reference to fellow members of the church—unless, indeed, such membership is understood as nothing less than membership in the heavenly court (cf. 2:6; cf. Best, 1998:168).

A different twist is placed on this phrase if *the wealth of the glory of his inheritance among the holy ones* refers not to the inheritance God *offers* the saints (as in 1:14), but to God's *own (his)* inheritance (Lincoln: 60; cf. 1:11-12, notes). While this interpretation seems somewhat strained, it highlights the importance of knowing that one is part of the wealth of God's own glorious inheritance. It remains ambiguous whether *in the holy ones* means that God's inheritance consists of saints, or that God enjoys his inheritance in the company of the holy ones who are members of the heavenly court.

Whatever the interpretation, this prayer for wisdom centers on knowing that the inheritance is sure. Furthermore, this prayer of intercession is important and needs to be ceaseless because such knowledge gives confidence for living in the *present*. Confidence in the future frees believers to give themselves wholly to the present. That point is much in evidence in the last item in the petition.

1:19a Knowledge of Power

The last item on the list of things to be known and understood is *the immeasurable greatness of his power for us who believe* (v. 19). Note the intensification from *hope of his calling* to rich and *glorious inheritance*, and now to *immeasurable power. Immeasurable* translates *huperballon*, from which comes our word *hyperbole*. In its verb form, it means literally "to throw over" or "beyond." As an adjective it can thus be translated as "exceeding" or "beyond measure." The root word is common in this letter (2:7; 3:19) and is typical of the underlying vision (cf. the only other instances of Pauline usage: 2 Cor. 3:10; 4:7; 9:14). The purpose of this choice of vocabulary is to say that God's power defies description. But that does not prevent the author from heaping up power terms in verse 19b, as we shall see shortly.

One thing is of first importance in the context of this prayer: believers come to understand that this great power is *for us* (so NRSV, NIV, NJB; similarly NASB, *toward us;* REB, *open to us*). The power is *for us* who *believe.* We should be careful to preserve here the dynamic quality of belief as "trust." (This is also how I read Rom. 3:22; 1 Cor. 1:21; 14:22; Gal. 3:22; 1 Thess. 1:7; 2:10, 13). God's power is exercised for the sake of those who trust God.

Some translations have *in us* (RSV, NAB, GNB/TEV), suggesting that God's great power is at work in and through those who believe. This shifts the sense from being *recipients* to being *agents* of divine power. Such a meaning is quite consistent with God's raising *us* with Christ (2:4-6), and with the call to put on God's powerful armor (6:10-20). However, the Greek preposition used here is *eis* (lit., *into*), and not *en*, which can mean "through" *["In"].* Mostly *eis* expresses direction and purpose. It appears nine times in chapter 1. *For us* is preferred (in 1:19a), even if the implications of *in us* would fit the objectives of Ephesians very well.

The Measure of Immeasurable Power 1:19b-22a

The phrase *according to the working of his great power* introduces the last part of this long sentence. The qualifying phrase *according to (kata)* is frequent in Ephesians, encountered repeatedly in the earlier section of this chapter (1:5, 7, 9, 11 [2 times]). Verses 20-22 are intended to qualify, to define, and somewhat ironically, to provide a measure for the immeasurable greatness of God's power mentioned in verse 19.

Literally, we should read, *according to the energy of the strength of his might, which [God] energized* . . . (also in 1:11; 3:20). We find a chain of terms for this divine energy: *power (dynamis), might (kratos), strength (ischus), energy (energeia).* As in the case of the numerous terms for wisdom in verses 17-18, little is to be gained from seeking differences of meaning. In English as in Greek, the terms are quite interchangeable and are intended to function together to express the incomparable power of God (cf. Arnold, 1989:73-5). Perhaps *energeia* is an exception in that it stresses the effective operative power of God in raising Jesus from the dead. Ephesians 6:10 is similar: *Be em**power**ed in the Lord and in the **strength** of his **might**!* Verse 19 also recalls Colossians 1:11: (lit.) *powered in all power according to the strength of his glory.*

In the background lurks a tradition in which such heaping up of power terms characterizes *God* as a great Creator and Warrior (cf., e.g., Deut. 3:24; Isa. 40:26; Eph. 6:10, notes). The present list is intended to jolt readers into an awareness that the power at work *for us* is nothing other than the power that has created, sustains, judges, and saves the universe, and that raised Jesus from the dead.

1:20 The Raising and Enthronement of Christ

This divine power is described first with a dense summary of what God has done for Jesus: God raised him from the dead and enthroned him in the heavenly places, above all powers. God subjected all things to him, making him head of all (1:20-22; cf. 1:10).

Notice first the theocentric perspective. It is not Jesus who rises, but God who raises him (Best, 1998:170-2). The power of the *Father of glory* puts Christ on the throne and thereby in the position of privilege at God's own right hand. This locates Christ *far above* all other powers and names *[Cosmology of Ephesians]*. It is *God's* power that places *all* powers under Christ's feet, in the process making him *head of all*. Throughout this scenario, Christ remains the recipient of God's intervention on his behalf.

Two biblical texts are used to shape the motif of Christ's exaltation: first, a clear allusion to Psalm 110:1 in verse 20; then, a quotation of Psalm 8:6 in verse 22.

The Lord says to my lord,
  "Sit at my right hand
until I make your enemies your footstool." (Ps. 110:1)

You have given him (them) dominion over the works of your hands:
  you have put all things under his (their) feet. (Ps. 8:6, RSV/NRSV;
  the Hebrew has the singular)

Two distinct traditions are fused (as they also are in 1 Cor. 15:25-27; Heb. 1:13; 2:6-8; cf. Best, 1998:171-2, 180-1). Psalm 110:1 is a part of a psalm that celebrates God's enthronement of his vice regent—his Messiah or Christ—and God's assurance of victory over his regent's enemies (TBC). Psalm 8:6 is part of a psalm that praises God and in the process reflects on the exalted place of human beings within creation (TBC). In Ephesians, Psalm 8:6 is interpreted messianically. A text that at one time intended to say something about humanity as a whole in God's creation serves now to celebrate Jesus' *special* status as the exalted Christ. By placing that text next to the royal psalm of victory, the phrase *he subjected all things under his feet* becomes an assertion of status and also one of subjugation and victory.

Even so, the messianic use of Psalm 8:6 does not obscure its original focus on the place of humanity in God's creation. On the contrary, in Ephesians 1 the rehearsal of what God has done *for Christ* is meant to indicate what God's power means *for humanity—for us* (1:19). That intention is well served by the use of Psalm 8:6 in that with Christ's restoration to a position of preeminence, humanity is restored to its intended position in creation (cf. 2:5-7). Christ is the true *Adam*, the true human being, under whose feet *all things* have been placed (cf. 1:10). Humanity is restored *in him* to its rightful place and role through the reconciling intervention of God.

1:21-22a The Subjection of All to Christ as Head

Before exploring more fully the connection between Christ and reconciled humanity in verse 23, a word about "the powers" *[Powers]*. Most readers already familiar with 6:10-13 will be predisposed to seeing the powers in 1:21 as hostile. That impression, supported through the allusion to Psalm 110:1 in verse 20 (cf. esp. 1 Cor. 15:25-27), will be reinforced in 2:2. However true such a perspective on the powers is for Ephesians as a whole (cf. 2:2; 6:12), that may not completely exhaust its meaning in this passage.

The hymn in Colossians 1:15-20 sheds some light on our passage. Briefly, this passage refers to Christ as *the image of God* (Col.

1:15), indicating contact with the tradition of Genesis 1:26 and Psalm 8. The Colossian hymn is more interested, however, in connecting Christ with the tradition of personified wisdom, the agent of creation [Wisdom]. It thus credits Christ, the firstborn of creation, with *creating* the powers (thrones, dominions, rulers, and powers; Col. 1:16). The powers are not seen as *inherently* hostile, however much they have become so. They are, instead, features of a divinely ordered cosmos (e.g., see Wink, 1984:6-11; 1992:10; J. H. Yoder, 1994:140-4) [Powers]. The concern in the Colossian hymn is to position Christ in a preeminent position over those powers (cf. also 2:15; E. Martin: 63).

As much as Ephesians is marked by a view of the powers as being aggressively hostile (6:11-12), the perspective captured in the Colossian hymn may have left its mark on this particular part of Ephesians. In contrast to 6:10-13, the quotation of Psalm 8:6 may indicate that the stress here is less on victory than on status (Perkins: 51). After all, the one clearly does not exclude the other, and victory over foes will soon move much more clearly into focus. Carr goes too far in viewing the powers here as heavenly hosts offering recognition to Christ as Lord (98-9).

Again we encounter a chain of terms—*all rule (archē) and authority (exousia) and power (dunamis) and dominion (kuriotēs) and every name (onoma) that is named.* Modern readers may find *name* out of place in a list of powers. And indeed, it may be no more than making sure no potency is left out (Best, 1998:173; Wink, 1984:22). But *name* equaled "potency" in the ancient world, as in many places today (cf. Phil. 2:9; Rev. 6:8; 13:1, 17; 14:1; and frequently in Gnostic literature). Note the importance of "naming" in Ephesians 5:3 (see notes on 5:3). Perhaps the author is alluding specifically to the practice of magic, where the utterance of names was an essential part of conjuring powers (Arnold, 1989:54-5).

Who or what are these powers? Roughly three interpretations are prevalent in our day: First, the powers are personal, spiritual, supernatural, and demonic. Second, the powers are political, either as rulers or as systems of control, and are not in and of themselves evil. Three, all of the above (2:2, notes; 6:12, notes) [Powers]. We are least likely to err if we opt for the third alternative, and that not as a matter of convenience. Early Christians and their contemporaries viewed all of life, individual and corporate, private and public, religious and political, as interpenetrated with spiritual forces and potencies governing events (cf. 2:2!).

Even if not all powers are in and of themselves evil, they are mostly so in the present evil age. The purpose of listing the powers here is less to provide an inventory of these powers than to state unambiguously that Christ has been made *head over* them *all ["Head"]*. The list of powers is intended to be so comprehensive as to leave no potency, no center of power, no force, great or small, seen or unseen, present or future *(in this age or the next),* beyond the rule of Christ (cf. Rom. 8:38-39).

Verses 19b-22 raise then an important question: If God has exalted Christ to his right hand and placed all things under him, including all powers, why do we still encounter hostile powers as *presently* active in chapters 2 and 6? What is the meaning of Christ's exaltation alongside the continuing rebellion of hostile powers and the call for believers to take up arms against them? One solution is to take these verses as indicating that the powers have been dealt with, as in Colossians 2:15. But that tends to diminish the importance of the struggle described in Ephesians 6:10-20. The other is to downplay the importance of the claim to lordship and victory in this passage in favor of ongoing conflict in chapter 6.

Neither option catches the perspective of this letter. Ephesians celebrates what God has done for, in, and through Christ precisely in order to empower the church to do what still needs to be done. These two emphases are equally important. Believers need to *know* of God's immeasurable power (1:17-18) precisely because of where they are located in relation to the powers who still need both to be informed (3:10) and overcome (6:10-20). Yes, believers are now already *seated with Christ in the heavenlies,* as we will see in the next section (2:6), but for the author of Ephesians, that places them into the thick of battle with those powers also residing *in the heavenlies* (6:10-12).

God's order of creation and salvation is still in the process of being realized in Christ (cf. 1:10). Such transformation is neither momentary nor without conflict and struggle. Hence, believers need *continual* prayer (1:16; cf. 3:14; 6:18) and a deeply rooted memory and knowledge of what God in Christ *has done* for them (Neil Elliott, 114-24, misses this point entirely, conflating or combining perspectives of Colossians and Ephesians and misreading both).

Two further observations support our interpretation. First, the celebration of Christ's status *over* the powers plays exactly the same role the assurances of victory do *before* the battles waged in God's name in the OT. The words "I [or the Lord] have given them into your hands" were spoken *before* battle (e.g., Josh. 8:1; 10:19; 4:14; cf. von Rad: 42-4). These verses thus anticipate battles yet to be fought (6:10-20).

The second observation is related. While it is doubtful that these verses derive directly from early hymnody, it is beyond dispute that the ideas and language in this passage have much in common with the blessing in 1:3-14 and the hymns in Colossians 1:15-20 and Philippians 2:6-11. Hymns characteristically celebrate as *already completed* what is still *anticipated*. That is because it is *God*, the Lord of time and space, who is praised.

The Church 1:22b-23

The final item in the recitation of God's acts of divine power is that Christ has been given headship (lit., *to be head*) *["Head"]* over all things *for* or *through the church* (1:22; on the church in Ephesians, see Best, 1998:622-41). Both the terms *church* and *body* appear here for the first time in the letter. *Church* translates the Greek *ekklēsia,* which means "assembly of those who are called." While that term enjoyed broad currency in the Hellenistic world, its meaning in Pauline circles is rooted in the biblical notion of the people of God who are "called out" (cf. the emphasis on call and election in 1:3-14). Usually in Paul's writings, *church* refers to a local congregation (but cf. 1 Cor. 10:32); here, however, as in the rest of Ephesians, it is used for the whole of the community identified with Christ (cf. Banks: 40-50; Meeks: 74-110, esp. 108).

The present text is somewhat ambiguous on how exactly the church is related to Christ as *head*. First, while the church is identified as Christ's *body* in verse 23, the wording at the end of verse 22 suggests that Christ is *head* of *all things*, not just the *church* (cf. 1:10) *["Head"]*. Second, *church* appears in the dative case, which allows a number of translations.

First, both NIV and NRSV understand this dative as a dative of advantage, translating it as *for the church*. The church is then the prime beneficiary of God's act of making Christ the head of all things, a claim consistent with the great blessing in verses 3-14.

A second and closely related possibility is suggested by the literal translation of God *giving* Christ as *head*. In Ephesians, *to give* is usually followed by the recipient in the dative case (dative of indirect object; e.g., 1:17; 3:2, 7, 8; 4:7, 8, 27, 29; 6:19). Literally translated, *God gave [Christ] to the church as head over all* (so NASB, GNB/TEV, REB). We should then not miss the startling assertion that the *head over all* is given to the *body*, the Lord of the cosmos to the church (cf. the reference to Christ as *gift*, a possible translation of 4:7; but note that the body grows into the head in 4:15-16) *["Head"]*.

Third, the dative can also have an instrumental meaning (dative of means). Our text is then best translated as *through the church*. God has made Christ *head over all through the church*. This interpretation is possible only if *to give* is used strictly in the sense of *to appoint* (cf. 4:11; Barth, 1974:157-8). This would imply that God uses the church to make real Christ's headship over *all things*. Such an interpretation finds support in 3:10, where the church breaks the news of God's wisdom (meaning Christ) to the powers. Support can also be found in 4:12, where saints build up Christ's body, and in 6:10-17, where believers battle the powers (cf. 1 Cor. 15, where Christ does battle).

Perhaps again it is foolish to choose one interpretation over another, especially since they all find support within the letter. In either interpretation the church moves to center stage as the body of the Messiah, benefiting from and implicated in Christ's headship.

1:23a The Body

The image of the *body (sōma)* comes as no surprise. It would have been well-known to the readership (Rom. 12:4-5; 1 Cor. 12:12-27; Col. 1:18, 24; 2:19; 3:15). It also has been implicit in the ascription of headship (1:22) and hidden in the image of *gathering up* (1:10). It will appear again in 2:16; 4:4, 12, 16; and 5:23, 30. We should notice that in neither Romans 12 nor 1 Corinthians 12 is Christ spoken of as *head* in distinction from the *body* (on head and body, cf. Barth, 1974:183-99; Best, 1998:189-96, 629-32; Lincoln: 67-73). For the image of *the body,* the author evidently draws on Colossians. Further, in some contrast to Paul's usual practice, where this image is used to address relationships within a local body of believers, here in Ephesians (as earlier in Col.) *the body* has taken on comprehensive dimensions; it refers to all those who hold to Jesus as Messiah, and more (cf. Banks: 72-81; Meeks: 89-90).

In Ephesians, the metaphor of the *body* expresses several crucial insights. First, it ties the church intimately to Christ the *head*. This stress conforms to the central burden of the prayer in 1:15-23 that believers might know what is true for Christ and also *for them*. The closer the tie between them and their *head*, the more the power at work in Christ can be said to be at work for, in, and through them too. Here hierarchy is less the point than identification. The point of referring to Christ here as *head* is to establish his redemptive rule over *all things* (cf. 1:10); the point of referring to the church as his *body* is to involve that church in his power and his task *["Head"]*.

Second, in light of Christ's headship over *all things*, to identify the church as his *body* is to imply a connection between *church* and *all things*. The universal outlook of the author draws the cosmological implications of the motif back into view. We would not overstate the connection to say that in Ephesians the *church* is already what *all things* are in the process of becoming. As Christ's body, the church is the reconciled or gathered-up cosmos in embryonic form (cf. esp. 2:11-22).

Third, to identify the church as the *body* of Christ is also to imply something about its task. In 4:12-13 the saints are to *build up the body* until it reaches the full stature of Christ. The church is a growing organism (cf. 4:15-16) that is intended ultimately to incorporate *all things* (cf. 1:10). This sense of church as reconciled whole within a world yet to be wholly reconciled comes to expression in the last phrase in the passage, *the fullness of him who fills all in all*.

1:23b The Fullness

The closing phrase of this sentence, *the fullness of the one who fills all things in every way,* presents us with some fascinating problems of translation. First, does *fullness (plērōma)* mean "something that fills," or "something that is filled"? Is *fullness* content and/or receptacle? It can mean both. Second, who carries this fullness, or who is being filled? Christ? The church? Third, who is doing the filling? Christ? God? At stake in finding an answer to these questions is the relationship of the church to God's overall plan for the cosmos as it is being worked out in Christ.

Paul uses the term *plērōma* in various letters, but usually in the restricted sense of "full measure" of time or people (e.g., Rom. 11:12, 25; Gal. 4:4). In later Christian (esp. Gnostic) thought, "the Pleroma" became the subject of a great deal of speculation, in which it came to signify the space closest to God, encompassing the divine emanations (on the rich variety of uses in literature of that day, cf. Barth, 1974:200-10; Best, 1998:183-9; Lincoln:72-6). In Hellenistic Stoic thought, the idea was widespread that everything in the universe is permeated with the divine spirit or presence. This concept left its mark on Jewish thinking (e.g., Wisd. of Sol. 7:24). We should hear such notions resonating richly in this passage, precisely because it is the author's concern to draw as largely as possible the circle of God's presence, Christ's headship, and the church's identity and task.

Colossians 1:19 locates *all the fullness of God* in Christ. The point is that in Christ, God is present *fully* (cf. Col. 2:9). Thus we might take the phrase here in Ephesians to refer similarly to Christ as the fullness of *God*, continuing the recitation of what God has done in and for Christ in verse 22. God's *gathering up of all things* in 1:10

would echo such a note. God is filling up Christ with all things, as it were. At the same time, God is filling the cosmos with himself in and through Christ (cf. 4:6).

Ephesians, however, we will frequently note, highlights the church sometimes precisely in places where other letters of Paul would speak simply of Christ (Introduction). The exact phrase from Colossians 1:19 (referring to Christ) is here applied to believers—a shift in focus hinted at, interestingly, in Colossians 2:10. If one takes into account that the author of Ephesians typically speaks of Christ and church in relation to each other, not least in this passage, then we should take *fullness* or *filling* to stand grammatically in the same place as *body*. The church is the receptacle of God's fullness, and as such it carries the fullness, even as it is in the process of being filled. As *Christ's* body, it also participates in being the *filling* (cf. 3:19).

Two further matters compound the difficulties surrounding the proper translation and interpretation of *fullness (plērōma)*. One, the participial verb *pleroumenos* can be either a passive participle ("being filled") or a middle participle, with either passive or an active meaning ("filling"), often reflexive ("filling oneself"). Most translators treat it as an active verb. The second issue is the phrase *in every way*, or *all in all (ta panta en pasin)*. The familiar *all things* is a translation of *ta panta* (1:10-11, notes). So we might take *ta panta* in this case to refer to "all that which is being filled," similar to all things being gathered up in 1:10.

The versions reflect the variety of possibilities. Here is a sample:

The fullness of him who . . .
1. [active voice]   fills all in all (NRSV)
                    fills everything in every way (NIV)
                    fills the universe in all its parts (NAB)
2. [passive voice] is filled, all in all (NJB)
3. [middle voice]   fills himself in every way (possible trans.)

In the first (active) translations, Christ is doing the filling, or God through Christ; either God is filling the cosmos with the church (*plērōma* as content), or he is filling the church in every way (*plērōma* as receptacle; cf. 3:19). In the second (passive) example, Christ is the one who is being filled with the church and, in the end, with the cosmos (cf. 1:10; 4:11-16). In the third proposal (with middle voice), God is the one who through Christ and his body is filling up himself with all things, so that in the end, God will be *all in all* (4:6; cf. 1 Cor. 15:28). All three possibilities find echoes in the letter. Translators must regrettably choose between them; interpreters need not. Perhaps the suggestive and imprecise nature of this choice of language is intentional.

None of these interpretations are excluded, and all are invited.

Obviously, it is impossible to fully catch the dynamic sense of the Greek vocabulary. But the clear implication is that the church, as Christ's body, is fully implicated in the filling up of all things. It is startling to say that the church is the recipient of God's *fullness* (3:19). But it is nothing short of breathtaking to think of the church as the *fullness* God is pouring out into the cosmos. To accept the first and reject the second is the height of selfishness; to accept the second while rejecting the first is the height of arrogance.

THE TEXT IN BIBLICAL CONTEXT

In addition to the following discussion, readers should refer back to "Christ and Wisdom" in TBC for 1:3-14, and forward to "Are the Powers All Bad?" in TBC for 6:10-20, as well as to the essays *[Wisdom] [Powers]*.

As the notes have shown repeatedly, this long sentence running from verse 15 to verse 23 reflects characteristic themes in Ephesians. At the same time, phrases and words utilized by the author are highly resonant of other Pauline writings, especially Colossians. We can summarize them as follows:

Ephesians		Colossians	Others
1:15-16	thanking, remembering, praying	1:3-4, 9	Philem. 4-6; Rom. 1:8-9
1:17-18	praying for wisdom	1:9-10	
1:18	wealth of glory	1:27	Rom. 11:33
1:20	raising	2:12	Rom. 8:11
1:20	seating	3:1	Rom. 8:34
1:21	powers	1:16	Rom. 8:38; 1 Cor. 15:24
1:21	name		Phil. 2:9-10
1:22	under feet		1 Cor. 15:27-28; Phil. 3:21
1:22	head	1:17-19	
1:23	church as body	1:24	Rom. 12:5; 1 Cor. 12:12, 27

The Vindication of the Just

The concentrated description of God's raising and exalting Christ over all things, including the powers (1:20-23), is a deeply rooted biblical paradigm. It was recited in various ways again and again, not least in the praise and hymnody of the church. Note, for example, the way the credal formula Paul cites in Romans 1:3 identifies Christ's resurrection with his exaltation to the status of divine Son. In the hymn of

Philippians 2:6-11, Christ, after emptying himself and living the vulnerable life of a slave to the point of death, is raised and exalted to the status of cosmic Lord, far above every other name (cf. Eph. 1:21!). The same scenario underlies 1 Corinthians 15:20-28.

This schema of faithfulness, suffering, death, and vindication by an all-powerful God is richly represented in biblical and related literature. Psalm 22 and Isaiah 53 are important examples. The latter is notable both for the decisiveness of God's intervention on behalf of his suffering servant and for the fact that the servant's enemies are not eliminated. Instead, they are reconciled through the suffering of that same servant, a theme that plays a significant role in Ephesians 2:11-22. Both the Psalm and Isaianic texts have had a profound effect on the passion narratives of the Gospels (cf. also Wisd. of Sol. 2–5, a text dependent on Isaiah 53). This tradition also played a very important role in the development of martyr theology (as in, e.g., 2 Macc. 7). So, at the time of the writing of Ephesians, this tradition is both old and contemporary.

Psalm 110:1 is of particular interest to NT writers and to the author of Ephesians. It is quoted or alluded to frequently as a way to celebrate Christ's resurrection and exaltation (e.g., Matt. 26:64; Mark 14:62; 16:19; Luke 22:69; Acts 2:33-35; 7:56; Rom. 8:34; 1 Cor. 15:25; Col. 3:1; Heb. 8:1; 10:12; see Hay). Its use here fuses the tradition of the enthronement of the anointed one (king or Messiah) with God's care and vindication of the just (note also how in Wisd. of Sol. 5:15-16 the vindication of the righteous is depicted as a coronation). The just can expect to suffer at the hands of evil tormenters. But even more certainly, they can count on God to vindicate them, first, by raising them up and rewarding them with royal status, and second, by dealing with their enemies. In later Jewish writings, such vindication of the righteous is frequently associated with resurrection, the ultimate reward for faithfulness (cf. 2 Macc. 7; Dan. 12:2-3; literature cited by Nickelsburg).

The Exaltation of the Many

The tradition of the vindication of the righteous speaks not only to the fate of a unique individual, whether king, servant, prophet, or righteous one. Exaltation to the full status of sons and daughters of God is also the hope of *all* who do God's will faithfully in the face of suffering and persecution. Whereas the suffering servant in Isaiah 53 may have originally referred to a king or prophet, in the end the text was understood to reflect the fate of *any* just and faithful servant of God or of the community of the faithful as a whole (note, e.g., the corporate exaltation of God's people that follows the exaltation of "one like a son of man" in Dan. 7:13-27, RSV; Perkins: 50).

In short, when early Christians proclaim and celebrate what God has done *for Christ,* they are also proclaiming a word of assurance for the *community* of the faithful and just. So in Ephesians 1:19-22, Christ's experience of God's power is rehearsed to indicate that the same power is there for *all* who are chosen to live a life of holiness, blamelessness, and love (1:4; cf. 2:4-6; in 1 Cor. 15:23, Christ is the "first fruits" of the [general] resurrection; in Heb. 2:10, he is "the pioneer of our salvation").

The use of Psalm 8 here and elsewhere in the NT illustrates this interplay between special individual and corporate experience, in this case between Christ and reconstituted humanity. Psalm 8 reflects on the place of human beings in God's creation (NRSV translates "man" in 8:4 as "human beings" and "son of man" as "mortals"). Understood this way, it is largely a restatement of Genesis 1:26-31. God has appointed humanity to a position of lordship "over all things," just short of being gods or God (8:5-6; the term is *elohim,* lit. "gods," common in the Hebrew Bible as a designation for God).

In the NT, however, Psalm 8 (esp. v. 6) is used to celebrate the special status of the risen and exalted Christ (cf. 1 Cor. 15:27, where, as here, it sits alongside Ps. 110:1; Heb. 2:6; cf. use of Ps. 110:1 in Heb. 1:13). However, as stated in the notes, the Christ who is raised and exalted is never understood to be a solitary individual. Christ is humanity reconstituted. That basic connection allows the authors of 1 Corinthians, Ephesians, and Hebrews to use Psalm 8 messianically: the exaltation of Christ means the restoring of creation. In Ephesians that tradition is employed, not to stress the distance between Christ and saints, but to minimize it, indeed to render Christ and saints one whole—*head* and *body.*

God as Divine Warrior

Behind the celebration of God's power in raising and exalting Jesus Christ over all the powers lies the theme of the reclaiming of creation and also the motif of God as divine warrior who intervenes to vindicate the oppressed. This tradition is widely present in the Bible (e.g., Exod. 14–15; Deut. 32-33; Pss. 18; 68; Isa. 59; 63; Hab. 3; cf. Wisd. of Sol. 5; work by Hiebert; Lind; Yoder Neufeld, 1997). Frequently the agent of God's coming as judge and liberator is God's Messiah (e.g., Isa. 11), especially also in the NT (e.g., 1 Cor. 15:24-26; 2 Thess. 1:5-10; Rev. 6; 19).

The concept of divine warfare is discussed more fully in relation to

6:10-20. Yet it is relevant here to stress the following: the motif of victory over enemies expresses God's sovereignty as judge and liberator, and thus also God's solidarity with suffering sons and daughters. The chief purpose of mentioning this victory is to assure both the just and their tormentors that God is not mocked. What God has created will be restored to its rightful place and function, even if the means of that warfare become the suffering and death of the warrior himself (2:16; notice how through his own death the peaceable "warrior" succeeds in "murdering enmity"; cf. the slain yet warring Lamb in Rev. 5).

The prayer in 1:17-19 that believers might come to know of the certainty of their inheritance and of the immeasurable power of God at work for them presupposes such a powerful and intrusive deity. Such a conviction can lead to a stance of patient waiting for God to act. As important and as deeply rooted biblically as is that tradition of courageous patience—often also dubbed "nonresistance"—it needs to be set alongside another dimension of the tradition of divine warfare. For the church to be the *body* of the Messiah (1:23) means that much more than patience and endurance is asked of the church, as will become abundantly apparent in the second half of the letter, especially in 6:10-20 (cf. Rom. 6; 13:11-14; 1 Thess. 5:8).

THE TEXT IN THE LIFE OF THE CHURCH

Knowledge and Revelation

Knowledge and *revelation* are celebrated as God's blessing of humanity in the great eulogy in 1:3-14 and are at the heart of the prayer in 1:17-23. Yet they have had a troubled history in the life of the church. Though all early believers, Jew and Gentile alike, valued knowledge and revelation, Gnostics in particular stressed knowledge (*gnōsis,* used in 3:19) as the core of salvation [Gnosticism].

Throughout the history of the church, mystics too have rightly treasured knowledge, wisdom, and revelation as intimacy with the divine. We find a similar perspective at the beginnings of Anabaptism with spiritualists like Sebastian Franck and Caspar Schwenckfeld, and such important Anabaptists as Hans Denck. In our day there also is a great emphasis on insight and knowledge, from the profound to the banal, from liberating hermeneutics (e.g., feminism, liberation theology) to so-called New Age consciousness.

A stress on spiritually imparted knowledge has always run the risk of making knowledge an end in itself, often vulnerable to losing touch with reality, sometimes succumbing in the process. Perhaps understandably, churches of all stripes—including, interestingly, charismatic and pentecostal—have feared, sometimes with good reason, an emphasis on spirit, knowledge, and revelation outside the control of the written Word and its authorized interpreters. However, the struggle to control and often to suppress this yearning for knowledge in the early centuries of the church, and many times since, has exacted a high price. The power of Easter and the operative knowledge of it in the lives of believers has too often been prevented from destabilizing the status quo, "the way things are" this side of the full realization of Christ's ingathering of all things.

Such fear of what has often been called "enthusiasm" has often also gone hand in hand with a pessimistic view of humanity in general and even of Christians. Thus, churches have typically propounded a Christology more concerned with the identity between God and Christ than with what that connection signifies for a humanity that is *in Christ*—the central christological and ecclesiological concern of Ephesians. The price has often been a disregard for the divine power that is *presently* at work *in* and *for* believers.

Easter Consciousness

Do contemporary Christians as individuals and especially as churches and communities possess knowledge of this Easter power, particularly as it pertains to their identity and task as the body of God's agent (Christ)? Do believers and churches "know" themselves to be filled with the one who is above all powers as they set their expectations for themselves individually and corporately? If the answer is no, then this prayer needs to remain unceasing (1:16).

These questions can be asked of Christian traditions that made their peace centuries ago with the way things are, as well as asked of those in the process of making such compromises. The powers do not flee such a church nor do they attack it. They make common cause with it. Insofar as such churches do not participate in the lordship of Christ *over* the powers, it is difficult to credit them with being *in the heavenlies* (2:4-6).

The question of how much Easter matters must also be asked of those who have made the cross more or less the sole lens through which the identity and task of believers is viewed (e.g., J. H. Yoder, 1994: esp. 51-3, 144-7). Do those who know that they are to take up the cross know just as strongly that they are empowered for such cross-bearing by God's Easter power—*now?* Elsewhere in his letters, Paul calls for the bifocals of cross *and* resurrection (e.g., Rom. 6). At this point in Ephesians, it is resurrection and exaltation that provide the glasses through which believers are to view themselves and their task (2:5-7, 10). To state it provocatively, Easter *precedes* Good Friday in the imitation of Christ (TLC for 2:1-10; Yoder Neufeld, 2000). Just as surely, Easter *leads to* Good Friday for those who make up the body of the one God raised above every name (5:2). Listen to the sequence of first Easter and then the cross in Paul's words in Philippians 3:10-11:

> I want to know Christ and the power of his resurrection and the sharing of his sufferings by becoming like him in his death, if somehow I may attain the resurrection from the dead.

These verses in Ephesians speak volumes to those in the church who struggle mightily and often at great personal cost to perform the messianic task of peacemaking. Today we might speak of a spirituality that must undergird the work of peace (e.g., Douglass; Snyder; Wink, 1992). Ephesians puts before us the need for a spirituality, a knowing *with the eyes of our heart*, and also insists that such a spirituality be informed by specific content: Easter (TLC for 2:1-10). James McClendon discusses "resurrection ethics" under the rubric of what he calls "the sphere of the anastatic" (1986:241-75; *anastatic* comes from *anastasis,* "resurrection").

> The central tasks of the Christian social life are exactly those fit to be informed by resurrection ethics—the worship, evangelism, service, and mission of the church either live by resurrection light, or they do not deserve to live. (McClendon, 1986:275)

Power over the Powers

This text is heard also as a forceful word of encouragement by those involved in deliverance ministries on behalf of those oppressed by evil forces (cf. Eph. 3:10, notes; 6:10-20, notes *[Powers]*; Arnold, 1997; Boyd; Wagner, 1991; Warner, 1991). As Alan Kreider has shown, healing and exorcism were already in the early centuries of the church a strong witness to the power of Easter in the life of the church, and a significant factor in drawing persons to faith (Kreider: 16-7).

But we can and should appropriate the encouragement to successful struggle within a much wider horizon of engagement with the powers. The past tense in the assertion that God *has raised* Christ from the dead and *has put* **everything** under his feet provides the necessary assurance for struggle with evil, regardless of its nature and manifestation. The call to live as sages in an evil time (5:15-17), as sages with *personal* knowledge and experience of resurrection power (5:14), is intended to inform engagement in *every* arena of life, including the ordinary, as the Household Code in 5:21—6:9 will remind us.

The *fullness* of God is in the process of filling up *all* things in every conceivable way (1:23). The church is inextricably related to this *fullness* as both recipient and dispenser.

Ephesians 2:1-10

From Death to Life Together with Christ

PREVIEW

Literally translated, chapter 2 begins with *And you* (pl.), indicating that the flow of the presentation continues without a real break from chapter 1. Marked by the same tone of grateful worship, these verses expand on the claim in 1:19 that the power that raised Christ is *for us*.

The syntax is less complex than that found in the two long sentences that make up chapter 1. A lengthy sentence (2:1-7) is followed by two shorter ones (2:8-9 and 2:10). Verses 1-3 form a parenthesis within the sentence, characterizing life under the control of an evil ruler. As usual, translators break up this long sentence (five sentences in NIV, three in NRSV), while preserving the central importance of verse 4. There God is said to have made *you* and *us* alive *together with Christ*. This is explicated further with two key terms that recall God's action on behalf of Christ in 1:20—*raising with* and *seating with*. With these main verbs of the first sentence, the author succeeds in depicting the drama of salvation in highly concentrated form.

The two concluding sentences (2:8-9 and 2:10) draw inferences from this concentrated summary. The first regards the basis of salvation—*grace*, the second the *purpose* of salvation—*good works*. The passage as a whole is framed by an *inclusio* (marking a section by repeating a beginning word or phrase at the end): in verses 1-2 the

89

once-dead *walked* in *trespasses and sins;* in verse 10 the now-living *walk* in *good works.*

The presence of an inclusio and the numerous stark contrasts— *once* and an implied *now, we* and *you, death* and *life, sins* and *good works*—have led to the suggestion that this passage reflects baptismal liturgy or catechesis (Lincoln: 88-91, with discussion and references). We do not have to be sure about whether our text is hymn or homily to be alerted to its nature as a celebratory and worshipful distillation of the pattern of salvation: in Christ a merciful and gracious God liberates rebellious humans to do the right thing.

Structure of 2:1-10

And you,
    dead in sins in which you once walked
        according to the ruler of this world
      among the disobedient
      among whom we all once walked as children of wrath, (2:1-3)
BUT GOD
    being rich in mercy
  made us alive, raised, and seated us with Christ,
    in order to show in coming ages
    the wealth of his grace. (2:4-7)

For by grace have you been saved through faith;
  it is a gift of God,
  not of works. (2:8-9)

For we are his product,
  created in Christ Jesus for good works. (2:10)

OUTLINE

You and We, the Walking Dead, 2:1-3, 5a
    2:2   Under Control of an Evil Power

The Merciful and Loving God, 2:4-7
    2:5-6   Made Alive Together with Christ

Saved by Grace Through Faith, 2:8-10
    2:10   For Good Works

EXPLANATORY NOTES

You and We, the Walking Dead 2:1-3, 5a

With language familiar to Jewish readers, the first three verses describe humanity in rebellion against God. Life apart from God is a living death. Such metaphorical use of *death* was widespread in early Christian circles, especially in connection with baptism (cf. esp. Col. 2:12-14, on which our text may depend; Rom. 6:1-14; 13:11-14; 1 Thess. 4:14-15; 5:1-11, esp. v. 11). *Death* carries also the suggestion of judgment, especially when set alongside *wrath* (see below).

These dead are highly animated—they *walk, trespass,* and *disobey.* In the Bible *walking* is a common term for manner of life or moral behavior (also Eph. 4:1, 17; 5:2, 8, 15; cf. Deut. 30:16; Ps. 119:1; Prov. 10:9; John 11:9-10; Rom. 6:4; Ps. Sol. 16:1-5). Walking rightly means obedience to God's will as codified in the law. Walking in *trespasses and sins* means breaking those laws (in 2:1 note plurals *trespasses, sins*).

The walking dead are called (lit.) *sons of disobedience. Sons of . . .* is a common Semitic way of referring to human beings (cf. Qumran's War Rule, 1QM, 4QM: The War of the Sons of Light Against the Sons of Darkness). But as in 1:5, the use of this Semitism carries additional freight obscured by the inclusive translation of the NIV and NRSV. Recall how important *sonship* is in this letter, notably in the introductory blessing, where it implies status as well as source of being (1:3-14). To refer to the dead as the *sons* of disobedience is to imply that they cannot but follow the orders being handed down to them. While they are called *disobedient,* they are, in fact, highly obedient to someone other than God. They are therefore also *by nature children of wrath* (cf. 5:6). The notion of obedience, which implies choice and thus responsibility, is thus augmented by the concept of nature, which suggests character or identity.

The author apparently feels no need to resolve this tension. One would think that we are either responsible for choices we make freely, or it is a matter of being controlled by some force, by our nature or by an outside force—"the devil made me do it." In Ephesians, as in Pauline and Jewish thinking generally, it is common to ascribe culpability to those who are at the same time believed to be under the control of someone or something else. In Galatians 5:16-25, humanity is viewed as a battleground for forces vying for control: "flesh" against "spirit" (cf. Rom. 7–8; Col. 2:18). *Flesh* is present here in verse 3 as well, along with the senses. The *sons of disobedience* serve their own wishes without hesitation, all the while following orders. Miroslav Volf speaks of this as being "colonized" by evil:

> [Evil] has colonized us to such a thoroughgoing extent that there seems to be no moral space left within the self in which it could occur to us to hate what we want because it is evil. We are ensnared by evil not only with full consent, but without a thought of dissent and without a sigh for deliver-

ance. With the inner workings of our will in its hold, evil can dispense with force and rule by lure. And so, paradoxically, we feel free only in the prison house of unrecognized evil. (Volf: 89-90)

We should not miss, finally, that this way of depicting human sinfulness adds victimization to culpability. Sinners are sinners because of the oppression of an evil that is greater than their own volition. They are in need of being *saved* (2:8).

2:2 Under Control of an Evil Power

Such willing servitude is a symptom of subjugation to what is variously referred to in verse 2 as *the aeon of this cosmos, the ruler of the authority of the air*, and *the spirit now at work among the sons of disobedience*. This is not a list of powers as we find it in 1:21 or 6:12, but various ways of naming and characterizing the ultimate center of evil ruling this world of death. We are reminded of the devil (*diabolos*, as in 4:27; 6:11), the opponent with whom the saints enter into intimate battle (cf. 1 Pet. 5:8). In this instance the image is more diffuse.

First, the controlling evil is called *the aeon (aiōn) of this cosmos*. *Cosmos* is well translated as *world*. *Aiōn*, on the other hand, is more difficult and often best translated as *age* or *epoch* (cf. 2:7), as in contemporary English usage. That is the meaning it usually carries for Paul.

Paul believed the "present age" to be passing away, giving way to the "new age" of the new creation (cf. 2 Cor. 5:17). Believers in Christ already live by the power and values of the coming age, at the same time doing so by that power within the confines and pressures of the present, old age. So Romans 12:2 reads, "Do not be conformed to this aeon" (TRYN). The NRSV translates *aeon* there as *world* (as in 2 Cor. 4:4), indicating that *aeon* can be understood as synonymous with *cosmos*. Perhaps that is why, like other translations, the NRSV renders the phrase here (Eph. 2:2) as *the course of this world* (cf. *ways of this world*, NIV; or suggestively, *ways of the present world order*, REB). Andrew Lincoln's "world-age" encompasses the spectrum of meaning (94-5).

Another meaning hovers in the background, however. Ancients sometimes viewed *aeons* as personal forces acting in the universe [*Powers*]. Such a view is hinted at here too, especially when set alongside the other characterizations of the controlling evil (e.g., Best, 1998:203-4; Schnackenburg: 91). While some commentators explicitly reject this meaning (e.g., Lincoln: 94; Perkins: 58; and to some surprise, Arnold, 1989:59-60), it is best to let words and concepts resonate richly, as often in this letter. The *aeon* signifies what we might today call "the spirit of the age," the zeitgeist (as in 2:2c), which both reflects and shapes the culture of the time (so Wink, 1984:84). We thus refer to "the dirty 30s" or "the greedy 80s," or just simply "the 60s." The author of Ephesians, however, wants us to think of such culturally pervasive attitudes and values (*principles,* NJB) as a personal force—tempting, cajoling, and enticing, indeed, acting upon humanity, forcing it into rebellion to God (so also Best, 1998:207).

The second characterization personalizes evil power more clearly: *the ruler (archōn) of the authority (exousia) of the air.* This image expands the notion of evil greatly by likening evil power to an atmosphere *(air).* Air provides a clue to how the author believed the universe to be organized. Many ancients held that, in contrast to the higher heavens (God's abode), the lower heavens (the air) were the realm in which evil or demonic powers held sway and influenced human affairs (note the *far above* in 1:21 *[Cosmology];* cf. 2 Cor. 4:4; 12:2; Arnold, 1989:60; Lincoln: 96; Perkins: 59). Thus a Greek magical incantation reads: "Protect me from every demon in the air!" (via Arnold, 1989:60). *The ruler of the power of the air* holds authority over those evil powers (cf. 6:11-12). The very air humanity breathes is an atmosphere contaminated by the lord of evil and his lackeys (cf. Wink, 1984:84).

The third and final characterization of evil contains a play on words. Immediately following the reference to *air,* we encounter the evil *spirit (pneuma). Pneuma* is usually translated "spirit," but it also means "wind," as in the case of the Hebrew *ruah* (note how the ambiguity of *pneuma* is exploited in John 3:5-8). The author wants readers to think of *spirit* as a superhuman force in a way analogous to the contrasting Holy Spirit in 1:13-14 (Fee, 1994:680, considers this to be a deliberate parody of God's Spirit). In addition to being a pervasive power, this evil *pneuma* is the air the disobedient breathe, the fake oxygen they use to live their death, to state it ironically, but no less the ferocious wind that sweeps them along in their rebellion.

As in 1:3-14 and 2:11-22, both first-person and second-person pronouns are employed—*we* and *you* were both *dead.* Does this refer to Gentiles and Jews, or to new and old believers? Perhaps we should not make much of this here since the pronouns are used almost interchangeably, and the characterization of life apart from God is clearly intended to apply to *us all* without distinction (2:3). We recall that Paul placed both Jews and Gentiles on a common footing with regard to judgment and salvation (Rom. 1:16; 2:9-10; 3:22; 10:12).

In the early years of the church, this distinction would have reflected the difference between new and mature believers as well and should therefore not be ruled out, especially if baptism plays some role in the background (1:3-14, notes).

At the end of verse 3, the dead are called *children of wrath*. This refers not to their own anger, but to *God's* wrath or judgment (cf. 5:6; Best, 1998:210). Divine wrath is an essential component of Pauline theology and inextricable from this tightly woven pattern of salvation. *Wrath* must be understood not as a divine fit of anger, however, but as God's meticulous attention to and response to rebellion, oppression, and the defilement of creation (e.g., Rom. 1:18; 2:5; 5:9; 9:22; 12:19; 13:4-5; 1 Thess. 1:10; cf. esp. Wisd. of Sol. 1–5; R. Martin, 1991:26-7). To be dead is thus to be unconscious and ignorant—asleep—and also to be subject to the judgment of God and thus as good as dead. Death is the natural consequence of the rebellion of those who are *by nature children of wrath* (cf. Rom. 5:12-21; John 3:36).

The Merciful and Loving God 2:4-7

Characterizing human life in such brutally stark brevity serves to set us up for the surprise of grace. The unexpected is introduced in verse 4 with *But God*—arguably the two most important words in all of Ephesians. Where we should have expected *wrath* (2:3), we (*you* and *we*) have experienced the wealth of God's *mercy* and *great love*.

Wealth (or *riches*) is a favorite term in this letter (1:7, 18; 2:7; 3:8, 16); here it describes a God who is *rich in mercy* beyond the wildest imagination. The radical discontinuity of *but God* is a reminder, however, that mercy is always and inherently a surprise. The dead toward whom God has shown mercy are drawn from precisely the ranks of the living dead described in 5:5. Unlike the righteous, they have no grounds upon which to be confident of God's intervention *for* them, only *against* them. They are *dead*—as is repeated for emphasis sake in 2:5a—and to be numbered with the transgressors and thus with the enemies of God. The poignancy of the surprise of grace increases when we remember that the objects of God's love are here in large measure Gentiles (*you*). Our text anticipates the exploration of the full reach of God's peacemaking in 2:11-22.

To say that mercy is a surprise is not to say that it is arbitrary. God's *mercy* is, after all, rooted in God's *great love*, a disposition that has governed God's actions from before creation (1:4). *Love* lies at the basis of God's covenant with Israel; *love* for creation lies at the root of God's wrath and judgment; *love* has received its most concentrated expression in the death of Jesus (1:5-8; 2:16; 5:2). *Love* is the seat of God's unsearchable ingenuity to see creation and its inhabitants reconciled in Christ (introductory blessing, 1:3-14; cf. Rom. 11:33-36). It could not have occurred to Jews such as Paul or his followers, steeped as they were in the Scriptures, that love and mercy on one hand, and judgment and wrath on the other, are mutually exclusive. Indeed, apart from judgment, mercy and grace have no meaning (cf. Yoder Neufeld, 1999, on Wisd. of Sol. 12).

2:5-6 Made Alive Together with Christ

Finally, the main verb of the sentence appears; it is a rare and distinctly Christian verb: God **made** *[us]* **alive together** with Christ *(suzōopoieō)*. This *making alive* identifies the experience of grace with Christ's resurrection. Early readers may well have heard in this an allusion to baptism (explicit in Col. 2:12-13, on which our text depends; Best, 1998:215-6; E. Martin: 111-3). Notably absent from the Ephesians passage is, however, any reference to dying with Christ, indicating that the emphasis falls on identification with the risen Lord (contrast Rom. 6:1-11). Jesus' death is stressed in the second half of this chapter (2:16), but even there participation with Christ is cast as new creation, not directly as identification with his death.

To what does *together with* in verse 5 refer? In the Greek *together with* is indicated with *sun-* prefixed to this verb as well as to *raised* and *seated* in 2:6. One obvious possibility is that *together* refers to *you* and *we*. A few manuscripts read *in Christ*, which implies that Christ is the means by which believers reconciled with each other have been brought to life (cf. 1:3-14; 2:11-22). Being made alive by God means joining a community that experiences divine life not individualistically but *together with* others. But Colossians 2:13 relates *together with* unambiguously to Christ by prefixing *sun-* to the verb and then repeating it as a preposition before *him*. Our text excludes neither interpretation and, as 2:11-22 shows, encourages both (Barth, 1974:220).

The weight and meaning of *made alive together with* is clarified in verse 6 by the verbs *raised with* and *seated with*. Recall 1:20, where *raised* and *seated* describe the actions of God on behalf of the Messiah. Recall also that the Messiah's resurrection, enthronement, and exaltation serve as a measure of the power of God *for us* (1:19). Now 2:6 makes it explicit that what God did for Christ, God does now for liberated sons and daughters of disobedience.

The wonder of this is heightened when it is kept in mind that the Messiah's resurrection and exaltation signified the intervention of God on behalf of a suffering and victimized Just One. That is a necessary backdrop for a full appreciation of the extent of God's grace in liberating the *disobedient* from the clutches of evil. God calls into their darkness, into their realm of death, and offers divine sonship and daughtership to any and all who will hear and respond, raising them *together with* Christ, and enthroning them *with him*. Best (1998:219) and Lincoln (107) believe the right hand of God is to be reserved for Christ (1:20) and thus is not mentioned here. Such distinction is out of character with the gist of this letter and underestimates the importance of identification of believers with and in Christ (cf. Rev. 3:21!).

God's intervention is characterized as an act of liberation, a fully accurate translation of *saved* in 2:5c. God invades the realm of the ruler of the air, snatching out of his clutches those who hear and respond to the word of truth, the good news of liberation (1:13; cf. 2:13, 17). Note once more: these are not the dead who have died a martyr's death (Rev. 6:9-11); they are dead in *their own* sins and trespasses. One cannot help but be reminded of the words of Paul in Romans 5:6-10, here slightly paraphrased: "While we were still weak, . . . sinners, . . . enemies, God liberated us in that Christ died for us." In contrast to Romans 5, however, the emphasis on salvation here falls less on Christ's death than on his resurrection. Markus Barth's title to this section, "Salvation by Resurrection," captures well the importance of the present emphasis (1974:211).

But should we take this to imply that everything is settled, that in having been raised, believers have been removed from the realm of sin and death? In Romans 6 Paul avoids that inference by carefully speaking of the resurrection of believers as a *future* event, even though he wants them now *already* to live in light of Easter (see 2:8-10, notes, and TBC). Has Paul's eschatological reserve (in Rom.) given way to a realized eschatology (in Eph.), to the conviction that what was hoped for has already come about?

Comparison with Colossians 2–3 is instructive. Through baptism, believers are said *already* to have been raised to the fullness of life *together with Christ* (2:10, 13). God has *already* vanquished the powers, humiliating them publicly in a victory procession (2:15; cf. Eph. 1:20-22, where God has put all powers under Christ's feet). Even so, in Colossians 3 the exhortation implies that believers are *not yet* in the heavenly realm, even though earlier they are said to have been transferred from death to the kingdom of Christ (Col. 1:13). While believers have been raised with Christ (3:1), their life is for now "hid with Christ in God" (3:3). They are thus to "seek the things that are above" (3:2).

Both Romans 6 and Colossians 2 are realistic in that they take into account *both* Easter *and* the brokenness of present reality. We might call this "Christic realism." Realism is usually thought of as the opposite of idealism; it commonly refers to the adjustments one makes morally and spiritually to sin and brokenness, whether individual or corporate—compromises with the way things are. But Paul and his students were realistic about this still-broken world and also especially about life in Christ. It is a betrayal of God's act in Christ to allow this world-age to define the limits of what is possible for those who are *together with* Christ. Christic realism takes seriously the *not yet* but especially also the *already* of what it means to confess Jesus as Lord.

Such realism is present in Ephesians but expressed slightly differently than in Colossians or Romans. Where the Colossians are called to seek "the things that are above" (Col. 3:1), such spatial distinctions are not respected in Ephesians. Believers are already *in the heavenlies together with Christ* (cf. Eph. 1:3; 2:6) *[Cosmology]*. Whereas in Colossians 2:15 the powers have already been paraded publicly as defeated foes, in Ephesians (as in 1 Cor. 15:20-28, esp. v. 25) the powers are still very much a force to be struggled with (6:10-20). Resurrection and enthronement need not imply *completed* victory, only *assured* victory (contra Lindemann, 1985:111-6).

We must then not read these euphoric words of the enthronement of believers apart from the larger context of struggle to which this letter summons believers. Indeed, these words are intended as encouragement for such struggle. To claim believers have been raised and seated with Christ in the heavenlies conveys to readers that they are pitted against that realm of death and its ruler from a position of superiority—in and with Christ, to be sure (cf. 1:22-23; so also Best, 1998:220-2). As chapter 6 will show, their "heavenly" struggle with the evil forces in the heavenlies takes the form of the earthly practice of truth, justice, peace, and proclamation of the powerful, life-giving word of God.

Verse 7 brings the theocentric perspective of Ephesians to the fore. Again we encounter God's *wealth* (cf. 2:4), now the *surpassing* or *exceeding wealth of grace and kindness*. As in the case of *love* and *mercy* earlier, *kindness* and *grace* usually describe God's disposition toward people *within* the covenant. This may provide the motive for the adjective *surpassing*, a favorite in Ephesians (cf. 1:19; 3:19; for the whole phrase *the surpassing wealth of grace*, see 2 Cor. 9:14).

The salvation of the sons and daughters of disobedience serves to *(in order to)* publicize God's grace and kindness to coming ages. The phrase *the coming aeons* is puzzling, especially in light of verse 2 (2:2, notes on *aeon, aiōn*). It is perhaps best to translate *aiōnes* as *ages* (so NIV, NRSV, and most interpreters). *Coming ages* implies an indefinite future during which God's grace will be shown, suggesting that this letter is not marked by an expectation of an imminent end or a drastic change, as typical in Paul's letters. In this interpretation believers *have been saved* (perfect tense, 2:8) and look forward to an indeterminate future of showing forth God's grace and kindness as the body of Christ in heaven and on earth.

On the other hand, as pointed out in relation to verse 2, *aeons* were sometimes conceived of as personal forces or beings. The meaning would then be that *in (to) the approaching (attacking?) aeons*, God will show or prove his kindness toward us (so, e.g., Barth, 1974:223; Lindemann, 1975:121-9). This is close to 3:10, where the church informs the powers of the manifold wisdom of God. While attractive and fitting for this letter, such a reading is grammatically difficult. We are on surest ground, while allowing for some notion of personal powers to resonate in the background, to take *in* as meaning *during* and *aeons* as temporal, and to wrestle rather with the eschatological difficulties that raises (Best, 1998:223-4; Lincoln: 110-1; Perkins: 62; Schnackenburg: 97).

Saved by Grace Through Faith 2:8-10

With a new sentence the central claim announced in verse 5c is now repeated and expanded: *You have been saved by grace **through faith***. This phrase may have had its home within the celebration of baptism (cf. also 5:14; Schnackenburg: 97). We notice, for example, that just as in verse 5c, the reference is to *you*, suggesting perhaps a saying usually spoken by the one doing the baptizing.

At first glance this saying is typically Pauline. Comparison with such central texts as Romans 3:26-30; 5:1, 9; 10:9-13; and Galatians 2:16 shows, however, that more typical of Paul is the phrase "*justification by faith*." Salvation is anticipated in the future (e.g., Rom. 5:9-10; 10:9, 13; 11:26; 1 Cor. 5:5; 10:33; 1 Thess. 1:10). Even occasions where present or past tense is used (e.g., Rom. 8:24; 1 Cor. 15:2) are marked by a strong eschatological tone. Ephesians does not mention justification and speaks of salvation chiefly in the sense (and tense) of completion. In Ephesians, salvation has taken the place of justification. Being saved is viewed then primarily as liberation from the oppression of the ruler of the authority of the air *in the present*, however much such liberation is inextricably connected to the future inheritance (1:14, 18; 5:5).

At the same time, this emphasis on *present* experience comes close to the way Paul understands justification. The more common forensic or legal understanding notwithstanding, Paul is clear in Romans 8 that justification implies liberation from the bondage of law wedded to flesh, sin, and death (8:2-8), and equally empowerment for a life of active "justness," the fulfilling of the demands of the law (8:4). That finds an echo in our immediate text, as we will see shortly in connection with Ephesians 2:10.

The perfect tense of *having been saved* does not mean that the future has been collapsed into the present. Just as surely as they *have been* saved from the power of the evil one, the saints await the coming day of redemption (4:30) when all things will be in Christ (1:10) and God will be all in all (4:6). Salvation means that the saints are *now no longer* under the control of the evil one, as they *once* were (and as the *disobedient* still are; 2:2); their *now* is defined as participation in the person, fate, and task of Christ, to whom all powers have been rendered inferior (1:22).

The once dead have been saved *by* or *through faith. Faith (pistis)* is a fundamental component of the Pauline gospel, especially with regard to how Gentiles become part of the holy community (cf. the role of Abraham in Rom. 4; Gal. 3). Members of this community are typically referred to as *believers (pisteuontes,* e.g., Eph. 1:13, 19; Rom. 3:22; et al.). Such faith is often best translated as *trust*—trust that God's offer of the *gift* of salvation is true (1:13). *Faith* is then often set in opposition to *works*, which are in turn understood to be deeds intended to assure God's favor.

As much as *pistis* means "trust," it can also mean "faithfulness" or "trustworthiness" (1:1, notes). We can ask then whether the *faith* spoken of here is the "trust" of believers (as in 1:13; e.g., Lincoln: 111; Patzia: 184; Schnackenburg: 98), or the "faithfulness" of God and his Christ (cf. 3:12; Barth, 1974:225, wants it both ways, perhaps rightly). Romans 3:3 refers to the *pistis* of God, there translated by NIV and NRSV and most translations as "faithfulness." Further, the "faith" spoken of in Romans 3:22, 26 and Galatians 2:16, 20 can be understood as the believer's "trust" *in* Jesus (NIV, NRSV, and most other translations). But it can also refer to the "faithfulness" *of* Jesus (so KJV; see note in NRSV).

It is better to interpret *pistis* in the present instance as referring not so much to human trust in God, as important as that is, as to *God's faithfulness.* This meaning suggests that salvation by grace is God's way of keeping faith with the human community, including Gentiles, who have been under the oppression of evil. Such fidelity is, of course, more appropriate to covenantal relationships. *But God reaches out to those who have either never been part of the covenantal relationship* (Gentiles, 2:12) *or who have broken it* (Jews, 2:3; cf. the hymn fragment in 2 Tim. 2:13).

Salvation—the liberation of oppressed sinners—is not a result of their own initiative, not *out of yourselves (ex humōn)* or *out of works (ex ergōn;* 2:8-9). The parallelism here reminds us to think, not of works of the law, but of human effort generally. After all, the sinners have been willing participants in their own victimization and are oblivious—*dead*—to the true state of affairs (2:1-3, 5). Their liberation is a result of God's loving initiative; hence, the importance of *grace* and *gift*. The Greek word for *grace (charis)* also means *gift*. The author adds yet another word for gift *(dōron)* at the end of verse 8 to give the point added emphasis.

2:10 For Good Works

The theocentric perspective shapes also the last sentence (2:10). Both salvation, a gracious gift of God, and those who have been saved are God's *product* or *work of art (poiēma,* related to the English *poem), created in (through) Christ Jesus ["In"].* The NRSV translates *poiēma* loosely but accurately as *we are what [God] has made us* (God's *workmanship,* NIV). So to be brought to life together with Christ is a divine act of rescue and also one of *re*-creation, a reconstituting of humanity to its intended state (2:15, notes; cf. also "new creation" in 2 Cor. 5:17; Gal. 6:15). Best says it well: "God is always 'making' and his 'saving' is just an aspect of his 'making'" (1998:230).

The purpose of this new creation is a new manner of life—*walking in good works* (cf. 4:24, the *new human* created in God's likeness *in justice/righteousness and the holiness of truth;* 1:4, the purpose of election, to be *holy and blameless).* Those who once *walked in transgression and sins* (2:1) have been re-created so as to *walk in good works.* Such walking is not a *precondition of* salvation—*not because of* or *through (ex) good works;* it is the *purpose of* or *reason for* salvation—*for (epi) good works.*

The plural *works* is found rarely in the Pauline writings (only in 1 Tim. 2:10; 5:10, 25; cf. Acts 9:36; singular in Rom. 2:7; 2 Cor. 9:8; Col. 1:10). *Works* may simply correspond to the plural *trespasses and sins* in 2:1. But to some the plural *works* suggests that ethics has become more moralistic for this author at the close of the first century (e.g., Schnackenburg: 101). In Ephesians, however, *good works* refers to more than virtuous deeds. In Colossians 1:10 "every good work" is synonymous with a life "worthy of the Lord" (cf. Eph. 4:1!). Ephesians, as much or more than Colossians, is intent on exploring the implications of the intimate connection between Christ and his body.

The church is identified with the Christ through whom all things are being reconciled to God (1:10; 2:13-16). We should then be alert to seeing *good works* as participation in that work of reconciliation, illustrated with such images as building up the body of Christ (4:12), transforming darkness into light (5:11-14), and defeating evil powers (6:10-18).

Good works have for centuries been tossed about in the faith-versus-works debate, often drawing a suspicious glance as an attack on grace. Ephesians 2:10 makes it abundantly clear that such suspicion is utterly misplaced. *Good works* are *God's* gift, as is emphasized by *pro-* (in Greek) prefixed to *prepared* (cf. 1:4-5, notes on *pre-*destination). These good works have been *pre-*prepared for those whom God *pre-*chose and *pre-*destined. Human boasting or self-congratulation has no place (cf., e.g., Rom. 3:27-28; 2 Cor. 10:12—12:10; Gal. 6:12-14). God gets full credit for any *good works* the saints perform. God's liberation of people from the realm of death is intended to restore them to their original purpose as doers of good. *Not* to do *good works* is nothing less than rejection of God's grace (cf. Rom. 6:1).

THE TEXT IN BIBLICAL CONTEXT

Two Ways of Walking

The description of sinners and oppressive evil in the first verses of this section is rooted in a notion, held widely in biblical times, that humanity is divided between the good and the bad, between those who can count on God's favor and those who will encounter God's wrath. Such a division was also held to separate Jews and Gentiles (see the characterization of pagan existence in Rom. 1–2; cf. Eph. 2:11-12; 4:17-19). A fitting metaphor, widespread in Jewish writings, was the doctrine of the *two ways*, the narrow one leading to life, the wide one to death; the narrow road is walked by few, the wide by many (cf. Matt. 7:13-14; Ps. 1).

Writers commonly characterized these two ways with lists of virtues and vices. This tradition also left its mark on early Christian writing (e.g., Ep. Barnabas 18-20; Didache 1-5), not least on the NT (e.g., Rom. 1:29-31; 1 Cor. 6:9-10; Gal. 5:19-23; Col. 3:12; 1 Tim. 6:2-11; Titus 2:2—3:7, parallel to Eph. 3:3-7). Second Peter

2:4-16 and Jude 4-16 clearly show the use of this tradition to malign those within the church believed to be perverting apostolic teaching (Charles: 237-42, 291-308).

A related variation on this theme, one particularly relevant to our text, is the notion found at Qumran of two "spirits" or "winds" that determine human action (1QS 3.17-26). As much as Ephesians presupposes such dualism and participates in it (e.g., 5:3-14), the author also believes firmly that in God's eyes such a division is never final. Indeed, in this text the stark dualism serves to emphasize God's initiative to overcome it (cf. 2:11-22)—*But God, rich in mercy.* The true measure of God's grace is the liberation or salvation of those on the way to hell and also their redirection onto the way of life, their resurrection into do-gooders.

Has the Resurrection Already Taken Place?

One of the more difficult issues in this section is eschatology. As indicated in the notes, Paul is generally quite careful about locating in the future central items of Christian hope such as resurrection and salvation (e.g., Rom. 6; 1 Cor. 15). Paul needed to be cautious in light of a tendency on the part of many to collapse the future into the present, obscuring the brokenness and hostility of the present age, and thereby underestimating the struggle for faithful living. Other Pauline texts (e.g., 1 Cor. 15; 2 Thess. 2:1-2; 2 Tim. 2:18) indicate that the relationship between resurrection, salvation, and eschatology was a troubling one for decades (Elias: 274-7). The Gnostic controversies of the second century sharpened the debate to the breaking point. Paul was enlisted on both sides of the struggle.

Ephesians is close to other NT writings such as Colossians and the Gospel of John. Those writings retain a clear-headed sense that the *full* appearing of salvation lies in the future, but also exploit with almost reckless abandon—we might call it the reckless euphoria of gratitude and worship—the implications of God's action in Christ *for the present* (e.g., Col. 1:13; John 5:24; 11:25). I say "reckless" because this emphasis on the *present* benefits of God's mercy and love repeatedly played into the hands of those who believed they already enjoyed all there is to experience of God, and who then ironically lost touch with the present, both ethically and spiritually.

Far from representing flight from material and social life, in Ephesians such language of assurance and status is meant to inform believers of their role in the cosmic scheme of God to save the world and further to buttress their resolve to live up to that calling amid the inevitable struggles that such participation invites. Hence, the emphasis on good works: the author intends to exploit to the fullest the implications of Easter for the daily exercise of holiness. Heaven is to be lived on earth.

THE TEXT IN THE LIFE OF THE CHURCH

Evangelical Separatism?

The characterization of humanity as the walking dead in collusion with evil should strike both familiar and dissonant chords in many churches. Some with a keen sense of difference between church and world are vulnerable to demonizing the "world." In many more faith communities, holiness, blamelessness, separation from evil, and resistance to evil have given way to normalcy. Some are discarding a conviction that difference is a necessary mark of faithfulness. They suspect that perfectionism can lead to individual and corporate self-righteousness and blindness to the reality of sinfulness in individual and, especially, corporate and institutional experience (cf. discussion in Sawatsky and Holland; Block).

Our text leaves no doubt, however, that the solution for the difficulties of the narrow path should not be sought on the freeway. The antidote lies rather in imitating a God who constantly leaves the narrow road, but only to raid the highway for new sons and daughters (in Matt. 5:43-48, "perfection" comes to fullest expression in the love of enemies).

Such a faithful, generous, evangelical separatism, if we may call it that, is relevant to the whole gamut of social and cultural issues—sex, greed, violence, racism, to name a few. To be different from the world—from the *sons and daughters of disobedience*—does not mean turning our backs on such issues, least of all on those caught up in them. It means, instead, trying to comprehend their complex nature, as well as recognizing them as the means of enslavement. Our text reminds us that evil is more like a deadly gas giving a false feeling of life to senses and imagination in rebellion to God. As unconscious as is breathing, so unaware is humanity of the depth of its alienation from God and of its victimization by the *ruler of the authority of the air*. Recall Miroslav Volf's words about being "colonized" by evil (Volf: 89-90, quoted in notes to 2:1-3, 5a).

In the view of Ephesians, the most Christian (Messianic) and thus both confrontive and evangelical act is to name and engage these issues as powers in rebellion against God (cf. 5:3-14; 6:10-18) *[Powers]*. Such naming will not be heard unless it emerges from a community of those who know resurrection in their individual and

their corporate life. However, believers have a task even more important than engagement with the issues and struggle with the powers.
They are called to imitate God in seeing through the issues to those
enslaved by the powers of evil, and to love them as God has loved
us, thereby participating in the process of salvation. Why else sit with
Christ in the heavenlies?

Lamentably, we can find a great deal of residual or renewed captivity and rebellion within the church. Ephesians acknowledges this: half
the letter is exhortation directed toward *believers* (chaps. 4–6). The
emphasis on mercy, grace, and liberation as well as the call to *walk
in good works* is directed to believers who have trouble staying on the
narrow road. With all the stress on resurrection and re-creation in this
passage, there is no room for smug arrogance in the church.

Ethics and Easter

Warnings against smugness and arrogance notwithstanding, our text
confronts believers with the central importance of resurrection. They
are to live out their resurrection and their exaltation in full view of the
ages (2:7), tirelessly doing *good works* (2:10). They are to perform
them, not as the weak, powerless, and suffering victims, but as the
raised and exalted kings and queens of heaven, as it were, as those
who participate in the *sovereignty* of Christ (2:5-6). Such royal faithfulness will find expression in loving-kindness, forgiveness, meekness,
and self-sacrifice, as shown in 4:31—5:2. It constitutes nothing less
than the imitation of God and his Christ (5:1-2) in exposing and transforming the works of darkness (5:11) and in the quality of domestic
love (5:25).

We need not be surprised that such sovereign faithfulness will be
met by resistance and will result in suffering. The cross belongs to
such a life, as the experience of Jesus shows. But the cross should not
be allowed to obscure the central importance of Easter for discipleship. Easter, and indeed Pentecost, *precede* Good Friday for walkers
of the narrow path (cf. Dintaman: 207; McClendon, 1986:242-75;
Yoder Neufeld, 2000:61-2; TLC for 1:15-23). The cross is inevitable
for those who have experienced Easter; that is finally why Ephesians
concludes on a note of conflict and struggle (6:10-20).

As stated in the investigation of this text, this part of Ephesians
may reflect a baptismal context. The Schleitheim Confession preserves precisely this sequence of resurrection and cross in its first
article, which deals explicitly with baptism:

Baptism shall be given to all those who have been taught repentance and the amendment of life and who truly believe that their sins are taken away through Christ, and *to all those who desire to walk in the resurrection of Jesus Christ and be buried with him in death*, so that they might rise with Him. (J. H. Yoder, 1972:36, italics added)

Menno Simons speaks similarly of two resurrections, the first one "a spiritual resurrection from sin and death to a new life and a change of heart," experienced by "putting on Christ" in baptism ("The Spiritual Resurrection," 1536; Menno: 53-62). It is this "Easter" that precedes taking up the cross in anticipation of the great resurrection to come.

Ephesians 2:1-10 represents a resource to reinvest baptism with the joy and exhilaration of Easter. Baptism will reflect fully the drama of salvation when it becomes a ritual that reenacts the movement from death to life, from the slavery of disobedience to the freedom of doing good works. As such, it will become a drama of empowerment for discipleship—a discipleship of participation in the sovereignty of the risen Lord (on baptism, see TLC for 4:17—5:2).

Ephesians 2:11-22

Christ Is Our Peace

PREVIEW

Ephesians 2:11-22 surely ranks at the top of the list of most memorable passages in Ephesians. It is one of the most profound and beautiful peace texts in the whole Bible. The image of the broken wall has exerted influence well beyond the borders of the Christian community. Events in recent memory such as the breaking down of the Berlin wall, and with it the rending of the Iron Curtain, have added special poignancy to this image. Yitzhak Rabin, late prime minister of Israel, spoke movingly of the breaking down of the walls of hostility between Israelis and Arabs at the opening of the border between Jordan and Israel in July of 1994.

Despite the positive associations this text and its imagery have in relation to peace, the terrible legacy of Christian anti-Judaism demands careful interpretation of this text. This is so because *the wall of division* (2:14) is related to enmity and also specifically to the defining element of Jewish identity, the law. Has the price of peace been too great?

The movement from alienation to participation in Christ in 2:1-10 is retraced in these verses. The contrast between *once* and *now* recalls the description of the "walking dead" in verse 2 and echoes Colossians 1:21-22. Further dualities sharpen the contrasts: far/near, strangers/family members, exiles/citizens, we/you. We hear echoes also of the opening blessing in chapter 1, where *you* (Gentiles) come also to believe in what *we* (Jews) have already participated (notes for 1:13 and 2:1-3).

The divine initiative in bringing about reconciliation (cf. 2:4) now takes the form of Christ the peacemaker destroying enmity by giving his own life—both in the sense that he gives up his life for humanity and that he gives life to humanity. Through his death, Christ does away with the law in its function as dividing wall. Insiders and outsiders now come to make up the church as household and family; Jews and Gentiles provide God with a dwelling place.

Verses 14-16 are of particular interest. Likely a hymn, or at least an adaptation of hymnic material, they celebrate the cosmic and social dimensions of Christ's work of peace on the cross. Readers of Colossians will recall the great christological hymn in 1:15-20, which also celebrates Christ as peacemaker (see esp. Col. 1:20; E. Martin: 59-77).

The passage is made up of five sentences: verses 11-12, 13, 14-16, 17-18, and 19-22. There are two ways of viewing the structure of the passage. One (Structure A) is determined by the *once/now* contrast, much like Colossians 1:21-22, present in the background. This makes verse 13 pivotal (*But now . . .;* Lincoln: 125, 148; see my Schematic Trans.).

Structure A

Remember that once you were Gentiles, strangers, aliens, without hope, without God, (2:11-12)

BUT NOW in Christ you have been brought near.... (2:13)

> For he is our peace
> who has made the two one. (2:14-16)

> He proclaimed peace to the far and the near. (2:17-18)

So then, you are no longer strangers and aliens but co-citizens with the saints, a dwelling place for God. (2:19)

The other view (Structure B) sees the passage as a *chiasm* (e.g., Bailey: 63; Houlden: 288; Kirby: 156-7; Thomson: 84-115; in contrast, Best, 1998:236-7; Lincoln: 126; on *chiasm(us),* see Introduction and literature cited there). A chiasm might simply repeat two phrases in reverse order, *A-B-B'-A':*

A Praise the LORD
  B with the lyre;
  B' with the harp of ten strings
A' make melody to him. (Ps. 33:2)

Other examples of *chiasm* have a concentric structure (e.g., *A-B-C-B'-A'*), drawing attention to the center, which presents the most important element in the passage. This appears to be the case in Ephesians 2:11-22. Around a hymnic celebration of Christ as peace—we might call it the central windowpane (2:14-16)—are placed two sets of mirrorlike panes, each roughly equal in size to its corresponding partner. The two outer panes (2:11-12 and 19-22) are contrasting treatments of the theme of exclusion and inclusion of Gentiles. The two inner panes (2:13 and 2:17-18) framing the peace hymn (2:14-16) depict Christ as one who has brought near those who were far off, preaching peace to both far and near.

Structure B

A Once strangers and aliens without God (2:11-12)
  B Christ has brought near the far (2:13)
    C Christ is our peace (2:14-16)
  B' Christ proclaimed peace to the far and the near (2:17-18)
A' Now no longer strangers, but part of God's home (2:19-22)

Both analyses (Structures A and B) are compelling in their own right; both are true to the thought of Ephesians. There is no need, as often in Ephesians, to force a choice (so also Thomson: 91). The first stresses the contrast between past and present, between the living death of alienation and hostility and the new creation initiated by God in Christ. The second draws our attention in an almost visual way—much like an icon!—to the Christ whose person and work is the peace that has made the contrast a reality.

OUTLINE

Once Excluded Strangers, 2:11-12

Brought Near in Christ, 2:13

Christ Is Our Peace, 2:14-16
    2:14a   Christ Is Our Peace
    2:14b   Peace in the Flesh
    2:14c-15a   Breaking Down the Dividing Wall
        The Fence   2:14c
        The Law of Commandments in Regulations 2:15a
    2:15b   The New Human
    2:16a   One Body
    2:16b   The Cross
    2:16c   Killing Enmity

Peace Brings Us Together Near God, 2:17-18

Now Welcomed and Integrated into God's Home, 2:19-22
    2:19   Restoring God's People
    2:20   Building God's Home

Building Materials: Jews and Gentiles!	2:19
Foundation: Apostles and Prophets	2:20
Cornerstone or Headstone: Christ	2:20-21
Power: The Holy Spirit	2:22
Inhabitant: God	2:21-22

EXPLANATORY NOTES

Once Excluded Strangers 2:11-12

In verse 11 the author forcefully reminds Gentile believers of their former state. With a bit of Jewish stereotyping, Gentile existence is caricatured with the vocabulary typical of "ethnic backbiting" (Perkins: 67). The author uses a derogatory nickname for Gentiles, *the uncircumcision*, (lit., *the foreskin*), contrasting them to *the circumcision*, Jews. Just as the Gentiles are *the foreskin in [the] flesh,* so the circumcision of Jews is *made by hands in [the] flesh.*

In Galatians 5:16-24 Paul uses "flesh" as a synonym for that which is not of God's Spirit. Note also Colossians 2:11, where "spiritual circumcision," "the circumcision of Christ," is distinguished from circumcision made "in the flesh with hands" (cf. Rom. 2:25-29). In our text, however, *flesh* serves mostly, but not exclusively, to identify the two hostile components of humanity as concretely as possible. Notice that Christ destroys that hostility *in his flesh.* Hostility, alienation, *and* salvation are all experienced *in the flesh.*

Gentile readers are reminded of what it meant—from a Jewish perspective, to be sure—for them to have been outsiders. *At that time* Gentiles were, first of all, *without Christ* (or *without a messiah*). The phrase *without Christ* does not simply state the obvious that they were once not believers in Christ and thus not beneficiaries of his saving work. Here *without Christ* is part of the inventory of what it means for Gentiles not to have been Jewish: they were excluded from the community *from whom* and *for whom* the Messiah would come (cf. Rom. 9:4-5; cf. the pseudepigraphical Ps. of Sol. 17:21-25). In other words, Gentiles were *without hope.*

Gentiles were *excluded from the commonwealth of Israel. Commonwealth (politeia)* refers to Israel as a nation that enjoyed the special relationship with God (Best, 1998:241; Houlden: 289;

Lincoln: 137). Outsiders are thus *strangers to the covenants of promise*, a somewhat unusual reference to the covenants God made with Israel containing promises of land, progeny, restored monarchy, and ultimate national restoration (cf. Rom. 9:4). It is unlikely that the author has the covenant with Abraham in mind, since it is interpreted by Paul as the basis of *hope* for Gentiles, and not *exclusion* (Rom. 4:1-12; Gal. 3:8-9).

To say that Gentiles have *no hope*, since hope resides in the favor of God, is much like saying they are *without God*. The author employs a term unique in the NT—*atheoi*, from which we derive the word *atheist*. Rather than a philosophical rejection of theism, it expresses the insiders' judgment on outsiders. In Jewish eyes Gentiles were as atheistic as were Jews in the eyes of Gentiles (e.g., Josephus, *Contra Apion* 2.148; Martyrdom of Polycarp 3.2; 9.2; Barth, 1974:260; Best, 1998:243). Nothing expresses more succinctly a state of hopelessness than to be *without God in the cosmos*. And that is exactly how Jews viewed Gentiles: hopelessly adrift in the universe.

This caricature is important and serves to set in sharp relief the shocking surprise of God's grace as it comes to expression in Christ, starting in verse 13. We are reminded of 2:1-3, which sets the stage for the great saving intervention of God in verse 4: *But God, rich in mercy* . . . . Like a divine echo, we encounter again the profound discontinuity of grace: *But now in Christ Jesus* . . . (2:13).

Brought Near in Christ 2:13

Verse 13 serves as a bridge between the description of Gentile life apart from God and the celebration of Christ's work of peace: *But now in Christ Jesus you who were far off have been brought near through his blood*. Whereas verses 11-12 describe what was *once* true for the Gentile readers of this letter, Christ has *now* changed all that. *You*—Gentiles, the *far*, the excluded outsiders—have *now* been brought *near*. The reference to *you* recalls the familiar contrast of *you/we* already found in 1:3-4 and 2:1-10.

In choosing this language, the author deliberately recalls the great announcement of peace in Isaiah 57:19: "'Peace, peace, to the far and the near,' says the Lord." To fully appreciate the significance of this quotation from Isaiah, we must pay attention to the context of 57:19. It is part of a poem anticipating the return of the exiles from Babylon. "The far and the near" refers to Jews taken into exile and those left behind in a decimated homeland. Exile was interpreted as punishment for disobedience. Humility and contrition changed God's disposition, and he now beckons home the contrite with assurances of peace. As for the wicked? "There is no peace for the wicked!" (Isa. 57:21).

Jewish rabbis would later come to use this text from Isaiah as a way of speaking about proselytes to Judaism (Lincoln: 147, referring to Num. Rab. 8.4; Midr. Sam. 28.6; cf. Smith: 41-2, esp. on Gen. Rab. 39.14). Yet we should not fail to marvel at the author of Ephesians employing this "welcome home" text from Isaiah for the Messiah's mission to the Gentiles. By recasting the estrangement of Gentiles as exile from home, this text is surely a profound act of peacemaking. Gentiles are invited to make the family history of their enemies their own, in effect, to come home (2:19-22). Thereby the family of God is opened to include those whose exclusion at one time defined the very borders of that family.

All this has taken place *in Christ*, specifically *in (by) the blood of Christ*. The *blood of Christ* refers, not to the circumcision earlier mentioned, but to the death of Christ on the cross, anticipating verse 16 (Best, 1998:246). The *blood of Christ* signifies redemption (1:7), reminding us of sacrifice and atonement (Lev. 17:11 shows the connection between blood, life, and atonement). What should not be missed here is that holy blood has been offered freely for the sake of those hitherto *outside* the covenantal arrangement. This dramatic insight is now celebrated in hymnic fashion.

Christ Is Our Peace 2:14-16

The grammatical structure of verses 14-16 hinges on the central assertion that Christ is peace. This is followed by four main (aorist) participles *(made, broken, abolished,* and *killed)*; the third participle *(having abolished)* is elaborated with two subjunctives showing the purpose of the abolition *(so as to create, so as to reconcile)*. *So as to create* is connected with a present participle to *making peace* (Schematic Trans.).

In these verses the main assertion is that Christ makes and proclaims peace and also *is* peace. *Peace (eirēnē)* in biblical texts means so much more than the absence of conflict. In the Greek version of the OT (LXX), *eirēnē* usually translates or is heavily colored by the Hebrew term *shalom,* as in NT. *Shalom* means well-being and wholeness, encompassing all of the concerns of human life—individual, personal, social, and religious (TBC).

At the same time, *shalom* is often found in close proximity to conflict and warfare. God the peacemaker is also God the warrior (e.g., Isa. 42:1-7, 13-15), as is God's Messiah (e.g., Isa. 9–10; 2 Thess.

1:5-10; Rev. 19:11-16; TBC for 6:10-20). This hymn celebrates both the creative energies of the messianic peacemaker *(making, creating, reconciling),* but also his militancy *(breaking, abolishing, killing).* We hasten to add that the destructive note is highly ironic, coming most forcefully to expression in the phrase *killing the enmity* or *murdering hostility.*

It is important to be aware of this deep biblical well from which the *peace* spoken of in our text draws meaning. At the same time, it is equally important to appreciate the distinctive contribution of this passage to our understanding of peace. To do that we should pay attention to the prehistory of this text. Though they may not agree on the exact shape of a hymnic source, many scholars believe that in these verses the author employs a hymn celebrating Christ as peacemaker (e.g., Barth, 1974:261-2; Dinkler: 177-81; Gnilka: 147-52; Lincoln: 127-30; Sanders: 88-92; Stuhlmacher: 337-58, with review of literature). Among them there is a relative consensus that underlying the present text is an earlier hymn celebrating Christ as *cosmic peacemaker,* which the author has adapted for the present context of Christ making peace between Gentiles and Jews.

Not all commentators agree (e.g., Schnackenburg: 107, 112, considering 2:13-18 to be a christological exegesis of three texts, Isa. 9:5-7; 52:7; 57:19; Best, 1998:247-50). An expansion of Colossians 1:20-22 may be sufficient to explain the origin of this text (Thurston: 108), but even then it would have hymnic roots.

While we cannot be sure in a final sense, the data point to the use of hymnic material in this passage. Following are elements that are likely to have been part of any earlier version of the hymn. Ellipsis points (. . .) indicate where additions were possibly added later to fit the hymn to the present context:

Hypothetical Original Hymn of Peace

He is . . . peace
    who made both into one
    and broke down the dividing wall, . . .
    having destroyed the enmity . . .
        in order to create the two . . . into one, . . .
            making peace,
      and might reconcile both in one body, . . .
    having killed the enmity. . . .

The cosmic dimension of Christ's peace emerges clearly in this reconstruction. Christ has healed the division in the cosmos by breaking down the dividing wall between heaven and earth. He united that which was divided *(the two, both)* into one new whole.

Admittedly, this bare skeleton leaves much room for interpretation. Some see in the background a Gnostic redeemer [Gnosticism] who brings peace by breaking through the wall separating true Gnostics from the heavenly realm (e.g., Fischer: 133; Schlier: 129-30). But the idea that reality is made up of divisions in need of mending found expression widely in Greek philosophy and also in Jewish writings influenced by Hellenism (Smith: 36-41, with citations), as well as in Jewish apocalyptic literature (e.g., 1 Enoch 14:9). This hymn, then, could have been sung by a wide spectrum of persons celebrating Christ's work of peace in the broadest terms possible.

In the present context, however, the hymn draws attention to the effect of Christ's peacemaking on the division between Jews and Gentiles—between those who have enjoyed a relationship with God and those who have hitherto been without God and without hope (2:11-12). We can illustrate the present concerns of the author by highlighting in italics the features that appear to have been added to the hypothetical original hymn above.

Additions to the Hymn of Peace

He is *our* peace
  who made both into one
  and broke down the dividing wall, *the fence,*
  having destroyed the enmity *in his flesh,*
  the law of commandments in regulations,
    in order to create the two *in him[self]* into one *new human,*
      making peace,
    and *might* reconcile both [groups] in one body
      to God through the cross
  having killed the enmity *in him[self]* (or *through it*).

2:14a Christ Is Our Peace

A number of key emphases emerge in such an exercise, regardless of how or even whether we reconstruct it in any particular way. First, Christ is *our* peace. The cosmic dimension of Christ's peace embraces the enmity between *you* and *us.* The peace of the Messiah is for Jews, the old covenant partners, and also for those who have been newly drawn near (2:13). The peace of Christ has to do specifically with social and religious enmities that are rooted in the very fabric of religious identity and hope.

Even so, a trace of the cosmic perspective of the earlier hymn has been retained in the neuter *ta amphotera* in 2:14, which the NRSV translates as *both groups,* and most others simply as *the two* (NIV, NJB). It is possible to refer to persons or groups with a neuter plural.

But the return to the masculine *hoi amphoteroi* in 2:16-17, where it clearly refers to Gentiles and Jews, allows for the possibility that the author in 2:14 has deliberately retained the neuter plural from the original hymn to point to a much larger sphere for peacemaking than human enmity (cf. the frequent *all things* (*ta panta* in Ephesians, as in 1:10, 23; 3:9, 20; 4:6, 10; 5:13; 6:16, 21).

In other words, the peace of Christ makes both *you* and *us*— Gentiles and Jews—the beneficiaries of Christ's overcoming of *all* enmities, *all* dualisms, and *all* divisions. The one who has broken down the wall dividing heaven and earth has also overcome *our* enmities—he is **our** peace.

2:14b Peace in the Flesh

Christ has made peace *in* or *through his flesh* (2:14b). Just as the distinction between Gentiles and Jews is one of *flesh* (2:11), so also Christ's work of peace has taken place, not at a cosmic distance but up close, *in his flesh*. In 5:31-32, the author likens the sexual union of man and woman becoming *one flesh* (Gen. 2:24) to the relationship between Christ and the church.

But what does *flesh* mean here? We might take it to refer to the incarnation. This would bring our text close to John 1, where the "word" (Christ) becomes "flesh." The point there, as it might be here as well, is to insist on the materiality and corporeality of Christ against those who disparage material creation and with it the fleshliness of both the enmity and Christ's peacemaking. The hymn, as adapted, wants to ensure that that does not happen.

Closer at hand is the connection to the *blood* of Christ in 2:13, anticipating the *cross* in verse 16 (cf. 1:7). In this case *in his flesh* points to the fact that Christ's act of peace required a costly personal intervention in human enmities. We recall Romans 5: "While we were still weak . . . , sinners . . . , enemies, Christ died for us." *In his flesh* (Eph. 2:14b) refers then to what Romans 5:18-19 identifies as "one man's act of righteousness (or justice), . . . one man's act of obedience."

Finally, *in his flesh* perhaps also anticipates the *new human* (*anthrōpos*, 2:15) and the unified *body* (*sōma*, 2:16). The church is then a "fleshly" sphere of peace where the "fleshly" hostility between erstwhile enemies has been and is being overcome. We should not rule out any of these possibilities. Both cosmic and immediately experienced social dimensions of peace are present in Christ.

2:14c-15a Breaking Down the Dividing Wall

The second major participle that expands on Christ's peace focuses on the enmity itself: Christ *broke down the dividing wall* between *you* and *us*, the *far* and the *near*, Gentiles and Jews. Although in the original hymn *the wall* may have referred to the division between earth and heaven (Best, 1998:254-5), it now refers to what has divided Gentiles and Jews from each other and Gentiles from God.

The Fence 2:14c

The *dividing wall (mesotoichon)* is identified as *the fence* or *hedge (phragmos)*. More than just another synonym, as often in Ephesians (NRSV does not bother to translate *phragmos*), it refers to something specific that has stood between Gentiles and Jews.

Some identify this broken wall with the partition separating Gentiles from the holier parts in the Jerusalem temple reserved for Jews (e.g., Houlden: 290). Perhaps this is what the NIV refers to with *barrier*. Such a suggestion carries an implicit critique of the temple as space hostile to Gentiles, an issue that seems to have been alive during the early years of the church (cf. Mark 11:17; Acts 6:13-14; 21:28). Such an allusion would have meant a great deal to a Jewish author, whether or not the temple in Jerusalem was still standing at the time of writing. It might have been less intelligible to Gentile readers (Best, 1998:253-4).

The Law of Commandments in Regulations 2:15a

More likely, *the fence* refers to *the law of commandments in regulations,* which Christ is said to have *abolished (katargeō,* 2:15). While *katargeō* can mean "to destroy," when related to law it means "to abolish," "annul," or "abrogate." Thus, we might take this to mean that Christ destroyed the source of enmity, the law. "Christ neutralized these negative effects of the law by doing away with the law" (Lincoln: 142). The radical nature of this view is reflected also in Perkins's comment: "Ephesians has no concern to affirm the divine character of the Law" (73). Though such a view meshes easily with a great deal of traditional Christian thinking about the law, it misreads, in my opinion, this *Jewish* author's celebration of the Messiah's act of including Gentiles.

Commentators on this passage face a difficult challenge. On one hand, an interpreter must account for the blunt word about the abolition of the law. On the other, one must acknowledge, first, the deliberate self-presentation of the author as a *Jewish* believer in Jesus; and second, the pervasive *Jewish* emphasis throughout this letter on holiness and righteousness (4:24; 5:3-5) and, not least, the specific use of the law as motivation and grounding for behavior (6:2). The motifs of light and darkness, holiness and licentiousness, as also the stark warning of judgment on those who violate God's will (as in 5:5), are rooted in a Jewish imagination shaped by Torah observance. The law is, after all, at heart the manifestation of the divine will for humanity. There is no evidence that *any* NT writer believed differently, including the author of Ephesians.

In the following we will explore whether the author *as a Jew* could have valued the law as God's will for Jews and for humanity generally and also celebrated the abrogation of the law as found in commandments and precepts.

First, we should pay careful attention to the wording. The interpretation in NIV and NRSV—*the law with its commandments and ordinances*—is not careful enough. The Greek says, literally, *the law of commandments in dogmas (regulations, decrees). In dogmas* is absent from the important early manuscript P[46], raising the possibility that this is an insertion (Roetzel: 86). However, since in the NT the phrase *in dogmas* appears only here and in Colossians 2:14, the pervasive dependence of Ephesians on Colossians leads us to take it as part of the original wording (so also Lincoln: 142).

Thus *in dogmas* specifies how the law is being thought of in this instance and in what sense Christ can be said to have annulled it. Instead of referring to the law as a whole, *the law of commandments in dogmas* suggests a more limited meaning and is open to several overlapping possibilities for its meaning:

1. *Abolishing the Law as Means of Separation?* The first possibility is that Christ has abolished, not the true and good law, but only its function of separating Jews from the rest of humanity (Barth, 1974:290-1). In view here are regulations commonly referred to as ceremonial laws, such as food laws and circumcision (Schnackenburg: 115). Relatedly, Christ is said to have destroyed only the *casuistic interpretation* of the law, the interpretation of the law as specific rules, rules which if observed in practice had the effect of separating Jews from Gentiles (Schlier: 126).

In this view the law *as such* still stands for believers in Christ, but not as an elaborate set of decrees to be interpreted in an even more elaborate system of regulations. Instead, the law provides the framework for the free exercise of holiness and righteousness, motivated and guided by the indwelling Spirit.

This suggestion has much to commend it. One should, however, be careful not to equate Jewish application of the law with legalism. The prime function of the so-called ceremonial law and the expanding code of rules was to express and solidify covenant faithfulness. One way of nurturing covenant faithfulness was to instill a clear sense of difference from those not of the covenant, as the widely referred to Letter of Aristeas (second century B.C.) illustrates clearly (cf. R. Martin, 1991:35; Mauser: 157; Schackenburg: 114):

> To prevent our being perverted by contact with others or by mixing with bad influences, [the Lawgiver/Moses] . . . hedged us in on all sides with strict observances connected with meat and drink and touch and hearing and sight. (Letter of Aristeas 139, 142)

In Deuteronomy 4, Moses asks the people to remember (Deut. 4:9; cf. Eph. 2:11) and keep the statutes and ordinances (Deut. 4:1, 5, 8, 40; cf. 6:1). Moses asks, "What other great nation has statutes and ordinances as just as this entire law that I am setting before you today?" (4:8). This follows immediately on the heels of a question strikingly resonant with our text: "What other great nation has a god so near to it as the Lord our God is whenever we call to him?" (4:7; cf. Eph. 2:13, 17!). The law as "statutes and ordinances" is meant to separate out those God has chosen for himself (Deut. 4:20). It signals, moreover, the nearness of Israel to its God (5:22-27).

The brutally sharp characterization of Gentiles in Ephesians 2:11-12 owes much to such instruction in the law (cf. Eph. 4:17-19). However, if Gentiles *as Gentiles* were ever to become part of the people of God—surely the very heart of the Pauline mission (cf. Eph. 3)—that dividing function of the law needed to be "drastically rethought" (R. Martin, 1991:36). In verse 15 the price of the integration of Gentiles and Jews into the *new human* is the termination of that specific function of the law. The *law of ordinances in dogmas* may thus refer, for example, to food laws and circumcision. These regulations were annulled insofar as they were expected of Gentiles becoming a part of God's household. What *Jewish* believers should continue to do is not specified.

2. Abolishing the Law as Means of Condemnation? Careful comparison with Colossians 2:14 raises the possibility that the author of Ephesians may more specifically have in mind the condemnatory function of the law. Aside from our present text, the only other place in the Bible where *in dogmas (en dogmasin)* appears is in Colossians 2:14. Literally translated, God is said to have "erased the handwritten note *in dogmas* that stood against us." In this case *dogmas* are legal decrees of judgment, recorded on a note of indebtedness. This note God "nailed to the cross," thereby canceling the "dogmas." With this pointer to Colossians, the author may want to clarify in what sense Christ's death on the cross is God's act of peace: in the cross, the dogmas of judgment against the Gentiles in particular have been canceled.

3. *"Abolition" as the Effect of Eschatology?* Another possible clue to the nature of the cancellation of the law lies in Jewish eschatology. Keep in mind that in verse 15 the death of Christ is related to the annulment of the *law of commandments in dogmas* and also to the creation of the *new human* (cf. 2:15c; 2:10; 4:24). This vocabulary reflects a basic set of convictions, including the understanding that with the coming of the Messiah Jesus, humanity is in the process of being re-created.

One aspect of this new creation relates to the law. As the great prophecy of Jeremiah indicates, when creation is mended, the law will be inscribed onto the heart, into the very consciousness of the people of God (Jer. 31:31-34; cf. 2 Cor. 3:3). There will no longer be any need for instruction—for *commandments in dogmas*, we might say. The law itself is not gone; it resides in the seat of human volition. The law as a set of rules has given way to the law inscribed in the heart as God's will and the exercise of human freedom become one.

The abolition of *the law of commandment in dogmas* should be viewed, then, as *Jewish* eschatological expectation having come true in Christ. That is bracing in and of itself. What adds to the shock value of this assertion is that the eschatological gift extends to those once outside the covenant. The good news of the Messiah's peacemaking turns out to be relevant for *us* Jews who have been *near* and also for *you* Gentiles who were *afar off*.

Conclusion. Each of these interpretations is compelling within the overall objectives of this letter. It is not necessary to choose between them. None of them are hostile to Jewish tradition itself, let alone to the law. Nevertheless, Jews not sharing Ephesians' eschatological, christological, and missionary outlook would understandably have reacted to this as an affront to Jewish identity and faithfulness, as a misreading of eschatological reality, and even as blasphemy.

In the view of this poet of peace, however, neither the law as God's wisdom and will nor the story of God's people—graced by covenants, intimacy with God, and the expectation of the liberator—has been abrogated (abolished) by Christ's radical act of peacemaking.

The author of Ephesians shares with Jeremiah the conviction that the law would be inscribed into the heart of humanity, including Gentile humanity. New creation has come to humanity as God originally purposed—before divisions, before enmity, before the chasm of the Jew-Gentile division, and before the law was forced, because of human sin, to serve those divisions (cf. Rom. 7; Gal. 3).

2:15b The New Human

As we have just seen, the breaking down of the wall is not an end in itself. The point of *destruction* is the *construction* of a new humanity (Barth, 1974:306). Christ the "Carpenter of new creation," to quote Brian Wren ("God of Many Names," *HWB*, 77, stanza 3), has destroyed the enmity *in order that he might create the two in him[self] into one new human, making peace* (2:15). Although the *new human* correctly translates the Greek, we should not think of this in individualistic terms. The *new human* is Christ, but Christ as reconstituted humanity (regarding *in Christ*, see 1:3-14, notes). Christ's act of peace is described as taking two groups (lit., *the two*), breaking down what has divided and defined them and fusing them into one being—Christ himself. At work here is the *gathering up* of humanity in Christ (1:10).

This notion has rich resonance in Pauline thought, in particular as it relates to the concept of the new Adam (see TBC). For Paul and his students, Christ *was* the one who died on the cross and who *was* raised from the dead (past tense; cf. Rom. 1:3; 1 Cor. 15:3-28; Col. 1:15-20). Just as important, Christ *is* the one "in whom" believers participate in the *new creation* (present tense; cf. 2 Cor. 5:17, Gal. 6:15). Christ *is* the *new Adam*, humanity re-created in the image of God (Rom. 5:12-21; 1 Cor. 15:21-28; Phil. 2:6-11; cf. esp. Eph. 4:24!). True, the full stature of that *perfect humanity* has not yet been arrived at (Eph. 4:13-14). But that should not obscure the eschatological vision undergirding this sweeping claim regarding Christ's peace. To be "one in Christ" is to begin again what it means to be human—*together with those who have been our enemies.*

2:16a One Body

This is further reiterated in what is largely a parallel statement in verse 16: *and might reconcile both in one body to God through the cross, having killed the enmity in (through) it* (or *in him[self]*). This phrase is dependent on the participle *abolishing*—*he abolished the law . . . so as to reconcile both groups.* The author draws heavily from the great christological hymn in Colossians 1:20, 22. Notice the connection in Colossians between universal peace and the cross, as well as Christ's fleshly body (lit., *in the body of his flesh through the death*). In particular, the author derives from Colossians the unique form of *reconcile (apokatallassō)*. It serves to identify the reach of Christ's reconciliation of "all things, whether on earth or in heaven," an emphasis consistent with Ephesians (1:10, notes).

Christ reconciles *both groups* (masculine plural for people: *hoi amphoteroi*) *in one body*. We are predisposed by 1:23 to hearing in *body* a reference to the church. The church is a *body* of reconciliation made up of erstwhile enemies who have been reconciled to each other. This parallels the creation of the *new anthrōpos*.

We are permitted to push this line of interpretation a bit further, however, by recalling that the word *in* can have an instrumental meaning *["In"]*, especially in Ephesians. That suggests that Christ's body, the church, is a means by which enemies are reconciled. Further, the very notion of *body* already implies activity. The church is the *result* of Christ's act of reconciliation and also an *agent* of reconciliation. At the same time, the close proximity to Colossians 1:20, 22 suggests that *body* might more obviously refer to Christ's own historical *body*, in his death on the *cross*.

Once again we do well not to make an absolute choice, given how compact and allusive our text is. It is clear from Colossians 1:24, and as well from Mark's recollection of Jesus' teaching in 8:27-38 and 10:35-40, for example, that early believers did not sharply separate the nature, quality, and meaning of Christ's suffering from theirs as participants in his body of flesh. Such ambiguity is particularly fitting as an interpretive key to Ephesians, where the membrane between Christ and church is extremely porous.

2:16b The Cross

It is not said *how* the cross brings about reconciliation. Perhaps for the author of this letter, that goes without saying. After all, there is every likelihood that this letter was meant to be read alongside other letters of Paul (Introduction). What is clear, however, is that the cross is set within a large horizon, one that goes far beyond application to the individual believer. The cross is related to the overcoming of hostilities between *groups* (so correctly NRSV). Its effect extends to the reconciliation and re-creation of humanity *in Christ*.

Nevertheless, the gift of peace granted through the cross is larger than a matter of overcoming hostilities between groups. They are not merely reconciled to each other. Those who were once *without God*

(*atheoi*, 2:12) are reconciled *in one body* **to God** (cf. Rom. 5:10;
2 Cor. 5:18-19). The importance of this cannot be overstressed. The
deepest chasm of enmity exists finally not between groups. In the end
such hostilities are evidence of enmity with God—with the God who is
Father of every family in heaven and on earth (3:15). Enmity in the
human community constitutes a violation of God's designs for humanity, and is thus a terrible affront to the loving Creator.

All of Ephesians is one long celebration of the fact that the same
God whom humanity has offended is the one who has taken the initiative to end the enmity (cf. 2:4). It is crucial to see that Christ does not
make peace between humanity and a vengeful God. *God* has taken
the initiative to reclaim humanity through Christ. The ultimate actor
in this drama of Christ as peace is none other than God.

2:16c Killing Enmity

The final phrase in this hymnic section captures succinctly the
central dramatic moment in the drama of peace: the killing of what
Ched Myers calls "the central antagonist in the Ephesian drama of
redemption"—*enmity* (Myers: 18). Enmity is murdered, ironically, by
Christ giving *his own* life on the cross. "Christ is killed and he kills!"
(Best, 1998:266). Or in the words of the hymn writer George Herbert
(1633):

> Come, my Way, my Truth, my Life:
> such a way as gives us breath;
> such a truth as ends all strife;
> *such a life as killeth death.* (*HWB*, 587, stanza 1, italics added)

However ironic, the motif of "killing enmity" as the work of peace
clearly reflects the reality that peace does not come about without a
life-and-death struggle. Though it certainly implies the death of the
"enemy," in this case enmity itself, it costs nothing less than the life
of the one making peace (cf. Rom. 5:1-11; 1 Cor. 15:3-28). The
endlessly wide embrace of peace that characterizes the vision of this
letter, and this passage in particular, is extended by the divine warrior
whose warfare in this case is waged against enmity itself by means of
his own blood.

There is some ambiguity as to how the end of the verse should
be translated. NRSV translates *en autō* as *through it*, referring either
to the cross (so explicitly NIV) or to Christ's body. But *en autō* can
also be translated as *in him* or *himself*, as in verse 15 (so NJB: *in his
own person*). A number of translations avoid the problem with *thus*
(NASB) or *thereby* (REB; similarly, NAB). Once again, the ambiguity

should be respected by retaining the full range of possibilities. In the end, Christ's death on the cross is an expression of Jesus' personal engagement on behalf of humanity caught in enmity with each other and with God. It is not finally Christ's enemies who hang on the cross, but he himself and, with him, enmity.

In the first century, the cross had the same meaning that torture chambers, firing squads, electric chairs, gas chambers, and lethal injections have for us today. Though early Christians might have heard of the emperor being called peacemaker, Caesar typically made "peace" by putting his enemies (including Jesus!) on the cross (for *eirēnopoios, peacemaker,* as an honorific title for the Roman emperor, see Foerster, 1964:419; Windisch: 251-6). The cosmic Peacemaker of our text dwarfs Caesar in might and power (1:22). But his way of dealing with hostile and unruly subjects is to offer up his *own* life, his *own body* (members beware!), for the sake of the reconciliation of humanity to each other and to God.

Peace Brings Us Together Near God 2:17-18

The theme of the *near* and the *far* introduced in verse 13 is now taken up again (see Structure B, above), only now closer to the wording of Isaiah 52:7 and 57:19. Verse 17 reads, literally, *And having come, he proclaimed the good news of peace (he "gospeled" peace [euangelizomai]) to you the far and peace to the near.*

We can tell from 6:15 that the author is quite aware of Isaiah 52:7 and is here pointing to that great text, linking Jesus to Isaiah's divine messenger of peace. Further, YWHW's announcement of peace in Isaiah 57:19 is related here to the word and work of the Christ. Christ's *having come* to proclaim peace is suggestive of both Jesus' Palestinian ministry and his post-resurrection appearances (cf. John 20:21-23; Acts 10:36-38). Making that specific connection may be seeking more precision than our text allows. More likely, guided by his Isaianic text that speaks of the messenger of peace, the author is referring to Christ's coming to make and proclaim peace as sketched swiftly in the preceding verses, the central feature of which is the cross (Barth, 1974:293-5; Best, 1998:271-3).

Isaiah 57:19, LXX, reads literally, *Peace upon peace to the far and to the near.* Our text's dependency on Isaiah no doubt accounts for the repetition of *peace* in relation to the far and the near. Both Gentiles and Jews have had peace announced to them in the coming of Christ. He is, after all, the Messiah of the Jews (cf. 2:12), but no less God's evangelist of peace to Gentiles.

Evidently this point still needed to be stressed at the time of the writing of Ephesians. Here a Jewish believer graciously reminds Gentiles of the grace of God to them who were still so recently outsiders. He may also be reminding less than fully loving fellow Jews of God's grace toward Gentiles and that their own full humanity cannot be experienced in separation from them. Throughout the passage our attention shifts back and forth from *you* to *we*: *you* were once *far* off and have been brought *near* by the one who is *our* peace. Verse 17 reintroduces the *you* of verses 11-12 only to move on in verse 18 to what Christ's peace means for *us*, an *us* which now explicitly includes but does not dissolve *you* and *us*.

For through him we have access—both (hoi amphoteroi) in one Spirit—to the Father (2:18). In this terse sentence, the whole Trinity is present—Son, Spirit, and Father (Barth, 1974:267). At this stage of Christian theological development, there is no fully developed notion of the Trinity, but the building blocks are present.

In this passage the way the ancient biblical understandings of holiness, majesty, and status are played out in highly concentrated form with respect to Gentile believers in Christ is important. In the Bible, the holiness of God is such that, given the sinfulness of humans, proximity is always dangerous (e.g., Exod. 3:5; 19:10-25; 20:18-21; 33:7-11; Isa. 6:5). For Jews of Jesus' time, this was concretely enacted in the temple by its various courts, marked off by walls, reflecting gradations of proximity to God. This background, already mentioned in connection with the wall of partition (2:14), gives special force to the word *access* (2:18).

Such access is made possible through God's *Spirit* (cf. 2 Cor. 3:18). The *one Spirit* is at work reconciling divided humanity and also creating access to God. *Spirit* is not a divisive phenomenon in Ephesians, but a unifying power emerging from God and returning to God with befriended enemies (Fee, 1994:682-5). This central function of the Spirit in making peace echoes the story of Pentecost: the outpouring of the Spirit allows diverse humanity to hear the good news of God's grace (Acts 2; cf. Joel 2; on such "Pentecostal peace," see Volf: 306).

Access then has to do with special status of those who can enter into the innermost dwelling place of the sovereign God. This privilege was much more understandable for first-century readers of this text than for modern heirs to a piety that understands relationship to God in casual or even cozy terms. Both errant Jewish believers and unclean, sinful Gentiles can now, as a result of Christ's work, walk *together* as one humanity into the very presence of God.

In Ephesians the term *Father* tends to have cosmic and comprehensive overtones (see notes on 1:17; 3:14; 4:6). But in 2:18, it is much like Jesus' use of "Abba" (Mark 14:36) at Gethsemane and "Our Father" in his instructions on prayer (Matt. 6:9-13//Luke 11:2-4). The effect of Christ's peace is that through the Spirit, erstwhile enemies can now stand in the presence of their divine parent as reconciled siblings—as chosen and adopted sons and daughters (1:4-5; cf. Rom. 8:14-16; Best, 1998:273-5).

Now Welcomed and Integrated into God's Home 2:19-22

Verses 19-22 build on the claims made in verses 17-18. At the same time, they constitute a contrasting mirror image of the strangers and outsiders of verses 11-12. In light of Christ's peacemaking, *you are no longer strangers and outsiders.* With an interesting mix of metaphors of organic growth and building, strangers and outsiders are said to have been brought into the family of God. They are growing into God's home (for a similar mix of metaphors, see 1 Cor. 3). Notice how the vocabulary itself has moved from terms of estrangement and alienation in verses 11-12 to that of house or home. The Greek word for house or home is *oikos* (the root word for *ecology* or *economics*). Six words in these few verses include the root *oik-*.

aliens, outsiders	*paroikoi*
members of the household	*oikeioi*
built	*epioikodomēthentes*
structure	*oikodomē*
built together	*sunoikodomeisthe*
dwelling place	*katoikētērion*

Whereas *at one time you* Gentiles were *strangers (xenoi)* and *aliens (paroikoi),* you are such *no longer (paroikoi* is literally *those outside the house;* cf. esp. 1 Pet. 2:11; Waltner: 25-7, 84).

2:19-20 Restoring God's People

Paroikos is used in the LXX to describe outsiders, but also aliens living within the borders of Israel, often referred to as sojourners (Lev. 25:6, 35; Deut. 23:7-8). At the same time, it is hardly a benign term, since the ground for treating the outsider well is that Israel too was once *paroikos,* away from home, in both Egypt and Babylon (cf. Ps. 39:12; 1 Pet. 1:1; 5:13). This vocabulary is thus suggestive of Israel's own experience of dislocation, estrangement, and exile, as well as of its high obligations to outsiders. Echoed here is the generosity we see in Ephesians 2:13 and 17, where Isaiah 57:19 is applied to Gentiles, in effect understanding their alienation from God as exile and their inclusion as homecoming.

Where once they were excluded from the *commonwealth (politeia) of Israel* (2:12), Gentiles are now *co-citizens (sympolitai)*. They enjoy citizenship *together with the saints*. *Saints* might be taken variously to refer to Israel as reflected in the implied contrast to alienated Gentiles, to the "golden generation" of early Christians (Houlden: 292), more generally to members of the church, or even to heavenly beings surrounding God in the heavenly places (notes on *saints* at 1:1; 1:18c; cf. 1QS 11.7-8). A clear choice is to be avoided. *Saints* should be taken broadly to refer to all those holy ones, human and angelic alike, who enjoy access to the presence of God (cf. 1:18; Schnackenburg: 121; Lincoln: 150-1). Yet another measure of the extent of Christ's peace is that those who once were by definition outside the sphere of holiness have now been brought so near that they share citizenship with all other holy ones.

To nation or city is now added the motif of household or home. Though Gentiles were once outside the household or family of God *(xenoi* and *paroikoi)*, they are now part of God's household *(oikeioi)*—from *paroikoi* to *oikeioi*.

2:19-22 Building God's Home

Building Materials: Jews and Gentiles! 2:19

In verse 20 the metaphor shifts yet again, now from home-as-relationship to home-as-house or home-as-building. Though Christ's peace has both horizontal and vertical dimensions, the light now falls on the peace Christ has effected between former enemies and God. Even so, a measure of the peace Christ has wrought between *us* and *you*, between Jews and Gentiles, is that Gentiles have now become the building blocks in God's home. Those stones everyone once assumed were refuse have become choice building material in the construction of God's holy temple. *You [Gentiles] were built upon the foundation of the apostles and prophets, with Christ Jesus himself as the cornerstone.*

Foundation: Apostles and Prophets 2:20

This text is in some contrast to Paul's reflections on Christ as the foundation of the church in 1 Corinthians 3:5-23 (esp. 3:10-17; see TBC). Here *the apostles and prophets* are the foundation. In Greek *built upon* is in the past tense, indicating that the author is

pointing back to the foundational origins of the community of faith
(Schnackenburg: 122). In the view of many commentators, including myself, this suggests a perspective appropriate to the years and
decades following the passing of the early apostles and prophets.
Apostles thus hardly refers to missionaries generally, as it might have
for Paul, but to those *notable* early leaders specifically commissioned
with the good news, who were witnesses to the resurrection.

The identity of *prophets* is more vague. They are not likely the
great Hebrew prophets, even if such an interpretation served well the
anti-Marcionite efforts of church leaders of the first centuries (Barth,
1974:315), and even if apostles like Paul saw themselves in continuity
with the great prophets of old (cf. Rom. 1:1-2; Gal. 1:15). *Prophets*
are here listed *after* the apostles (as in 3:5; 4:11). The term *prophets*
is not simply a synonym for *apostles*, even though there is no definite
article before *prophets* (Best, 1998:281; contra R. Martin, 1991:38).
The author has in mind prophets of the early church.

In Ephesians these prophets are an important way the spirit of
Christ communicates in an ongoing way with the church (note the
turn of phrase in 3:5; cf. Acts 13:1-3; 1 Cor. 12; 14; Perkins: 76).
Didache 11 clearly shows that late in the first century, churches were
still struggling to accommodate itinerant prophets within the increasingly defined structures of the churches. To list prophets as part of the
foundation speaks, not to *their* stability, but to that of the One who
communicates through them (1 Thess. 5:19-21). Even so, the vista
here is more to the past than to the present activity of prophets, even
if it in no way excludes it (Eph. 4:11, notes).

Cornerstone or Headstone: Christ 2:20-21

If Christ is not identified as the *foundation* in this text, he is intimately related to the foundation as the *cornerstone, headstone,* or
keystone (akrogōniaion). While it is impossible to be precise in translating the term, *akrogōniaion* is usually translated as *cornerstone*
(NIV, NRSV). In that case, Christ is the most important and deter-
minative part of the foundation, providing its orientation (Isa. 28:16;
R. Martin 1991:38; Schnackenburg: 124). On the other hand, it also
makes good sense to think of Christ as the *headstone* or *keystone*
(Jeremias, 1964:792; 1967:275).

Perhaps the author is thinking of the stone set at the very pinnacle
of the temple (cf. Ps. 118:22, referred to in Mark 8:31; Luke 20:17;
Acts 4:11; 1 Pet. 2:4, 7). Or it might refer to the stone at the apex
of an arch against which the other stones lean and by which they are
given their structural integrity. Best prefers the neutral "angle-stone"

(1998:284), although it is not clear what that would communicate other than a relationship to the foundation. The notion of Christ being "the head" is already present in 1:22, as is the somewhat peculiar idea of growing up into the head in 4:15 (so also, e.g., Barth, 1974:317-9; Lincoln: 154-6).

In either case, as verse 21 makes clear, Christ is central to the growth of the building. Christ is the one *in whom*—through whose work on the cross and in whose body—Gentiles have been *joined together* into a holy temple of God. The church is God's dwelling, not simply by virtue of being a community of erstwhile enemies at peace, but because it is being created *in Christ*. The phrase *in the Lord* may simply re-emphasize this intimate relationship of Christ, church, and God's dwelling, even as it points to the creative and restoring presence of God as reconciler throughout this passage (Lincoln: 152, 161-2).

The term *joined together (sunarmologoumenē)* is unique in the NT, reappearing in 4:16 in a similar context. It expresses well the notion of organic growth in either an architectural or physiological sense. Erstwhile enemies are fused together into one new temple for God. This anticipates 4:3, where the readers are asked to be *eager to keep the unity of the Spirit in the* **bond of peace** (4:3, notes; Yoder Neufeld, 1993:211-32). Given the imagery of the temple, there is no reason to interpret this in terms only of individual believers rather than of Gentiles and Jews (contra Best, 1998:287).

Power: The Holy Spirit 2:22

In verse 18, the *Spirit* gives breath to the *new human* and enables communication with God (cf. Gen. 2:7; Ezek. 37; 1 Cor. 12). In verse 22, the Spirit provides the energy for the construction of the temple: *in [through] whom you also are built together into a dwelling place for God in (or by) [the] Spirit. En pneumati* (lit., *in spirit*) is translated by the NRSV as *spiritually* (similarly REB, *spiritual dwelling*), and only in a footnote as *in the Spirit* (so NAB and NJB; NIV, *by his Spirit;* TEV, *through his Spirit*) *["In"]*.

Spiritual can often mean little more than "metaphorical." That is clearly not its meaning here (so also Best, 1998:290). *In Spirit* parallels *in the Lord (en kuriō)* and *in him (en hō, 2:21)*. Together with the explicit reference to God, we thus again find an early basis for later understandings of the Trinity—God, Christ, Spirit. The *Spirit* represents God's presence and power giving energy to the *building* of a temple.

Such a *building* is not *spiritual* if it means something other than the concrete material reality of human social life lived out amid the conflicts and enmities of everyday existence. It is the church made up of real Gentiles and real Jews—who once lived out their enmities of prejudice and mutual rejection in specific social, cultural, and religious ways—that is the dwelling of God. So now it is the church concretely and experientially breaking down the walls of hostility between groups and individuals, reaching out to those still at a distance, that is the holy temple of God. Holiness is Spirit-filled energy for making peace.

Inhabitant: God 2:21-22

Verse 22 restates verse 21. Just as *in the Lord* the whole building grows into a temple, *you yourselves* are now being built into God's dwelling. *Together* is emphasized with the prefix *sun—joined together* (*sunarmologoumenē*, 2:21) and *built together* (*sunoikodomeisthe*, 2:22). As before, it can refer to being *joined to* Christ the cornerstone or headstone (cf. use of prefix *sun-* in 2:5-6). This would be consistent with the image of the body, especially as seen in 4:15-16. But it surely can also refer to Jews and Gentiles being *built together with each other*, especially given the gist of that meaning in 2:19. However, since this reconciled community exists *in Christ* (2:15), it should not be seen as an alternative to the previous interpretation, but as an aspect of it. The temple of God, the dwelling of God, is made up of erstwhile enemies now at peace with each other and with God *in Christ*.

Several simple but important points need to be stressed. First, the emphasis on *together* precludes an individualized understanding of the temple of God. In some contrast to 1 Corinthians 6:19, not the individual believer but *the whole structure* (2:21), made up of Gentiles and Jews together in Christ, is the temple of God. The emphasis falls on the corporate dimension of the church, not on the individual believer.

Second, the image of the growth of the building suggests more than edifying what already exists. The divine mason is still on the lookout (present tense, *are built together*) for stones once rejected (cf. 1 Pet. 2:4-10, esp. 2:5). That suggests "intensive" (Schnackenburg: 126) and "qualitative" growth (Lincoln: 158) and also *necessarily extensive and quantitative* growth (4:12-16, notes).

To conclude, through his proclamation of peace, and most especially through his own death, Christ has violated sacred space by breaking down the dividing wall. His purpose is to reconstitute sacred space through the inclusion of those whose presence would at one time have been an abomination. In the process, he has re-created humanity in himself, a fitting abode for the God of peace.

THE TEXT IN BIBLICAL CONTEXT

Many connections to the larger biblical context have been made throughout the notes. The many points of contact with Romans, 2 Corinthians, Galatians, and Colossians are of special importance. Isaiah 57:19 and 52:7 figure prominently in the mind of the Ephesian author, and demand that the audience listen to this text in light of inherited scriptural tradition. A number of issues are worth highlighting in addition.

Biblical Peace

Ephesians 2:11-22 is widely held to be one of the most important biblical peace texts (e.g., Dinkler: 176-81; Mauser: 151-65; Stuhlmacher). It is the most far-reaching treatment of the theme in the NT. This text draws together many of the important dimensions of biblical peace by identifying Christ with peace, in particular his giving of his own life on the cross, within the context of the historic enmity between Jews and Gentiles. The "dual element" of peace (Dinkler: 180)—peace with God and peace within the human family—is of particular importance.

This text does not *directly* reflect the earthiness of *shalom* (e.g., land, health, and security; Westermann: 16-48; P. Yoder, 1986). Nevertheless, the universality of Christ's peacemaking, especially the reconstitution of creation implied in the motif of *the new human*, invites attention to such material concerns as well (for recent survey of biblical scholarship on peace, see Swartley, 1996).

In this passage God's peacemaking through Christ is focused on enemies. As such, this text stands as a beacon within the Bible for what is finally at the heart of the gospel in both OT and NT: God goes after both the stubborn elect (cf. Deut. 9–11; Hos. 2) and alienated enemies beyond the pale (Zech. 8; Rom. 5). Divisions are overcome, creation reconstituted, the human family mended, and the dwelling place of God extended. Any notion of peace that does not include that wide reach clearly falls far short of the biblical understanding of peace.

Peace and Christology

In this hymn, peace has taken on christological significance. Ephesians is not the first letter to identify the special relationship between Christ and peace. Romans 5 and Colossians 1 make this connection explicitly, and the Gospels do so implicitly and explicitly (cf., e.g., Matt 10:13//Luke 10:5-6; but see Matt 10:34//Luke 12:51; John 14:27; 20:19-26). But in Ephesians, peace has become a christological attribute. The rabbis read Isaiah 9:6 as identifying the Messiah's name as Peace and hear that echo again in Isaiah 52:7, as does the author of Ephesians in 2:14 (cf. Mauser: 153).

Christ does make peace, and *Peace* also is his name. To put it another way, *peace*—between God and individual human beings, and even more emphatically also between social entities defining themselves by their enmity toward each other—is inseparable from what it means to identify Jesus as the Christ. This makes the issue of enmity within the human community central to salvation.

Peace and Identity

Ephesians 2:11-22 raises some troubling questions regarding identity. Our passage would have raised for Jewish readers the question of whether peace with Gentiles must be purchased with the destruction of that which has defined the community—in this case, the *law of commandments in dogmas* (2:15). Has Christ's peacemaking abrogated being Jewish? Some commentators suggest as much and thus speak of Ephesians anticipating the church as a "third race," as did postapostolic leaders of the church such as Origen (e.g., Best, 1998:267-9; R. Martin, 1991:31).

Such Gentile triumphalism made Paul nervous already in Romans 9–11, especially in 11:13-32. However true such alienation from Jewish roots was to become for many within the Christian movement toward the end of the first century and especially in the second (e.g., Ignatius, To the Magnesians 10.3), it is neither recognized nor celebrated in this passage. In my view, the Jewish author of Ephesians views Christ's work as an act of *inclusion* (of Gentiles) and not *exclusion* (of Jews), of growth (2:21), not amputation (so also Barth, 1974:310). That such inclusion implies a recasting of identity, as all radical peacemaking does, is not thereby denied (Volf: 99-165). The toehold may thus be there for later generations removed in time and culture from their Jewish matrix to read this text as anti-Jewish. But that requires, in my view, a fundamental misreading of the letter and the spirit of this passage.

Law and the New Human

In the notes we explored how the eschatology of Ephesians provides the context in which the author can speak of the annulment of the *law of commandments in dogmas* (2:15). In commenting on the Creation and Fall narrative, the great Jewish philosopher Philo, roughly contemporary with the author of Ephesians, claimed that the law of commandments, injunctions, and prohibitions was necessary for the "earthly Adam," who needed instruction like any child (*nēpios;* cf. Eph. 4:14). The "heavenly Adam," in contrast, being "perfect" (*teleios;* cf. Eph. 4:13) and "wise" (*sophos;* cf. Eph. 5:15) needs no set of rules and instructions with sanctions and rewards (Roetzel: 87). It would not have occurred to Philo that he was thereby disparaging the law or declaring it void.

Paul is no stranger to Adam-imagery, even if he is more likely to speak of the "first" and "second Adam" than of an "earthly" and "heavenly Adam," and then in an eschatological sense (Rom. 5:12-21; 1 Cor. 15:21-22, 45-49). For Paul the "new Adam" is Christ, in whom reconciled humanity lives by the Spirit, even as it waits for the redemption of the body. In Christ, believers already participate in the "new Adam."

This has profound implications for the law in Pauline thought. In 2 Corinthians 3:1-6, for example, Paul alludes to the great eschatological prophecy in Jeremiah 31:31-34 (cf. also Heb. 8:6-13). Jeremiah prophesied that the time would come when the law would be "written on their hearts." It would become a part of the consciousness of the people to such an extent that obedience to the law would not be compelled from the outside with written rules and regulations. Obedience to the law would, in effect, become an expression of freedom.

For Paul, the gift of the Spirit present in the lives of Jews and Gentiles alike was the greatest evidence that such a state of affairs had dawned. That is why he became so exasperated with Galatian Gentile believers. They had received the Spirit and become a part of the new creation, the body of the new Adam, but they felt they needed to become Jewish to participate fully in the new creation (Gal. 3:2; 5:22-23; 6:15). Hence also, Paul insists to Roman believers, Jewish and Gentile alike, that he in no way disparages the law, let alone wants to open the door to what the law abhors as licentiousness and immorality (Rom. 3:31; chaps. 6–11).

At issue for Paul was not God's law itself, but the mode of its presence, given the new eschatological circumstance. The letter (of the law) may kill, but just as surely the Spirit (of the law) gives life (2 Cor. 3:6; cf. Rom. 8:1-8). We should read Ephesians 2:15 through the prism of such Jewish eschatological convictions.

The Temple of God

Temples were everywhere in first-century Asia Minor. As a metaphor it would have been equally understandable to Jews and Gentiles. Our author, however, draws heavily on its biblical meaning. In Israel the temple became the symbol for God's abode with the people (e.g., Pss. 11; 48; 84; Ezek. 43; Hab. 2:20; Mal. 3:1; Rev. 21:22). Even when the actual temple and the cult fell into disrepute because of the sinfulness of sovereigns, subjects, and priests alike, the purification or rebuilding of the temple became identified with the hope for a restored people and land (e.g., Neh., Ezek.). Even the Dead Sea covenanters at Qumran, who rejected the temple cult in Jerusalem as illegitimate and impure, dreamed of a new and ideal temple (Temple Scroll, 11QT).

The importance of the temple is expressed in the NT as well. The letter to the Hebrews, written at much the same time as Ephesians, also uses the motif of the temple and the sacrificial cult to describe Christ's work. Christ is the ideal high priest at work in the heavenly temple (Heb. 7–10). Willard Swartley has explored ways in which OT temple traditions shaped the synoptic Gospel traditions (1994:154-97).

The themes of purity and holiness are always central to the motif of the temple. That is why Paul uses the image, albeit in highly altered form, to counsel purity in terms of personal lifestyle (e.g., not having intercourse with temple prostitutes, 1 Cor. 6:19). The church is the *body of Christ* and also the *temple of God* (1 Cor. 3:16-17). The idea of purity and holiness gives special force to the image in Ephesians, where the temple of God is made up of those once excluded. The Gentiles are now welcome to enter the presence of God (cf. 2:18) and also have become building blocks in the dwelling itself. So, this passage echoes Isaiah 9:6; 52:7; and 57:19, and also 56:3-8, where "foreigners" gain access to the temple, a temple that is to be a "house of prayer for all peoples" (or "Gentiles," *ethnoi,* LXX; cf. Mark 11:17).

The Foundation of the Temple

First Corinthians 3:5-23, especially verses 10-17, shares much with our present text. In both passages, organic and architectural images of growth and building sit alongside each other. Notice especially the motif of the temple of God built on a foundation. But there are differences as well. First, in 1 Corinthians, Paul wants to clarify his and his fellow apostles' role in building and nurturing the church. Paul insists that neither he nor apostles such as Peter or Apollos are the foundation of the faith of the Corinthians. Only Christ can be that foundation, one upon which he and his fellow apostles build the temple of God like wise architects (1 Cor. 3:10-11).

In Ephesians the importance of the apostles and prophets within the new movement has moved to a new level. *Apostles and prophets* have themselves become the foundation (see esp. how Paul appears in Eph. 3; Paul does refer in Gal. 2:9 to Peter, James, and John as "pillars," *stuloi,* but not as *foundation;* cf. Rev. 3:12). For a generation removed in time from the first witnesses of Jesus the Messiah, apostles and prophets have become an essential basis for the further growth of the church.

THE TEXT IN THE LIFE OF THE CHURCH

Peace and Mission

For church traditions committed to the importance of peacemaking, Ephesians 2:11-22 should enjoy the status of a classic. Ironically, this text does not figure prominently in early Anabaptist writings, nor does it today. It is not mentioned in the *Declaration on Peace* sponsored by the Historic Peace Churches (Gwyn, Hunsinger, Roop, and Yoder; cf. Loewen; some rare exceptions: Marlin Miller; J. H. Yoder, 1985:108-15; 1994:218-9). When it comes to peace texts, the Sermon on the Mount and related passages are the texts of choice (Loewen). The Pauline literature is generally viewed as carrying the agenda of theology, doctrine, church order, and evangelism, not of peacemaking. Beyond its obvious relevance to matters of peace, Ephesians 2:11-22 should find rich resonance with the concerns of mission and evangelism.

One might wonder whether this text's limited popularity in peace churches is due to the wall that has grown up between those who view peace as social and political and those who view it chiefly in terms of personal reconciliation with God. Each side has developed vocabulary that hardly engages the other: what has conflict resolution to do with evangelism? Sadly, what God put together the church has succeeded in rending asunder (Sider; cf. J. H. Yoder, 1979:68-103). Our text challenges both camps.

Peace and the Cross

Ephesians 2:11-22 defines peace in radical relationship to Christ and his death on the cross. Christ *is* peace—but not all that is called peace is of Christ. In short, in this letter, as in all of Paul, the scandal of the cross and the particularity of the Christian claims regarding the centrality of Christ's death and resurrection are inextricably related to peace. Behind the crumbled dividing walls stand the cross, the resurrection, and the new creation. Thus, while the image of crumbling walls of hostility has achieved currency well beyond the Christian community (Preview) the *christo*-centric nature of this text renders it somewhat unwieldy for secular use. Increasingly, however, that is precisely the arena in which much of the church's engagement in peacemaking takes place. Will the church remember *what* and, more importantly, *who* is peace?

Peace and the Community of Befriended Enemies

This text requires that evangelism and peacemaking be seen as indivisible. The one who *is* peace *made* peace through his death on the cross, and came *announcing* the gospel of peace. Enemies have thereby been reconciled with God *and* with each other. *Together* they have become part of God's family. The church is not a collection of individuals, each with their own personal peace arrangement with God. The church is the familial community of reconciled enemies (J. H. Yoder, 1983:281-3; 1985:110-2; Yoder Neufeld, 1999a).

If true to its Lord and its calling, the church is as such always a community on the lookout for walls to breach, for enemies to befriend—with each other and with God. With respect to a reconciling and re-creating God, God's home is never big enough; better yet, God's family is never big enough. With respect to those people and peoples still estranged from God and God's family, there will always be room. God's home is permanently under construction (cf. John 14:2-3).

This is a true peace text in that it has, first, the potential to break down the walls of division *within* the church. Second, it represents a solid christological foundation for mission to all who are still estranged from each other and from the family of God, who still do not know access to God's gracious presence—whether in evangelism, the work of justice and peace, or meeting material human need.

The Role of Boundaries (Walls)

Some church traditions, such as Anabaptism, have stressed separation from and resistance to the world (TLC for 5:3-21). Churches in this stream know something about being different and have found many ways to nurture such difference—to maintain the boundaries. Like radical Jewish communities, they know the importance of radical obedience to God's commands. They know it is important to maintain the boundaries to ensure the integrity of the community's faith and practice.

Despite the deep affinity of Ephesians for such separatism (see esp. 5:3-21), this particular text is deeply unsettling for such communities. After all, it celebrates breaking down boundaries through Christ as the price of peace. Inevitably questions arise: Which boundaries are of the essence, and which are obstructions or barriers? Which boundaries safeguard the gospel of peace, and which suffocate it? Which boundaries nurture a vision and identity that empower a community to participate in the *gathering up of all things in Christ* (1:10), and which impede such peacemaking?

The battle over boundaries took place in the first century. The struggle between openness to those deemed unclean and insistence on holiness and faithfulness can be seen in every stratum of the NT (cf. Matt. 5:17-20; Acts 10; Rom. 14; 1 Cor. 10:6—11:1). It has been fought in the context of the church's missionary work during the past two centuries. In past decades many Mennonite missionaries, for example, felt that the church's peace stance was one such a barrier that should not be allowed to stand in the way of peoples' encounter with God's grace and salvation (see, e.g., Gallardo: 152; Ramseyer, 1979; 1984; Shenk, 1984).

Attempts to reach out in North American and European contexts have likewise been marked by such questions (e.g., struggles over worship, peacemaking, and denominational designations). Recently churches have been struggling with identity and boundaries in relation to race, class, worship styles, pacifism, and sexuality, to name a few of the most contentious issues. Various attempts at church growth have exposed the complex tensions between the "science" of growth and the demands of the biblical gospel or between the demands of the "market" and the intransigence of tradition (e.g., Yoder Neufeld, 1999a). For those finding security and direction *within* walls of tradition, however much they have been erected in the service of faithfulness and holiness, this text presents a constant challenge, if not outright irritant.

This text is equally troubling, however, for those who would like to see all walls come down, all boundaries erased. Ephesians 2 still knows who *we* and *you* are. The church has a "bicultural history" (J. H. Yoder, 1997a: 39-40) or "hybrid identity" (Volf: 54-5) and also retains a distinct memory as to where both *you* and *we* came from as distinct from the newly created *we*. This text asserts that the wall of enmity has come down and also that *Christ* brought it down through his death on the *cross*. Peace is rooted in that specific event.

Moreover, the wall between enemies has come down to create a *new humanity*, the body of *Christ*. This text stresses the central place of the church as *the new human*, as a holy temple of God, built upon the foundation of the apostles and prophets, with Christ as the headstone or cornerstone. For many people, such a foundation seems too limited, and such a building too confining. But for the author of Ephesians, there is finally no more embracing and comprehensive a peace than that found specifically in Christ. To mix metaphors, without the boundaries represented by Christ, the embrace has no capacity and no strength to gather people in.

Jews and Gentiles

Our present text is a sharp prod to make peace between Gentiles and Jews. The work of Christ is identified centrally with that divine objective. At the same time, the celebration of the abrogation of the *law of commandments in dogmas* is a *skandalon* (stumbling block), precisely because of the text's central emphasis on *peace.*

Given the long history of anti-Judaism in churches of every tradition, including the heirs of the Radical Reformation, we can no longer read this text innocently. What at the time of writing was a courageous recognition—*by a Jew!*—of how far God was prepared to go to include *outsiders—Gentiles!*—became, in the hands of Gentiles with a short memory, a means of dismissing the community whose hope they had inherited. The door flung open by messianic Jews with costly generosity was slammed shut by the guests from within, leaving the hosts outside.

That *Gentile* followers of a *Jewish* Jesus and his *Jewish* apostles should have taken these euphoric words as a basis for disparaging the Jewish inheritance is nothing less than a betrayal of Christ's act of peace. The effect of considering the law *itself* as outmoded severed the (Gentile) Christian community from its Jewish roots. This step essentially abrogated not law itself—which Christianity reinvented for itself in any case, ironically utilizing the letters of Paul for this. Instead, it abrogated the movement of reconciliation, of bringing to full realization a new humanity made up of erstwhile enemies. In effect, Gentile believers in Christ erected a new wall. Calvin Roetzel's comments on this are sobering:

> Whatever the author's intent, the unity he hoped for eluded the church. By the second century, Justin spoke of the exclusion of Jewish Christians from salvation (*Dial. with Trypho* 47), and Jerome later criticized Jewish Christians: "While they wish to be both Jews and Christians, they are neither Jews nor Christians" (*Ep.* 112.13). The vision of our author was noble, but his strategy was flawed. Consequently, by the second century, even the vision had soured, and the way to the union of Jewish and Gentile Christians was barred. (1983:88)

In my view, the author of Ephesians cannot be allowed to bear the blame for what amounts to a most profound breach of trust with God's people. Without denying the obvious difficulties this text and its logic raises for Jewish-Christian relations, it places at the very core of Christ's work overcoming division amid the diversity of identities and histories. It especially deals with the division between those who have known God long enough to construct a culture of familiarity, and those who have not. How might Gentile Christians, who long ago became insiders, read this text in relation to those into whose family circle they were once invited? After all, these Gentile Christians have, at least from their own perspective, rendered the original family members as outsiders and strangers. This text celebrates what happened to *that* wall *then*, and it indeed forces us to ask about *ours now*.

Singing Hymns So They Change Us

Finally, I give an observation on the use of the hymn in this passage. The point was made in the notes that likely a hymn extolling Christ as peace was incorporated by the author and possibly edited to fit a particular issue—Gentile-Jewish relationships. This is surely a sharp reminder that there is no point in singing general hymns of salvation and reconciliation unless they are brought into specific contact with the animosities, enmities, hurts, and oppressions that are lived by the singers. It's too easy to praise Christ as God's peacemaker if such praise is not offered in the conscious presence of the strife the worshipers know: home, church, nation, and nature.

Thus, to sing a song of peace is to commit oneself to its realization. To thank God for the gift of peace in Christ becomes a pledge to participate in that ministry of gathering all people and all things into Christ. Only such worship "makes sense" (a carefully translated phrase from Rom. 12:2, TRYN). Liturgical renewal should have its beginning and end in such peaceable integrity.

God's peaceful man of Galilee,
   Love's triumph, we shall follow thee—
      to crumble ev'ry bound'ry wall,
      build highways to the hearts of all.
   Love's triumph, we shall follow thee,
God's peaceful man of Galilee.

(H. W. Farrington, "Strong, Righteous Man of Galilee," *HWB*, 540,
   stanza 4)

Ephesians 3:1-13

The Secret Revealed

PREVIEW

In Ephesians 3:1-13 we encounter Paul as one of the most important building blocks in the *foundation of the apostles and prophets* (2:20; 3:5). He is *the* guide into the mystery of God's grace toward Gentiles. The secret he has been charged to divulge is that Gentiles have become part of God's inner circle (3:6; cf. 2:19-22). Paul's trustworthiness has been tested in suffering as *prisoner of* and *for Christ* and for the sake of his beloved Gentiles (3:1, 13). The theme of Paul's suffering frames this passage.

Structurally, verse 1 is an incomplete sentence, taken up again in verse 14 (see next section). It serves, nevertheless, as the opening to the lengthy digression on Paul's task and message as an apostle (3:2-13). Verse 2 begins the digression with another incomplete sentence that does not end till verse 7. Verses 8-12 form a full sentence, restating the content of verses 2-7 while shifting the focus to the cosmic arena in which, not Paul, but the church makes known the wisdom of God with boldness and confidence. Verse 13 forms the closing parenthesis to this digression by bringing the sufferings of the apostle back into view, as an *inclusio* (bracket).

Some see this as "by far the most personal" section in Ephesians (e.g., Houlden: 294; cf. Best, 1998:293); others see all the hallmarks of an official portrait by the respectful hand of a follower of Paul. Lending support to this view are several observations: There is a rather stylized presentation of Paul as guide into the mysteries. The text shows evident dependence on Colossians 1:23-29 (TBC, Chart 2). It implies that readers might lack familiarity with Paul's task and message (3:2). Finally, the text possibly refers to previous writings (3:3; TBC, Chart 1, for suggested points of contact with other Pauline letters; cf. Lincoln: 168; R. Martin, 1991:39-40; Schnackenburg: 131).

Structure of 3:1-13

For this reason I, Paul, the prisoner of Christ for you—(3:1)

> assuming you have heard
>> of the mystery made known to me
>>> (as I wrote earlier in brief),
>>> now revealed to his holy apostles and prophets,
>>> that the Gentiles fully share in the promise in Christ. (3:2-7)

> To me, the least of all the saints, this grace was given,
>> to bring to light the plan of the mystery,
>>> in order that now the multivaried wisdom of God be made known
>>> to the rulers in the heavenlies through the church. (3:8-12)

> I ask not to lose heart in my sufferings for you, which is your glory. (3:13)

OUTLINE

Paul the Prisoner, 3:1

Paul the Steward of the Secret, 3:2-7

The Church Makes God's Wisdom Known, 3:8-12

A Request Not to Lose Heart, 3:13

EXPLANATORY NOTES

Paul the Prisoner 3:1

Verse 1 begins, *For this reason*. This phrase might refer to the immediately preceding description of God's inclusion of Gentiles in the house of God (Best, 1998:294; Lincoln: 172). Yet there is every reason to see the author as bringing the whole of the first half of the letter, which sets the basis for the exhortation in chapters 4–6, to a climactic and prayerful conclusion. Verse 1 is, after all, an incomplete sentence, continued in verse 14, where the prayer-report begun in 1:16 is brought to conclusion with a doxology that provides a fitting complement to the eulogy of 1:3-14.

Before that prayer finds full expression, the focus shifts from the mystery of God's work of peace to Paul, who has been entrusted with giving away the secret. The shift is forceful: *I, Paul, the prisoner of* (or *for*) *Christ*. The emphatic *I* draws our attention toward Paul. The definite article before *prisoner* has the effect of further highlighting the special status of Paul as *the* prisoner of Christ par excellence. There is here a special irony, entirely consistent with Paul's understanding of his apostleship. *Prisoner* would normally suggest the opposite of special status, if it were not for Paul's frequently stated view that suffering, not glory, marks the true apostle of the Christ who went to the cross (cf. 2 Cor. 11).

Is Paul a prisoner *of* Christ or *for* Christ? Both translations are equally possible. The first implies a metaphorical understanding, the second physical imprisonment. Paul was quite capable of referring to his imprisonment in both senses. Philemon 1 and 9 and Philippians 1:12-17 show that for Paul actual imprisonment also had theological importance. Later texts show that being a prisoner became part of the character profile of the great apostle (2 Tim. 1; Col. 4:3, 18), reflecting a constant in Paul's life, but also the *necessity* with which he performed his duty as an apostle to the Gentiles (cf. 1 Cor. 9:16-17). "He is Caesar's prisoner because he is first of all Christ's prisoner" (Best, 1998:296).

Paul is a trustworthy guide into the mystery of God's grace precisely because he is *a messenger in chains* (cf. 6:20, TRYN). This is much more than a "detail in the Pauline façade" (Houlden: 297). However incomplete as a sentence, it provides a fitting introduction to the portrait of Paul's mission that now grammatically interrupts the flow of the sentence.

Paul the Steward of the Secret 3:2-7

A certain lack of familiarity with Paul's mission and message is suggested with *assuming you heard*. This is puzzling if the letter was written to Ephesus by Paul himself. Acts 19:10 and 20:31 indicate that Paul spent up to three years in Ephesus. The phrase is less jarring if the letter was intended not for Ephesus but for a wider circle of congregations, some of which may have had little knowledge of Paul (Introduction; 1:1-2, notes). On the other hand, if this letter was written after Paul's death, then such a phrase acknowledges the need for following generations to come to appreciate or, as the case may be, not to lose their appreciation for Paul (Lincoln: 173).

Perhaps the reference in verse 3 to *brief words written earlier* sheds light on this matter. Some take this to refer to earlier parts of the letter, notably 1:9-10 and 2:11-22 (Barth, 1974:329; Best, 1998:302; Lincoln: 175; Schnackenburg: 133; so also NRSV). But it is also possible that this is a pointer to Galatians 1:11-12, where Paul speaks similarly of his gospel coming through "a revelation of Jesus Christ" (cf. Gal. 1:16! Houlden: 298).

In Galatians, this identification of Paul's gospel by revelation is immediately followed by a phrase similar to the one we find in Ephesians 3:2: *You have heard, no doubt . . .* (Gal. 1:13, NRSV). This statement presupposes, however, that readers of Ephesians, knowing only secondhand of Paul's work (3:2), are nevertheless familiar with the letter to the Galatians. That would be less likely during Paul's life-time than for a time *after* Paul, when readers could be assumed to be familiar to some extent with letters of Paul already in wider circulation. The emphasis on *reading* so as to assess Paul's *insight* also suggests a context after Paul's death, when his writings were increasingly becoming the object of study and reflection (cf. 2 Pet. 3:15-16).

Two key phrases describe Paul's mission: *the administration of God's grace* (3:2) and *the mystery made known according to revelation* (3:3). *Administration* is a translation of *oikonomia*. In NRSV, *oikonomia* is also translated as *plan* (1:10; 3:9), *management* (Luke 16:2), and *training* (1 Tim. 1:3). In NASB, *oikonomia* is *steward-ship* (Eph. 3:2) and *administration* (3:9). Curiously, NJB does not translate the term in 3:2 and offers *inner workings* for 3:9. NIV has *administration*. Obviously the term is elastic. *Oikonomia,* the ances-tor of our word *economy,* literally means "rule or law *(nomos)* of the house" (on *oiko-,* 2:19-22, notes). It is the work of an *oikonomos,* one who oversees or manages the household (cf. 1 Cor. 4:1; Gal. 4:2). Thus we have a variety of possibilities in translation: *administra-tion, commission, stewardship,* and even *office* (BAGD: 559; Eph. 1:3-14, notes).

Paul's apostleship is here related to God's "economy of grace" in the sense that he has been given the task of managing or administer-ing the grace of God on behalf of the Gentiles. We might call him an "economist of grace" or, with Letty Russell, the "housekeeper" in God's household (57). *Oikonomia* can also refer to the *arrange-ment* or *plan* of God's economy, and thus it parallels the *mystery,* or *secret,* made known to Paul. As apostle, Paul has been given man-agement responsibilities, but he has also been given *insight* into the economy of God's grace toward Gentiles.

This economy of salvation is said to have remained a secret *in other generations* until God decided to divulge it to *his holy apostles and prophets in spirit* (or *by the Spirit,* 3:5). Giving structure to this thought is a "revelation schema" (Lincoln: 170, 177), present in 1 Corinthians 2:7-10 and notably in Colossians 1:26-27, familiar from Jewish and especially apocalyptic writing. In such a schema, what was *once* hidden, God has *now* finally disclosed. The present manifestation of grace is a long-held secret, a plan hatched before the dawn of time (cf. Eph. 1:3-14).

Holy apostles and prophets are identified in 2:20 as the *foundation* upon which God's house is built. The fact that they are called *holy* here in verse 5 suggests dependence on Colossians 1:26, where the mystery has been revealed *to his saints* (lit., *holy ones*). In our passage the more general label *saints* is reserved for the church as a whole. With the term *holy apostles,* the author may also want to show respect for apostles and prophets of the church as special recipients of revelation (Barth, 1974:335; Best, 1998:307-8; Lincoln: 179).

These *holy apostles and prophets* have received this mystery *in spirit.* This is not enough to provide a basis for a theory of revelation, but the text makes it absolutely clear that the information given to the apostles and prophets was mediated from God *by the Spirit* (cf. 1 Cor. 2:10-13; Fee, 1994:692-3).

Ephesians makes an important claim regarding Paul, one we might miss given his prominence in Christian tradition. Paul at times had to fight fiercely for his place among the apostles (see, e.g., 1 Cor. 1:10—4:21; 15:3-11; 2 Cor. 10–12; Gal. 1–2). In Ephesians we find him firmly inside the circle of recipients of divine revelation, with the *holy apostles and prophets.* His version of the secret and his administration of it are consistent with that made known to the larger community of apostles and prophets.

Paul's administration of the mystery is *according to revelation* (*kata apokalupsin,* 3:3). The author wants to draw attention both to *how* Paul came to know the secret (Best, 1998:299-300) and to the fact that his *administration of God's grace* (3:2) is consistent with the "norm" of *revelation* (Lincoln: 175). Paul's *insight* into the secret of God's grace is not something for which he is taking credit or being credited, but it is rooted in the initiative of God to make the secret known to him and to the *holy apostles and prophets.*

The secret hitherto hidden from *humankind* (lit., *sons of humans,* a Semitic expression) was earlier identified as the *secret* or *mystery of Christ* (3:4). This leads some to interpret the mystery in Ephesians in light of the closely related Colossians 1:26-27, where the secret is identified as *Christ in you, the hope of glory* (Barth, 1974:331; E. Martin: 91-2). However, while verse 6 suggests that Christ is clearly at the center of the mystery (cf. 1:9-10), the specific content of the secret in Ephesians is news regarding Gentiles: *in Christ.* Gentiles have become **co**heirs (cf. 1:13-14, 18), **co**members of [Christ's] body (cf. 1:23; 2:16), and **co**sharers of the promise (cf. multiple use of prefix *sun-* in 2:5-6, 19-22; 4:16).

Numerous points of contact with preceding chapters indicate that *mystery* subsumes the whole of what the author has been laying out in the first three chapters, as 1:9-10 anticipates. Even so, under the impact of 2:11-22, *mystery* is in this case related specifically to the inclusion of Gentiles.

The final words of 3:6—*through the gospel*—reemphasize Paul's work as bringing *good news. Gospel*—both proclamation and content—is the means by which the inclusion of the Gentiles is being realized. Paul's work is thus an essential component of Christ's own proclamation of peace (2:17, notes; cf. Rom. 10:14-15, where Paul applies Isa. 52:7 to himself!).

Verse 7 pursues this thought further by identifying Paul now not as a prisoner or steward, but as a *servant (diakonos)* of this gospel, a term also well suited to the administration of household matters (cf. Russell's "housekeeper," 57). NIV and NRSV make 3:7 part of the next paragraph, but grammatically it brings the sentence begun at verse 2 to an end. It also returns to the theme of Paul being given the task of stewardship.

Paul is *servant* (lit.) *according to the gift of the grace of God* (3:7). God is the gracious giver; his gift of grace makes the ministry and message of Paul authoritative and trustworthy. This gift of grace is, moreover, given *in keeping with (kata) the energy of [God's] power. Energy (energeia)* and *power (dunamis)* are encountered together in 1:19, where with two more power terms they serve to describe the overwhelming might of God at work for the sake of believers (1:19, notes). These two terms also appear together in 3:20, where they again identify the power of God in believers.

Thus in 3:7 Paul's ministry is credited to the dynamic energy of God. There is a special irony here, given that Paul has been introduced as *prisoner* in verse 1. This would be a surprising characterization of one so empowered were it not for the Christ whose ambassador he is. The irony is encountered again in 6:20, where Paul appears as an *ambassador in chains.*

The Church Makes God's Wisdom Known 3:8-12

The second sentence in this section (3:8-12) is a reprise of the first (3:2-7), but by no means simply a repetition. Paul has been *given the grace* to tell to the Gentiles the good news of the *unsearchable wealth of Christ* (3:8), and to divulge *the plan of the mystery hidden from the ages in* (or *by*) *God* (3:9). The revelation schema again provides the structure: what was *once* hidden is *now* made known (3:9-11).

Familiar terms are now recast. The *mystery of Christ* encountered in verse 4 is now referred to as the *wealth of Christ* (3:8; *mystery* and *wealth* are held together in Col. 1:27). The Greek term *oikonomia* appears here in immediate relation to *mystery;* in this case it refers to God's economy of grace and not specifically to Paul's administration of it—hence *plan* (Best, 1998:319). The *mystery* has been hidden in and/or by the God *who created all things* (3:9), clearly evoking 1:9-10, where the *mystery* is identified as God's strategy to *gather up all things in Christ* (1:9-10, notes).

While verses 8-12 restate the thought of verses 2-7, we notice an important shift of focus. Even though the emphatic *To me* begins verse 8, highlighting the apostle as in verse 1, the text subtly redirects attention from Paul to the church. Paul is now *the very least of all the saints* (lit., *the leaster*), bringing to mind 1 Corinthians 15:9, where Paul calls himself "the least of the apostles." That obvious exaggeration is here intensified, first by adding a comparative to what is already a superlative—*less than the least*—and second by comparing Paul, not with the apostolic elite, but with *all the saints*. This is especially noticeable given the highlighting of the *holy apostles and prophets* in verse 5 (cf. 2:20). Paul puts himself, or is put by the author, at the very back of the line.

As in 1 Corinthians 4:8-13, Paul does not cease to be the leader. It is only as one at the back of the line that he wants to be imitated (cf. 1 Cor. 4:16; cf. also Phil. 2:1-11; Rom. 15:1-3). Being *less than the least* goes to the very heart of what it means to serve a Christ who emptied himself and took on the form of a servant (Phil. 2:6-11). It is also consistent with Paul's conviction that he is little more than a facilitator in bringing about the *new human*—the church (cf. 2:15). Even so, Paul and his followers knew full well that he could only be that facilitator, that *servant* (3:7), that *foundation* (2:20), that *economist of grace* (3:2), if he was recognized as carrying the full authority of a divine emissary, a *holy apostle* (3:5). To safeguard the authority of this suffering servant of grace is, in the end, the main purpose of this passage.

Whatever the phrase *least of all the saints* might say about Paul, it also serves to draw attention to those saints who come into view as the *church* in 3:10. At the time of the writing of Ephesians, a *church* made up of old stock Jews and Gentile outsiders must still have been a source of wonder (see 2:11-22). Such a church is by its very existence (Best, 1998:325; Arnold, 1989:62-4) and by its proclamation a witness to *the multivaried wisdom of God* (Wink, 1992:84-5; J. H. Yoder, 1994:147-9). Bengel refers fittingly to the church as a "theater of God's works" (cited in Barth, 1974:364). The church is thus not simply a beneficiary of God's peace in Christ, but an active participant in the realization of that divine economy of grace, "tending to God's housekeeping chores," as Letty Russell puts it so well (1984:59).

The revelation schema is here employed to show the significance of the church in the process of revelation. What was *once* hidden is *now* being brought to light *through the church*, not only through the ministry of Paul and his fellow apostles and prophets. The church is the secret disclosed, the realized mystery cf. 2:7; cf. 2 Cor. 3:1-6, Paul's image of the church as a revelatory "letter of Christ"). The church's task is nothing less than to make known the *multivaried wisdom of God [Wisdom]*.

Wisdom may in this instance refer to Christ (1:3-14, notes). At the same time, we should remember that *wisdom* is called *multi-varied* (*polupoikilos*, 3:10), which means "many-sided" or "much variegated," a warning against limiting too much what the author has in mind. This is, after all, the *wisdom* of the God who created *all things* (3:9) and the God whose wisdom extends to reclaiming *all things* (1:10). *Wisdom* may thus refer more generally to what God is up to in reconciling and re-creating the world *in Christ*. It draws less on the tradition of personified wisdom and more on the notion of God's wise will undergirding and guiding the economy of grace from creation (3:9) to re-creation (2:14-16; so Best, 1998:322).

However varied the divine wisdom is here, it is particularly important that the *church* is at the center of making this *wisdom* known in the cosmos. Here this point is made compactly; its transformative aspect will be more fully explored in 5:3-21, and its confrontive dimension in 6:10-18.

The church's audience is *the rulers and authorities in the heavenlies* (3:10; cf. 1:21; 2:2; 6:12). Recall that these rulers and authorities are not simply invisible spiritual realities residing in a distant heaven, but centers of power deeply affecting human life. In Ephesians, their impact is experienced largely as evil (contra Barth, 1974:365 who reads this text too much in light of Rom. 13 and Col. 1; cf. Arnold, 1989:62-4; Wink, 1992:68, 85) *[Powers]*. The church's participation in making God's wisdom known takes place, as we will also see in chapters 4–6, in the everyday contexts of social, political, and cultural life, and at the same time, at the highest levels

(Wink, 1992). The author of Ephesians has prepared the readers for this thought by placing the believers with Christ *in the heavenlies*, meaning in a sovereign position of power (2:6, notes).

On the content of the wisdom the church communicates to the powers, there is no need to restrict it to news of the inclusion of Gentiles (contra Best, 1998:324), as critically important as that is in this passage and indeed in the letter. For that, the adjective *multivaried* would hardly have been necessary.

All this is taking place *according to the plan of the ages which [God] made in Christ Jesus our Lord* (3:11; cf. 1:11). The central importance of Christ in this drama of salvation is shown in verse 12, which brings the sentence begun in verse 8 to a close: *in whom we have boldness and access with confidence through his faith[fulness]* (or *through faith in him*; on *faith* and *faithfulness*, see notes on 1:1-2; 1:15-23). On one hand, this draws attention to both the status and the intimacy believers now enjoy *in* and *with Christ* (cf. 2:18!). On the other, we can read the final verse in light of the overwhelming task laid upon the church, to confront the rulers and authorities in the heavenlies with the world-changing multivaried wisdom of God.

To do this, the church needs every amount of *boldness, access* (to God's power), and *confidence* it can receive (3:12). *Boldness* (*parrēsia* with its verbal form *parrēsiazomai*) appears again in 6:18-20, in the context of Paul's request for prayers on behalf of himself and of all the saints engaged in the task of proclaiming the *mystery of the gospel*.

We note that whereas in 3:1-11 readers are addressed in the second person plural *(you)*, in verse 12 the first person plural *we* reappears. The apostle and the church *together* share in this boldness and confidence (cf. Phil. 1:29-30).

A Request Not to Lose Heart 3:13

Verse 13 is the final sentence in this section. While it seems to change the subject rather abruptly, the *therefore* indicates that it follows from what has preceded. Indeed, as stated in the Preview, it forms an *inclusio* by bringing the apostle's suffering *for you* back into focus (cf. 3:1).

A number of ambiguities confront the translator. First, NRSV translates *aitoumai* as *pray*, implying that God is the one to whom the request is made *not to lose heart* and further that the readers are the ones who are not to lose heart (so also Barth, 1974:348-9; and others).

However, another view is possible: Paul may be praying that *he himself* not lose heart in his sufferings on behalf of Gentile believ-

ers, much the way he requests prayers on his behalf in 6:18-20 (cf.
2 Cor. 4:1, 16, where Paul relates "not losing heart" to his apostolic
ministry). Such an interpretation makes verse 13 flow more smoothly
from the preceding verses.

Finally, *aitoumai* need mean no more than *ask* or *request*, and
since the prayer does not properly begin until the next verse, *ask* or
request may be the more likely translation (Lincoln: 191). In this case,
Paul is pleading with his readers that *they* not lose heart in face of his
suffering on their behalf (so NIV).

As often in Ephesians, translators should find a way of preserving
the ambiguity, since each of these is grammatically possible (Best,
1998:330-1). At the center of the verse is the motif of the apostle's
suffering on behalf of Gentile believers. As such, the verse builds on
a notion that comes to startling expression in Colossians 1:24, where
Paul's "sufferings *(pathēmata)* for your sake" are said to complete
what is lacking in the "sufferings *(thlipseis)* of Christ." In our text,
then, the *sufferings (thlipseis)* of the apostle participate in some way
in the passion of Christ, even if Ephesians does not state it as explicitly
or as radically as does Colossians.

The clause *which is your glory* poses more riddles. For one, it is
not clear to what *glory* refers. Is it Paul's sufferings? NRSV's loose
translation *they are your glory* (similarly NIV) makes the connection between sufferings and glory immediate. This implies a highly
ironic understanding of glory: Paul's suffering on the Gentile believers'
behalf is their glory. Believers can glory in suffering, in this case not
their own, but Paul's—a notion close to the irony of speaking of the
power of the cross in 1 Corinthians 1:17-25.

On the other hand, does *glory* refer more generally to Paul's
efforts on behalf of the Gentiles, which will result in eschatological
glory (so Lincoln: 192; Schnackenburg: 142; cf. 2 Tim. 2:10)? *Glory*
figures prominently in chapter 1, where at least one case can be
taken to refer to the eschatological inheritance (1:18). Most of the
instances, however, suggest less eschatological hope than awe and
wonder at the grandeur and power of God's *present* action *in Christ*
(1:6, 12, 14, 17). *Power* and *glory* are twins in the Bible, especially
in Ephesians 1:15-23.

Colossians 1:24 and 27 are more to the point: the sufferings of
Christ, participated in by the apostle, are juxtaposed with the *glory
of the mystery of Christ in you, the hope of glory*. Comparison
with Colossians suggests that one should not force a choice between
a present and a future understanding or between sufferings and the
larger administration of the mystery (Eph. 3:2). In the end, they are

inseparable. Both the present and the future are filled with glory, even if presently the glory is refracted through the suffering of Christ's apostle and his church.

THE TEXT IN BIBLICAL CONTEXT

Paul the Apostle

Verse 3 draws attention to what was *written briefly beforehand*. As indicated in the notes, this may refer to earlier parts of the letter or to Paul's earlier letters. There are many points of contact with both other parts of Ephesians and Pauline letters. The features of the portrait offered here are typical of Paul's characterization of his mission, as indicated in Chart 1 (the pastoral letters, written after Ephesians, are placed in brackets). This text's special affinity with Colossians 1:23c-29 is shown in Chart 2.

Chart 1

Eph. 3:1-13		*Eph. 1–6*	*Related Pauline Texts*
v. 1	Paul, prisoner	4:1; 6:20	Philem. 1, 9 (2 Tim. 1:8)
1	you Gentiles	2:11-22	Rom. 11:13; Gal. 1:16
2, 9	commission, plan (*oikonomia*)	1:10	1 Cor. 4:1; 9:17 (1 Tim. 1:4)
3, 4, 9	mystery	1:9; 6:19	Rom 11:25; 16:25; 1 Cor. 2:7-8; 4:1
3	revelation	1:17	Gal. 1:16
5	apostles, prophets	2:20; 4:11	1 Cor. 12:28
6	heirs	1:14, 18	Rom. 8:17; Gal. 3:29
6	fellow (*sun-*)	2:5-6, 19, 21-22; 4:16	Rom. 8:17
7	servant according to the gift		Rom. 15:15-16
8	the least of		1 Cor. 15:9
8	boundless riches of Christ	1:7	Phil. 4:19
10	rulers and authorities	1:21; 2:2; 6:12	1 Cor. 15:24-28
10	wisdom	1:17	1 Cor. 1:24, 30
11	purpose, plan	1:11	Rom. 8:28 (2 Tim. 1:9)
12	boldness, access	2:18	2 Cor. 3:12
13	suffering, glory, not losing heart		2 Cor. 4:1, 15; Phil. 3:8—4:20

Chart 2

(Clear affinity between the two letters shown in bold.)

Colossians 1:23-29 (NRSV)	Eph. 3:1-13
[23] **I, Paul, became a servant of this gospel.**	3:1, 7
[24] I am now rejoicing in my **sufferings for your sake,**	3:1, 13
and in my flesh I am completing what is lacking in Christ's **afflictions** for the sake of his body, that is the church.	3:13
[25] **I became its servant according to God's commission that was given to me for you,**	3:2, 7
to make the word of God fully known,	
[26] **the mystery that has been hidden throughout the ages and generations**	3:4-5, 9
but has **now been revealed to his saints**.	3:5, 8
[27] To them God chose to make known	
how great **among the Gentiles are the riches of the glory of this mystery,**	3:8-9
which is **Christ in you,** the hope of glory.	3:11-12
[28] It is he whom we proclaim,	
warning everyone and teaching everyone **in all wisdom,**	3:10
so that we may present everyone mature in Christ.	
[29] For this I toil and struggle with all **the energy**	
that he **powerfully** inspires within me.	3:7

In its major emphases, our present text is consistent with the way Paul presents himself in his letters. This is particularly true of the main features of the portrait of Paul as suffering and bound messenger, as one whose message has been given by revelation, and finally, as one whose message is good news for Gentiles. Reading Paul's letters to the Corinthians, Galatians, and Philippians shows that virtually all the features of this portrait were often sources of great controversy and difficulty for Paul. This trouble appeared in Paul's relationships either with his congregations or with fellow missionaries (cf. 1 Cor. 4; 2 Cor. 3–12; Gal. 1–2; Phil. 3:2—4:1).

Good News for Gentiles

One fundamental difficulty in Paul's apostolic ministry lay at its very core: the breathtaking distance God was evidently willing to cross to bring in the harvest of Gentiles *as Gentiles* (explored in relation to 2:11-22, above). Galatians shows the tenacity with which Paul pursued his mission, which he saw as nonnegotiable because it was rooted in divine revelation (Gal. 1). In Romans 9–11, Paul is more nuanced in presenting his mission, showing much concern for his fellow Jews and impatience with emerging Gentile-Christian arrogance. In our text the profile of Paul as administrator of grace to Gentiles has become an essential part of his portrait; here he is more a cause for celebration than a source of strife. Nevertheless, this matter continued to be a source of strife in the church into the second century.

The Suffering Apostle

Another official part of the portrait in Ephesians 3 is the irony at the heart of God's economy of grace: God has chosen to make a new start with humanity via the shameful death of his Messiah rather than through the elimination of rebellious humanity. Second, God has chosen to make that message known through a suffering prisoner, *the least of the saints* (3:8), rather than through a "super-apostle" (2 Cor. 11:5). As Paul's wrenching second letter to the Corinthians shows, he was fully aware that their inability to accept such irony in his style of apostleship was nothing less than inability to accept the kind of Lord they had been given. This also meant that they did not really accept their own calling (see esp. 2 Cor. 10–13; Shillington: 202-52).

The Gospels also attest to difficulty with this crucial irony, most notably in Mark. There the disciples' difficulty with the notion of a suffering Son of Man, a Messiah who dies, is consistent with their difficulty in accepting the cross for themselves (8:27-38).

As we see in our present text, suffering had become part of Paul's heroic profile. This can be observed also in the report of Paul's farewell speech to the elders of Ephesus (Acts 20:18-35), as well as in 2 Timothy. Is the pervasiveness of this theme in the late writings within the Pauline letter collection evidence that Paul's ironic view of weakness and power, humility and glory, had won the day? Perhaps. But the vulnerability of such success is that the church made such suffering the *unique* characteristic of its great hero, much as happened with its crucified Lord.

In contrast, by placing the church at the center of the divine strategy of salvation, here as elsewhere in Ephesians, the author does not allow the church simply to glory in the suffering of its hero (3:13). When they remember their hero, they are forced to count the cost of their own calling to make known the wisdom of God (3:10). The Paul encountered here as elsewhere is to be imitated. The church will find its leader, as it will its Lord, at the back of the line (cf. Matt. 20:25-28; Mark 10:42-45; John 13:3-10). In the least among its membership, the church has a fitting hero—the only hero who could be an emissary of the crucified Messiah.

The Multivaried Wisdom of God

The mention of *the multivaried wisdom of God* in 3:10 is, however brief, a window on a rich and variegated tradition in Israel. For a Jewish author, *wisdom* is overflowing with meaning (cf. notes on 1:3-14 and 1:17-19a). Wisdom encompassed the wise designs of God for the world (Prov. 8:22-31; Wisd. of Sol. 6–7; cf. Eph. 3:9!), expressed most succinctly in the Law (Ecclus./Sirach 6:23-31; 24:1-23; cf. Matt. 11:19, 28-30). Wisdom could also be personified as God's daughter or even companion in the creation of the world (Prov. 8:30) and as a companion for faithful human beings (e.g., Prov. 9:1-6; Ecclus. 24; Wisd. of Sol. 7:1-14). The reference in 3:10 can only be appreciated within the expansive context of the biblical wisdom literature as a whole (canonical and apocryphal) *[Wisdom]*.

THE TEXT IN THE LIFE OF THE CHURCH

Heroes of Faith and Action

No matter what the church tradition, heroes of faith and action have played a significant role in the moral and spiritual imagination of the church through the centuries. The cloud of witnesses and martyrs (the same term in Greek) is large indeed. One of the most significant influences on the Anabaptist wing of the believers church tradition has been van Braght's *Martyrs Mirror*, a treasury of suffering heroes of the faith (Waltner: 148-50). Dietrich Bonhoeffer, Dorothy Day, Martin Luther King Jr., Mother Teresa, and Oscar Romero are more recent examples (Waltner: 153-4). In 1998 Guatemalan bishop Juan José Gerardi was added to this great cloud of witnesses. Beyond the confines of the church, one of the greatest modern examples is Nelson Mandela, who while in prison for a quarter of a century served as a rallying point for a people struggling against injustice.

There are countless witnesses in this cloud, some heroes known to only a few for whom they have been life-giving models of faith and courage. Our greatest moral and spiritual models appear to be those who voluntarily subject themselves to hardship or who bear up with great courage under the hardship and suffering their commitments have brought with them.

Such heroes play double and somewhat contradictory roles in church culture. On one hand, they are models for everyone in that they are seen to live up to the values that everyone in the church holds dear. On the other, heroes are *heroes* because they are different, set apart from ordinary folk who live in the real world and have to make practical decisions, who often accommodate and compromise with values prevailing in the larger society. In the Roman Catholic tradition, this is illustrated in the arduous process by which extraordinary persons become saints.

Our text begins with a heroic Paul and then pushes him to the back of the crowd of saints. The implication is that church members are not simply to venerate those whom God has blessed in a special way—even if their names are Paul, Teresa, or Oscar. Christians are saints *together* on the front lines, as it were, encouraged, pushed, and prodded *from behind* by their heroes in the faith.

The church as a community of *holy ones* shares the profound calling of informing those in high places of the endlessly varied and manifold wisdom of God. This is a task as important as that assigned to Paul, even if his is foundational in a distinctive and normative apostolic way. In the end, the church's character will not be measured by its heroes but by the extent to which it heeds their word and emulates their example. Only such a church is in a position to inform those in high places of the mystery of Christ, the manifold wisdom of God.

Informing the Powers of God's Wisdom

How does the church inform the powers of the wisdom of God? (on the *powers*, see 6:10-20, notes) *[Powers]*. First, the church communicates God's wisdom in Christ by the quality of its existence (see Arnold, 1989:62-4; Berkhof: 41-2; Wink, 1992:85; J. H. Yoder, 1994:147-53). "Let the church be the church!" (J. H. Yoder, 1994a:168-80). The church is most powerful in its "communicative being" when it is diverse ethnically, racially, culturally, and socioeconomically—when it is made up of those who should not be able to coexist.

Such a church is the peaceable body of the Christ who embraces in himself people and peoples at odds with each other and re-creates them into one new human in himself. By *being* that way, the church sends a strong message to the powers that control and nurture hostilities that divide humanity: a new order is invading the earth and the heavens. A homogeneous church is severely hampered in its ability to carry out this evangelistic task.

Second, the church communicates this wisdom by being itself, and yet to *be* the church of Christ as described above also requires a great deal of *work*. Such a church *exists* only when its members *participate* in taking up the cross in relation to those outside their fellowship and especially in relation to each other. For the church to be a peaceable community requires the reenactment in large and small ways of the drama of salvation so forcefully expressed in 2:11-22 (cf. 4:32–5:2). The church's *being* is inseparable from its *doing*.

The church also specifically goes beyond merely maintaining itself in its courageous *confrontation* of the powers with the wise gospel. Its message is that God is reclaiming humanity and all that God has created from the grip of evil and rebellion. A faithful church can never simply be a passive recipient of grace. When believers receive the peace of Christ (2:14), they are set at odds with the rulers and authorities in charge (even if only apparently) of this present age. Communication is thus often confrontation. Hence, the church needs boldness and confidence (3:12; cf. esp. 6:18-20).

The Comprehensiveness of the Church's Witness

Whenever the church's critique of oppression and injustice, violence and destruction, emerges from its own transformation into a new humanity in Christ, then it is proclaiming the *good news* of God's wisdom. Such communication will be as varied as the multivaried wisdom of God. It will be as specific as the resistance to that wisdom. The church's grasp of good news, of wisdom, and thus its task of informing the powers is not restricted to a few slogans or to a narrow agenda. The formulation of 3:10 invites a broad agenda, an ever-widening articulation of wisdom.

The key element is God's action in Christ. But as 1:10 already indicated, that action is the gathering up of everything and everyone into Christ. There can be no room for cynicism and hopelessness, even if there clearly is ample room for the honest probing of why the gathering up in Christ is taking so long and appears to be so hidden.

Such a stance may well collide head-on with "the wisdom of this world" (Paul's language, 1 Cor. 1:18-30), as the second half of Ephesians repeatedly suggests (e.g., 4:17-24; 5:6-17; and esp. 6:10-20). At other times, thankfully, the church finds a hearing.

For example, the commitment to peace among the offspring of Anabaptism was once largely restricted to nonresistance and simplicity of life. Today this passion is being applied to arenas as diverse as domestic violence, sexual and power abuse within and outside the church, judicial correctional systems, and national and international conflict. A body of practical wisdom has emerged as a direct result of the *practice* of the wisdom of God as it relates to peace and justice. It is finding institutional expression in Victim-Offender-Reconciliation Programs (VORP), numerous academic programs for the study of peace and the transformation of conflict, JustaPaz in Colombia, and Christian Peacemaker Teams.

Such wisdom is finding ready acceptance well beyond the church community—an important reminder that not all informing of *rulers and authorities in the heavenlies* need be experienced as confrontation "down on earth." Nonetheless, the vulnerability of such popularity is that this wisdom will lose its moorings in the mystery of Christ and thus cease to truly inform those in high places of *God's* multivaried wisdom. In the end, God's multivaried wisdom is nothing more or less than the *gathering up of all things in Christ* (1:10).

Ephesians 3:14-21

An Apostolic Prayer

PREVIEW

The sentence begun in 3:1 is now brought to completion. The prayer initiated in 1:16 is thereby also brought to a conclusion, and with it the end of the first panel of Ephesians (Introduction). Capping the prayer, and indeed the first half of the letter, is a doxology.

Verses 14-19 constitute one lengthy sentence. Directed to *the Father (patēr)* who has named every *family (patria)* in the universe, the prayer consists of three related requests, increasing in intensity (Schnackenburg: 146). The first is that believers might be renewed at the core with power and love (3:16-17; note the importance of how *the inner human [anthrōpos]* is interpreted). The second is that they might have the power to grasp reality *(the width, length, height, and depth)* and the love of Christ (3:18-19a). The third request is that believers might experience the fullness of God (3:19). The prayer concludes with a joyous and confident doxology offered to the God who is able to exceed any and all needs and expectations (3:20-21).

Structure of 3:14-21

For this reason I bow my knees before the Father, (praying)—
- that *(hina)* he might strengthen you in(to) the inner person,
- that *(hina)* you might be able to grasp the width and length and height and depth,
- that *(hina)* you might be filled into the whole fullness of God.

To the one who is able to do more than all we can ask or think,
be glory in the church and in Christ Jesus.
AMEN.

OUTLINE

Kneeling Before the Father, 3:14-15

Empowerment, Love, and the Indwelling Christ, 3:16-17

Power to Grasp and to Know, 3:18-19a

Power to Be Filled with/into God's Fullness, 3:19b

Doxology: Praising the Empowering God, 3:20-21

EXPLANATORY NOTES

Kneeling Before the Father 3:14-15

Verse 14 takes up the sentence begun in 3:1 and shows us the imprisoned apostle at prayer. The specific term for prayer here is *bow* or *bend the knees*, a somewhat unusual prayer stance since Jewish prayer was usually performed standing. Perhaps it emerges from the motif of the imprisoned apostle. In Luke-Acts bending the knee is associated with impending death (e.g., Luke 22:41; Acts 7:60; 20:36; Perkins: 88). Bending the knees is also, however, an expression of awe and reverence before God (e.g., Isa. 45:23; cf., Phil. 2:10-11). Such a sense of awe is present here in that prayer is directed to the God who is *Father of every family in heaven and on earth*. The concluding doxology fittingly gives the whole the ambience of grand worship.

The picture of Paul on his knees serves an important theological interest as well. It provides some sense of balance to the strong assurances of full access and boldness of sons and daughters of God that we see in the previous verses. Believers can approach God with the confidence and freedom of family members (2:18-22; 3:12); nonetheless, they come with prayer into the presence of the Creator and Savior of the whole universe (3:9). The intimate way Jesus taught his followers to address God as Father—*Abba*—was well known to Paul and his churches (cf. Mark 14:36; Rom. 8:15; Gal. 4:6). In this case, however, *Father* is more a term of respect than of intimacy. It expresses the recognition that all families in the cosmos, in heaven as on earth, owe their existence to God and are under his authority.

Not surprisingly, God is called the same name in the opening eulogy and in the first prayer-report in chapter 1: *our Father* (1:2); *the Father of our Lord Jesus Christ* (1:3; some manuscripts expand *Father* in 3:14 to conform to that wording); and especially *Father of glory* (1:17). The wording in our text also anticipates 4:6—*one God and Father of all.*

Related to the word *Father (patēr)* is *family (patria),* an unusual word and thus likely a play on words. It is not an abstraction like "fatherhood," as it is erroneously translated in NJB, but instead it denotes every family, group, tribe, people, or nation that claims the same ancestor (*BAGD:* 636; Barth, 1974:368, 382; Gnilka: 181; Lincoln: 201). NIV mistakenly translates *every family* as *the whole family,* which has a quite different sense. The absence of the article before *pasa (every)* demands, however, that it be translated as *every* and not *whole* (Barth, 1974:381; Best, 1998:338; Lincoln: 202).

This reach of God's parenthood should not be obscured, even if it presents us with some difficulties. For one, these families reside in the whole cosmos—*in heaven and on earth.* With respect to earthly families, the most dramatic expression of God's parental reach has been explored in relation to Jews and Gentiles in 2:11-22. "Social groups" rather than "families" might thus be a preferred translation (Best, 1998:338). Speculation is rife as to who the heavenly families are, however. Are they angelic families? (e.g., Lincoln: 202; Schnackenburg: 149). Are they churches of which some members have already died and gone to heaven? (Mitton: 237-9).

Furthermore, how many is *every?* Does it mean that God is Father of *every* family on earth, even those outside the boundaries of the church? Does it mean that God is Father of *every* family in the heavens, including the hostile rulers and authorities (cf. 1:21; 6:12)? If so, what is the meaning of such paternity? Since there is not the slightest interest on the part of the author to speculate on these questions, let alone to argue for some kind of universalism, the answer may lie in the prevailing ambience of worship and adoration. The formulation *every family in heaven and on earth* uses the lavish expression of worship to indicate the extent of God's care as Creator and Savior of the *whole* cosmos, heaven and earth (Perkins: 89). It also serves to reassure believers that God is directly Lord of heaven and earth and those who inhabit them (Best, 1998:339).

God's relationship to all these families has been established by *naming.* In the ancient world, to give a name could mean to claim paternity. But it could also mean to claim authority over, to establish dominion over. Closely related to this is the sense that those who bear a name are given the power and authority that such a name carries. Names are potencies (cf. esp. 1:21; 5:3; also Phil. 2:9-10; Rev. 2:17; 14:1; 19:12).

Two important ideas combine in this case. One is that in some mysterious sense, God is progenitor of all families in heaven and on earth and gives them their names. That says nothing, of course, about the state of the relationship between those families and their divine parent. In the view of Ephesians, many or perhaps most of these families or groupings are living in broken relationships with God (e.g., 2:1-3, 12; 6:12). However, the fundamental conviction that God is the parent of *all* families and groups corresponds to the conviction that God's designs for redemption and restoration also know no limits. Hence, we see the repeated *all things (ta panta)* at crucial points where God is mentioned as Creator, Lord, and Savior (e.g., 1:10, 23; 3:9; 4:10). God is reclaiming *all* of creation, and that surely includes every grouping of human beings.

The second idea is related: God's claim on creation is being asserted in his work in and through Christ. So the naming of all families is God's act of asserting authority and dominion over all the families of heaven and earth. This is couched in patriarchal terminology. In the first century, a father was considered the ruler of the household. If we think of the cosmos as in some sense God's household (2:19-22; Russell, 1984; 1985), even if presently still in disarray, then we should think of God's *naming* of families as the reestablishing of lordship over them. In the end, this conviction underlies the confidence with which the church undertakes to confront the rulers and authorities residing in the heavenlies (3:10, 12). God is Lord over them all, and they need to be *informed* of that great life-giving wisdom—a wisdom as multifaceted as there are families to be reconciled.

Empowerment, Love, and the Indwelling Christ 3:16-17

The first part of the tripartite petition is that the church be empowered by God. This is the core concern of this prayer and of the whole letter (so also Arnold, 1989:137-9; R. Martin, 1991:44; Schnackenburg: 150). The concern is so important because of the breathtaking scope of the church's calling and task. The church is to be the body of the Messiah (1:23; 2:16), the *new human* (2:15), the holy temple of God (2:21). It is charged with making the wisdom of God known to the rulers and authorities in the heavenlies (3:10) and, finally, with taking them on in battle (6:10-20). Hence, the author makes the concern for empowerment the center of his prayer, just as it was in 1:15-23 and will be again in 6:10-13.

God is asked to *empower the church with power*, a typical redundancy with which the author intends to strongly emphasize his point (cf. notes on 1:19 and 6:10). Readers are thereby reassured and bolstered in confidence. Not surprisingly, we observe this in the militant literature of Qumran (1QM 10.5-6; 11.4-5, 9). Such heaping up of synonyms for power, as we see here, ironically witnesses to the inadequacy of human words to measure the power, grace, and love of God in Christ (as made explicit in 3:19-20).

Believers are divinely empowered *according the wealth of [God's] glory* (cf. 1:18; Rom. 9:23; Phil. 4:19; Col. 1:27). God's *glorious wealth* (3:16) is an inexhaustible source of power as much as it was of grace in 1:7 and of mercy in 2:4. God's *glory* is God's power at work within and for believers (2:5-6). Ralph Martin's apt rendering of glory as "God's presence-in-power" captures the connections of glory and power perfectly (1991:45).

The means of empowerment is God's *Spirit*, which could be captured just as well by Martin's phrase cited above. Just as *glory* and *power* are virtual equivalents in the Bible, so the word *spirit* is also a way of speaking of the palpable presence of God's power (Fee, 1987:695). In Greek, *pneuma* is the word for "spirit" as it is for "wind." God's Spirit is power that moves.

A most difficult phrase in 3:16 is (lit.) *into the inner human* (or *person*). Both NIV and NRSV translate the phrase as *in your inner being*. If this is the correct understanding, then we have a glimpse into the anthropology of the author, one he would have shared with many others in his day: a person is made up of an outer being and an inner being. The inner being is that part of a person with which God communes, "the base of operation at the center of a person's being where the Spirit does his strengthening and renovating work" (Lincoln: 205; so also Best, 1998:340-1; cf. Rom. 7:22; 2 Cor. 4:16). The immediately following reference in 3:17 to Christ dwelling *in your hearts* is then taken to parallel being strengthened *in the inner being*. *Inner being* and *heart* thus complement each other (Fee, 1987:695-6).

However, close attention to the exact vocabulary invites a rather different understanding in 3:16. The phrase is literally *into the inner human* (or *person, anthrōpos*). *Into* suggests a direction in which the prayer asks the power of God to move the believers. Further, we already know *anthrōpos* from 2:15, where it is the term for reconstituted humanity *in Christ* (2:15, notes). If such a meaning of *anthrōpos* informs its use here (so Barth, 1974:388-94; rejected by Fee, 1987:696; Lincoln: 205), then God is being asked to empower the believers so that they might become more like the one who inhabits them—Christ.

The coexistence of notions of *being in Christ* and *Christ being within* (understood both individually *and corporately*) is typical of Paul (cf., e.g., Gal. 2:20; 4:19). In Ephesians, the emphasis falls more on

being *in Christ* (cf. 4:13, 15-16). At the same time, the church carries
the fullness of Christ (1:23). The complement to *the inner human* is
thus not the *heart* of the believer, but the *Christ* who has become a
"permanent tenant" (Best, 1998:341) in the heart, as made explicit
in 3:17. The author's concern is Christology—or the church in light
of Christology, not anthropology. To speak of *inner* is therefore to
speak of social, public, and communicative reality, not of private reality. The Christ who lives *within* finds expression in the *outer* social
reality of a holy community made up of reconciled enemies—the new
humanity of whom the rulers and authorities in high places must take
note (3:10).

This latter point is emphasized by the phrase *rooted and grounded in love* (cf. Col. 1:23; 2:7). Botanical and architectural imagery are
combined (cf. 2:20-22). Believers are *rooted* in God's love as experienced in Christ (2:4), in the sense that they owe their very lives to it
and continue to draw strength from it. But they are also *established
upon* it as their foundation (*tethemeliōmenoi*, 3:17; cf. *themelios,
foundation*, 2:20). Their existence is thus governed and shaped by
the love that finds expression in their own lives. There is no need to
decide, as many commentators do, between God's love, Christ's love,
or the believers' love (cf. Best, 1998:343; Lincoln: 207). In the end,
the one is meant to effect the other. That is the consequence of being
in Christ.

Power to Grasp and to Know 3:18-19a

The second request is again couched in the vocabulary of power:
that *you may have power to grasp what is the breadth and length
and height and depth. Grasp* can mean "comprehend," an adequate
rendering of *katalambanomai* (middle voice). In other contexts, active
forms of this verb can mean "grasping," "taking hold of," "seizing,"
even "overpowering" (e.g., Mark 9:18; John 1:5; 1 Thess. 5:4). For
this, the divine power stressed throughout is clearly required.

The "four dimensions" (Best, 1998:344, rejects this since there
are only three spatial dimensions) are preceded by only one article
and thus should be taken together as four facets of one whole. They
have been the source of a great deal of speculation. Some see in this
an allusion to the cross (Houlden: 304-5), others to the new Jerusalem
(cf. Ezek. 48:16; Rev. 21:16), and others an adaptation of a magical formula intended to conjure up the powers of a deity (Arnold,
1989:89-96). More in keeping with the concerns of Ephesians, the
four dimensions have been related to dimensions of the cosmos, to
the mystery of Christ, to Christ himself (cf. esp. cosmic dimensions

implicit in 1:10), and to the love of Christ, mentioned in the following clause (3:19; discussion and citations in Barth, 1974:395-7; Best, 1998:344-6; Lincoln: 208-13).

Most connect the four dimensions to the love of Christ, as do many translations (e.g., NAB, NIV, REB, TEV). The immediately preceding reference to being *rooted and grounded in love* (3:17) and the immediately following text, *to know the love of Christ, which surpasses knowledge,* would commend such an understanding. After all, in the end it is the love of God (2:4) as it comes to expression in the love of Christ (2:13-18) that is the core of the mystery now revealed.

However, there is also a persistent emphasis on wisdom in Ephesians, not least in 3:10, where wisdom is referred to as *multivaried* (cf. also 1:17; notes on *wisdom* for 1:3-14; 3:1-13 *[Wisdom];* for background on dimensions of wisdom, see esp. Job 11:5-9; Ps. 139:8-10; Perkins: 90). By its very nature, the biblical understanding of wisdom is holistically and comprehensively related to the will of God as expressed in creation, law, and salvation. This letter's vision emerges out of that conviction perhaps more than the vision of any other NT document.

We thus should understand grasping the four dimensions as an invitation to grasp reality fully. That includes viewing reality from the vista of God's secret now disclosed in Christ, and also taking hold of reality in the sense of participating in the gathering up of all things in Christ (1:10). The grasping of the four dimensions should thus be seen in the light of the church's experience of being saved and reconstituted in Christ and in light of its task as articulated in 3:10. Such an interpretation does not rule out a close connection to the love of Christ in verse 19. On the contrary, the love of Christ is limitless, beyond grasping, and extends to *all things* and thus to the edges of the four dimensions of the cosmos.

Nowhere does the infinite wisdom of God come to more creative expression than in the love of Christ, which like all true wisdom surpasses human comprehension. At the same time, believers are to be empowered to grasp reality and to know the unknowable—the incomprehensible love of Christ—because it is their task to communicate that fathomless wisdom to the rulers and authorities in high places.

Once again, the brevity of the vocabulary invites comprehensiveness, not precision. The biggest mistake would be to force a choice between a wide range of possible understandings. In the end, comprehending and knowing are not an intellectual exercise, even if they require all of the intellectual powers God has granted humans. Such knowing is nothing other than receiving God's gracious gift of revelation. Further, such knowing encompasses the experience of the love of Christ and also a life and a mind nurtured by and built upon the exercise of such divine love. To know is to love.

This is not a private or individualistic empowerment or knowledge. Believers get hold of the true nature of reality and participate in its gathering up in Christ (1:10) *together with all the saints.* Christian knowledge is not private; it is public and social, and thus it is intimately related to living out the love of Christ in the community of the saints (Barth, 1974:394-5).

Some see in this a polemic against the Gnosticism beginning to take root in Pauline churches (Houlden: 305). Both the emphasis on *knowledge (gnōsis)* and its rootage in *love (agapē)* would have found resonance as well as resistance in Gnostic circles. But nothing in this text, including the highly allusive reference to the four dimensions, represents an invitation to the speculations of the privileged few, as in the Gnosticism of the second and later centuries.

Power to Be Filled with/into God's Fullness 3:19b

The three-part petition reaches its climax in verse 19: *that you may be filled into all the fullness of God.* Again the grammar allows for a number of interpretations. As already indicated at 1:23, *fullness (plērōma)* can refer to that which is filled and to that which fills it. Here the passive form of the verb *to fill,* meaning *that you may be filled,* is first followed by the preposition *eis,* usually translated "into" or "toward," implying process or direction (*BAGD*: 228-9). NRSV has **with** all the fullness, obscuring this important point (so also KJV, NJB, REB). We understand the text to imply that believers are *to be filled up to all the fullness of God* (so, e.g., Best, 1998:348; Lincoln: 214; cf. also similarly NAB, NASB, NIV). This more careful translation also preserves the element of growth and development, visible also in 4:13.

The church is *already* the body of Christ, bearing his fullness (1:23, notes; 3:19 is in close contact with Col. 2:9-10). At the same time, the apostle must still be in constant prayer (1:16-17) for the church that it might in fact be so filled. We catch the sense of Ephesians this way: as the filled body of the filled Christ, the church is in constant need of being filled **toward** all the fullness of God. The element of direction and process must not be obscured in this text.

Even with such qualification, this request is breathtaking in its implications. It suggests a level of "participation in divinity" that might make us nervous. Such reticence does not fit the author of Ephesians, however. Whereas the awesome holiness and the love of God are beyond measure and understanding, the wondrous extent of that love is shown most profoundly, first, by drawing rejects into God's family (chap. 2) and, second, by graciously making them the receptacles of God's own fullness in Christ.

Doxology: Praising the Empowering God 3:20-21

The final two verses of chapter 3 provide a conclusion to the prayer of verses 14-19. They take up the theme of power by glorifying the giver of power. Such power is said to exceed infinitely what can be asked (referring to prayer) and thought (alluding to the theme of knowledge and understanding throughout the prayer-report, 3:14-19).

This doxology is surely a fitting conclusion to the first half of Ephesians. Much as in Romans 11:33-36, the recitation of the grace of God provokes a doxology—an expression of praise to the God who has made it all happen and who will bring the work to completion. Further, as in Romans 11, the doxology prepares the ground for the exhortation that follows. It is a reminder that all ethics, all *walking in good works* (2:10), is possible *only* because of God's grace and power. A gracious God stands before and after all doing of good. All ethics, all discipleship, must begin with praise and worship. More, ethics itself is to be worship.

A number of features of this doxology reflect the character and vision of Ephesians as a whole. First is the emphasis on *power*, an essential component of the preceding prayer-report (3:14-19; cf. 1:15-23). The English terms *dynamic* and *energy* are reflected in the Greek: *To the one who is able (dunamenos) according to the power (dunamis) at work (energoumenē) within us* (cf. *energeia* and *dunamis* together in 3:7; 1:19). The phrase *within us* holds particular interest because in 1:19-20 God's power is at work *in Christ*, but *for us*. That such power is now at work *in us* shows the extent to which the church has taken an exceedingly prominent place in Ephesians. This will explain the unique inclusion of *the church* in the final clause of this doxology (see below).

Second, *the power at work in* and *through us ["In"]* brings about more than we can ask or imagine or, as the NRSV puts it, *abundantly far more than all* . . . Lincoln captures well the deliberately prepos-terous language: "infinitely more abundantly above all" (216). Once again, the hyperbolic style of the author serves him well. It illustrates that even the most exaggerated human language cannot possibly provide adequate expression for what the power of God is able to bring about. In Ephesians, exaggeration is understatement. "Neither the boldest human prayer nor the greatest power of human imagination could circumscribe God's ability to act" (Lincoln: 216). Again, we must stress the author's emphasis: this power is at work *in and through us.* Doxology is thus in the end thanksgiving.

Third, the glory ascribed to God is *in the church and in Christ Jesus.* The prominence of the church in such a doxological climax fits the overall emphasis in Ephesians on the church. As such, it is unique among the doxologies of the NT (cf. Rom. 16:25-27; Jude 24-25). It is open to question whether the Greek *en* should be taken simply as *in* (NRSV and other versions) or instrumentally as *through* or *by ["In"].* We see the stress on Christ as the agent by whom God's power is at work and the stress on the church as the recipient of God's grace and power and also as a participant in it. Both these emphases invite us to see the church as a means by which God is glorified (so also Houlden: 305). Thus God's glory is visible *in* the church and *in* Christ and also is generated, so to speak, by Christ and the church. God is glorified in the life and mission of the church.

All this plays itself out against the background of eternity. The author uses two motifs already familiar from the earlier part of chapter 3—*generations* (*geneai,* 3:5) and *ages* (*aiōnes,* 3:9). Here they are combined with *all* in a way typical of the style of Ephesians. Just as God will show forth his overwhelming wealth of grace to *coming ages* (2:7), so in and through the church and Christ, glory will be given to God *for all coming generations and ages. Amen*—so be it!

THE TEXT IN BIBLICAL CONTEXT

God the Father

One of the most prominent features of this prayer is the way God is referred to without qualification as *the Father* ("Father," TLC for 1:3-14). As the notes explain, the motif of God as Father is prominent in this letter (cf. 1:2, 17; 2:18; 4:6; 5:20; 6:23). This is particularly distinctive. The term is found everywhere in Paul's letters as a designation for God, characteristically as a way of addressing God at the beginning of his letters (e.g., Rom. 1:7; 1 Cor. 1:3; 2 Cor. 1:2; Gal. 1:3; Phil. 1:2; Col. 1:2; Philem. 3). More broadly, the designation of God as Father is conspicuous in the Gospels, especially in Matthew and John. This often shows in the way Jesus refers to God as *his* Father, and also in the way he invites others to relate to God (e.g., Matt. 5:16, 45, 48; 7:11, 21; 11:25-27; John 3:35; 10:15; 14:23).

The rare personal form of address, *Abba,* which appears in the Gospels only in Mark 14:36 in connection with Jesus' wrestling with his impending death, was evidently retained for prayer also in Pauline churches (cf. Rom. 8:15; Gal. 4:6). However, it is clear in Ephesians 3:14 that *Father* is used to describe God as Creator, sustainer, and restorer of creation as a whole, in particular the groupings that make up the varied network of relationships in the world—*all families on earth as in the heavens* (cf. also 2:18). It is not focusing on *Father* as a title of intimacy or familiarity.

Prayer

The Gospels Matthew and John contain two other important examples of prayer. The Lord's Prayer is found in Matthew 6:9-13 (cf. shorter form, Luke 11:2-4). Jesus models how one prays to the divine Father. Ephesians 3:14-21 shows clearly that same confidence, boldness, and access to God that Jesus attempted to instill in his followers (cf. Eph. 2:18; 3:12). The postbiblical form of the Lord's Prayer, as it is known and recited today, concludes with ascriptions of power and glory to God similar to those in the Ephesian prayer—*for thine is the power and the glory, for ever and ever, Amen* (cf. Didache 8).

One might ask whether the prayer of 3:14-21 (begun in 1:16) is also meant to teach the church how to pray. This is how the church is to pray in light of its identity and task: with boldness and confidence the church is to request power, knowledge, love, and fullness. Might this be a Pauline "Our Father"?

The prayer in Ephesians also has points of similarity with Jesus' high priestly prayer in John 17. It also begins with an address to the *Father*. It touches on themes we see in Ephesians 3, such as *glory* (John 17:1, 4, 5, 22, 24), *power* (17:2, 18), *knowledge* (17:3, 7, 8, 25, 26), the *name* (17:6, 11, 12, 26), *holiness* (17:17, 19), *sharing Christ's task in the cosmos* (17:18, 21, 23), *love* (17:26), *oneness with God and Christ—being in God and Christ* (17:21, 24), and *Christ and his love being in the believers* (17:10, 13, 22, 23, 26).

I am not suggesting dependency of one prayer on the other. Nevertheless, both emerge out of profound care for the church. That might be the greatest point of similarity between these two prayers. The prayer in Ephesians can rightly be seen as the Pauline high priestly prayer. Such a view of the prayer is equally compelling if it is seen as a post-Paul retrospective on the great apostle's relationship to the church as a whole and a crystallization of his pastoral concern.

To liken the prayer in Ephesians 3 with both the Lord's Prayer in Matthew 6 and the high priestly prayer in John 17 fits well the designs of the author of Ephesians. Here the great apostle intercedes on behalf of the church. In 6:18-20, the tables are turned, and the recipients of the letter are asked to pray for all the saints, but especially also for the apostle himself, that he might be given the boldness to fulfill his calling to speak the good news fearlessly.

THE TEXT IN THE LIFE OF THE CHURCH

Praying to God the Father

The content of this prayer is as timely in our day as it was then. Believers today are just as much in need of empowerment, renewal, knowledge, and the courage to fulfill the church's task as believers were then. Sadly, because the prayer is directed to God as *Father*, many cannot hear its profound and majestic strains. For most of the church's history, the fatherhood of God has not been a matter of controversy. *Father* has been a term of respect for God's authority and generativity, but mostly it has offered an opportunity for believers to practice in prayer their status as daughters and sons with full access to God their heavenly parent. To begin a prayer with *Father* witnesses as much to a personal relationship with God as it does to God's lordship.

In recent years, naming God as *Father* has been caught up in great social change ("Father," TLC for 1:3-14). Fatherhood is often equated with patriarchy, which literally means "the rule of the father." *Father* can carry the burden of hierarchy, domination, and top-down models of relationship, and thus imply the victimization and abuse of the less powerful, notably women and children. So in some churches, God is seldom if ever addressed in prayer as Father.

Much is at stake. On one hand, those who have been injured by male privilege, especially as concentrated in the role of the father, may find the terminology of fatherhood as encountered in Ephesians to be unhelpful or even offensive. The critique often goes beyond individual experiences of power and sexual abuse, however. It encompasses the ideological and cultural undergirding for such structures and behaviors. In many circles, patriarchy holds pride of place as a chief example of the wicked *principalities* and *powers* (6:12, KJV) with which especially women in the church must contend (5:21—6:9, notes). On the other hand, some have sounded the alarm that rejecting the image of God as Father lays siege to fatherhood as a cultural institution and also one of the essential foundations of the faith (Kimel; J. W. Miller).

To call God *Father* recognizes God as creator and sustainer of all that is. It recognizes God's relationship to "the all" as one of authority. It implies that God can make demands on "his" families. That much would have been taken for granted in the first century as inherent in the meaning of father. Letty Russell believes such a perspective too easily views fatherhood as the power to dominate, a view of authority she rejects for human fathers as for God (Russell: 30-32, 62, passim).

Today one might search for a better way to express God's sovereignty. Yet such authority and lordship, power and glory, are, in the view of Ephesians, the basis of the confidence with which the church undertakes its mission. God's grace, kindness, forgiveness, love, and peace are strong and authoritative initiatives, not to be separated from the conviction that only God can guarantee the ultimate success of the assault on evil, hostility, and brokenness.

After all, it is the *Father of glory* who raises the crucified one from the dead and with him all those who belong to him (1:17, 20; 2:4-6). Whatever difficulties such a view may present to us and our contemporaries, the conviction that God can and will see to it that things will turn out right in the end is one that pervades the biblical imagination *at its core*. This conviction cannot be removed without dismantling the gospel (cf. Rom. 8:28, NRSV note; 8:38-39).

As an alternative to a patriarchal view of authority, Russell proposes "partnership." With that term she has, perhaps ironically, hit on by far the most important implication of fatherhood in Ephesians, as she herself recognizes (32, 62). In addition to the explicit summons to *imitate God* (5:1), such partnership is implicit in the understanding of the church that underlies this passage and indeed all of Ephesians. That is what it means to sit *with* Christ, indeed *with* God, in the heavenlies (2:6-7), informing rulers and authorities in high places of the wisdom of God, thus participating with God in the "naming" of reality (3:10).

Most strikingly, the church is being filled up to and with the very fullness of *God* (3:19)! As applied to God, *fatherhood* is in Ephesians first and foremost a way to signify that God's authority, power, and glory is *for us*, for God's sons and daughters (1:19; 3:20). To call God *Father* also communicates the kind of respect for God's daughters and sons that implies partnership, to the extent of flirting dangerously with divinizing human beings (see 3:19; cf. Col. 2:9). But such is the measure of a love that *exceeds understanding*. This is a Father who liberates and empowers those who have hitherto been outside the family (2:11-22).

Only *after* seeing God's fatherhood in such terms should we approach the image critically. Alternative ways of addressing God should be no less profound in their capacity to evoke the mix of access, assurance, hope, and glory (see also Swartley, 1990; Volf: 167-90).

To apply *Father* to God is, of course, an analogy drawn from the realm of human experience. Are we permitted to turn the analogy around and ask to what degree the divine Father becomes normative for human fathers? Are human fathers encouraged to see themselves as "fathers of glory" through whom and to whom all things in the family are to be oriented? The answer may lie in the fact that when the issue of male family behavior is specifically raised in Ephesians, the injunctions are not that fathers imitate the Almighty, but rather the *Christ* who gives up his life for his bride, the church (5:25). Fathers are not to provoke their children to anger, but rather to nurture them to be Christlike (6:4). So God in the role of father is not the model for human fatherhood in any obvious sense.

Only one place in Ephesians *explicitly* calls for the imitation of God (4:32—5:1), a feature unique in the Pauline writings and a strong witness to the high level of partnership this letter envisions for believers. *All* the saints, men and women alike, including fathers, are to be tenderhearted, forgiving, kind, and loving to the utmost. A notion of fatherhood premised on such a foundation would ill fit a patriarchy slanted to serve the interests of fathers at the expense of mothers and children.

Doxology as the Basis of Ethics

The location of the doxology of 3:20-21, *after* a lengthy recitation of God's gracious intervention in Christ (chaps. 1–3) and immediately *before* the exhortation (chaps. 4–6), carries some significant lessons. First, any recitation of God's grace appropriately results in grateful worship. A deep awareness of God's love and grace should make a hearty "Thanks be to God!" a constant in the lives of believers.

The second lesson follows from this and is related to the doxology's location as a preamble to the exhortation. Worship, however much shaped by gratefulness, is not complete or true without a life in which "obedience" is experienced, not as compulsion, but as the free expression of gratitude to God. Such an insight is not easy to appreciate in a tradition such as Anabaptism, for example, which has viewed Christian ethics as obedience and discipleship rather than as worship. This text is intended to instill in readers a disposition of active gratitude, regardless of how costly and struggle-ridden it might be.

Ephesians 4:1-16

Growing Together into Christ

PREVIEW

The prayer and doxology at the end of chapter 3 provide a fitting conclusion to the first half of Ephesians. They also anticipate the believers' grateful response to God's grace. The second half of the letter thus begins with an urgent exhortation *to lead a life worthy of the calling* explored in the first half of Ephesians.

The stress falls first on *unity*. At the center of the rehearsal of grace in the first half of the letter is Christ's work of peace to make **one** *new human* out of erstwhile enemies (2:11-22; Introduction). Keeping that unity now becomes the work of the church (4:3). This is followed by a list of seven essential items with which that unity is secured (4:4-6). Verses 7-16 continue the focus on unity by emphasizing Christ's act of giving gifts to the church (4:7-11) so that the church can make unity a reality (4:13). Verses 9-10 are a brief parenthesis, applying Psalm 68:18 to Christ as gift-giver. Whereas 4:1 begins the exhortation half of Ephesians, verses 7-16 are more accurately a theological reflection on the church's growth and Christ's role as gift-bearer and head. The exhortation proper is taken up again in verse 17.

Lists are a prominent feature in this passage (see Structure below and Schematic Trans. in an appendix). Most obvious is the "unity list" in verses 4-6, the list of gifts Christ has given the church in verse 11, and the various ways Christ is identified as the goal of the church's growth in verse 13.

Structure of 4:1-16

I therefore beg *you*
  to walk worthy of the calling to which you were called—
    [a list of "virtues required for unity"]
  —eager to keep the unity of the Spirit in the bond of peace:
    [a list of "unity items" of the "chain of unity"] (4:1-6)

But to each one of *us* was given the grace according to the measure
  of the gift of Christ. (4:7)
    [Parenthesis: a brief interpretation of Psalm 68:18 in light of
    Christ as victorious gift-giver] (4:8-10)

And he *himself* gave
  [a list of gifts: persons with particular tasks]
  . . . for the *equipment* of the saints for the work of ministry,
    [which is] *building up* the body of Christ,
    . . . who is the *head* out of whom the whole *body*
  builds itself up in love. (4:11-16)

Readers should pay close attention to the interplay between the unity of the body, on one hand, and the empowerment and giftedness of individuals, on the other. Second, note how leadership *(gifts)* and general membership of the church *(saints)* relate to each other and the ministry of the church. Third, whereas the church is again identified as the *body of Christ* (4:4; cf. 1:23), the sense of incompleteness is strongly emphasized in these verses (4:13, 16). The task of the church is to become what it already is.

It is unclear whether the emphasis on unity reflects a specific division among the recipients of the letter. More likely, disunity was a constant danger or even reality for Paul and his followers (Introduction). Issues of ethics and mission are often divisive because they expose theological and doctrinal differences. Perhaps the concern for unity is at the head of the exhortation to respond to growing fractiousness in Pauline churches in the decades after Paul's death.

OUTLINE

Summons to Unity, 4:1-6
    4:1   The Prisoner's Request
    4:2-3   The Bond of Peace
    4:4-6   Bonds of Unity

Equipped to Grow into Christ, 4:7-16
  4:7   The Gift of Christ
  4:8-10   Christ the Ascending and Descending Giver
  4:11   The Gifts
  4:12-16   The Purpose of the Gifts
        To Equip the Saints for Ministry   4:12
        To Arrive at the Fullness of Christ   4:13-14
        To Grow into Christ   4:15-16

EXPLANATORY NOTES

Summons to Unity 4:1-6

4:1 The Prisoner's Request

As in 3:1, Paul appears in chains. *I urge you, therefore, I, the prisoner in the Lord . . .* Presenting Paul thus as a captive *in the Lord* has clear metaphorical and theological significance, whether or not the letter is from his own hand and whether or not actual incarceration lies behind the phrase (3:1, notes). The urging comes with the weight of someone who has no alternative but to exhort the saints—Paul is a captive of his apostolic commission from the Lord (cf. 1 Cor. 9:15-23). He has no choice and neither do his readers, who have been led into the gracious mystery of their salvation by the great *ambassador in chains* (6:20).

Perhaps that accounts for the emphatic *I*. With a rather clever wordplay, the one in *bonds (desmios)* exhorts his readers to *keep the unity in the* **bond** *of peace (sundesmos,* 4:3). As bondservants of the same Lord, both exhorter and exhorted share the same gracious captivity.

The exhortation begins with the important *therefore (oun)*. The importance of this little word for Christian ethics can hardly be over-stated. Exhortation *(paraenesis)* typically appears in Pauline letters *after* a recitation of what God has done for believers. The faithful life of a believer is nothing other than a grateful response to grace. Salvation is not *by* works (2:8) but *for* works (2:10). Romans 12:1 makes clear why: "I appeal to you therefore, ..., by the mercies of God, to present your bodies as a living sacrifice."

Here the image is not sacrifice but *walking (worthily) in keeping with the calling. Walking* is a common biblical expression for how people live out their lives (cf. 2:2; "Two Ways of Walking," TBC for 2:1-10; 4:17; 5:2, 8, 15; cf., e.g., Deut. 10:12; Prov. 2:20; Isa. 30:21; Mic. 4:5; John 8:12; 12:35; 1 John 1:7). Today one might speak of "lifestyle." The biblical image is less static, however. It implies that human life is heading somewhere, either to life or to death (see esp. 2:1-10).

Call and *calling* (*kaleō* and cognates) are prominent in this opening to the exhortation. Even the term we have translated as *urge* is related in the Greek to *call* (*parakaleō;* Liddell and Scott; cf. Best, 1998:361; Schmidt; Schmitz). What is *the calling* in which and toward which believers are called? For a Jewish writer, walking as *holy ones* or *saints* means, first of all, doing God's will, the *good works* God has prepared for humanity (2:10). Further, in verse 4 as in 1:18, this *calling* is directly linked to *hope.* God's call to believers is that they *walk in hope* toward that for which they hope.

At the beginning of this exhortation, we thus observe the characteristic Pauline tension between the *already* and the *not yet.* Believers are to live *presently* by the power and the values of that which they will most certainly receive fully *in the future.* They are *already* the body of Christ (1:23; 2:16), and *already* enjoy the fullness of God (1:23; 3:19), but they together with *all things* (1:10) have not yet fully grown into Christ. They are still in the process of being filled. They *have been saved* (2:5, 8) to participate in bringing salvation to completion (6:17, notes).

4:2-3 The Bond of Peace

The irony inherent in the image of an imprisoned messenger (3:1; 6:20), as in that of a crucified pacifier (2:14-18), is to characterize the lives of all believers. The *chosen* (1:4) have been *raised and seated with Christ in the heavenlies* (2:5-6); as living temples they furnish God with a home (2:21-22) and bear the *fullness of God* (3:19). Now they are asked to *walk* (2:1) in keeping with that grand and lofty calling *with all humility and gentleness, with patience.*

This collection of virtues, likely derived from Colossians 3:12, hardly reflects the strutting of the privileged sons and daughters of God or of the enlightened elite. Indeed, in the broader Gentile culture such humility would have been viewed as embarrassing nonassertiveness and hardly as a virtue (see Best, 1998:362; TBC). But Paul understood it to be the necessary glue to hold the body of the Christ together (e.g., Rom. 12:16; Phil. 2:3, 8; Col. 3:12). The exercise of *patience (makrothumia)* imitates a God of patience (cf., e.g., Exod. 34:6, LXX; Ps. 85:15, LXX), and anticipates the imitation of God in 4:32—5:1. *Bearing with one another in love* aptly captures these virtues and gives them their integrity and community-building character (Russell: 76; on these virtues, TBC).

The next directive dispels any notion that such a disposition is in any sense passive. Believers are to be *eager to maintain the unity of the Spirit in the bond of peace. To be eager* or *to hurry (spoudazō)* captures the urgency with which *unity* is to be maintained. In the NT, the term for *unity (henotēs)* is unique to Ephesians (cf. also 4:13). It is a unity *of the Spirit*, meaning a unity the Spirit makes possible (cf. 2:18). *Unity* is a divine gift to humanity and has been purchased at enormous cost (2:14-16). Even so, this gift is fragile, and its maintenance and ongoing realization require all the energy and resourcefulness, all the eagerness and zeal, with which God has endowed believers through the Spirit.

The irony returns to full view in the final image of this sentence: *the bond (sundesmos) of peace. Sundesmos* can mean "joint," "tie," "band," or "chain"—anything that binds things. *Peace* is the fetter of unity. Humility, gentleness, patience, and forbearance are the links in this chain of peace (4:2-3).

Peace is more than harmonious relations in a particular congregation, however, as much as it includes them. As chapter 2 shows, Christ's work of peace results in a new humanity, a body of reconciled enemies. The horizon of such peace clearly extends beyond the local congregation to the church at large and then beyond to *all things*. The church is the beachhead for a peace that is to extend to the cosmos (notes for 1:10 and 2:11-22). So the focus shifts now from the interpersonal relations (4:2-3) to the universal church (4:4-6), and indeed, to the one God and Father who is *over* and *through* and *in* **all** *things* (4:6).

4:4-6 Bonds of Unity

Attached to the exhortation to maintain unity is a list of seven items in relation to which unity is to be experienced and preserved. Some interpreters believe this to be traditional creedal material (e.g., Barth, 1974:429), associated perhaps with the celebration of baptism. No one doubts that the author has shaped this list as we presently have it, whatever the traditional background might be (Best, 1998:357-9; Lincoln: 228-9; Perkins: 96, suggesting it is constructed using 1 Cor. 12:12-13; 8:6).

Notice, first, the number of affirmations—seven. This is no mere happenstance. The number *seven* is a well-known biblical number of completion. Here it serves well the theme of unity. Second, whereas a hierarchy in the order is not obvious, the importance of the church in Ephesians is shown by the fact that the first item is the *body*. By saying *body* and not *church,* the point is made that in both its identity and its task the church is inseparable from the head, Christ, whose body the church is (4:15-16). In characteristic Pauline fashion, the *body* is inseparable from the *Spirit* that gives it breath and energy (cf. 1 Cor. 12:13).

The next item echoes verse 1—*just as you were called to the one hope of your calling*. Both mission and hope are inextricably connected to *body* and *spirit*. After all, *body* is not a static or institutional concept. The body is an organism, enlivened by the breath (*pneuma*, wind, spirit) of God (2:5, 18), whose growth will not be complete until *all things are gathered up in Christ* (1:10; 4:13). And the *Spirit* is always the wind blowing from the future, quickening the church with that which is yet to come, enabling the church to live toward that future (cf. 1:13).

To many readers, the compact triad in verse 5 sounds like a baptismal acclamation (the last item is *one baptism*). Each item is a noun of a different gender, which contributes to the formula-like nature of the triad: *one (heis) Lord, one (mia) faith, one (hen) baptism*. At issue in *one baptism* is not the mode of baptism, but the one into whom believers are baptized: Jesus Christ, the *one Lord*. *One faith* has as its content the conviction that God has called a church into being through Christ's death, that such a church is made up of both Jews and Gentiles, and that this church shares the Christ's identity and task as it awaits its hope.

The theocentric vision underlying this whole letter comes to expression in the final acclamation of faith in verse 6: *one God and Father of all, who is above all and through all and in all*. God is ultimately the author and the goal of unity (cf. esp. the opening blessing in 1:3-14).

The acclamation that God is *one* is deeply rooted in Jewish faith (cf. 1 Cor. 8:6). At daily prayer, Jews affirmed it in the *Shema*: "Hear, O Israel: The LORD our God is one LORD" (Deut. 6:4, KJV/RSV). It is not surprising for us to find this at the center of Christian affirmation. Even so, we see the germ of later trinitarianism in these affirmations (Fee, 1994:702; Perkins: 96). The *Father* and the *Lord* and the *Spirit* are all present. But note that in this list they stand alongside the *body*. In this list, it is God *the Father of all*, not only of the Son, who stands above, before, and after all, and whose fullness pervades *all things* (cf. 3:19; cf. Rom. 11:36; Best, 1998:370-1, on how encompassing *all* is).

Is this exhortation to unity a call for uniformity? Is the insistence on *one* body, *one* faith, and *one* baptism an assertion that only the view held here can claim legitimacy? Verse 14 suggests that the author is deeply concerned about the destructive effect of false teachings on the unity of the church and the spiritual health of vulnerable believers. In chapter 5 the author will draw sharp distinctions between light and darkness.

Even so, the governing vision in Ephesians is one of gathering, not elimination. Unity is clearly understood as adherence to the *one Lord* and the peace he created *in himself* (2:15; cf. 1:10). But it is a unity that is generous and inclusive at its core, one to be zealously maintained by all who have been liberated from the realm of death and called to life in the *new humanity* (Yoder Neufeld, 1993:211-32).

Equipped to Grow into Christ 4:7-16

4:7 The Gift of Christ

With verse 7 attention shifts from inclusive unity to *each one of us*, and the *gift* each receives. Three different words for "giving" and "gift" appear in verse 7. *Each one of us* has been *given (didōmi)* the *grace (charis)* according to the measure of the *gift (dōrea)*. The term translated here as *grace (charis)* can also be translated as gift (cf. the "gifts of the Spirit" *[charismata]* in 1 Cor. 12:4). This heaping up of synonyms fits the style of this letter very well (e.g., 1:19, 21; 3:20; 6:10). Its purpose is to bring special emphasis: the church is supplied with *every gift* it needs for the task of unity.

The identity of both giver and receivers is not immediately obvious. In biblical language the passive *(was given)* usually implies God as actor. God is thus the implied giver. The *measure* of the *gift* (or *grace*) God gives *to each one of us* is that which God has already given to and in Christ. Such a line of thought is already present in 1:19-23 and is clearly implied in 2:4-7 (notes).

However, as the author interprets Psalm 68:18 in verses 9 and 10, Christ himself is the giver of gifts. The *measure* of Christ's gift is then *the boundless riches of Christ* (cf. 3:8). The text obviously implies that God remains the ultimate Giver because the Messiah, God's agent of grace and salvation, delivers the gifts.

Though earlier in this passage the emphasis was on the *one body*, here the emphasis falls on *each one of us* as the recipients of Christ's gifts (cf. 4:16). There is some ambiguity as to who is included in the category *each one*. Some interpreters prefer to see *each one of us* in close connection with verse 11 (*apostles, prophets, evangelists,* and others). The first person plural—*each one of **us***—would then refer to Paul and other leaders of the church, and not to all members (so, e.g., Schlier, 1971:191). However, verse 11 makes clear that the apostles, prophets, evangelists, and teachers are themselves *gifts* that

Christ has given to all *the saints* (4:12)—to the church as a whole. In this instance, they are the gifts, not the gifted.

There is little in Ephesians to support the idea of a gifted elite (cf. 3:8, notes). *Each one of us* should be taken to refer to each of the saints who make up the body (cf. Rom. 12:3). The gifts the saints have been given are in this case the special messengers, teachers, and pastors listed in verse 11 (Barth, 1974:480; Best, 1998:376-7; Lincoln: 241; R. Martin, 1991:53; Schnackenburg: 177-8). The emphasis on unity is not allowed to obscure or devalue the individual who receives the gift or the grace from Christ. Likewise, the gifts are received and exercised only in the unity of the body, even if, as here, the emphasis falls on the gifts of leaders and teachers.

4:8-10 Christ the Ascending and Descending Giver

By means of a "midrash pesher" (a rabbinic style of biblical interpretation stressing recent or present fulfillment; Lincoln: 242-4; cf. Best, 1998:375; Perkins: 97), the author now employs Psalm 68:18 to illustrate the giving of gifts. Psalm 68 is one of the great hymns extolling God as victorious warrior (cf. notes on the divine warrior at 1:15-23; 6:10-20). God ascends Mount Zion after liberating his people and vanquishing his foes. On his ascent he receives gifts of tribute from the people. In Ephesians the quotation has undergone some significant alterations.

Psalm 68:18 (NRSV)	*Ephesians 4:8 (NRSV)*
You ascended the high mount, leading captives in your train and receiving gifts from people.	When he ascended on high he made captivity itself a captive; he gave gifts to [his] people.

The reader encounters several surprises when comparing Ephesians 4:8 with Psalm 68:18. We will distinguish between changes the author has made and differences permitted in the process of translation.

First, the second person *you ascended* is changed to the third person *he ascended* (lit., *having ascended*, which can mean either *when*, as in NIV and NRSV, or *after*). This allows the author to transform an acclamation of worship directed to God into a claim about Christ (KJV, NKJV, TEV translate Ps. 68:18 in the third person).

Second, NIV and NRSV present the final phrase in the first line in Ephesians 4:8 as *he took captivity captive*. This might seem like the complete opposite of *leading captives in his train* and thus a major change from the Psalm text. However, as most translations have it, and as virtually all commentators agree, the abstract noun *captivity* is an idiom for *captives* themselves (cf. Num. 31:12, LXX; *BAGD:* 26; Barth, 1974:431; so NAB and NJB in both Ps. 68 and Eph. 4:8). The Greek OT (LXX) translates the Hebrew in such a way that in English it can accurately mean both "taking captives" and "taking captivity captive" (hence *leading captivity captive* appears in KJV/ NKJV of both Ps. 68:18 and Eph. 4:8).

We should respect the ambiguity of the text. If we translate verse 8 as *taking captives*, we should perhaps think of Christ taking captive the powers (cf. 1:21; 6:12; cf. also 1 Cor. 15:24; and esp. Col. 2:15; the psalm thus anticipates the activity of the church's participation in divine warfare in 6:10-20; cf. also Perkins: 98). Early commentators often took this to refer to Christ's liberation of Satan's captives (see Best, 1998:382). We might even hear an echo of the "captivity" of Paul and those who zealously keep the chain of peace secure (4:1, 3; cf. 2 Cor. 2:14). On the other hand, *taking captivity [itself] captive* conforms perfectly to the irony encountered in 2:16, where Christ *murders enmity*. Where the text does not force a decision, interpreters should avoid making one. Instead, we should savor the interpretive possibilities.

The most important difference from Psalm 68 is that the one who ascends or has ascended the heights does not *receive* gifts but *gives* them. Christ's *giving* gifts in verses 7 and 11 is no doubt the reason for this change. It is not a change, however, unique to Ephesians. The Jewish Pentecost liturgy used Psalm 68:18 to celebrate Moses' *giving* of the law after ascending Mount Sinai (Best, 1998:378-82, with documentation; Lincoln: 242-4; Yoder Neufeld, 1997:100). The author's freedom in adapting Scriptures to his purposes is rooted in precedent, and it is anything but arbitrary.

In Ephesians, the identification of Christ is not with Moses, however, but with the victorious God of Psalm 68. The identification with God is further made clear in verse 10, where Christ's ascension leads to his filling *all things*, the whole of the cosmos (cf. 4:6; cf. also 1:10, 23; 3:19).

Victorious warriors receive tribute; they do not pass out gifts. But in our text, Psalm 68:18 has been turned on its head. The note of victory is loud and clear, but here the victor *offers* gifts to those from whom he might have expected to receive them. This point becomes even sharper when it is observed that in Psalm 68 the divine victor receives gifts of tribute from the rebellious. In Ephesians, the divine victor *gives* gifts to those who were once rebellious *sons of disobedience* (cf. 2:1-3).

Verses 9 and 10 are a parenthesis (explicitly so in, e.g., NIV, NRSV, NASB). The author attaches an interpretive comment ("christological midrash," Lincoln: 244) to the citation of Psalm 68:18 to draw attention to a particular point of the biblical text. *What does it imply that "he went up" other than that he also came down into the lower [parts] of the earth?*

There are roughly three ways of understanding this difficult sentence. The first view takes *the lower [parts] of the earth* to refer to the underworld, the realm of the dead (cf., e.g., Rom. 10:7; 1 Pet. 3:19; Rev. 1:18). This connection has found considerable scholarly support; it also was the preferred interpretation in the first centuries of the church (survey in Barth, 1974:432-4; Best, 1998:383-6; Lincoln: 244-7; Russell: 76). Ephesians expresses no interest, however, in going any lower than the earth.

It should be noted that *parts* is not supported in the best manuscripts (hence square brackets in my translation); more carefully translated, we should say *the lowers (ta katōtera),* much as we speak elsewhere of *the heavenlies (ta epourania;* 1:3-14, notes) *[Cosmology].* Lincoln thus suggests that the genitive *of the earth* be understood rather as a genitive of apposition, *the lower regions, that is, the earth* (245; so similarly NIV: *lower, earthly regions*). A visit to hell, as it were, is not likely what the author has in mind.

But to what then does the descent to these *lowers* refer? One suggestion is that it refers to Christ's incarnation (Best, 1998:386), reading verse 9 in light of the christological wisdom hymns in Philippians 2:6-11 and John 1. The affinities of the Christology of Ephesians to the wisdom tradition have been noted earlier (notes on 1:3-14; 1:15-23) *[Wisdom].* Some manuscripts indeed include the word *first* (he **first** *descended to the lowers,* hinting at incarnation). The *gift* would then refer to Christ's coming to earth.

A third view takes the descent to refer to Christ's *post*-Easter descent at Pentecost in the form of the Spirit (e.g., Lincoln: 247; R. Martin, 1991:50). The role of Psalm 68:18 in Jewish Pentecost celebrations was noted earlier. Christ, the risen and exalted victor, descends in the form of the Spirit to give gifts to his body. The pattern observed throughout the letter is again visible: the best measure of the power and might of God, even when depicted as military conquest, is ironically the offering of love, grace, and gifts to rebellious humanity (cf. 2:4, 13-18). Divine power expresses itself in the empowerment of others.

While the third interpretation might be preferred, given the emphasis in verse 11 on *gifts* rather than *gift,* it is important not to be stingy in our interpretation. In the end, the generosity of God in Christ knows no limits. It includes the gift of Christ, for which God is blessed at the beginning of the letter (1:3-14), the gift of his peace (2:11-22), and here the ongoing generosity that accompanies the church in its growth into Christ.

Verse 10 should be read in such a light. It stresses again the ascension of Christ *far above all the heavens*. The one who came down—meaning the one who has touched the lives of those on *the lowers of the earth*—is none other than the one who has *ascended far above all the heavens* and who *fills all things*. How many heavens there are is of no interest here. The only point of interest is that the exaltation of the one who gives gifts knows no limits; nor, importantly, does his generosity.

4:11 The Gifts

Verses 11 to 16 are one long sentence, exploring the nature and purpose of Christ's gifts. Verse 11 provides a list of these gifts. Careful translation is key to understanding the gist of the argument. NIV, NRSV and other translations (e.g. NJB, REB) rather carelessly, in my view, leave the impression that Christ gives gifts to certain people, enabling them to be apostles, prophets, and teachers (as in Rom. 12:6-8; 1 Cor. 12:8-10, 28-30). They are the "gifted ones," just as *each one of us* has been given a gift of some sort (Eph. 4:7) "for the common good" (1 Cor. 12:7). However, our text quite literally lists *apostles, prophets, evangelists, pastors, and teachers* as the gifts themselves (Best, 1997:160-73; 1998:389-95).

Careful comparison with Romans 12 and 1 Corinthians 12 allows the distinctiveness of our text to emerge (chart in TBC). In Ephesians, the list is of persons rather than ministries. Further, the list is much shorter than even Romans 12:8-10. The kinds of persons listed are essentially ministers of the word (cf. Barth, 1974:436): *apostles* and *prophets*, and proclaimers and teachers of the word that came through them—*evangelists, pastors and teachers*.

Apostles and *prophets* are already known from 2:20 (notes) and 3:5 (notes), where they are viewed as the *foundation* on which the edifice of the church is built. Their role is to receive and then authorize the teaching and beliefs of the church (Lincoln: 249; Schnackenburg: 184). If the working hypothesis in this commentary is correct, that Ephesians is written fairly late in the first century (Introduction), then the *apostles and prophets* are seen as an early gift of Christ to the church, Paul being one of the most important.

In some areas of the church, *prophets* continued to play a significant role in the period following the first generation of apostles. The late first-century Teaching of the Twelve Apostles (Didache) provides a set of instructions on how to recognize a true prophet among the many itinerant ones making their way through the churches of Asia Minor (Didache 11-13). It is not clear that these are the prophets the author of Ephesians has in mind. More than likely, the author lists them with the apostles as founding "specialists in mediating divine revelation" (Lincoln: 249), and less as gifts presently operative in the churches he is addressing. That does not rule out the ongoing missionary and prophetic activity in Pauline congregations, as we see in the gift listed next.

New to the list of gifts are the *evangelists*, the *proclaimers of good news* to those both within and outside the church. Here the emphasis lies on service to the *saints*, who also must hear *good news*. Early on, that task was carried out by apostles—missionaries. But after their death, the apostles were increasingly viewed as founding authorities (2:20), and the ongoing task of proclaiming the gospel fell to evangelists (so also Best, 1997:163-6; 1998:391; Lincoln: 250; Schnackenburg: 184). Acts 21:8 may reflect this shift in vocabulary, even as it describes events taking place during the time of Paul and Peter (cf. 2 Tim. 4:5).

Pastors and *teachers* are listed last. Pastoring, literally *shepherding*, is mentioned elsewhere in the NT as service to the church only as an action rather than an office (cf. 1 Pet. 5:2). As 1 Peter makes clear, this ministry imitates "the chief shepherd" (1 Pet. 5:4; cf. 2:25), "the good shepherd" (John 10:11), or "the great shepherd of the sheep" (Heb. 13:20)—Jesus Christ. Only in Ephesians 4 are *shepherds* or *pastors* listed as designated gifts to the church. Their responsibility was likely to give guidance and direction to the church and to oversee the life of the flock (cf. John 21:15-17).

First Peter 2:25 identifies Jesus as both "shepherd" and "overseer/guardian" (*episkopos*, "bishop" in KJV; the cognate participle is present also in 1 Pet. 5:2; cf. Waltner: 156-8, 183-4). The proximity of *pastor* to the function of elder is also apparent in that passage. The wording in Ephesians may thus reflect that toward the end of the first century, "pastor," "bishop," and "elder" have become similar in meaning and function, referring to the exercise of oversight responsibilities in local congregations.

The term *teachers (didaskaloi)* is not preceded by an article; *pastors and teachers* may thus be much the same group. Barth refers to them as "teaching shepherds" (Barth, 1974:438; cf. also R. Martin, 1991:52; but see Best, 1998:393). That may be so. Nevertheless, to list *teachers* explicitly fits well the importance Ephesians placed on knowledge, wisdom, and insight (cf., e.g., 1:17-18; 3:14-19; 4:13-14). "Teachers" are mentioned in the earlier list in 1 Corinthians 12:28 and thus played a role in the very early stages of Pauline church life as well. Their importance as guardians of the apostolic "deposit," as the pastoral letters put it (1 Tim. 6:20; 2 Tim. 1:14), increased exponentially in the postapostolic period. If we think of the author of Ephesians as one such teacher, then we see that they were guardians and also inspired developers of the apostolic legacy.

There is not enough information in Ephesians and too ambiguous a set of data outside of Ephesians to allow for more than strong hunches on how ministries and leadership were organized in early churches. There is no mention in Ephesians, for instance, of elders, deacons, or bishops. Furthermore, we cannot be sure that this list of *gifts* reflects a structure of offices for which individuals were ordained, as in the pastoral letters. We can glean from this passage that in the author's mind these gifts of Christ to the church are of particular importance to the church's identity and mission. Importantly, the gifts that predominate are those that have to do with preserving and inculcating the apostolic legacy and teaching.

4:12-16 The Purpose of the Gifts

A crucial matter in this passage is the relationship of the *gifts* (apostles and others) to the *saints* as a whole. Christ is said to provide the gifts *for the equipment of the saints, for the work of service (ministry), for the building up of the body of Christ.* Notice the different Greek prepositions translated as *for* (Schematic Trans.): the first phrase is introduced by *pros*, the second and third by *eis*.

At issue is whether the second and third phrases depend on the first (so, e.g., Best, 1998:395-9) or whether this is a list of three parallel phrases defining the task the gifts perform (so, e.g., Houlden: 315; Lincoln: 253). If it is the latter, then the *gifts* are in effect the *ministers* who do three things: equip the saints, perform the work of service, and build up the body. Such an interpretation would undergird the practice in the majority of churches up to this day (with varying degrees of clerical definition, to be sure).

If, on the other hand, the two phrases introduced by *eis* indicate the task of the *saints* as a whole rather than only that of the leaders-gifts, then an entirely different understanding of church relationships and of ministry emerges. Then the *apostles . . . teachers* are there to enable *all the saints* **together** to do *the work of ministry* and *to build up the body* (so correctly NRSV and most translations).

Thus on one hand the author is concerned that apostles and prophets, evangelists, pastors, and teachers are accorded proper respect as Christ's gifts to the church—the "royal largesse" of the giving Christ (Lincoln: 248). On the other hand, they are also no more and no less than Christ's gift *to the saints* so as to enable *them* to do the work of ministry (Russell: 77). Lincoln, who holds a contrary view of the grammar (see above), believes verses 7 and 16 safeguard the importance of the ministry of all the saints, and that the focus in verse 12 is strictly related to the *apostles . . . teachers* (Lincoln: 253). It is preferable, however, to see verse 12 as corroborating the emphasis on *each individual's ministry* in verses 7 and 16 by placing the leaders-*gifts* in verse 11 in proper relation to the *saints* to whom they have been given.

The arena of sports provides a useful analogy. The list of gifts in verse 11 might be seen as the coaches, trainers, team physicians, and equipment handlers. The saints as a whole are the team that does the actual playing. Each member of the team has a role to play for which he or she is prepared, given direction, and kept in shape by the coaching and training staff. Without the coaches and trainers, the team functions poorly, if at all. Coaches may achieve a remarkable position of authority. Indeed, they require the respect and the deference of the players. But with few exceptions, they are not the players. Without the team, there would be no game, let alone a victory.

Likewise, it is the responsibility of pastors, teachers, and other leaders, to see to it that the team—*the saints*—is completely equipped and functions *together* as a team (NJB aptly translates the phrase as *to knit God's holy people together*). With expert teaching, guidance, watchful care, and encouragement on the part of the leaders-*gifts*, each of the saints functions together with other team members (4:16) to do the work of ministry and build up the body of Christ. That is the "game."

This analogy has a limitation. It draws too sharp a distinction between coaches and trainers and the team. Both leaders-*gifts* and *saints* are part of one church. Both play the game: apostles, pastors, and teachers as players-coaches, together performing the work of ministry. The analogy is useful, however, in identifying the distinct responsibilities in the church as the author envisions them, while safeguarding the emphasis on the importance of *all the saints* in playing the "game."

Distinctions between "officials" and the whole of the church appear to have become more pronounced in the author's day than they were in the early years of the church. Only a decade or two after the writing of Ephesians, Ignatius, the bishop of Antioch, commends a highly stratified leadership model centered on the bishop, to whom everyone is subject, especially the faceless "laity" (e.g., Letters of Ignatius: Eph. 6.2; Magn. 6; 8; Trall. 3.1; 7.2; Philad. 3.2). The present text is often taken to be supportive of this increasing differentiation between clergy and laity (e.g., Best, 1997:172; 1998:399). But others notice the absence of bishops in the list and wonder whether they are deliberately left out as an attempt to reassert a more Pauline notion of ministry (Fischer: 15, 38).

Regardless, in Ephesians we can observe with what skill the distinction between leadership and the church as a whole is both acknowledged and qualified at the same time. Apostles, prophets, evangelists, pastors, and teachers are to be held in high esteem, consistent with instructions given by Paul in the earliest extant letter:

> We appeal to you, brothers and sisters, to respect those who labor among you, and have charge of you in the Lord and admonish you; esteem them very highly in love because of their work. (1 Thess. 5:12-13)

Nevertheless, in Ephesians as in 1 Thessalonians, *ministry* or *service* is entrusted to *all* the members of the church (Elias: 214-23). Ephesians addresses *both* those who are Christ's gift to the church *and* the members of the church are addressed in Ephesians. Leaders and teachers truly are Christ's gifts, but they have been given for the sake of the ministry of all the saints! It might have become quite necessary to make this point for leaders at the time this letter was written. It is a message also to members of the church who are tempted to translate deference to leaders into their own insignificance. To see oneself as not a minister is to betray the ecclesiology of this letter, and with it the costly work of Christ.

At the same time, this text is a clear message to those saints whose sense of self-importance leads them to disparage the *gifts*. First, they lack appreciation for the apostolic roots of the faith. Second, they lack respect for those whose task it is to guard, nurture, and develop the faith and the church's fidelity to it. That too betrays the vision of this letter.

To Equip the Saints for Ministry 4:12

Equipment (katartismos) appears in noun form only here in the NT. In verbal form it means "to put in order," "restore," or "complete" (cf. 1 Cor. 1:10; Gal. 6:1), or more generally "to prepare," "make," or "create" (cf. Rom. 9:22). The noun is used, for example, for "setting a bone," and thus carries overtones of equipping in the

sense of restoring, binding, training, and discipline. This rich resonance should not be overlooked in light of the predominant metaphor
of the body (see esp. 4:4, 16).

The *gifts* are to *equip* the saints for *ministry*. *Ministry* translates
diakonia, which for our purpose is more accurately translated as *service,* even demeaning service. *Diakonia* acquired noble associations
only through identification with early Christian leaders like Paul, who
emulated their Servant-Lord Jesus. In time the term became caught
up, ironically to be sure, in the struggles for power and authority,
eventually losing its moorings in humble service and becoming perhaps the most important designation for Christian leadership. Hence
the confusion among scholars on how to interpret this verse.

In Ephesians, this confusion has not yet set in. The leaders of the
church are to enable all to offer *service,* to engage in *ministry.* Such
servanthood requires resilience, energy, and fitness. It also requires
models who remember that they themselves have no better teacher
than the Christ who washed feet and in the end went to the cross.
Paul knew that (see esp. 2 Cor.); Ephesians wants to remind both
leaders-*gifts* and the other *saints* of that (cf. 2:13-18; 5:2, 25).

To Arrive at the Fullness of Christ 4:13-14

The goal of ministry is for *all* believers to *arrive at the unity of the
faith and of the knowledge of the Son of God, at the perfect man,
at the measure of the stature of the fullness of Christ.* The ministry
of building up the body of Christ (4:12) is to be exercised *until all of
us* arrive at Christ.

An element intrinsic to the vision underlying Ephesians comes
to expression here. The conjunction *until* makes it clear that even
though the church is already the *body* (cf. 4:12) and the *fullness* of
Christ (cf. 1:23; cf. 3:19), all the energies and gifts at work in and
among the saints are to be put to work so that we *all* might *together
arrive* at that *fullness. Ministry* has to do with becoming what we
already are.

This apparent contradiction—"already/not yet"—is an essential
component of Pauline eschatology and ethics. To relax either element in this tension threatens the church's faithfulness. The church
is *already* the incarnation of Christ (2:15) and thus participates in
the messianic task of *gathering up all things in Christ* (1:10). But
the church is *not yet* all that it can and will be. The *saints* must be
conscious of the fact that they must draw on the *gifts* of Christ to live
up to their identity as Christ's body, and to grow more fully into that
identity.

When placed alongside each other, verses 12, 15, and 16 produce an almost absurd but illuminating picture: The body is to arrive at its head. It is to grow into the head to which it is already connected and by which it is defined. And it is to grow into the head from which it receives its growth.

The goal of ministry is defined in a number of ways. The first is to *arrive together at the unity of the faith.* In this case *the faith* is a better translation than "fidelity," as much as being faithful to each other and to God is an essential part of how the body grows together into Christ (4:16; notes on 1:1; 2:5, 8; 6:16). *The faith* is also here a better translation than "trust" in God, as much as that is an essential component of salvation (2:8, notes). Here the view is on the unity of the church as it is constituted and preserved by holding to and rehearsing shared convictions (cf. 4:5).

More is at stake, however, than common assent to a set of propositions or doctrines. This unity is identified as shared knowledge of the Son of God. In 3:17, 19, *knowledge of the unknowable love of Christ* is a result of Christ *dwelling in the hearts* of believers. To "know," as anyone trained in the Scriptures would have known, means to *experience,* to become *one flesh,* in this case with Christ (cf. 5:31).

The intensity of this identification is indicated by the goal of arriving (lit.) *into the perfect man.* In this phrase, *anēr,* the gender-specific term for an adult male, suggests an intense identification with Christ and should not be read as an idealization of maleness per se (1:13; Russell: 82-3; Barth, 1974:441, 484-7, who also sees connections to the marriage motif of 5:25-32). NIV, NRSV, and other translations render this phrase as *maturity,* contrasting it to *children* (lit., *infants*) in verse 14 (also Lincoln: 256, who nevertheless wants to retain the primary sense of the church's *corporate* maturity).

A contrast is no doubt implied between verses 13 and 14. However, as the preceding reference to *the Son of God* and the subsequent phrase *the measure of the stature of the fullness of Christ* indicate, *the perfect man* is none other than Jesus Christ. In chapter 2, Christ re-creates hostile humanity into *one body,* into *one new human (anthrōpos).* Here the process is described from the other direction. By his gifts Christ has enabled the church to arrive at himself, *the perfect man* (so also with some hesitation, Best, 1998:402).

Perfect (teleios) can certainly imply *mature,* as most translators render it. To speak of arriving at *the perfect man* would then be the equivalent to arriving at what in the next phrase is called *the stature of the fullness of Christ.* Everything in that understanding is consistent with the "developmental ecclesiology" of Ephesians. However, without claiming anything more than common vocabulary, it is worth noticing that the term appears in Matthew 5:48, where "perfect" *(teleios)* refers to God's righteousness as expressed in enemy love, a perfection, moreover, that is to be imitated by all who would be sons and daughters of God (Matt. 5:45).

In Ephesians, Christ, *the Son of God,* has already been introduced as the embodiment of enemy love (2:11-22). His perfection in love finds its fulfillment in the creation of a new humanity *in himself* (2:15). In Christ, humanity regains its perfection, as at creation. In Christ, the *fullness* of God (3:19) and the *fullness* of humanity (1:23; 2:15) meet. This *perfect man* becomes the goal for those who already constitute his body. Whereas the church is "already" the *fullness* of Christ (1:23), its ministry is geared to having it arrive at a *fullness* that is "not yet" perfect. How better to reach that goal than to practice the enemy-loving perfection of God's Christ?

Readers are jolted into an awareness of the vulnerability they experience this side of perfection, as verse 14 indicates. For all the power at work in members of the body of Christ (notes for 1:19-20 and 3:14-21), Gentile believers as "toddlers in the walk" are still vulnerable to the deceitful wiles and teachings of ill-intentioned persons. Such deceit is part and parcel of the strategies of the devil himself (cf. 6:11), here served by human cunning (the image is taken from dishonest dice playing; Best, 1998:405). This does not refer explicitly to persons in the church, but it is strongly suggested (cf. Col. 2:22, where the same terminology is employed in warning about false teaching).

Thus, while growing into Christ is much more than a matter of right belief, of adherence to *the faith,* matters of right belief are of great concern to the writer. At issue is the survival of the church as the presence of a Christ whose mission is to reconcile all of reality to God. We see here the flip side of the emphasis on the church as Christ's body. For the church to fail to hold to a *faithful* unity (4:1-6)—for the corporate body to disintegrate into a plurality of toddlers being pushed in any number of directions by gusts of ill wind (cf. 2:1-3)—imperils the mission of Christ to gather up all things in himself and in the process to create humanity anew.

There is an element of stark realism in this terse image of being adrift at sea. For all the generosity that pervades Ephesians, for all its celebration of the universal scope of God's grace, the author firmly believes that there are ideas and modes of life leading to shipwreck *(tossed to and fro by waves;* so also REB; cf. 4:17-19!). Ephesians has little of the polemical ambience of some earlier Pauline letters (e.g., Gal., 1–2 Cor.) and the writer's vision is irenic to the core, but this urgent note of warning must not be overlooked in a discussion of unity. Given the image of infants tossed about on the turbulent seas of life, empathy more than blame is in the mind of the author with respect to these still new believers. There is also an implicit message to the leadership of the church regarding the gravity of its task in outfitting the church for its vulnerable voyage.

The emphasis on unity in the faith and growth into oneness with Christ, coupled with warnings of what can arrest development, may be occasioned by the kind of church the author envisions. That church is made up of those who were once strangers and outsiders, of groups typically in conflict with each other, and of those whose former way of life was the opposite of what God intended (e.g., 2:1-3; 4:17-19). If such a church continues to grow by the incorporation of ever-new reconciled enemies, it will always be made up of those who are vulnerable to losing their way. Because of their newness to the faith and the novelty of the peace they share, they will be easy prey for deceit of all kinds.

A missionary peace church as envisioned in 2:11-22 will by its nature always have vulnerable "babies" who will need to grow with the guidance of the gifts Christ gives (4:11, notes). Having said that, notice that vulnerability to deceit and false teaching is something all share—*so that* **we** *might no longer be infants.* This is both pastoral solidarity of the Jewish writer with his Gentile readers and a frank recognition that such vulnerability marks the life of all believers who have not yet arrived fully at Christ.

To Grow into Christ 4:15-16

Verse 15 returns to the positive goal of growing into Christ. The participle *being truthful (alētheuontes)* is a verb form of *truth (alētheia)* and could be translated as "truthing." While NIV and NRSV translate it as *speaking the truth*, some translations rightly wish to extend its meaning beyond *speaking* (e.g., NJB, *living by the truth;* REB, *maintaining the truth*). *Being truthful* incorporates both speaking and acting. Such *truthing* stands in immediate contrast to the falsity that puts believers adrift on the stormy sea. Just as coming to unity in Christ (4:13) enables believers no longer to be infants tossed about on the rough seas of deceptive teaching, so truth-full existence becomes the way to grow into Christ.

Truthing most certainly includes speaking "with integrity." But its horizon extends much beyond personal honesty (cf. 4:21, 25; 6:14). *Truthing* means *professing the truth* (NAB) rehearsed in the first three chapters of Ephesians (cf. 4:4-6). It thus stands in direct contrast to the deliberate deception of cunning false teachers (4:14). It means *speaking the truth* (NRSV), first of all proclaiming the gospel to each other (Best, 1998:407), but surely also to the powers, announcing the *multivaried wisdom of God* to the rulers and authorities on high (3:10). It means also *living by the truth* (NJB), maintaining the unity of the faith and the knowledge of the Son of God (4:13).

Such speaking and acting is not *truthful* unless it is done *in love*. *In love* appears frequently in Ephesians (1:4; 3:17; 4:2, 16; 5:2). *Love* is the means by which truth comes into the community *["In"]*. Since we recognize the Creator's designs for all of creation and the love that drives and shapes those designs (cf. 2:4!), we know that truth and love are indivisible (4:25, notes). Thus for believers, "ultimately, at the heart of the proclamation of the truth is love, and a life of love is the embodiment of the truth" (Lincoln: 260; cf. Best, 1998:407; Russell: 79-80; Schnackenburg: 191).

Living by, in, and for the truth is the means of *growing in every way* (or *in all things*; both can translate *ta panta*) *into Christ, who is the head ["Head"]*. In this instance most translators and interpreters prefer *in every way* (NRSV; *in all things*, NIV; similarly Barth, 1974:444; Best, 1998:408; Lincoln: 260; Schnackenburg: 191; Gnilka: 218). *Ta panta* is elsewhere translated *all things*, a typical way the author of Ephesians likes to refer to the cosmos and all that is in it (4:10; cf. 1:10-11, 23; 3:9). Some interpreters then translate the phrase as *causing all things to grow into the head—Christ*, in which *to grow* is treated as a transitive verb (notably Schlier, 1965:680-1; 1971:190).

In such a reading, the verse would point to the missionary task of the church as participation in the *gathering up of all things in(to) Christ* (cf. 1:10). Some perceive this interpretation to be an imperialistic and triumphalistic understanding of the church that is unbecoming the author's ecclesiology (e.g., Barth, 1974:444-5; Schnackenburg: 191; Schlier, 1965:681, admits that it does sound like that). There is, however, no good reason to dismiss such a reading on those grounds. That the church is a full participant in the messianic project is implicit in calling the church Christ's *body*—a notion explored as profoundly in Ephesians as anywhere.

The terseness of the language is not intended to suggest an easy universalism, anymore than does 1:10 (notes). But neither does it allow a restriction to only an "intensive" notion of the church's growth (contra, e.g., Best, 1998:408; Lincoln: 260-1; Schnackenburg: 191).

The image of *head* and *body* may be a blending of two originally independent traditions, one of Christ as head of the cosmic body (as in Col. 1:16-18), the other of the church as Christ's body (as in 1 Cor. 12 and Rom. 12; Best, 1998:195; Lincoln: 262). The combination of cosmos and church is already present in Colossians, however, which indicates that these traditions had been combined before the writing of this letter. *Head* carries implications of authority (cf. esp. 1:22), but also of source (cf. 1 Cor. 11:3, 7) *["Head"]*. Here both ideas are present. As *head,* Christ is the *governing goal* of the church's growth (cf. 4:13); as *head,* Christ is also the *source* of the church's identity, task, and empowerment (4:7-12), as well as of its growth (4:16; lit., *out of whom*).

Verse 16 is as grammatically difficult as it is uncommonly rich in meaning. The bewildering complexity appears to result from the intention on the part of the author to bring this passage to a climactic summation. The terms *each one* and *measure* in verse 7 reappear to form an *inclusio* (marking a section by repeating a beginning word or phrase at the end). Grammatically, the verse is dependent on the previous assertion that Christ is the *head* (4:15), while the focus of the verse is now on the *body*. Further, the vocabulary of Colossians 2:19 is integrated into the complex sentence and expanded with some medical vocabulary related to joints and ligaments (though we cannot be sure what these terms actually mean; Best, 1998:411).

Two words with the prefix *sun-* *(with/together with), joined together (sunarmologoumenon;* cf. 2:21) and *knit together (sumbibazomenon),* recall similar strings of *sun-* compound words in 2:5-6, 21-22, and 3:6, drawing attention to the interrelationship of believers with each other and with Christ. Though in 2:21 *joined together* functions in the architectural image of a building, here it is combined with the similar *knit together* to depict the organic growth of a body. Even so, the individual does not disappear from view. The availability to individual believers of God's power as well as Christ's "sourcing" of the body is reasserted in the final clause: *Each* individual contributes to *growth* (cf. 4:15) *according to the energy* (cf. esp. 3:20) *appropriate to* (lit., *in [the] measure of) each part* (paralleling 4:7, *according to the measure of the gift of Christ given to each one of us*). To sum up, the church's *growth* is to happen *in love* (cf. 4:15, notes).

The phrase *for the purpose of building itself up is* particularly puzzling. Perhaps it should be translated *into his building,* as some manuscripts allow (Schematic Trans.). The two alternatives are closely related. The one has the church *building itself up in love* as it becomes more and more Christlike (the identical *eis oikodomēn is* used in 4:12). The image of the organic growth of a body controls such an interpretation. The alternative translates *oikodomē*, not as building up, but as *a building*, a term already used in connection with *joined together (sunarmologoumenon)* in 2:21 to describe the church as God's holy temple. Christ creates in himself a new human who is to serve as God's own home; the church as his body also participates in the construction of that temple.

Grammar is evidently the small price paid for such a successful compression of central themes and imagery. The gist remains clear: Christ the head gives the body, the church, what it needs to grow in love into a new humanity—into Christ. Notice also that, in keeping with Paul's vision in 1 Corinthians 12, special emphasis is given to the importance of *each individual part* for the growth of the whole body.

The effect of 4:16, as of the whole of verses 7-16, is that the exhortation of the following chapters is always addressed to the whole church as a corporate reality. Unity is the premise and objective of the exhortation. At the same time, *each individual* believer is to hear and respond to the challenge directed to the whole *body*. Not surprisingly, the challenge to *hold **each other** up in love* (4:2) lies at the heart of the opening exhortation to unity in verses 1-3.

THE TEXT IN BIBLICAL CONTEXT

Affinity to Colossians is again evident: Ephesians 4:2-3 appears to be dependent on Colossians 3:12-14, verse 4 on Colossians 3:15, and verse 16 on Colossians 2:19. Indeed, much of Colossians 3:1-17 is taken up, reworked, and reordered in Ephesians 4:1—5:20, as will be seen also in following sections of text.

Unity

Few passages in the NT are as eloquent in their call for unity as are these verses. The high priestly prayer of Jesus in John 17 is the only other text used as frequently to give a scriptural warrant for the church's struggle for unity. I have already drawn attention to John 17 ("Prayer," TBC for 3:14-21). Both texts stress the central importance of unity for the identity and mission of the church.

In the case of Jesus' prayer (John 17), such unity means fidelity to and participation in the divine Word become flesh. The unity of the Father and the Son becomes the measure of the union believers are to have with each other and especially with God and his Christ. In Ephesians 4, unity means fidelity to the apostolic and prophetic foundation; it means being *chained together in peace* (4:3); it especially means *growing together into Christ* (4:16) and thereby into union with God (4:6).

Such unity requires deliberate and energetic adherence to *the faith*. In both the Gospel of John and Ephesians, the call for unity is understood to have the potential to cause renewed division. When unity is to be found specifically in union with Christ, then who that Christ is believed to be also becomes a critical point of division (the Johannine letters illustrate this for that community; the pastoral letters for the Pauline churches). Unity is always more than unity among people, even Christians. The unity for which Jesus prays in John 17 and to which Ephesians 4 exhorts is the unity of all together *with and in Christ*.

Unity Virtues

To be one with Christ is to participate in his mode of being. This accounts for the central place of the virtues of unity—*humility, gentleness,* and *patience.*

In Judaism, the "piety of the poor" valued *humility* as the proper stance of the believer. God has a special preference for the poor, and so those who want to enjoy God's favor need to humble themselves (Grundmann, 1972:6, 11-15; cf. esp. the Beatitudes in Matt. 5:3-12; 1QS 4.2-6). However, in the wider Hellenistic world, such humbling of oneself was seen more as humiliation, self-denigration, and servility unbecoming of self-respecting free persons (Grundmann, 1972:1-5).

In the Pauline view, such a slavelike stance is precisely what makes church life possible. Nowhere is this more clearly seen than in Philippians 2:3-11, where Christ himself models such *humility* by choosing the form of an obedient slave over equality with God. In Ephesians, it is the servile captive of that Christ (4:1) who calls on believers to make themselves slaves to each other, prisoners to each others' needs. That is their high calling, just as it was for Christ and for their apostle (3:8; cf. 1 Cor. 4:8-13 and 2 Cor. 4:7-12). They have been empowered for humble servanthood (cf. 5:21).

Gentleness is a virtual synonym of *humility* in Christian usage, but in wider Greek use it communicates friendliness more than servility. By placing these two terms next to each other, the self-denigration suggested with *humility* is mitigated by the *gentleness* expected of friends. Such use of vocabulary is consistent with earlier Pauline letters. In 1 Corinthians 4:20-21, for example, Paul places "gentleness" opposite "the rod" as alternative ways for him to exercise power in relation to the Corinthians. *Gentleness* is one of the manifestations of divine empowerment, one of the fruits of the Spirit in Galatians 5:23.

Patience, also listed by Paul in Galatians 5:22 as one of the fruits of the Spirit, literally means "long temper" (as opposed to "short temper"; Lincoln: 236; Thurston: 123). An essential element of community, it refers to the ability to put up with each other. If, however, such patience is to be anything other than a stoic "putting up with," it needs to be a *chosen* disposition of respect and love for the sister and the brother.

Gifts

The most immediate point of both contact and contrast is with other Pauline texts that deal with "gifts"—Romans 12 and 1 Corinthians 12 (Eph. 4:11, notes). The following renders the three texts literally:

Rom. 12:6-8	1 Cor. 12:8-10, 28	Eph. 4:11
having gifts *(charismata)* that differ according to the grace *(charis)* given to us, prophecy ministry *(diakonia)* one teaches another exhorts another shares another leads another shows mercy	given through the Spirit a word of wisdom a word of knowledge faith gifts *(charismata)* of healing works of power prophecy discernment of spirits various kinds of tongues interpretation of tongues [. . .] God has appointed first apostles second prophets third teachers then miracles gifts *(charismata)* of healing helping administration kinds of tongues	[Christ] himself gave apostles prophets evangelists pastors teachers

Careful comparison reveals that in Romans 12:6-8 and 1 Corinthians 12:8-10, the important word is *gifts* (*charismata,* related to *charis,* "grace" or "gift"). The lists show a diversity of gifts, with little apparent attention to whether they are given to only some persons then recognized as holding an "office." Most scholars believe correctly that *function* rather than *office* marks these passages. Even 1 Corinthians 12:28, which appears initially to rank church officials, continues the list after *teachers* with functions rather than with the functionaries themselves. The impression is clearly left that *everyone* in the church has some gift for the common good (12:7).

Despite the emphasis on gifts and grace in Ephesians 4:7, the term *charismata,* "gracious gifts," is absent from Ephesians. Does this suggest that Ephesians represents a development away from the early "charismatic" church life to more organized and defined church "offices," as many argue? Perhaps so. That is of less significance, however, than how Ephesians engages this increasing institutionalization. Our analysis in the notes has shown that the author views the gifts—however specialized in defined roles—as enabling the *whole* church to practice its ministry of building up the body.

The Peaceable Warrior

Psalm 68:18 is not the only war-text that is used and transformed in Ephesians. Isaiah 59:17 will be taken up in 6:14-17 and radically transformed (6:10-20, notes). Biblical traditions were appropriated with great creativity in light of the surprising gift of Christ. In Ephesians, such appropriation and transformation takes place particularly in light of the special grace toward those once on the outside, the Gentiles. Such freedom to adapt stands in some contrast to the carefulness a commentator exercises to recapture as closely as possible the intentions and meanings of biblical texts. However ironic, without such care, the bracing freedom and inspired creativity of biblical writers observed in such reworking of biblical texts would go unnoticed. In this way, careful and meticulous exegesis becomes the pursuit of the wondrous ways of the Spirit.

THE TEXT IN THE LIFE OF THE CHURCH

Unity and Peace

We discover in verse 3 a pacifism eager to keep the unity of the Spirit. It is a pacifism, moreover, that exhibits itself in the irenic and ironic energy and power of meekness. Meekness-values are historically endemic to the culture of Anabaptist piety. Today, however, they are often suspect as displaying weakness or at least reluctance to become involved. For the most part, the phrase *"die Stillen im Lande"* ("the quiet in the land," as applied to churches separated from larger society) is increasingly an epithet, not a compliment.

In Ephesians, meekness and patience are the mode in which the high calling of God's sons and daughters is lived out. Can humility and deference be recovered by a generation increasingly distant from the culture of meekness? Our text suggests that the unity of the church depends on such pacifism.

Unity and Diversity of Belief

At the same time, unity as envisioned in Ephesians 4 is not simply the result of deference to the opinions of others, least of all the avoidance of conflict over fundamental issues of faith and practice. Such a unity would not be the unity of *faith*, but the unity of fools tossed about by every wind of human teaching (4:14). God-given unity is brought about by the wind of God, the Spirit (4:3). It is a unity of adherence to the *one body*, the *one Lord*, and the *one God*. It is, further, a unity that goes beyond the microcosm of the local congregation. This letter is written quite consciously to the church as a whole.

A double-edged challenge emerges at this point. On one hand, the sectarianism of the believers church tradition, as that designation suggests, has resulted from making adherence to the one Lord in both belief and practice the test of unity. The effect has often been to make the circle of unity tight. The smaller the circle, the greater the faithfulness and the more intense the unity—an understandable rationale. We know from Anabaptist history that when such circles of unity become too tight and too small, unity becomes suffocating uniformity, not the unity of the *reconciling* body of the cosmic Christ.

Ephesians is sympathetic to drawing the line sharply between truth and falsehood, between light and darkness, both in matters of belief (4:4-6) and practice (4:17—5:21). At the same time, its vision of the church as the reconciled body of the one who is *gathering up* **all** *things* (1:10) at the behest of the one who is *Father of* **all** *families* (3:14) condemns all *intentional* sectarianism. In other words, being labeled a sect or a minority may be the predictable result of faithfulness to Christ. But for those who follow and embody the Christ who is engaged in re-creating humanity as a whole, such a status is at best a *lamented* effect of faithfulness. The church must have the courage to be "separate," but only for purposes of the larger inclusion of all things. In short, a smug minority sells short the all-embracing reach of Christ's reconciliation.

Our text also stands in critical relationship to the "catholicism" that came after the writing of Ephesians. Notwithstanding its service as a prooftext for such efforts, it also asks critical questions about attempts at organizational and structural unity. The stress in our text is on unity made possible and enlivened by the *Spirit* (4:3) and defined by adherence to the sevenfold "ones" (4:4-6). Unity born of the lowest common denominator is thus no more faithful to the vision represented here than is a smug separatism.

Leadership and Empowerment

With respect to ministry, our text has been read from early times in quite different ways. Some have read it as supporting a clearly defined leadership stratum in the church, as can be seen in the Roman Catholic and Reformation traditions (Schnackenburg: 328-31, surveys the history of interpretation). Others have read it through the lens of 1 Corinthians 12 and thus interpret it in an egalitarian way. One might characterize this as the tension between spiritual gift (as in 1 Cor. 12) and office. Still others, as do I, read the text as *reflecting* an emerging officialdom in the church, but *engaging* that development critically in the light of Christ. As such, the text offers some important challenges to contemporary churches, regardless of where they find themselves structurally on the gift-office spectrum.

In the believers church tradition, for example, there are various models. At one end of the spectrum are congregations with a single pastor as CEO, religious expert, and jack-of-all-trades (J. H. Yoder, 1987:5, 59). At the other end is egalitarianism, with all members sharing in ministry. In such congregations, leadership may be ill-defined or at most strictly functional and temporary, as in some fellowships and house-churches (for helpful studies of models of ministry in the believers church tradition, see J. H. Yoder, 1987; Bauman; D. B. Eller; Esau; Lebold: 24-31; Toews: 217-37).

Most congregations inhabit the large and fluid middle ground: ministry happens through a professional ministerial staff, an array of committees, and the informal efforts of members generally. Leadership (usually exercised by "ministers," egalitarian disclaimers notwithstanding) is often heavily bureaucratized at both congregational and denominational levels. Leaders are as often as not chosen for their skills at, and training for, getting jobs done. Often endangered, absent, or unacknowledged is leadership (paid or unpaid, professionally trained or experientially forged) that is grounded in character, piety, or spirituality (as endowed by the Spirit and expressed in a life of humble self-sacrifice to the church).

The frequently conflictual relationships between congregations and their pastors over questions of leadership and expectations of ministry are born of a volatile mix. First, members may have a lingering memory of other more participatory albeit also more authoritarian models, such as an unpaid multiple ministry of elders—"the bench." Second, congregations may express a burgeoning demand for competent and trained professional pastoral staff. Third, members may have a matching wariness of any expertise that would disenfranchise "ordinary" members of the congregation. Fourth, they usually have a shared sense, regardless of where persons or congregations find themselves on the spectrum, that getting the relationships and structures of ministry right goes to the heart of being a faithful church.

How does our text relate to these concerns? Great respect is shown in Ephesians 4 for those entrusted with the leadership of the church. They are nothing less than the *gifts* the *head* gives to the *body*. Do congregations accord their leadership the grateful reception befitting Christ's gifts? The temptation not to do so is as old as the church and is addressed in the earliest of NT writings (cf., e.g., 1 Thess. 5:12-13; 2 Cor. 8–12).

Pastors and other leaders might ask themselves the equally hard question: Do we see ourselves and comport ourselves as Christ's gifts? For such a relationship between leaders and congregations to be present, our text insists, such leaders must see themselves as *at least* gifts of Christ but also *no more* than gifts for the ministry of *all* the saints (4:12-16, notes on analogy of coaching staff).

For this to be true, *leadership* and *ministry* must not be treated as synonyms. Stated differently, leadership is only one specific form of ministry. As exercised by apostles, prophets, evangelists, pastors, and teachers, leadership is the ministry of enablement (cf. 3:7; cf. 1 Cor. 3:5; 2 Cor. 6:3-4). Leaders offer service or ministry as they enable the whole body, more specifically each and all of its individual parts together, to perform the ministry of building up the body of Christ. This does not exclude leaders from participating in the broader ministry of the body. As "player coaches," they enable others by modeling what selfless and caring ministry looks like. But as leaders, their participation in the ministry of the saints as a whole (4:12) finds its characteristic expression in enabling and equipping all the saints.

Diversity of expertise is mandatory (4:12-16, notes on sports team). There is room and need for the specific skills we today identify with professional expertise. But the fact remains unchanged that *ministry* is as comprehensive and as diverse a task as are the individual parts together constituting a body.

Authority and Servanthood

Can authority and servanthood coexist in the same person(s)? The answer *must* be yes if Christ is to be the model for leaders. Paul understood well that this issue goes to the heart of what it means to confess that the one who took on the form of a slave is "Lord" (Phil. 2:5-11). It goes to the heart of Paul's apostleship as a slave of the congregations for which he was responsible (1 Cor. 4). A servant-leader, a "slave-lord," was difficult for the Corinthians to accept then (2 Cor.

10–13); it is almost impossible for congregations to accept today, just as it is for their leaders who are taught to view themselves as experts, consultants, and CEOs.

Then as now, the concept of a leader who is truly a servant rubs hard against prevailing assumptions about how expertise goes together with income, power, and status. Even if one should be wary of the centralization of ministerial tasks in the one hired pastor, priest, or "minister" (J. H. Yoder, 1987:1-8), it may be, ironically, that it is the jack-of-all-trades who is in the best position to express such servanthood.

Even so, to relax *either* servanthood *or* authority in this tension-filled image fundamentally subverts Christ's lordship, renders Jesus and his apostle Paul unintelligible, and subverts this text's ability to renew the church's ministry. If we relax the tension between authority and servanthood, it will render the ministry of the leaders a betrayal of the Lord in whose name they exercise leadership. It will also render the church unable to recognize and acknowledge the leadership and ministry of true servants in its midst who fall outside the definitions of professional competence and training.

Leaders as Diverse Gifts

The list of *gifts* in verse 11 is, of course, not a complete inventory of leadership functions nor is it intended to be (contra Best, 1998:393). Even if we restrict ourselves to the larger collection of Pauline letters, we find other leader-*gifts:* "bishops" (Phil. 1:1; 1 Tim. 3:1; Titus 1:7), "elders" (1 Tim. 5:1-2, 17-21; cf., e.g., Acts 20:17; 21:18), "deacons" (male and female; e.g., Rom. 16:1; Phil. 1:1), "presidents" (male and female; Rom. 16:2; 1 Thess. 5:12), and "widows" (1 Tim. 5:3-16). Various church traditions have institutionalized these diverse *gifts*, functions, or offices in different ways.

Our text shows little if any interest in the issue of structure or institution. Instead, it asks whether those who inhabit the various functions or offices serve to empower a church made up of a host of diverse individuals, enabling them together as a body to perform the work of ministry of building up the body of Christ. That is the far more important question than which structure a church has.

Structures themselves do little to empower. The most egalitarian structures can suffocate the growth and mission of the church if they inhibit or even prohibit the exercise of the diverse ministries, one of which is leadership. Conversely, those who exercise their structure-given authority as slaves of the people can wonderfully subvert the most hierarchical and ostensibly oppressive structures. This text forces *all* to reorient themselves *together* to build up the body until *all together* arrive at the unity of the Son of God, at the fullness of Christ.

Discipleship and Mission

The *head* into which the *body* grows is *Christ*, the one in whom *all things* and *all people* are being gathered (1:10), the one in whom both *the near* and *the far* are gathered and made into one new humanity (2:13-18). This means that the growth envisioned in verse 13 is *intensive* (discipleship) and also necessarily *extensive* (mission).

This passage must not be read apart from the great peace text in 2:11-22. The church grows into the Christ who is peace (2:14) to the degree to which it participates in the healing of the cosmos in all its dimensions. This includes reconciliation between warring peoples, reconciliation of the alienated and lost with their loving divine parent, restoring people to their full humanity, and not least the reconciliation of *all things* with God in Christ.

Such a view welcomes the impatience of various church-growth movements to see persons find God. But it is deeply suspicious of any notion of church that would betray the *inclusive* nature of the church racially, ethnically, and socioeconomically (Yoder Neufeld, 1999a:69-82). A church that is homogeneous *by design* is no longer the body of the Christ who fuses enemies and strangers into *one new humanity* (2:15), nor is it the church of the one who is *Father of **all families*** (3:14-15, TRYN).

A church insensitive to attempts at healing conflicts in the world (peacemaking or peacebuilding, justice-making, conflict resolution, mediation, hunger relief, and development) and to the need for restoring a spoiled earth (ecology)—that church is not growing into the Christ in(to) whom **all things** are being gathered (1:10). On the other hand, a church callous to the fate of unforgiven, unreconciled, and spiritually unrestored persons is also not growing into the Christ whose peace-work opens up access to God, membership in God's family, and the joy of worship in the presence of God (2:18-22; 5:18-20).

We urgently need a vision of mission as integrated as the one that informs Ephesians. In this vision, peace with God and peace on earth are experienced, understood, articulated, witnessed to, and struggled for as one seamless whole, woven on the loom of God's gracious, loving, and mysterious will (cf. Eph. 1).

Ephesians 4:17—5:2

The Old and the New Human: Two Ways of Walking

PREVIEW

It is rather artificial to break up 4:1—5:21 into distinct sections. Even so, we are helped by stylistic and thematic features to mark off distinct parts of the text for the sake of manageability. Ephesians 4:17 repeats the *therefore (oun)* initiating the exhortation section in 4:1 (reduced by NIV to *so,* and by NRSV to *now*), thus taking up the exhortation in earnest with an emphatic appeal: *Walk* (NIV and NRSV: *live*) *no longer as the Gentiles do!* The section concludes in 5:2 with an equally emphatic *Walk in love as did Christ! Walk,* as in 2:1-10, serves as an *inclusio* (marking a section by repeating a beginning word or phrase at the end).

Adding to this frame is the contrast between Gentiles *handing themselves over* to vice (4:19) and Christ *handing himself over* to God as an act of sacrificial worship (5:2). The focus of contrasting lifestyles is not brought to a close at 5:2 (cf. *walk* in 5:8, 15, in addition to further contrasts), but the striking contrast between "two ways of walking" serves as a useful theme under which to consider this section of Ephesians.

The contrast between the two modes of life is sharpened here in two ways. First, 4:20-24 challenges readers to recall their bap-

199

tism as a ritual of *taking off* or *putting off the old human (the old anthrōpos)* and *putting on the new human (the new anthrōpos)*—Christ. Second, verses 25-32 illustrate life in *the new human* with exhortations on truth-telling, anger, theft, speech, and grieving the Holy Spirit. Prohibited behavior is contrasted with what should replace it. The contrast is sharpened further in verses 31 and 32 with lists of vices and virtues, likely drawn from Colossians 3:8, 12-13. The first two verses of chapter 5 bring the exhortation to a climax with the call to imitate God and to *walk* like Christ. We hear an echo of 4:1 with its call to *walk in a way worthy of God's calling.*

Here is a summary of the many contrasts in this passage:

the old human	*the new human*
decaying	being renewed
walking like the Gentiles	imitating God
walking like the Gentiles	walking in love as Christ
who have given themselves up	who gave himself up
to every unclean work	for us
alienated from the life of God	forgiven and loved children of God
ignorance	learning
empty mind	renewed in the spirit
darkened thinking	of the mind
the lie	the truth
every evil	the good
stealing	working with one's own hands
rotten language	truthful and grace-full language
bitter, angry, and wrangling	kind, compassionate, and forgiving

As to structure, verses 17-19 form one sentence, as do verses 20-24. Verses 25-32 are shorter sentences exhorting to various kinds of behavior.

Structure of 4:17—5:2

For this reason I testify in the Lord—
  You are no longer to walk as Gentiles.   (4:17-19)

You did not so learn Christ, the truth in Jesus.
  You are to have taken off the old human
  and to have put on the new human.   (4:20-24)

Therefore, having "taken off" the lie—
  • Speak truth with the neighbor.
  • Be angry, but do not sin.
  • No longer steal, rather give to those who need.
  • No rotten words, rather impart grace.
  • Do not grieve the Holy Spirit of God.

- Let all vices [list] be removed from you.
- Rather be like God in Christ [list of virtues].   (4:25-32)

Therefore, be imitators of God
and walk in love just like Christ.   (5:1-2)

OUTLINE

On Not Walking Like Gentiles, 4:17-19

Learning Christ by Putting on the New Human, 4:20-24
    4:20-21   Learning Christ, the Truth in Jesus
    4:22-24   "You Are What You Wear"

No to the Lie and Yes to the Truth, 4:25-32
    4:25   Saying No to the Lie and Speaking Truth
    4:26-27   Sinless Anger
    4:28-29   Meeting Need with Hands and Words
    4:30   On Not Grieving the Holy Spirit
    4:31-32   Contrasting Ways of Relating to Others

Imitating God and Walking Like Christ, 5:1-2

EXPLANATORY NOTES

On Not Walking Like Gentiles 4:17-19

This section begins with an emphatic double statement: *For this reason I therefore declare and testify in the Lord.* Notice first that *therefore* appears as it did in 4:1, indicating the resumption of exhortation premised on grace. As the exhortation of 4:1 was premised on God's grace as explored in the preceding chapters, so now again the exhortation follows necessarily from the rehearsal of Christ as gift-giver and growth-giver (4:7-16).

Testify is a translation of *marturomai,* from which we derive the English term *martyr.* Readers hear the following exhortation as emerging from someone who is a witness *in the Lord* and for that reason is to be heeded. A more intimate tone is set in 1 Thessalonians 2:11-12, where Paul as "father" (2:11) exhorts, encourages, and "testifies to" *(marturomai)* his "children" to "lead a life worthy of God" (cf. Eph. 4:1!). In Ephesians 4:17 the tone is less of parental intimacy and more of apostolic authority. Recall 2 Corinthians 2:17 where Paul speaks as "from God before God in Christ" (TRYN).

As in 4:1, the exhortation has to do with *walking.* This motif first arises in 2:2 (notes; 4:1, notes). Life is not static; it leads somewhere—either to ruin or to *the life of God* (4:18). The direction in which believers are to walk is first suggested by its opposite, the *walk* of the Gentiles. Since most of the recipients of the letter are Gentiles, the use of *Gentile* is here meant to bring to consciousness their former manner of life (cf. 4:22; 2:1-2, 11-12; 5:3-7).

The description of Gentile existence is brutal in both brevity and one-sidedness, owing much to a tradition of Jewish characterizations of Gentile life (TBC). Here its function is to hold up an ugly mirror to the readers, reflecting their former *walk* for purposes of warning, encouragement, and reinforcement of identity. Readers are *no longer* to *walk* as they once did (and presumably are still tempted to do—hence the exhortation). *No longer* fits well the *once-now* schema observed also in chapter 2 (notes) and sets the scene for the baptismal reflections to come in 4:22-24.

Alienation from God and God's will for human life is first a matter of corrupted consciousness, from which flows corrupt behavior. This is sketched in broad strokes with a string of virtually interchangeable images: the *mind (nous)* of such persons who are *alienated from the life of God* (cf. 2:12!) is *futile* (4:17; cf. Rom. 1:21; Wisd. of Sol. 13:1). Their *thinking (dianoia)* is *darkened* (cf. again Rom. 1:21; Wisd. of Sol. 17:2-3, 17, 21). "The light has gone out in the seat of Gentiles' understanding so that they are no longer capable of apprehending ultimate truth" (Lincoln: 277). All this is a result of the *ignorance* residing in them (cf. 1 Pet. 1:14; similarly, Wisd. of Sol. 13:1), a result as much as cause of their alienation from God.

Ignorance thus cannot be claimed as an excuse (cf. Rom. 1:20-22). From a Jewish perspective, Gentile ignorance is culpable ignorance, particularly because of its delusions of knowledge and wisdom (cf. emphasis on delusion in Eph. 4:22; 1 Cor. 1:18-25). The author is not describing "a defect in the ability of his readers to reason" (Best, 1998:417) but an inability or unwillingness to perceive life and its demands in accordance with God's will.

A parallel to ignorance is, not surprisingly, *hardness of heart* (4:18). The *heart* is a virtual synonym for *mind* in the Bible (1:18, notes). *Hardening* is a frequent biblical way of describing resistance to truth or to God (cf. Mark 6:52; 8:17; John 12:40; Rom. 2:5; 2 Cor. 3:14; the prime example is Pharaoh, Exod. 7–14; Rom 9:18). Such *hardness of heart* (Eph. 4:18) leads strikingly to *callousness,* to a "loss of sensitivity to pain," as *apalgeō* can be translated literally (4:19; Liddell and Scott)—in this case moral pain. As the NJB translates it, *Their sense of right and wrong [has been] dulled.*

Once such hardening has happened, people *hand themselves*

over or *deliver themselves up* to licentiousness, every kind of impure practice, and greed. The similarity to Romans 1 is striking, but there Paul says three times that God has *given up* such persons to a life of dissipation (1:24, 26, 28). The verb *paradidomi* is the same term used of Judas handing Jesus over to the authorities (e.g., Matt. 26; Mark 14; Luke 22; John 13). It is the same term used of Jesus in Ephesians 5:2, who *hands himself over* for us as an offering and a sacrifice. Here the term has a tragic and fateful ring to it. These are, after all, the sons and daughters of disobedience, the "walking dead" under the rule of the evil authority of the air (2:1-3). Even so, they have *handed* **themselves** *over* to that authority as living yet deadened sacrifices.

Their life is marked by three interrelated categories of vice, all of which appear repeatedly in lists of vices (Best, 1998:422): *licentiousness, impurity, and greed*. *Licentiousness* or *debauchery (aselgeia)* is already linked with *impurity (akatharsia)* in 2 Corinthians 12:21 and Galatians 5:19, where both are listed with *fornication (porneia)*. Jewish and Jewish-Christian believers viewed sexual sin as a representative affront to the holiness of God and characteristic of "unclean" Gentiles and their idolatry (cf., e.g., Wisd. of Sol. 14:26). Tellingly, this trio of vices is echoed in 5:3, 5, with the exception that *fornication* has replaced *licentiousness*.

The concern about *purity* has in this instance less to do with personal spiritual and moral hygiene, as important as that is, than with the fact that Gentile readers are now a part of God's holy temple (2:21-22). God's home cannot abide the defilements of sin *(every unclean work)* so heedlessly engaged in by those whose minds and hearts have become inured to purity and holiness (cf. also 1 Cor. 6:9-20).

Greed (pleonexia) here signifies the force that drives *license* and *impurity* (NRSV: *greedy to practice*). Some link it more closely to sex by translating it as *lust* (e.g., NIV). While that restricts its meaning too much, it draws attention to the fact that greed as *insatiability* is at the root of sexual excess as well. In that sense, sexual sin is symbolic of all other greed, the most prevalent being not sexual but economic! Biblically, *all* such greed is closely linked to *idolatry*, as is explicitly the case in 5:5 (cf. Col. 3:5; also Rom. 1:29 in light of Rom. 1:24-25; 1 Cor. 5:9-13; Isa. 2:6-20).

Such a bleak picture of *the Gentiles* might easily play into moral arrogance toward outsiders. However, its purpose here is to hold up a mirror to *the saints*, reminding them of their *former* way of life and regrettably also their *present walk*. This is, after all, exhortation. In this way the finger pointed at them becomes a prophetic/ apostolic word reminiscent of the OT, where such a mix of motifs of debauchery, ignorance, darkness, and hardness of heart is used to depict *Israel's* apostasy (cf., e.g., Isa. 59, which furnishes an important background to Eph. 6:10-20).

The author thus attempts to create a chasm between who the readers *once* were and who they are *now* to be. Another example of how such stereotyping of a life of vice could be used *within* the church is found in 2 Peter 2, which characterizes false teachers in much the same way: ignorance, deceit, falsehood, and moral turpitude (Charles: 237-44). In short, the walk of the Gentiles is perilously near for both new and seasoned believers.

Learning Christ by Putting on the New Human 4:20-24

4:20-21 Learning Christ, the Truth in Jesus

Pointing a finger at others is not at the heart of the exhortation. Instead, at its heart is a summons to a new life, reminding readers what it means that they were baptized into Christ and thereby have embarked on a course of learning and discipleship. Again, the contrast to the former way of life is stated emphatically: *But you did not so learn Christ.* As Barth puts it, "You have become students of the Messiah" (1974:504). Being faithful believers is a matter of learning how to walk in the school of Christ. The term for *learning (manthanō)* is the verb form of *disciple (mathētēs).*

The turn of phrase—*learning Christ*—is surprising and indeed unparalleled. Some versions try to clarify it: *learning about Christ* (TEV) or *coming to know Christ* (NIV). Most correctly retain the peculiar *learning Christ.* Similarly, Colossians 2:6-7 combines "receiving" with "being taught." "As you therefore *received* Christ Jesus the Lord, walk in him, rooted and built up in him and established in faith *just as you were taught,* abounding in thanksgiving" (TRYN).

Does "learning Christ" mean learning the tradition "about Christ"? (so Lincoln: 279; Schnackenburg: 199). Yes, but that is too limited. In Colossians, what has been taught and what has been received is a *person* rather than a teaching *about* him—though that surely would not have been excluded from any instruction in the faith. We recall the prominence given to teaching ministries in the gifts listed in Ephesians 4:11. Clearly, teaching is more than imparting facts and dogmas; learning is more than the acquisition of information. It is *growing into Christ* (4:13, 16), becoming more fully a part of Christ as *members of Christ's body* (cf. the similar "Christ being formed in believers,"

Gal. 4:19). To *learn Christ* is to encounter and commune with the risen Christ present in the church (so also Best, 1998:426-7). Hence the clause *You were taught in him* (Eph. 4:21).

Verse 21 repeats the clause encountered in 3:2, *if indeed you heard.* Here it is a reminder of what the author can assume has been heard and taught to the recipients of the letter. It is the premise upon which the author builds his appeal *(if indeed you heard and were taught in him)*. However, just as in 3:2, the turn of phrase carries an implicit invitation to self-examination. Also as in 3:2, the phrase serves to introduce a major emphasis: there it was to rehearse the content of the apostolic legacy; here it refers to what it means to *learn Christ.*

Believers are said to have been *taught in him,* meaning *in Christ. In* can have spatial and instrumental meaning, but can also express agency *["In"].* Believers learn *within* Christ as members of his body (1:23; 2:15-16; 3:16-17; 4:15-16); they learn as those who have been raised to life *with* Christ (2:5-6); they are taught to live by what they see *in* Christ; finally, they are taught *by* Christ. We should resist choosing one interpretation over another. Through his example (2:14-18; 5:21-33), his gifts *(apostles . . . and teachers,* 4:11), and his Spirit (1:17; 3:5, 16; 4:3-4; note that in 5:18-21, *being subject to each other* is a consequence of *being filled with the Spirit;* cf. 6:4, notes), the risen Lord is himself the teacher of the church.

The following phrase is as puzzling as *learning Christ. As truth is in Jesus* ties truth to the specific person of Jesus. It is relatively rare in Pauline letters to refer to *Jesus* without the addition of "Lord" or "Christ" (Rom. 3:26; 8:11; 1 Cor. 12:3; 2 Cor. 4:10-11, 14; 11:4; Gal. 6:17; Phil. 2:10; 1 Thess. 1:10; 4:14). Surely the author intends to draw specific attention to Jesus in a way "Christ" or "him" would not have accomplished. But why? He may want to point to the content of what is to be learned, in particular the life, death, and resurrection of the man Jesus (Schnackenburg: 199). The evidence is too scanty for us to see the phrase as referring to traditions of Jesus' sayings and deeds as recorded in the Gospels.

More likely, it refers to the faithfulness of Jesus in giving himself entirely to God and to humanity, to the point of giving the ultimate gift of love, his life (2:14-16; 5:2! cf. Phil. 2:6-11). In other words, *learning Christ* must have content in terms of the life of the man *Jesus.* It is that man who is to be followed (so also Best, 1998:429-30). Such *truth* (known in following Jesus) is vulnerable to being ignored in favor of truths *about* Jesus, which more easily allow believers to avoid the implications of that example for them as participants *in Christ.*

4:22-24 "You Are What You Wear"

With three interrelated infinitives, verses 22-24 continue the sentence begun in verse 20. They are sometimes translated as imperatives (e.g., REB), but should be seen as dependent on the verb *you were taught* (so correctly NIV, NRSV, and most versions). The essential gist is as follows: *You were taught, in keeping with the truth which is in Jesus*, first, *to have taken off the old human*, second, *to be renewed in mind*, and third, *to have put on the new human*. The exhortation is thereby inextricably related to the identity believers have in Christ.

One might well choose as rubric for this motif Letty Russell's "a change of uniform" (81) or the well-known aphorism "You are what you wear." The specific vocabulary of *taking off* and *putting on* likely reflects the baptismal ritual in Pauline churches (TBC). Here it is dependent on the imagery and thought pattern found in Colossians 3:9-10, where it is part of a larger context of having died and risen with Christ (Col. 2:20; 3:1; note also the baptismal formula in Col. 3:11; cf. Gal. 3:27-28; Best, 1998:431-3, doubts the connection with Col.). Dependency on Colossians is by no means simple copying, however, as the following chart illustrates (e.g., see how the terms for *new, kainos* and *neos, can be interchanged*):

Ephesians 4:22-24	Colossians 3:9-10
put off *(apotithēmi)*	take off *(apekduomai)*
the old human *(anthrōpos)*	the old human *(anthōpos)*
renewed *(ananeoomai)*	renewed *(anakainoomai)*
in the spirit of your minds	in knowledge
put on the new human	put on the new [human]
(kainos anthrōpos)	*(neos [anthrōpos])*
created according to *(kata)*	according to *(kata)*
God	the image of its creator

Together these texts are witness to the importance of baptism in Pauline churches and to the creativity with which exhortation could appeal to baptism.

The basis of exhortation is that believers have left behind an old life and taken up a new one (the first and third infinitives are in the past tense), expressed in terms of *taking off the old human (anthrōpos)* and *putting on the new human (anthrōpos)*. Does this refer to the individual's nature or orientation? Or is something larger at stake? Romans 6:6 speaks of *our old anthrōpos* being crucified with Christ, which lends a somewhat individualistic understanding to *anthrōpos* ("self," NIV, NRSV; cf. 2 Cor. 4:16, referring to the "outer" and the "inner *anthrōpos*"; Shillington: 105-7). Most versions cast this phrase in Ephesians 4:24 individualistically as *self* (NRSV, NIV, NASB, TEV) or psychologically as *human nature* (REB).

However, chapter 2 already introduced *kainos anthrōpos* as referring to hostile and fractious humanity reconstituted in Christ as *the new human* (2:15, notes). The NJB recognizes this by making a distinction, translating *old anthrōpos* as the *old self* and the *new anthrōpos* as the *New Man* [sic], indicating an awareness of the connection to 2:15 and also to 4:13 *(the perfect Man)*. There is no reason, however, to conceive of the *old anthrōpos* as any less comprehensive than the *new*.

At the core of this imagery is the fundamental issue of what it means to be human. In Ephesians, this is definitely *not* understood individualistically. Human identity is understood both negatively and positively to be shaped by corporate experience (cf. 2:1-3, 15-16; 4:1-16, 17-19). People either participate in "the first Adam," to put it in language not used here but which informs the author's "anthropology," or they participate through Christ's peace in the "new Adam" (cf. esp. Rom. 5:12-21; 1 Cor. 15:45-49). To speak of *the old human* and *the new human* is a way of describing a "culture of humanness" more than any one individual's character (so also Martin, 1993:152, on Col. 3:9-10).

The *old* way of being human is marked by decay, by the rot that sets in through deceitful desire (cf. 4:17-19; 2:1-3). This is "life" lived in a pact with death (cf. Prov. 8:36; Isa. 28:15, 18; Wisd. of Sol. 1:16—2:24). It is the "life" readers of this letter *once* lived. The presence of this urgent exhortation shows that they *still* struggle not to live it. After all, their *new* life takes place in the midst of and alongside sons and daughters of disobedience (2:2). Believers in Christ are "in the world but not of it," as John 17 says, and for that reason are in a constant struggle to define themselves over against the world (5:3-21). Such a struggle takes place in each individual, to be sure. However, both *old human* and *new human* point to an intricately interconnected social and cultural existence in which values and imagination are forged on an anvil much larger than the individual human mind or heart.

In contrast to *the old human, the new human* is Christ. Christ is the *head* attached to a *body* (4:15) made up of many individual members (4:7, 16). Christ is *the new human* (2:15) *created according to God* (4:24; 2:10). This is a new "self," but a self large enough to encompass the whole church and more—the same *new anthrōpos (human)* in(to) whom all things are being gathered (1:10; contra Best, 1998:439-40, who individualizes the *new anthrōpos* radically throughout Ephesians). The identity of individual believers is defined by the whole—Christ. So the struggle to live as *the new human* in a world in which the *old human* is still much "alive" is not one engaged in alone but *together* with other members of the body of Christ. *Putting on the new human* (4:24) is another way of referring to becoming one with the body of Christ and together with others growing into Christ (4:15-16).

The use of the past tense in the first and third infinitives (*to have taken off* in 4:22, and *to have put on* in 4:24) can leave the impression of a past momentary experience of conversion and/or baptism. In these verses, however, the radically transformative imagery of baptism is linked with the motif of *hearing, teaching,* and *learning* (4:20-21). This implies a *moment* of transformation and also a *process* of formation. While initiated and undergirded by grace (cf. 2:5, 8), life in *the new human* requires all the energy, discipline, and effort believers can muster, individually and together (4:11-16).

In keeping with this insight, the second infinitive *to be renewed* (passive) or *to renew [yourselves]* (middle, acting on oneself) is in the present tense, implying ongoing present experience. Recall the similar Romans 12:2: "Be transformed by the renewing of [your] mind." Surprisingly, such a "passive" experience as the renewal of the mind is stated in Romans 12 as an *imperative*. Here the reminder about *having been taught* (past tense, 4:21) *to be renewed* (present tense! 4:23) carries an implicit imperative. Renewal of *the spirit of the mind* is an ongoing process related to *hearing, teaching,* and *learning Christ*.

The phrase *the spirit of your* (pl.) *mind* is as puzzling as it is unique. Notice the variety of translations. NRSV translates fairly literally *in the spirit of your minds*. Others are more interpretive: *in the attitude of your minds* (NIV); *acquire a fresh, spiritual way of thinking* (NAB); *your mind renewed in spirit* (NJB); *in mind and spirit* (REB); *hearts and minds* (TEV). Interpreters typically take one of two paths. One is to take *spirit* as more or less synonymous with "mind," "heart," or "inner person" (cf. 4:18; 3:16-17, but see notes; cf., e.g., Barth, 1974:508-9; Best, 1998:436; Lincoln: 287). The other takes *spirit* to refer to the divine Spirit, whatever the grammatical difficulties (e.g., Houlden: 319; Schnackenburg: 200).

Gordon Fee has taken into account both interpretations. In his view, early readers would have taken *spirit* to refer first to the "human spirit," as we should. But they and we should "be prepared also to recognize the Holy Spirit as hovering nearby," the agent and power of renewal (Fee, 1987:712). As stated repeatedly in this commentary, where grammatical ambiguity invites equally important and illuminating readings consistent with the gist of the letter as a whole, one should resist resolving the ambiguity.

Verse 24 draws attention specifically to the creation of *the new human* (cf. 2:10, 15). *The new human* has been created *according to God (kata theon)* in (or *with* ["*In*"]) *righteousness* (or *justice, uprightness* [NJB]), *and in* (or *with*) *holiness of the truth.* NRSV and many other versions correctly understand the phrase *according to God* as referring to the image of God: *according to the image of the one who created him* (cf. Gen. 1:26; not as obvious as in Col. 3:10). Believers put on *the new human*—Christ—and thus become *like* God (cf. 5:1!); they become part of the *new human* who has been *created in justice and holiness of the truth.*

Translations vary greatly in how they render this last phrase. Along with the NIV and NRSV, most take *the truth* adjectivally (e.g., *true righteousness*). There is every reason, however, to allow *the truth* a higher profile, as the following contrast in verse 25 regarding *the lie* will show. *The truth* is characterized by both *righteousness* or *justice* (both equally well translate the Greek *dikaiosunē*) and *holiness*. This is a familiar pairing. God, for example, is characterized by *justice* and *holiness* (Deut. 32:4, LXX; Ps. 145:17 [144:17, LXX]; cf. also Luke 1:75; Wisd. of Sol. 9:3).

Truth and *God* are inextricably linked as well, as are *doing* or *speaking the truth in love* and *growing into Christ* in 4:15. *Truth* is thus intended to encompass reality as shaped and re-created by God in Christ. *Truth* is a rubric for life as the *new human*. Should we be surprised to find it as the first item of the armor of God in 6:14? To speak of *righteousness* and *holiness* as "virtues" (Lincoln: 288) is not wrong, but it does undervalue their roles as divine gifts and as modes of participation in the *new human*.

No to the Lie and Yes to the Truth 4:25-32

4:25 Saying No to the Lie and Speaking Truth

Putting off the lie in verse 25 echoes *putting off the old human* in verse 22. Several translations (e.g., NIV, NJB, REB) take the aorist participle as an imperative, as is grammatically possible. However, the aorist participle can also serve, as I have translated, to express the basis for the subsequent appeal: *Since you have put off the lie,"* where *the lie* is the equivalent to *the old human*.

As in the case of *the truth* in verse 24, translators typically underplay the significance of *the lie*. No doubt under impact of the subsequent command *to speak truth with the neighbor*, they see in this little more than a prohibition against lying, the first in a series of prohibitions running to the end of verse 31 (cf. Col. 3:8-9). However, the use of the noun *the lie* and the strong echo of *to put off* or *take off* in 4:22, suggest that in Ephesians *the lie* stands for much more than making statements that are not true. This parallels *the truth* in verse 24 being much more than a matter of words that are trustworthy (notes on 4:15, 21; and 6:14). *The lie* represents nothing less than *the old human* in rebellion against God (cf. Rom. 1:25; so also Barth, 1974:511; contra Best, 1998:445; Lincoln: 300).

Deception of self and of others is often used in the Bible to describe a society in rebellion against God. Zechariah, from where the injunction to *speak truth with the neighbor* is taken (Zech. 8:16; cf. Lev. 19:17-18), identifies love of "false oaths" as a fundamental characteristic of rebellion against God (see esp. Zech. 8:17; cf. also Lev. 19:11, 15-16). Isaiah 59, which underlies 6:14-17, also makes the absence of truth the hallmark of an unjust society ripe for judgment (esp. Isa. 59:3-4, 13-15). *The lie* is thus not simply "telling a lie"; it is shorthand for the life of the *old human*. *The lie* refers to callous disregard for truth in relationships, inside and outside the church, in both private and public spheres. But it refers just as well to the fundamental misreading of reality by those who mistake slavery for freedom, and such "freedom" for impunity (cf. 2:1-3; 4:17-19; 5:3-5).

In verse 14 the author has warned about no longer living as infants vulnerable to the deceits and wiles of those who would lead them astray. Now 4:25-32 treats old and new ways of walking, the old human and the new human, and the truth and the lie as an essential part of exhortation. And the exhortation is directed to those who already have (past tense!) *put on the new human*—Christ.

This tells us that, despite all the reminders of what was *once* the case and assurances of what is *now* true, the "culture" of the old way of being human remains the context in which the *new human* learns to exercise *justice* and *holy truth*. However much believers are *holy ones* **already** *in the heavenlies with Christ* (2:5-6), their identification with Christ is lived out in immediate proximity to *the lie*. Light shines in and into the darkness (5:8-14; cf. John 1:5), even when found in the lives of believers.

The reference to *speaking the truth with the neighbor* (4:25) must then also mean more than simply "telling the truth to the neighbor." It is surely shorthand for living the life of *the new human* (cf. 4:24). The words are virtually identical with Zechariah 8:16. But since there is no quotation formula that introduces the phrase, we cannot be absolutely sure the author is specifically quoting Scripture. He may have simply drawn it from Jewish ethical tradition (so Best, 1998:446; Lincoln: 300; cf., e.g., Test. Dan 5:1-2). However, since Ephesians frequently cites the OT, and since Zechariah 8 resonates with the concerns in Ephesians, it is likely that the author is consciously quoting Zechariah.

There is, however, one small difference between Ephesians 4:25 and Zechariah 8:6, LXX. Zechariah has "to *(pros)*" rather than *with (meta) the neighbor,* as in Ephesians. Speaking "to" the neighbor is of course to be speaking "*with*" or "*in the presence of*" the neighbor. But the nuance is somewhat different. *Speaking truth* is what believers do together, *each* **with** *his neighbor, since we are members of each other.* This can imply the sometimes hard words of loving confrontation (see Eph. 4:26!), but it can also suggest the truth members of the body speak together—to each other and to the world, including to the powers (3:10; 6:14).

Notice, incidentally, that in Zechariah 8, *truth* and *peace* are practiced before an audience of Gentiles who through this witness have their interest in God awakened (8:18-23). So also in Ephesians the good news of peace goes out to the *near* and the *far* (see esp. 2:13, 17). Hence, though *neighbor* should be taken first to refer to a fellow member of the body of Christ (so also Lincoln: 300; Schnackenburg: 206), nothing precludes the term from having much wider resonance (so also Best, 1998:447). A truthful corporate life is an inherently evangelistic enterprise.

Several exhortations now illustrate what it means to say "No to the Lie and Yes to the Truth." They are not simply prohibitions, however. They are accompanied by a positive alternative to the old way of being human. The prohibitions are in some ways no more than a foil for the real point of the exhortation, to encourage participation in the life of *the new human.*

4:26-27 Sinless Anger

At first glance, the prohibition not to sin in relation to anger seems to be mostly negative: readers are *not* to sin, *not* to let the sun go down on their anger, and *not* to give room for the devil. When read this way, these verses anticipate the prohibition of anger or wrath in 4:31 (cf. Col. 3:8; James 1:19-20). Nursed or unresolved anger appears to be the central concern. To paraphrase: *Deal with your anger before the sun sets, or the devil will get a foothold in your life!* This is, however, not the only or even the best understanding of the text.

The prohibition not to sin in relation to anger is taken verbatim from the Greek translation (LXX) of Psalm 4:4. In the Hebrew, the Psalm text is a warning against sinning when angry, and that is how translators render the Psalm text (NIV: *In your anger do not sin; NRSV: When you are disturbed* [or *angry*], *do not sin.*) In short, deal with your anger before it becomes sin! The Greek, however, has an imperative: *Be angry, but do not sin!* Ephesians evidently employs the Greek version of the Psalm.

One way of explaining this strange text is to understand the imperative as a "concessive" imperative, and thus not really an imperative at all: *Be angry [if you must], but do not sin* (so NIV, NAB, NJB; Barth, 1974:513; Best, 1998:449; Lincoln: 301; Schnackenburg, 207). In this case there is no real difference between the Greek and the Hebrew text of Psalm 4:4. The following clause *Do not let the sun set on your anger* only reinforces the urgency of dealing quickly with anger. In this interpretation it is *anger* that is the problem (cf. 4:31!). And it is sin not to get anger out of the way by sundown. Such anger is an open door through which the devil will find entry.

An alternative interpretation emerges, however, when careful attention is given to the vocabulary of the second sentence in verse 26, in particular the term usually translated as *anger—parorgismos—* which appears only here in noun form in the NT, but several times in the Greek OT. It is best translated as "provocation to anger" rather than "anger" (this is even the case in Jer. 21:5, where it can very well denote God's furious baiting of Zedekiah; contra Lincoln: 302). That is also its meaning when it appears in verb form in Ephesians 6:4: *Fathers, do not provoke your children to anger!*

If *parorgismos* is translated in 4:26 as "that which provokes to anger," then the focus shifts from anger to that which provokes it. The problem is "out there," an objective offense that requires a response, and not the emotional response to that offense. The devil gains a foothold less through anger than through leaving the provocation to anger in place past sundown.

Whose anger is being provoked? On one hand, the command to be angry in verse 26 suggests that it is the readers who are to deal with what has provoked *them* to anger. Without attributing any inherent value to anger, there are things that will and *should* anger those whose view of life is shaped by *the new human*, the indwelling Christ. Injustice and falsehood are provocations to those who have been created for *justice* and *truth* (4:24). More importantly, however, such violations of God's will provoke *God's* anger or wrath. *God's* judgment urges dealing with such matters before sundown.

That understanding of God's will and wrath raises questions: Is it the neighbor's provocation of yourself and/or of God that must be pointed out and dealt with? Or is it your own provocations to anger that must be confessed and corrected? (cf. Ecclus./Sirach 5:4-7!). In either case, these provocations should be dealt with *immediately*.

Ephesians 4:25-26 should be seen as part of a tradition running from Leviticus 19 to Qumran and to Matthew 18 (so also Gnilka: 235-6; TBC). It sees sin as provocation to anger, most importantly, God's wrath. It also draws the implications of Leviticus 19:17 for life in the communal *new human*. In the process, one of the most central concerns of the law—the love of neighbor—has moved to the center of the elaboration of life in the *new human* (2:11-22, notes on the ongoing relevance of the law).

The command in 4:27, *Do not give room to the devil*, is thus more than a call to avoid giving the devil an opening. Speaking *the truth with the neighbor* and dealing with *provocations to wrath* before the sun sets reflect the courageous if sometimes conflictual intervention of love. Just so, *not giving room to the devil* is a matter of courageously opposing the devil. Indeed, this little phrase anticipates the full picture in 6:10-20 of the armed body of Christ confronting *the devil* and his minions with truth, justice, peace, faith, and salvation. The way the devil is denied space is through the courageous and sometimes angry speaking of truth in love whenever there are provocations to divine wrath. We catch a glimpse here of the conflictual dimensions of the gathering in of all things.

4:28-29 *Meeting Need with Hands and Words*

On the surface the commands against *stealing* and *foul language* appear ill suited to serve as paradigmatic or representative exhortations for life as *the new human*. One might, of course, see *stealing* as representing selfishness and greed (cf. 5:3, 5). Likewise, rather than simply "speaking garbage" (Fee, 1987:712), *foul language* might be viewed as communication alienated from *the truth*. It emerges from the mouth of the *old human* (cf. 5:4, 6; cf. also James 3:1-12; 1QS 7.2-11).

The real weight in these two exhortations falls not on stealing and rotten speech, however, but on the alternative. *The new human* does not steal, but *works the good with the hands*. Such labor is not for self, which can itself be a form of stealing within God's economy. It is performed *in order to have something to share with the one who has need*. Members of *the new human* do not speak *rotten* words, but *good* words, again, not for the sake of personal purity, but *for the building up of that which is lacking, so that [the words] might give grace to those who hear*. The references to stealing and trash talking are thus little more than foils (contrasts) to bring out the real emphasis in these exhortations—living for the well-being of others.

Here we encounter up close the *good works* prepared by God for those who have been *saved by grace* (2:8-10): laboring to meet the needs of others, building up those in need, and dispensing grace to those with ears to hear. Although the injunctions are general and find echoes in many other biblical and nonbiblical texts, they are powerful. Indeed, the specific wording may hint at the imitation of Paul, who says that he "worked hard with his own hands" (1 Cor. 4:12; cf. 9:6).

Speaking words that bring grace to those who hear is also evocative of the prime task of the apostle: to bring words of healing, grace, and salvation to those who hear (e.g., 3:7-10; 6:19-20; cf. Rom. 10:5-17; 2 Cor. 5:20—6:13). In short, an apostolic mission awaits those who turn their back on the old ways of being human.

4:30 On Not Grieving the Holy Spirit

Verse 30 is a clear and unambiguous warning not to *grieve the Holy Spirit of God*. That exhortation can stand on its own, and it is often read that way. Pauline writing often groups exhortations that do not have any relationship to each other. That does not take away from their importance. It only means that there is no clear progression of thought or logic.

Nevertheless, there is ample reason to interpret this warning in the larger context of life as *the new human*. For one, the exhortation touches on the power that undergirds living as *the new human*. Second, the emphasis on speech in both the preceding and immediately following verses reflect the close relationship between *Spirit* and speech elsewhere in this letter (5:18-19; 6:17; cf. e.g., Rom. 12; 1 Cor. 14; 1 Thess. 5:18-19).

At the basis of this exhortation lies the awareness that God's empowerment through the *Spirit* is vulnerable to callous disregard in both deed and word—this despite the reminder that it is the *Spirit* by which believers have been *sealed for the day of redemption*. *Sealing* may refer to the experience of baptism (e.g., Perkins: 110; Russell: 83-5; Schnackenburg: 210; contra Barth, 1974:521; Lincoln: 40; Best, 1998:458, believes the sealing relates equally to baptism and prior conversion). This would imply, on the surface, that the status of believers on that *day of redemption* is assured: they *were sealed* (cf. 1:13). But the warning here not to grieve that Spirit is intended to dispel any glib sense of security. Indeed, the exhortation may be heard as a warning of dire consequences for grieving the Spirit of God. Callousness can impede the power of God to transform.

It will be understood as such an obstruction especially by those familiar with the words of Jesus in Mark 3:29: "Whoever blasphemes against the Holy Spirit can never have forgiveness, but is guilty of an eternal sin" (cf. Matt. 12:32). The context of that warning is clearly different from Ephesians. In Mark 3, Jesus responds to the accusation that he is empowered by an unclean spirit. In Ephesians, the concern is the betrayal in word and deed of the empowering and re-creating presence of God (cf. 3:18).

The consequence of such betrayal is to subvert and undo the work of the Spirit. The Spirit brings unity to the body of Christ (4:3), assures access to the presence of God for those who have been reconciled through the peacemaking Christ (2:18), makes them into a fit dwelling for God (2:22), enlivens their worship (5:18-19), and provides them with the needed armaments for struggling with the principalities and powers (6:17-18). So, even though the context is different, the heavy weight of Mark 3 is felt with reason.

The gravity of the exhortation is heightened by the fact that the wording echoes Isaiah 63:10, LXX, where the prophet decries Israel's rebellion as *grieving* [God's] *Holy Spirit* (Fee, 1987:713, n. 175; Lincoln: 306). In response, God becomes Israel's enemy (Isa. 63:1-6). Evoking that important prophetic warning is quite intentional.

The logic is straightforward: You have been liberated from the sway of the evil spirit now at work among the sons and daughters of disobedience (2:2). You have been brought to life, empowered by the Spirit of God (3:18), brought into unity with Christ by the Spirit (4:3), brought near to God by the Spirit (2:18, 22), and sealed for the great day of redemption by the Spirit (cf. 1:13). You insult God if you return to the old ways of being human, or do not avail yourselves of the spirited power of God for life in *the new human*. Such sinning is *grievous* because it happens in the presence of God, in full view of God's enabling grace—"murder in the cathedral."

The presence of this exhortation is a sobering reminder that life in *the new human* this side of the *day of redemption* is fraught with vulnerability, danger, and struggle for faithfulness. It is a life that believers begin with the promise of God's enabling nearness in the Spirit, but also against the backdrop of God's judgment. It is a life marked by countless daily choices that either draw on the power of the Spirit or give room for the devil to wreak havoc.

4:31-32 Contrasting Ways of Relating to Others

"Exhortation by catalogue" (Barth, 1974:550) was a common tradition of moral education in Jewish and Christian circles. The use of lists of vices and virtues was typical of what is often referred to as "the doctrine of the two ways." It provided a handy way of contrasting faithfulness and rebellion. We find this well-known motif in the Sermon on the Mount: "Enter through the narrow gate; for the gate is wide and the road is easy that leads to destruction, and there are many who take it. For the gate is narrow and the road is hard that leads to life, and there are few who find it" (Matt. 7:13-14; in Pauline writings, see also, e.g., Rom. 1:29-31; 1 Cor. 5:9-11; Gal. 5:16-26; beyond the NT, cf. Ps. 1; Prov. 2:12-13; esp. Ep. Barnabas; Lincoln: 296-7, with texts and literature).

In this case the author is highly dependent on Colossians 3:8 and 12. As in Colossians, the list of vices comes first, immediately following the warning about not grieving the Holy Spirit. Again the matter of *anger*, already identified in Ephesians 4:26, emerges as a major concern. In verse 26 *anger*, or not dealing with the *provocation to anger*, had the potential of giving a foothold for the devil. In 4:31 anger in its various guises constitutes the sure way to grieve the Holy Spirit, to frustrate and undermine the work of God. Thus believers are, literally, to *remove* or *get rid of* (GNB, NIV, NAB) all forms of anger from their midst (Col. 3:8 uses the term *putting/taking off*, familiar from Eph. 4:22, 25).

Verse 31 is a virtual catalog of anger: *bitterness, rage, wrath, angry yelling, slander, and every (other) evil*. Evidently at least some terms are synonymous. At the same time, we can observe a certain progression in a "cycle of anger" (so also Best, 1998:460-2). Anger emerges out of a disposition of bitterness and resentment; it bursts forth in fits of rage, but is also nursed as persistent hostility; it is abusive and destructive of others, knowing no limit in its destructive potential *(every kind of evil)*.

We entertained the possibility that the imperative in 4:26, *Be angry but do not sin!* reflects a context in which there are provocations to anger that need to be dealt with, where anger is *not* the opposite to the love of the neighbor (4:26, notes). What is being criticized in 4:31 is anger that grows out of the *absence* of love (cf. esp. 1 Cor. 13:5), anger that is *not* a result of witnessing the breaking of covenant and community, but is out to destroy relationships.

Just as in the case of *stealing* and *rotten speech*, an alternative is held out to those who have chosen to walk the way of *the new human*, again by means of a catalog: *Be kind to one another, com-*

passionate, forgiving each other just as God in Christ forgave you (us) (5:32). Over against bitterness and anger are placed *kindness, compassion,* and *forgiveness* (or *graciousness*). The focus is less on actions than on the disposition out of which actions emerge. It is a matter of character. Importantly, the character of *the new human* who has been created in God's own image (4:24) is patterned after the divine creator.

Though the terms together describe a positive and generous disposition to fellow members of the community of faith, each term retains important dimensions of meaning. Kindness translates *chrēstos,* a common term for a good person (Best, 1998:462). Significantly, it often appears in the Greek Bible in expressions of praise to God, frequently translating the Hebrew *tob* ("good," as in Pss. 25:8; 34:8; 86:5; 100:5; 136:1; cf. also Wisd. of Sol. 15:1-3). To say that the Lord is good is to describe God in his kindness toward humanity. In the context of relationship, "good" becomes kind, generous, and gracious (cf. esp. 2:7! also Rom. 11:22; Titus 3:4; 1 Pet. 2:3)—even to enemies! (Luke 6:35). It is this kindness that is to characterize humanity made in the image of God.

Compassionate translates *eusplanchnos* (lit., "good intestines," cf. "gut feeling"), which appears in the NT only here and in 1 Peter 3:8, and not at all in the Greek OT. A very telling if rare use of the term appears in the apocryphal Prayer of Manasseh 7 (Ode 12:7, LXX), where the arch-sinner, King Manasseh, appeals to God for mercy, describing him as *Most High, of great compassion (eusplanchnos), long-suffering, and very merciful. Tenderhearted* gets closer anatomically to the literal meaning of *eusplanchnos* than does *compassionate.* But since the guts were understood to be the seat of feeling, the term refers literally to a "gut feeling" for others.

In his blessing of God for the birth of a son, Zechariah refers to God's "bowels of mercy" (*splanchna eleous,* Luke 1:78). God's saving intervention in the affairs of humanity emerges out of deep feelings for humanity. It is this kind of love for others that is to define the character of those who are on the way to becoming more fully *the new human* created in God's image.

Forgiving translates *charizomenos,* which can mean "to grant favor" in the sense of "to grace" or "to be gracious," but can also mean *to forgive,* the translation of choice in most Bibles. While that may be the best reading, it is important to note that *charizomenos* is a verbal (participial) form of the meaning-laden *charis (grace* or *gift)* encountered frequently in Ephesians (e.g., 1:2, 6, 7; 2:5, 7, 8; 3:2, 7, 8; 4:7). One should therefore think of forgiveness first as practicing grace in imitation of God. Notably, in 2:7 the limitless wealth of God's *grace (charis)* comes to expression in God's *kindness (chrēstotēs,* a cognate of *chrēstos).*

Imitating God and Walking Like Christ 5:1-2

The first two verses of chapter 5 bring this section to a climactic conclusion. Ephesians 4:17 exhorted the readers *no longer to walk as the Gentiles;* now 5:1-2 exhorts them *to imitate God and walk in love, just as Christ loved* them.

The close connection to what immediately precedes these two verses is shown first in the repetition of the emphatic *Be, therefore* . . . (cf. 4:32). And just as 4:32 grounds the positive disposition of graciousness in God's own grace, so now readers are exhorted to *be imitators of God.* The specific command to *imitate God* is unique in the Bible and relatively rare in Judaism generally (extensive discussion in Barth, 1974:556, n. 10; 588-92; Best, 1998:466-8; Lincoln: 311). Its rarity is no doubt related to the deference shown to God in Judaism. Recall that the sin of the first humans was to want to be "like God" (Gen. 3:5).

Such deference notwithstanding, the implicit call to imitation of God is there already in the Holiness Code of Leviticus 19:2: "You shall be holy, for I the Lord your God am holy." This finds a striking echo in the Sermon on the Mount: "Be perfect as your heavenly Father is perfect" (Matt. 5:48). The parallel "Be merciful" in Luke 6:36 comes close to Ephesians. That familial connection is evident also in our text. Readers are to imitate God *as beloved children* (cf. Matt. 5:45).

In Paul's letters, *imitation* is an important concept. Usually it is a matter of imitating Paul and his associates (1 Cor. 4:16; 11:1; Phil. 3:17; 1 Thess. 1:6; 2 Thess. 3:9), and thereby Christ (1 Cor. 11:1; 1 Thess. 1:6); but Paul can also speak of believers imitating other congregations (1 Thess. 2:14). Also for Paul, the familial dimension of parent-child marks much of this tradition of moral formation as imitation (cf. 1 Cor. 4:14-16; Best, 1998:467; Perkins: 114).

Only in our present text do we find the call to imitate God directly. This reflects the thoroughly theocentric perspective of Ephesians. But it also reflects the exalted view of the church as sons and daughters, *beloved children* created in the divine parent's image. Here the parent of these beloved children is depicted as a model of kindness, compassion, and forgiveness. The imitation of God is breathtaking in 6:10-20, where the new human receives God's own armor for the task of combating the principalities and powers.

This is not to say, however, that believers are to imitate God in all the ways in which God is active in the affairs of humanity. There are hints at believers' participation in divine judgment in the command to be angry in 4:26, in the summons to expose the works of darkness in 5:11, and in the call to enter into battle with the forces of evil (6:10-20). Yet *grace* and *love* rather than judgment (e.g., 5:5) are the principal areas of imitation.

Nowhere does God's love and grace come to greater expression than in verse 2 in the self-offering of God's Son, the Christ. The nature of Christ's love is described in cultic terminology: *He handed himself over for us as an offering and sacrifice to God, as a pleasing odor.* In contrast to the Gentiles who *handed themselves over* to *licentiousness, impurity, and greed* (4:19), Christ *handed himself over for us as an offering and a sacrifice.* Just as Christ offered up his life as a pleasing sacrifice to God *for us,* so *we too* are to *walk in love,* to offer ourselves as a pleasing sacrifice for the sake of each other and God (cf. Rom. 12:1-2; Ezek. 20:41). God's *beloved children* are to *walk in love, just as* Christ loved them. *Just as* appears already in 4:32 and is sometimes called a "conformity pattern" (Lincoln: 309, 311).

Christ's walk was marked by love and boundless generosity, but it was a costly walk (2:16). The reference to *sacrifice* may echo Colossians 1:24: "I am now rejoicing in my sufferings for your sake, and in my flesh I am completing what is lacking in Christ's afflictions for the sake of his body, that is, the church" (NRSV; cf. Rom. 8:17). Christ's death was *for us* (cf. Rom. 5); and it was *for us* also in the sense that it provides the model for what it means for us to love, to take up our own crosses, as Jesus puts it in the Gospels (Mark 8:34 and par.). Most immediately, however, the language of Ephesians 5:2 is drawn from the realm of worship, a reminder that the true and faithful *walk* is a grateful offering of a *living* sacrifice in imitation of Christ (cf. Rom. 12:1-2; on ethics and worship, see Eph. 3:20-21, notes; "Doxology," TBC for 3:14:21; for more on imitation of Christ in the NT, see J. H. Yoder, 1994:112-33; Swartley, 2000:218-45).

THE TEXT IN BIBLICAL CONTEXT

As manifest throughout the analysis, there is much resonance in this passage with other parts of Ephesians as also with Pauline letters. These verses retrace the steps taken in 2:1-10, which begins with a description of life apart from God as *walking in trespasses,* obeying the evil ruler of the air, following the desires of the flesh (2:1-3; cf. 2:12). God's merciful raising of these dead *sons and daughters of disobedience* (2:5-6) parallels the *taking off* of the decaying *old human* and the *putting on* of *the new human*—Christ (cf. 2:15). The purpose of being re-created in Christ into God's image is *good works* (2:10). Our present text can rightly be viewed as an elaboration of what it means to practice "the good" (esp. 4:28-29).

In addition to recalling chapter 2, the author appears to draw on Colossians 3:5-15, with its baptismal imagery of "taking off the old human" *(anthrōpos)* and "putting on the new" (3:9-10). Notice also lists of vices (Col. 3:5, 8-9) and virtues (3:12-15), matched by several items appearing in Ephesians 4:17—5:2. Romans 1:18-25 likely also figures in the formation of this passage, as may Wisdom of Solomon 13–15 (see below).

Negative Stereotyping of Gentiles

The negative characterization of Gentile existence in Ephesians 4:17-19 owes much to a common tradition in Judaism that served to mark off the people of God and to reinforce that boundary (2:11-12, notes; discussion in Best, 1997:143-6, 152; 1998:416-25). Romans 1:18-32 (esp. vv. 21-25) provides a precedent in the Pauline letters for a characterization of Gentile life as vacuous and futile. Such character sketches are found in other roughly contemporaneous Jewish writings, most accessibly in Wisdom of Solomon 13–17.

The elements of such a benighted existence are a life of mindless and ruinous self-indulgence, accompanied and precipitated by a morally bankrupt and self-deluded consciousness. Practice and thought, body and mind, go hand in hand. Ignorance is thus more than simply lack of information (cf. 1 Pet. 1:14). It is chosen and therefore culpable ignorance (cf. Rom. 1:20-22), masquerading as knowledge and wisdom (cf. 1 Cor. 1:18-25). In our text this tradition serves as reminder and warning more than it does as an accurate and balanced depiction of Gentile life. It was and remains a common device in moral exhortation (on Jewish and Gentile examples, see Best, 1998:423-5).

One danger in such stereotyping is the exaggeration of the *other's* badness; just as dangerous is the exaggeration of one's own goodness. The rest of the exhortation in the present passage is intended to dispel such blindness.

Taking Off and Putting On

At the root of the motif of *putting* or *taking off* and *putting on* (4:22-24) lies the drama of the baptismal ritual (Meeks: 155; so also Lincoln: 284-5, despite his skepticism on how much we know about specific Pauline baptismal practice; Best, 1998:432-3 is even more dubious). While we have hard evidence only for later years, it is a safe guess that in Pauline churches those being baptized took off their old clothes to symbolize leaving the old way of being human (so also Jeschke: 126). They were then immersed as a symbol of their participation in the death and resurrection of Christ (cf. Rom. 6). Emerging from the watery grave, they put on new clothes, symbolizing investment with a new identity as participants in the body of Christ, *the new human* created in the image of God (4:24).

Chapter 2 shows the same movement from a "living death" under the tutelage and dominion of the ruler of the air to life as a new human *created in Christ Jesus for good works* (2:1-10). And chapter 6, with its clarion call to *put on the armor of God*, will show with what militancy baptismal vows could be taken. Paul earlier speaks similarly in Romans 13:12 of "taking off the works of darkness" and "putting on the weapons of light," synonymous, it turns out, with "putting on Christ" in 13:14.

Anger and Speaking Truth

In the notes, the interpretation of Ephesians 4:26-27 regarding provocations to anger—whether one's own provocations of God or another's provocation of oneself or of God—finds support in Leviticus 19:17. Members of the covenant community are to "reprove" or "expose" the sin of the neighbor lest it bring judgment on themselves as well (on exposing sin, see Eph. 5:11; cf. also Prov. 17:10; 27:5-6). *Speaking* such painful *truth* is nothing other than a deep if potentially conflictual expression of love for the neighbor, required (!) of members of the same covenant community. Leviticus 19:17 no doubt underlies the command taken from Zechariah 8:16 and quoted in Ephesians 4:25, to *speak truth each with his neighbor*. In Zechariah 8:14, LXX, the sins of the fathers are referred to as *provoking [God] to wrath* (*parorgisai*, "to be angry!" Cf. the rare *parorgismos* in Eph. 4:26).

Such neighborly love is reflected also in the Community Rule of the Dead Sea covenanters at Qumran. That rule repeatedly appeals to Leviticus 19:17 as a warrant for members of the community to deal straightforwardly and quickly with the sins of others. This means handling provocations to anger or wrath—*one's own and God's*—by reproaching the erring fellow member of the community (e.g., 1QS 5.24—6.1; CD 20.4-6, 17-19; 4QD^e [4Q270] 10.3.13; 4.11-12). To be sure, such reproof is not to be done in the spirit of vengeance but rather "in truth, in meekness, and in compassionate love for the man [sic]" (1QS 5.25; cf. CD 20.4, 17-18; cf. Eph. 4:15, 25, 32).

Responding to such provocations must not be delayed; they must be dealt with "before sunset" (CD 9.6; 1QS 5.26). In striking similarity to Ephesians 4:27, the covenanter pledges that he "will not retain Belial within [his] heart" (1QS 10.21). The urgency is rooted in the concern for the covenant partner in light of the wrath or vengeance of the divine judge. "I shall enclose him with a solid fence to maintain faithfulness and staunch judgment with the justice of God" (1QS 10.25).

That same urgency to deal with the sin of the brother or sister through truthful and loving confrontation finds expression in the familiar Rule of Christ in Matthew 18:15-20. The objective is twofold. First, it is an act of love, motivated by the desire to win back the brother or sister, and thus to reconcile with the erring sibling and to reconcile the sinner with the family of God (18:15). The second objective is intricately related: to reclaim the erring brother or sister in light of the otherwise inevitable judgment or wrath of God. Indeed, "binding and loosing" (Matt. 18:18) amounts to participation in both the mercy and the judgment of God (on Matt. 18 and related passages: J. H. Yoder, 1992:1-13; 1997; in relation to church discipline: Huebner, 1997; Schroeder, 1993).

THE TEXT IN THE LIFE OF THE CHURCH

This text has evident interest for a believers church tradition born from the conviction that faithfulness means taking the road less traveled, the *renewed* way of life (4:23-24; cf. 2:10, NRSV) instead of the *former way* (4:22). The stark contrast of the two ways of "walking" resonates strongly with the values of nonconformity and separation from the world (4:17; 5:2; see also 5:3-21).

Baptism as Ritual of Transformation and Re-Creation

The central image of "taking off" and "putting on," rooted in the drama of baptism, represents a major point of contact with Anabaptist and believers church traditions (4:22-25). This will be of special interest to churches that practice baptism by immersion. They witness an oft-repeated ritual of transformation, of clothes that need to be replaced after being drenched in the waters of baptism.

This text is a reminder that baptism is more than a membership rite, or even an act of obedience. It is the point of entry into the body of *the new human*—Christ, together with whom we have been raised to new life (2:5-6). As such, baptism marks the beginning of a new way of walking, a pledge of fidelity to participate in the life of *the new human* marked by justice, truth, and holiness (4:24; the Latin word *sacramentum*, from which comes the English term *sacrament*, referred to the military oath of Roman soldiers). Just as baptism represents a pledge of loyalty and faithfulness on the part of a believer, the new creation is *God's* act of grace. (On baptism, TLC for 2:1-10; cf. Finger, 1989:342-8; J. H. Yoder, 1992:28-46, 71-3; McClendon, 1986:255-9, esp. relevant on relating baptism to "resurrection ethics.")

Struggle *Inside* the Church with Old Ways of Walking

Our text can leave the impression that the problem with *the old human* (4:22) lies out there with *the Gentiles* (unbelievers, 4:17-19); truth, justice, and holiness prevail inside the church. Churches, including those that are heir to a tradition of radical commitment to holiness and separation from *the old human*, are deeply conscious and increasingly willing to admit openly that the old ways are still much in evidence in their homes and congregations. One need think only of the areas of consumerism, entertainment, and especially sexuality (TLC for 2:1-10). Two disparate responses to this reality vie with each other.

Realism Versus Perfectionism

One response is to become more "realistic" about the church. "Perfectionism" has thus been roundly criticized as arrogant and self-deluding (cf., e.g., Block; Sawatsky and Holland, 1993). A more pervasive example is the virtual disappearance of church discipline in many churches of the (once) radical stream (see, e.g., Resources Commission: 97-103; Huebner, 1997).

In response, it is important to observe that in our text the exhortation to *walk* (conduct ourselves) like *the new human* is inseparable from the conviction that the church—made up of mostly reclaimed sons and daughters of disobedience (2:2-3)—is the *body* of *the new human*—Christ. The indicative (the church *is* the body of Christ) is the premise for the imperative (it therefore *ought* to walk like Christ). To paraphrase Galatians 5:25: "If you are the new human, walk like one!" (5:8-10, notes). The discomfort with perfectionism easily becomes an attack on that premise, re-creation in Christ. Grace becomes then absolution for persistent stumbling rather than empowerment to walk like Christ in imitation of God (cf. 2:1-10, notes). Thereby the messianic character of the church is fatally subverted, and the Spirit is grieved.

Zero Tolerance

Another response runs in the opposite direction, mostly in relation to a specific set of concerns. There is quite rightly growing alarm in the church about abuse—abuse of power, privilege, and of sex. In that context, a consensus has emerged in both church and society about the importance of naming the reality of abuse, establishing rigorous standards of behavior, and developing stringent disciplinary procedures for dealing with those who have violated others, especially in the area of sexual behavior (see, e.g., Heggen, 1993; Melissa A. Miller). In short, in the context of dealing with matters of abuse, the church is rightly rediscovering the importance of truth, justice, and holiness.

In some measure the church is beginning to live by the wisdom of Leviticus 19 and its offspring (TBC). Sadly, it is often the broader social consensus that has pulled the church kicking and screaming into dealing with these issues. "Gentiles" have been holding the feet of the "saints" to the fire. However ironic, the "world" is giving the church an opportunity to rediscover the hard work of "walking" like *the new human*.

Ironically, those who are critical of perfectionism and of the old church discipline are often wholeheartedly supportive of zero tolerance for sexual abuse, whether in homes or church institutions. Might churches, whether mainstream or radical, see in the broad social consensus around the importance of dealing with sexual abuse, an opening to recover truth, justice, and holiness in relation also to *other* dimensions of life? These include relational, economic, political, and institutional dimensions. Churches might thereby recover what discipline could look like in a community committed to being the *new human* in an old world.

Anger: Virtue or Vice?

Our text suggests that anger is an inevitable and even mandatory response to injustice and violence, both inside and outside the church (4:26). Such anger is the experience of pain and the expression of outrage at the experience of violation or at witnessing it happen to others. In the same breath, our text warns us not to nurse anger into bitterness and vengeance (4:31). Instead, anger is to give way to loving if forceful speaking of truth to the neighbor (Augsburger on "care-fronting") so as to bring about confession and transformation, and finally lead to forgiveness.

Anger, truth, love, and forgiveness are a volatile mix in relation to the abuse of power and sex within the church. Presently the issue of abuse is getting a lot of attention in North American churches. In the struggle for wholeness and healing, we are learning not to discount anger and not to coerce forgiveness. We are learning to work in a context of truth and to search for justice and holiness. Ephesians is wholly supportive of such a search. But, as stated above, it encourages us to expand that learning to other dimensions of life in the community of the new human. There are places on the globe where members of Christ's body identify economic and political oppression and violence as primary arenas in which truth, justice, anger, and love are to be exercised. In such places it may be that the hunger for justice needs to be expanded into the more private arenas of domestic violence and sexual abuse.

The stress in Ephesians falls fundamentally on what makes for wholeness in the body, what builds up, what meets needs, and what communicates grace (4:28-29). Nothing quite succeeds at this like the imitation of a merciful, kind, and compassionate divine parent (4:32—5:2). It is of critical importance for churches in the "meekness" stream of tradition (TLC for 4:1-16) that such kindness, compassion, and forgiveness must never be severed from justice, truth, and holiness—the hallmarks of the *new humanity*. If they are severed, they leave the provocations to anger in place and expose brothers and sisters to abuse and their abusers to the judgment of God.

Ephesians 5:3-21

"Walk as Children of Light!"—Transforming Nonconformity

PREVIEW

This section of Ephesians continues the exhortation on "walking properly" begun in 4:1 and taken up in earnest in 4:17. In 5:21 it also introduces the Household Code. The first half of the title is taken from verse 8 and reiterates the familiar emphasis on *walking* in a way that is worthy of the high calling of sons and daughters of God (2:10; 4:1; 5:2). The second half of the title expresses the strong emphasis on nonconformity.

Strikingly, such nonconformity is understood as a matter of turning away from the darkness and also as a means of transforming darkness into light—nonconformity as transformation of the world. This rather surprising twist appears at the point where radical nonconformity would seem to require radical separatism (e.g., 5:3, 7, 11). The *children of light* (5:8) are not to share in the deeds of darkness; they are to *expose* them (5:11) and thus to transform them into light (5:13-14).

At the point where this twist is introduced, we encounter a fragment of a baptismal hymn:

Arise, sleeper,
and rise from the dead,
and the Christ will shine on you! (5:14; cf. 2:1)

Those who have been awakened from death are now to *walk as the wise* who are *filled with the Spirit* (5:15-18). Such Spirit-filled nonconformity finds expression in worship, in mutual instruction, in the praise and thanksgiving of God, and in mutual subordination (5:19-21).

The call to mutual subordination in verse 21 is usually taken to be part of the following section on the Household Code, as it should be (5:21—6:9, notes). However, 5:21 depends grammatically on the command to *be filled with the Spirit* in 5:18. This means that the call to *mutual subordination* is premised upon divine empowerment (cf. 4:1-3, notes). In this context mutual subordination is an essential part of the intoxicating worship that results from being "drunk" with the Spirit of God (5:18) and should thus be treated also as part of this section of text.

Structure of 5:3-21

Sexual sin, uncleanness, greed,
base behavior, silly talk, coarse joking—
all are to be replaced by thanksgiving! (5:3-4)

For know this for certain:
such persons are subject to the wrath of God.
Therefore do not become their co-participants! (5:5-7)

Walk as children of light
in all goodness and righteousness and truth!
Do not co-participate in the fruitless works of darkness,
much rather expose [them]! (5:8-11)
All things that are exposed by the light are revealed,
for everything that is revealed is light.
So,
Arise, sleeper,
and rise from the dead,
and the Christ will shine on you! (5:12-14)

Walk as the wise,
exploiting the time!
Do not be drunk with wine,
rather be filled with the Spirit,
• singing,
• giving thanks,
• being subject to each other! (5:15-21)

OUTLINE

Transforming Nonconformity, 5:3-14

5:3-7, 11	Separation from the Darkness
5:8-10	Walking as the Children of Light
5:11-14	Transforming Darkness into Light

Walking as the Wise, 5:15-17

Filled with the Spirit, 5:18-21

5:18	Drunk with Wine Versus Filled with Spirit
5:19-20	Inspired Worship
5:21	Inspired and Empowered for Servanthood

EXPLANATORY NOTES

Transforming Nonconformity 5:3-14

5:3-7, 11 Separation from the Darkness

We pick up the stream of exhortation from the previous section. *Walking in love as Christ loved us* (5:2) is contrasted now by a list of three vices: *sexual sin (porneia), impurity* or *uncleanness (akatharsia),* and *greed (pleonexia).* The NAB translates the series as *lewd conduct, promiscuousness, and lust,* suggesting that the element tying these three terms together is sexual vice (so also Lincoln: 321-2). The usual translation of *porneia* (behind the word *pornography*) is "fornication," but it should be taken as referring to a much broader range of sexual misconduct (Best, 1998:475-6).

The three terms are taken from a slightly longer catalog in Colossians 3:5 and may have been adapted to highlight sexual vices. But it also echoes the characterization of how the Gentiles *walk* in 4:17-19 (notes). Especially the presence of *greed,* however much fueling sexual misconduct, has much wider meaning, including an economic dimension. At the same time, sexual sin is viewed as a prime characteristic of a life alienated from God's will (cf. Rom. 1:18-32; Hos. 1–2; Ezek. 22–23). When sex is linked to greed, and the greedy thus become insensitive to persons and their covenants (cf. biblical injunctions against lust and adultery), then sexual license becomes cultic defilement—*impurity*—defilement of the holiness of God's people who constitute the temple of God (2:21).

This brief catalog of vices is repeated in 5:5 and recast to list sinners rather than sins. They are appropriately identified as *idolaters* (cf. Col. 3:5; Rom. 1:23-25; on the connection between greed, immorality, and idolatry: Wisd. of Sol. 14:12, 22-27; Matt. 6:24// Luke 16:13).

Such vices should *not even be named among you, as is fitting for holy ones* (5:3). NRSV translates this line as *not even be mentioned among you*; NIV has *there must not be even a hint.* These translators read 5:3 in light of the prohibition against vile speech in 5:4. Clearly, the prohibition against obscenity in verse 4 is directed squarely at talk that makes light of sexual sin and abuse, trivializing its importance by making it a matter of entertainment. As in verse 3, such talk is not fitting for the holy. The inappropriateness of such talk becomes all the more clear when we remember that *the holy ones (saints)* can refer equally to members of the church and to heavenly beings (1:1-2, notes; Perkins: 115).

The radical covenanters at Qumran censured such behavior severely (thirty days for someone who "giggles so that his voice is heard," along with such inappropriate behavior as spitting, exposing oneself, speaking ill of fellow members of the community, or falling asleep at meetings; 1QS 7.16-17).

Naming has, however, already appeared in Ephesians in the great prayer of 3:14-21. God is said to have *named every family on earth and in the heavens.* As the notes on that passage showed, *naming* has to do with both engendering and claiming ownership over those named. By *naming,* God declares paternity. If one allows that to affect the meaning of *naming* in 5:3, then the concern is less with mentioning such sins than with engendering them, with allowing such sins to take on existence in the community of holy ones. Perhaps both senses are present, especially if trivializing talk of sexual sin tends to lower the threshold of acceptability (Best, 1998:476-7; Lincoln: 322; Thurston: 134).

On the other hand, *naming* has quite a different meaning today and has come to have an important place in dealing with sexual abuse. The prohibition of *naming* here clearly does not preclude the naming of sexual sin in the sense of identifying it and exposing it for what it is. Indeed, such naming is entirely consistent with the call to *expose the works of darkness* (TLC). There can be no intended contradiction between 5:11 with its call to *expose,* and 5:12, which suggests that some things are too shameful even to talk about. Obviously, the concern is with *how* and *for what purpose* the church talks about these or any other sins. Does such talk give life and power to sin, or does it expose it, disempower it, and transform darkness into light (5:13-14)?

Verse 4 should be understood in this light. *Obscenity and silly talk* or *vulgar joking* have no place among those whose task is to expose sexual license and all other forms of greed. Instead, the speech of believers is to be marked by *thanksgiving (eucharistia).* *Thanksgiving (eucharistia)* is to replace *vulgar joking (eutrapelia;* in broader Hellenistic culture, the term could mean "wittiness"; Lincoln: 323). This clearly recalls 4:29, where *bestowing of grace* is to replace *rotten speech.* The importance given to speech in this passage, as in chapter 4, reflects the understanding that words do matter; they express character and disposition, and they also give life to both good and evil (cf. Mat. 15:16-20; James 3:10-12).

Thanksgiving (eucharistia)—in effect, worship (5:4; cf. 5:20)—is to replace destructive sexual behavior and talk. This does not imply estrangement from sexuality itself. The presence of the Household Code later in this chapter shows that this author is a friend of family and having children, and of patterning the relationship of Christ to the church after a model of marital relations (5:23-32). Walking the path of holiness, however narrow, is to be marked by celebrative sounds of thanksgiving.

Grave warnings accompany the catalog of vices. Verse 5 states emphatically *(Know this for sure!)* that those who practice these vices *will have no inheritance in the reign of Christ and of God.* Verse 6 warns readers not to be misled by *empty words,* possibly another reference to ribald speech (cf. 5:4), but more likely to false reassurances that such behavior has no serious consequences. Readers are to know that the *wrath of God* falls on *the sons [and daughters] of disobedience* (cf. 2:2; 4:17-19; 1 Cor. 6:9-10; Gal. 5:21).

The unique and puzzling reference in 5:5 to a "double kingdom"— *the kingdom or reign of **Christ** and of **God***—merits closer consideration. On one hand, the reference to Christ *and* God may be no more than a heaping up of synonyms, as often happens in Ephesians. On the other, it may be derived from the double emphasis on God and Christ in 5:1-2 (Perkins: 117). It is also possible that the wording here betrays familiarity with 1 Corinthians 15:24-28: Christ's reign or kingdom is marked by battle against the powers, culminating in the defeat of death. When that reign is accomplished, Christ hands the kingdom over to God.

In the notes on Ephesians 1:20-22, we suggested that the author may be directly dependent on 1 Corinthians 15 for the combination of Psalms 110:1 and 8:6. Such dependency may extend to the present text. The author may have in mind a two-stage notion of the kingdom: first, the *present* reign of Christ, marked by both reconciliation and defeat of the rebellious principalities and powers (1:20-23; 6:10-18); second, the *future* kingdom of God (the anticipated inheritance; cf. 1:14). All this is at best only hinted at in this cryptic phrase (Schnackenburg: 220), but should not be rejected outright (as do Barth: 564-5; Best, 1998:482; Lincoln: 325).

Verses 7 and 11 are radical in their simplicity of calling for non-conformity and nonparticipation in the life of darkness. Two words with the prefix sun- *(with)* describe participation with darkness and those who walk in it: *Do not be their* **co***-participants (summeto-choi, 5:7); do not* **co***-participate (sunkoinōneite) in fruitless works of darkness* (5:11). Typical of the style of Ephesians, the prefix is somewhat redundant. But such redundancy gives greater emphasis to participation (cf. positive uses of the prefix *sun-,* "together with," in 2:5-6, 19, 21-22; 3:6; 4:3, 16; see Schematic Trans.).

Those who do not heed this warning become vulnerable to the *wrath* or judgment *of God.* Interestingly, in this case the distinction of the kingdoms or reigns of Christ and of God suggests that the author has in mind the future judgment of God, even as the ongoing vigilance and judgment of God also fits the eschatology of Ephesians (Schnackenburg: 221; cf. Best, 1998:485-6).

5:8-10 *Walking as the Children of Light*

Verses 8 to 10 express the heart of the exhortation in concentrated form. The premise for the call to separation and nonconformity is found in verse 8: *For* **once** *you were darkness, but* **now** *[you are] light in the Lord. Therefore, walk as children of light . . . , discerning what is pleasing to the Lord.*

Several important features typical of Pauline thought shape these verses. The *once-now* schema employed to great effect in chapter 2 is present here as well (cf. Col. 3:7-8). Its home is the drama of the baptismal ritual of taking off the former *old human (anthrōpos;* cf. 4:22) and being renewed by putting on *the new human* (cf. 4:23; chap. 2, notes; chap. 4, notes; cf. Col. 2:20; 3:1; Lincoln: 326). Here it is combined with one of the starkest contrasts in the Bible—*light and darkness* (TBC).

Ephesians pictures the realm in which believers "walk" as the light. The text further intensifies this: they themselves also are *light* (5:11-14, notes). At the same time, they are light only *in the Lord* (5:8). Their relation to the light of God is therefore that of being the offspring of light, the *children of light* (with *tekna,* the inclusive term for children). The strength of the identification also applies to the negative: *Once you were darkness* (5:8).

In Ephesians, the contrast of *light* and *darkness* is an ethical dualism. It draws a line, not so much through the heart of each believer or even through the community of the church, but rather through humanity. The line is between *the sons of disobedience* (5:6; cf. 2:2) and the *beloved children of light* (5:8; cf. 5:1), between those who are under the sway of the *prince of the air* (2:2) and those who have been brought from darkness to light (5:14; cf. e.g., 2 Cor. 4:6; 1 Thess. 5:4-5; 1 Pet. 2:9). At the same time, that line also describes the distinction between what the children of light *once* were and what they *now* are.

This stark contrast is a reminder that something fundamental and radical has taken place in the lives of believers. They are *no longer* what they *once* were (cf. 2:11-22). This is an assertion of fact, a change that must now find reality in believers' lives. Interpreters of Pauline theology often call this concept "the indicative and the imperative" (Best, 1998:489).

> Indicative: You were once *darkness;* you now are *light.*
> Imperative: So live as children of *light!*

This is highly reminiscent of Galatians 5:25: "If we live by the Spirit, let us also walk by (line up with) the Spirit" (TRYN). Such exhortation assumes the Spirit's transforming and empowering presence in the lives of believers, who are a part of *the new human* created by God. If it is true that believers participate in this *new creation* (cf. Gal. 6:15; 2 Cor. 5:17; cf. Eph. 4:24), one would expect their "walk" to emerge as natural "fruit" from such a renewed nature.

This is the language used in Ephesians 5:9: *For the **fruit** of the light [is found] in all goodness and justice and truth.* Galatians 5:22-23 has a fuller catalog: "The fruit of the Spirit is love, joy, peace, patience, kindness, generosity, faithfulness, gentleness, and self-control" (some manuscripts of Eph. 5:9 have *spirit* rather than *light,* no doubt influenced by Gal. 5:22).

Such virtues do not come as automatic *fruit,* however. Despite the certainty of what is *now* true of the children of light, the existence of exhortation is witness to something Paul and his students know well: what is *already* true *(now you are light)* is yet much in need of realization. In his writings, Paul is quite concerned to preserve what is sometimes called "eschatological reservation," realism about life this side of what in Ephesians is called *the day of redemption* (4:30) or here *the kingdom of God* (5:5). In Ephesians this comes to expression in the exhortation to *grow into Christ* (4:13, 16), to *learn Christ* (4:20), or to struggle against *the powers* of evil (6:10-20).

At the same time, no Pauline letter celebrates the *present* effects of conversion, baptism, and the Spirit as freely and enthusiastically as

Ephesians does. The *fruit of light* is *now already* to be abundantly real in those who *are* light, and as we are about to see, apparent to those yet sitting in darkness.

The fruit of light is introduced with a familiar three-item catalog in 5:9—*goodness (agathōsunē), justice (dikaiosunē: justice,* NAB; *uprightness,* NJB; *righteousness,* NIV, NRSV, REB), and *truth (alētheia).* All three virtues are prominent in Ephesians: *justice* and *truth* are constituent elements in the creation of the *new human* in the likeness of God (4:24) and are the first items listed in the divine armor in 6:14. They are thus related to the "nature" of *the new human* and also constitute the way *the new human* acts. No other virtue is as frequently stressed in Ephesians as *truth* (1:13; 4:21, 24, 25; 6:14; Schnackenburg: 224, renders it as "fidelity" and misses this point). At the same time, *goodness* takes on a comprehensive quality, especially in 2:10 where it is explicitly related to *works* (applied in 4:28-29).

These virtues are related to *discerning what is pleasing (euareston) to the Lord* (5:10). Believers are to *discern (dokimazō: find out,* NIV, NRSV; *discover,* NJB; *learn to judge,* REB) what gives the Lord pleasure through the practice of goodness, justice, and truth. Though in Pauline writings, *Lord* usually refers to Christ, in this case we should think more generally of God. "Pleasing the Lord" is a common biblical way of referring to the sacrificial worship of God. This is true both in the case of actual sacrifices or offering up a pleasing odor (e.g., Lev. 1–2; Num. 15) and in the metaphor of offering up one's life and one's deeds as a proper and pleasing offering and sacrifice to God (e.g., Ps. 51; Heb. 13:16).

Ephesians 5:2 has already mentioned how Christ offered himself up to God as a sacrifice with a *pleasing odor* (5:2, notes; cf. Phil. 4:18). Romans 12:1-2, is particularly relevant where believers are to present themselves as a "living" sacrifice, "pleasing" to God. In Romans 12, such a pleasing sacrifice is nothing other than the transforming practice of nonconformity *and* the means by which to "discern what is good and pleasing [to God] and perfect" (TRYN).

Nonconformity and the practice of *the good, the just, and the true* gives God pleasure (5:9). Their exercise constitutes the worship of the *children of light* (cf. Pss. 50:14; 69:30-31). The call for *thanksgiving* in 5:4 anticipates this characterization of life in the light. We will not be surprised that this section of Ephesians reaches a climax in the call to thanksgiving, praise, and worship in verses 19 and 20.

5:11-14 Transforming Darkness into Light

The contrast between fruitless darkness and productive light needs continually to be sharpened: *Do not co-participate in the fruitless works of darkness.* The word *co-participate (sunkoinōneō),* while not unique to Ephesians (cf. Phil. 4:14; Rev. 18:4), certainly fits the author's love for words with the prefix *sun-* (5:7, notes). Here it means that believers are to have no share in a darkness too awful even to talk about.

One might expect the community of believers now to turn their back on the darkness and to separate itself, as happened at Qumran and countless times since. Radical nonconformity is often buttressed with hostility toward those who do not meet the standards of righteousness and truth. Ephesians, however, proposes something better for believers than turning their backs on the darkness and those who sit in it and pushing the *works of darkness* out of mind (5:12). Instead, the *children of light* are to *expose (elenchō)* evil works (so NIV and NRSV; *bring them out to the light,* GNB; *show them up for what they are,* NJB, REB; *condemn them,* NAB).

As the various translations show, the Greek word *elenchō* has a range of meaning (Büchsel, 1964). "To condemn" (NAB) clearly fits a community taking a hard and absolute line against the *works of darkness* (as in Wisd. of Sol. 4:20). This passage leaves no doubt that actions, words, and dispositions that grow out of *darkness* are to be condemned (note esp. 5:5-6).

Elenchō has a rich association with several texts already discussed in relation to 4:25 (notes; "Anger and Speaking Truth," TBC for 4:17—5:2). In Leviticus 19:17-18, to "reprove" (NRSV; *elenchō* in LXX) is an expression of covenant obligation to love the neighbor. In Matthew 18:15, Jesus calls on his followers to *expose (elenchō)* the sin of the brother and sister—a generous if often conflictual act of love meant to bring repentance and restoration (cf. 1 Cor. 14:24-25).

Ephesians 5:13-14 suggests that such an understanding of *elenchō* is present also in this passage. However, the focus of the exposure is not on the misdeeds of *fellow* members of the community (Best, 1998:492-3; cf. Lincoln: 329-30), but on the goings on among the *sons of disobedience* (Schnackenburg: 226, n. 34). Now the act of neighborly love seen in 4:25 is to be extended to the *sons of disobedience,* whether or not they heed the confrontation or consider it an act of love (on "evangelistic exposing," see 1 Cor. 14:24-25; John 4:29). Preaching peace to *the far* (2:13, 17) now finds expression in relation to the confrontation with a culture of darkness.

Verse 13 expresses a proverb: *All things that are exposed by the light become visible* (or *are revealed,* or *made visible by the light*).

The grammar is ambiguous, but the meaning is clear: *the light* shows up things for what they truly are (so also NJB, REB). Up to this point, the meaning could still be chiefly condemnatory. But verse 14 adds a further maxim: *Everything that is revealed is light.* NIV's translation, *for it is light that makes everything visible,* does not capture the surprising twist. In this instance, exposing the works of darkness is not primarily directed at the works of darkness still present among fellow Christians (as in 4:25). Here it is participation in God's comprehensive project of reclaiming creation and those who inhabit it, including the *sons of disobedience* who sit in *darkness* (cf. 1:10; 2:4; Perkins: 119). To expose is to transform.

This explains the otherwise baffling presence in verse 14 of a hymn fragment (Best, 1998:497-8; Lincoln: 331), likely at home in the baptismal celebration of coming to life with Christ (cf. Rom. 6:1-11; Eph. 2:4-6; Schnackenburg: 228-30). This "three-line baptismal chant" (R. Martin, 1991:63) must have enjoyed wide currency in Pauline circles and have achieved something approaching canonical status. This status is shown by the fact that it is introduced with a formula otherwise reserved for quoting Scripture (cf. 4:8; James 4:6).

> Therefore it says:
> Arise, sleeper,
> and rise from the dead,
> and the Christ will shine on you! (5:14)

This hymn or chant contains a number of important items. First, since it typically would have been sung by those attending the baptism of new believers, it in effect becomes an evangelistic wake-up call, echoing Christ's preaching of peace to *the far and the near* in 2:13, 17. It also reminds believers that they are themselves the beneficiaries of Christ's gracious and transforming illumination. With this disposition of gratitude, they are to direct the light into the darkness.

Although the hymn celebrates Christ as the one who shines on the sleeping dead, Jewish readers will surely have heard echoes of the great blessing in Numbers 6:24-26 and, more specifically, of Isaiah 60:1-4. In that instance, the faithful are summoned to arise and shine, reflecting the glory of the Lord. Moreover, the peoples who sit in darkness shall be drawn to this great light emanating from the people of God. In Ephesians, "Christ" includes those who have become part of Christ's body. Not surprisingly, those who were once drawn to the light of Christ have themselves become identified as light (5:8). They are light *in the Lord.* As such, they participate as members of Christ's body, as members of *the new human,* in shining the light into the eyes of those sleeping in the darkness (cf. Matt. 5:14, 16; earlier, Isa. 42:6-7).

Separation and difference have given way to reconciliation, restoration, resurrection, and re-creation ("Light" and creation, TBC). Stated differently, separation and differentiation have as their fundamental motivation the *gathering up of all things in Christ* (1:10). That, in the mind of the author, is impossible if the distinction between light and darkness is not maintained.

Walking as the Wise 5:15-17

Verses 15-21 are structured around three contrasts:

Do not walk as the unwise,	*rather* as the wise.
Do not be fools,	*rather* know the will of God.
Do not be drunk with wine,	*rather* be filled with the Spirit.

The first two contrasts place the wise over against fools. This comparison can be found frequently in the Bible, especially in prophetic and wisdom literature (e.g., Wisdom and Folly, personified as two women in Prov. 7-8; 4:11-19 links contrasts of wisdom/foolishness and light/darkness as in Eph. 5:15-17). After the text reminds the children of light of who they are, it exhorts them to *watch very carefully how [they] walk* (for *walking* as a metaphor for living, cf. 2:1-10; 4:17—5:2).

It is important to keep in mind the connection between Wisdom and Christ (TBC for 1:3-14 *[Wisdom]*). Sages are those who have **learned** Christ (4:20) and who have come to *understand* the **mystery** of God (1:9-10, 17-18; 3:8-9). They also have been entrusted with the grand task of making the *multivaried* **wisdom** of God known (3:10). They can **discern** *what pleases God* (5:10) and what is *God's will* (5:17; in Rom. 12:1-2, the will of God and what pleases God are virtually equivalent). *The wise* are friends of God and intimates of Wisdom herself (Wisd. of Sol. 7:26-30) or, as in Ephesians, members of Christ's body, participants with and through him in *the new human* (chap. 2). To be addressed as *the wise* in 5:15 presupposes that believers are fully implicated in the task of Christ, God's *multivaried wisdom* (3:10).

The wise are asked to *watch carefully* how they *walk*. One might initially interpret this in light of the vulnerability of the children of light to stray from the way of goodness, justice, and truth (5:9). It is more likely, however, that *watching carefully* should be understood in relation to 5:16—*exploiting the moment to the full, because the days are evil*. The meaning of that line is not immediately clear, however.

The Greek behind *exploit (exagorazō)* means "to buy" or "redeem" something; in its middle form (as here) it can also mean "to buy off" or "pay off" someone. If interpreted in the latter sense, the wise "pay off" wrath (alluded to with the phrase *the evil days*) and thus "redeem the time" *(BAGD:* 271), much the way Christ "redeems" those under the curse of the law in Galatians 3:13 and 4:5. Time is thus "saved" from wrath (Barth, 1974:578; Best, 1998:505; Lincoln: 341).

A less fanciful and more common interpretation understands the word *exagorazō* in a "commercial" sense of "snapping up all chances at a bargain that are available" (R. Martin, 1991:66; so also at Col. 4:5). Applied to time, it means "gobbling up every available opportunity" (E. Martin: 200; cf. Büchsel, 1964a: 128; Schnackenburg: 235). Time is not neutral, but it is laden with opportunities to be seized—hence the term *kairos* ("opportune time") rather than *chronos* (time as "duration"). To *watch carefully how one walks* is thus to "purchase" every opportunity to expose the darkness (5:11) and thus to participate in the redemption of time, the transformation of darkness into light (5:13-14).

What lends urgency to this call? Interpreted in light of Paul's typical apocalyptic eschatology, time is to be exploited because it is short. The *evil days* are the time of intensifying crisis before the day of judgment and redemption (cf. the *evil day* in 6:13). Similarly, Romans 13:11-14 exhorts that since the day of salvation is nearer than ever, believers are to "take off the works of darkness" (TRYN; cf. Eph. 4:22; 5:11), "put on the weapons of light" (TRYN; cf. Eph. 6:10, 14-18), and say no to drunkenness and sleep (cf. Eph. 5:14, 18; 1 Thess. 5:2-8). In short, the *wise* had better know that they are living in the last days and that there is no time to waste. Whatever time there is must be used to get ready for the day of redemption.

Ephesians does not, however, easily fit into an apocalyptic framework (Best, 1998:503-4). In 2:5-7, for example, the author celebrates as *already* true what is more often only anticipated in other Pauline writings—believers have **already been raised with Christ and seated with him in the heavenlies.** Further, the reference in 2:7 to the *coming ages* appears to allow for a protracted future during which the grace of God is to be shown forth (2:7, notes). While Ephesians does retain a sense of a *future* reckoning and time of salvation (1:14; 4:30), as in the present section (5:5), there is no *explicit* anticipation of the return of Christ in Ephesians.

Instead, in Ephesians the present is loaded to an unparalleled degree with both blessing and struggle. *All* time is "loaded" *(kairos),* however much of it remains until that day of redemption. Many days are *evil* and with them comes the challenge of exposing the evil to the light. The urgency of the exhortation is related to time. But it is related just as much or more to the identity of the church. To walk as *fools* is to miss grasping that the *present* time is loaded, even if the present age is not being wrapped up tomorrow (contrasting with 1 Thess. 4:13—5:11; cf. Elias). To be *fools* is also to undervalue the nature and task of the church as a community of *sages* who as *light* are to seize every moment *(kairos)* to transform darkness into light (cf. Matt. 5:14).

To be *wise* is *to know the will of the Lord* (5:17). Here *Lord* is not restricted to Christ (contra Best, 1998:506; Lincoln: 343), even if it includes Christ. The phrase has both a large and a specific meaning. On one hand, it refers to knowing the height, depth, width, and length of the mystery of the will of God as revealed in Christ, which is to *gather up all things in Christ* (cf. 1:9-10; cf. 3:18-21). This entails an appreciation for God's gracious intentions for the disobedient (2:1-10), specifically for Gentiles (2:11-22; chap. 3). It also means understanding what kind of behavior God expects from the community that constitutes God's home. It means *imitating God* and *Christ* (4:32—5:2). It means *learning Christ* and the *truth in Jesus* (4:20-21). All this can be summarized as discerning what gives God pleasure (cf. 5:10).

Filled with the Spirit 5:18-21

5:18 Drunk with Wine Versus Filled with Spirit

Verse 18 introduces the third of the contrasts, this time being *filled with wine* versus being *filled with the Spirit*. To a modern reader, the focus appears to shift abruptly from wisdom and insight to sobriety. This impression is aided by the fact that the injunction *Be not drunk with wine!* appears to be a direct quotation of Proverbs 23:31, where it is a part of an extended description of the effects of over-consumption of wine (23:29-35). Yet the difference between Ephesians 5:18 and the previous contrasts may not be so great after all. In Proverbs 20:1, drunkenness is contrasted to wisdom, much as is foolishness. We should be prepared for the fact that this is more than "clearly spelled out" and "easily understood" ethical instruction on immoderate drinking (contra R. Martin, 1991:63-4; Schnackenburg: 236), even if warnings against over-consumption of alcohol are fitting, now as then (Best, 1998:507, citing literature).

Drunkenness is a metaphor for life in the darkness (TBC). Here it serves to describe the inebriated walk of the foolish sons of disobedience in 5:3-5 or of the ignorant Gentiles in 4:17-19. Early readers also might have heard in this an allusion to the uninhibited intoxication that characterized many pagan religious observances; this aspect aids its suitability as a metaphor (specific references to worship appear immediately following, in 5:19-20). The injunction not to be drunk with wine is likely not motivated by any particular problems with alcohol consumption (as in 1 Cor. 11:21) or inappropriate worship, but both would have been familiar to the readers. Instead, being drunk is associated with the "walk" of *fools*.

Sometimes a direct connection to Proverbs 23:31 is contested, on the grounds that the injunction against getting drunk with wine had already become widespread in Jewish moral teaching and made its way into Ephesians that way (cf. Lincoln: 340). Testament of Judah 14, for example, contains an identical injunction against getting drunk with wine, connecting Judah's sin against his daughter-in-law Tamar (cf. Gen. 38:12-26) with the destructive effects of intoxication.

There is good reason, however, to think that Proverbs 23 is being used, in particular in its Greek form. Proverbs 23:31 (LXX) uses the *not . . . but rather (mē . . . alla)* formula, just as we see in Ephesians 5:18. Further, sounding much like Ephesians 5:19-22, the Greek text of Proverbs 23:31 (LXX) carries an alternative to drunkenness: *Do not be drunk with wine, but converse (homileō, the verb form of "homily") with righteous persons.* In Ephesians, the alternative to being drunk with wine is to be filled with and by the Spirit, which then finds expression in *speaking to each other with psalms and hymns and spiritual songs.*

The center of the exhortation is the summons to be *filled in* [*with and by the*] *Spirit* [*"In"*]. Here again we see the pattern observed in 4:25-32, where a negative injunction is followed by a more important positive exhortation. The alternative to being *drunk with wine* is not simply sobriety, but being *filled with the Spirit.* It is correct not to over-read this as "don't be drunk with wine, but do be drunk with the Spirit" (so also Fee, 1987:720-1); yet one should not miss the parallel, either. The two have more than once been mistaken for each other (cf. Acts 2:14-21!).

In Ephesians, being *filled with the Spirit* is not focused on ecstatic manifestations of the Spirit, as is the case in 1 Corinthians 14. But we will miss the energy and enthusiasm that is to pervade the corporate experience of the church if we allow no spillover from the image of intoxication ("sober inebriation," Schnackenburg: 236-7). Keeping in mind that these words are directed to sages, Sirach (Ecclus.) 1:16

comes to mind: "To fear the Lord is fullness of wisdom; she inebriates mortals with her fruits."

The Spirit enjoys considerable prominence in Ephesians, referring to the nearness of God's renewing and sustaining power in the lives of believers (a few relevant instances: 1:13; 2:18, 22; 3:16; 4:3-4, 30). As in 3:19, which our present text echoes, believers are to open themselves to the *fullness of God* by being *filled with the Spirit*. Remarkably, whereas *being filled* is a passive imperative, it is nonetheless an imperative. This command leaves no doubt that *the wise* have considerable responsibility for the degree to which they are able to discern what pleases God, what God's will is, and what it means to walk in the light (cf. Gal. 5:16).

Even so, believers need the energizing presence of God to exercise that responsibility. Ultimately, it is the gracious *Spirit* of God who empowers the wise children of light in their walk (notes on 1:15-23; 2:1-10; 3:14-21; esp. on 1:17; 2:8; 3:16, 19, 20).

To be sure, it is the community *together* that is *filled with the Spirit*. Being filled with and by the Spirit is not an individualistic experience. Instead, it enables the body of *the new human* to breathe the very breath of God (cf. Paul's discussion in 1 Cor. 12 and 14, where the gifts of the Spirit have as their sole purpose the enlivening and coordination of the body of Christ, "for the common good" [12:7]). Importantly, *grieving* the Holy Spirit also takes place in the corporate life of believers (4:30, notes).

5:19-20 Inspired Worship

Verses 19 to 21 are grammatically dependent on the imperative, *Be filled with the Spirit* (5:18). Here the author elaborates what it means to be so filled, using a series of participles: *speaking* (or *addressing*), *singing*, "*psalming*," *giving thanks*, and *being subordinate*. The function of these participles is open to considerable interpretation. Many versions translate them as further imperatives (e.g., GNB, NAB, NIV, REB). That obscures the grammatical dependency on the main imperative to *be filled with and by the Spirit*, leaving the impression of a series of disconnected exhortations. NRSV is most faithful to the grammar with *as you sing . . . , singing . . . , giving thanks . . . .* Only on the last participle does NRSV reintroduce the imperative: *Be subordinate . . . !*

But what is the relationship between the participles *(singing, giving)* and the main imperative *(be filled)?* Do they describe the attendant circumstances or *effects* of being filled, as the NRSV has it? *Be filled . . . as you sing*, etc. Or might the participles indicate the *means* by which believers are filled with the Spirit? *Be filled . . . by singing,* and so on. This suggests that the corporate life of worship and mutual relations is the context in which it is possible to grieve the Spirit (4:30), and it is also the context in which the filling with the Spirit takes place. Even more important, believers participate in "filling each other up" with the Spirit. Such an understanding is entirely in keeping with the strong emphasis on building each other up in the process of growth into the Christ who is *the new human* (cf. 4:3, 12-16).

An interpreter should always be respectful of grammatical ambiguity. Nevertheless, taking the participles in an instrumental sense shows the most sensitivity to the author's profound respect for the status and responsibility of the church as the community of the *wise*, as the body of *the new human*.

The first participle, *speaking (laleō),* illustrates this point. The choice of the verb *speaking* may seem peculiar, since it appears that with *psalms, hymns,* and *spiritual songs* the readers are to "speak" to each other. It is not clear whether this is a heaping up of synonyms, a common stylistic feature of this letter, or whether it represents an inventory of various kinds of hymnody in the early Pauline churches: psalms known from the Scriptures, hymns to Christ (see 5:19b), and inspired songs born in the moment (Fee, 1987:650, 653-4, calls them "Spirit songs"; cf. 1 Cor. 14:26). What is clearly in the picture is the corporate musical experience of the gathered church. NRSV thus translates the Greek verb *laleō* as *singing*.

However, *laleō* bears great weight in the Pauline writings. With few exceptions it refers to communicating profound truth, often divine revelation. Paul frequently uses *laleō* in relation to his apostolic witness (e.g., 1 Cor. 2:6-7; 2 Cor. 2:17; 12:19; 13:3; 1 Thess. 2:2, 4). It is also the verb of choice when referring to the communication of divine truth in the congregation. Especially in 1 Corinthians 14, *speaking (laleō)* is referred to in a way that builds up the church, whether through tongues or prophecy (cf. most immediately, Eph. 4:25!). It is thus a fitting alternative to the parallel in Colossians 3:16, which has *teach and admonish.* So the call to *be filled with the Spirit* finds realization in sages *speaking* (in this rich Pauline sense) *to each other with psalms and hymns and spiritual songs.*

With the possible exception of *spiritual songs* (Fee, as above), there is thus little hint in this passage of ecstatic inspired speech, such as tongues or prophecy. There is recognition, rather, of the instructive, corrective, and motivational power of the church's hymnody. Such *singing* is then a way of addressing *one another*, of *speaking truth to each other* (cf. 4:25; 2:11-22, TLC), of having a *good word* that communicates grace to those in need of grace (4:29) and, as in the present text, of helping to fill each other with God's *Spirit*. The brief hymn fragment in 5:14 may be such a form of speech (cf. the use of christological hymns for exhortative purposes, as in 2:14-16 and Phil. 2:6-11). If *to each other* hints at antiphonal singing (Best, 1998:511), so much the better: form and intention buttress each other.

The most immediate audience for the church's hymns is the community of believers, and the second is *the Lord: singing and psalming with* or *from your heart to the Lord*. Singing and psalming, virtual synonyms, create the sense of worshipful music-making. *Heart* does not refer to silent inner singing, but singing from the very depth of one's being, where Christ has taken up residence (cf. 1:18; 3:17). *Lord* would have been heard by Jewish worshipers as a reference to God, but in Pauline churches, *Lord* was also the preeminent way to refer to Christ.

The presence of several christological hymns in the Pauline letters suggests that what is in view here are hymns to Christ as Lord (cf. e.g., Phil. 2:6-11; Col. 1:15-20; 1 Tim. 3:16; most immediately, Eph. 2:14-16!). Beyond that, we recall John 1 and the numerous hymns to Christ in Revelation. As we see, the confession of faith in Christ as *Lord* is often expressed in music and worship. Paul's claim in 1 Corinthians 12:3 that such acclamation of Jesus as Lord can only be the result of the Spirit's presence fits the present context well.

Verse 20 slightly shifts the audience of worship again, this time to *the God and Father in the name of our Lord Jesus Christ*, to whom *thanksgiving* is to be offered *always for everything*. The term *thanksgiving* appeared in 5:4 as the alternative to useless and base talk. Here it is evidence of being filled with the Spirit as well as the means for such filling. As in the case of 5:19, it appears that Colossians 3:16 has also had an influence on 5:20.

Despite the allusions to wine, it is highly unlikely that *thanksgiving* is here a reference to a particular part of a worship service, let alone to communion itself (*giving thanks, eucharisteō*, related to *eucharistia, thanksgiving* = eucharist; so also Best, 1998:515; Schnackenburg: 239). Worship is in view, true, but as a worshipful stance of gratitude generally, expressed in any number of ways. While *giving thanks* has deep roots in the psalms of Israel, here it describes the disposition of those who have been blessed (1:3-14), graced (cf. 2:5, 8; 4:32), and filled with the God's Spirit (cf. 3:14-21).

Thanks is to be given *always for everything*, echoing the words of Philippians 4:4-7. This is somewhat of a rhetorical exaggeration. The author does not have in mind the experiences—individual and corporate—for which thanksgiving becomes blasphemy. The wisdom tradition of Israel knew the inscrutable nature of suffering and how deeply wrong it is to force dishonest gratitude on the suffering (see Job). At the same time, this rhetorical flourish is witness to the depth of the experience of grace and love, often mysteriously in the most painful circumstances. It is intended to evoke a life in which gratitude to God informs *every* facet of life, including the struggles of family (5:22—6:9) or the battle against the forces of darkness (6:10-20). All of life is to be marked by grateful worship (1:3-14, TLC).

Such *thanksgiving* is offered *in the name of our Lord Jesus Christ.* Thus it gives witness to where and how that grace has been encountered (see all of chap. 2).

5:21 Inspired and Empowered for Servanthood

Translators typically begin a new paragraph with verse 21 (NAB is a rare exception). They see the call to subordination as introducing a new topic, the Household Code (next section). The participle *being subordinate (hupotassomenoi)* is read as a new imperative *(Be subordinate!)* rather than as the last in the chain of participles elaborating on what it means to be filled with the Spirit (so also Schnackenburg: 231-2, 244).

It will be important to consider 5:21 as an integral part of the next section, dealing with the Household Code. The Code is grammatically attached to it (5:21—6:9, notes). At the same time, 5:21 must also be read by itself as elaborating what it means to be filled with the Spirit (so also Best, 1998:515-6; Perkins: 125). We should thus consider 5:21 as "transitional" (Lincoln: 338, 365), related *both* to the exhortation to be filled with the Spirit *and* to the Household Code. Here we will consider it in light of the injunction to be filled with the Spirit, and in the next section in relation to the Household Code.

Much is at stake in how the verb *hupotassō* is understood and translated. Literally, the word means "to order under." Sometimes it can mean "to subject" as in "to vanquish" (e.g., Eph. 1:22; 1 Cor. 15:27-28). The passive is "to be subject" or "to be subjected." In the middle form, likely here, it means "to place *oneself* under the other" (Delling, 1972; *BAGD:* 847). In Hellenistic culture, such servility would generally not have been seen as a virtue. The feature of mutuality saves this call to *subordination* from idealizing servility and self-denigration and from locking in place a rigid hierarchy of power and status. Such *subordination* is envisioned as a corporate experience: *Place yourselves under **each other*** (*allēlois, mutually;* cf. esp. Rom. 12:10; Gal. 5:13; Phil. 2:3-4). So its usage here is consistent with the central emphasis in Pauline writings on a disposition of putting others first, of seeking their welfare above one's own.

There is an inherent irony in being subordinate *to each other*. If everyone is a slave of the other, then everyone is also a master. It is this irony that the choice of vocabulary exploits. In Philippians 2:3-4, Paul specifically calls on the saints in humility to put others before themselves. He goes on to quote the famous Christ hymn (Phil. 2:6-11) to root such deference in Christ's own disposition of voluntary slavery in relation to both God and the human community. Such is the intended meaning here in Ephesians. In imitation of Christ, believers are to take on the position of subordinates *to each other* (cf. 5:2). This is in contrast to understandings of subordination in which everyone "knows their place" and humbly and stoically accepts it (cf. 1 Clem. 37.1—38.2; 1QS 2.19-25).

Christ's servitude was nothing less than a radical expression of his sovereignty. His lordship found expression in his servanthood. It is as such a lord that he is to be imitated by his followers (5:25-31, notes). In them, such "servitude" becomes the expression of the sovereignty of the sons and daughters of God, of those who have been raised and exalted with Christ (2:5-6). Hence, it is important for us to see the grammatical dependency of this phrase on being *filled with the Spirit*. Mutual subordination requires full endowment with the power of God (so also Best, 1998:518).

The servant-Lord who is to be emulated by the believers is also a Christ to be *feared*. Believers are to subordinate themselves to each other *in fear of Christ (en phobō Christou),* a phrase unique in the NT. It finds its closest parallel in 6:5-9. Christ is a self-sacrificing reconciler (2:11-22) and also an exacting and demanding master and judge (cf. 5:5; cf. Barth, 1974:521; Best, 1998:518, rejects the suggestion of a hint of judgment here).

Modern translators understandably shy away from *fear* as a motivator for mutual relations in the church community. They are also reluctant to depict Christ in this way, given how differently he is depicted elsewhere in this letter (cf. 5:2, 25-27). Usually *phobos* is translated as *reverence* (as in NIV, NRSV, NJB, TEV). However it is translated, the phrase is roughly parallel to "the fear of the Lord" (or the less-common "fear of God") found frequently in the Bible (a few manuscripts offer these variants here; KJV). In these texts, *fear* often means reverence, awe, respect, and even gratitude (e.g., Pss. 25:12, 14; 34:4-11).

The shock effect of *phobos* should not be entirely eliminated, however (so Barth, 1974:608, 662-8; Lincoln: 366). *Fear of Christ* should be heard as more than reverence or respect. It should also be taken as a reminder of the awe and fear accorded the divine judge. The *fear of Christ* might be intended to carry such a mix of awe and gratitude, as well as a recognition of the obligation to live in keeping with the will of Christ, as *slaves of Christ* (6:6). Such an understanding of *fear of Christ* is not in tension with being *filled with the Spirit* (TBC). Many of these issues will be taken up again in the next section. Here it is enough but also crucial to relate mutual subordination and the fear of Christ to being filled with the Spirit.

THE TEXT IN BIBLICAL CONTEXT

Light and Darkness

In the Bible *light* is identified with God. God is the source of light as at creation (Gen. 1:3; cf. 2 Cor. 4:6). Moreover, God *is* light (cf. James 1:17; 1 John 1:5; Rev. 21:23), whose face shines upon those who do God's will (Num. 6:24-26; Ps. 89:15; and perhaps most dramatically Isa. 60:1-4). This adds to the sense of surprise when we read in Ephesians that believers are themselves *light* (5:11-14, notes). They are so, however, only *in the Lord* (5:8). Their relation to the light of God is therefore that of being the offspring, the *children of light*—a phrase that echoes "sons of light" in 1 Thessalonians 5:5 (cf. John 12:36). James also depicts God as "Father of lights" (1:17).

Nevertheless, those who now are *light* were *once* actually *darkness* (5:8). The term *darkness* is deeply resonant in biblical literature. It represents the chaos out of which God creates the light (Gen. 1:2-4; cf. Job 12:22). It also serves to depict death, the cessation of life (e.g., Job 10:20-22; 38:17). Frequently *darkness* denotes sin, rebellion, and oppression (e.g., Job 24:13-17; Ps. 44:19; Isa. 59:9). Its overtones of chaos, death, and alienation suggest God's fearsome wrath and judgment (e.g., Isa. 47:5; Jer. 13:16; Ezek. 32:8; Joel 2:2, 31; Amos 5:20; Zeph. 1:15).

Not surprisingly, such a stark contrast can lead to a dualistic view of human life and of the human community. Some view this passage in light of a material dualism as found in Gnosticism (e.g., Russell: 96-7). But conceptualizing humanity and its practices in this manner has stronger affinities with the radical sectarianism of Qumran, at the Dead Sea. In the view of those covenanters, humanity is made up of two camps, those with a "spirit of deceit" who "walk in darkness," and those with a "spirit of truth" who "walk in light" as "sons of justice" (1QS 3.17—4.1).

The hostility of Qumran to those deemed to live in darkness is expressed in the title of their famous scroll The War of the Sons of Light Against the Sons of Darkness (1QM). The piety of Qumran, or one like it, may have influenced this section of Ephesians in particular (so also Perkins: 117). It may also have influenced 2 Corinthians 6:14-15: "What fellowship is there between light and darkness? Or what does a believer share with an unbeliever?"

In the Gospel of John, *light* and *darkness* function as mutually exclusive realms, which nevertheless interpenetrate. Thus in John 1 the "light" (Christ) enters the "darkness," which can neither absorb it nor overcome it (1:4-9). While the light enlightens every person (1:9; 8:12), only those who believe become "children of light" (12:36). They "do the truth" and act "in God"; therefore they seek the "light" (3:21). For both John and Ephesians, the transition point of persons moving from darkness to light is "believing" (e.g., John 1:12-13; Eph. 2:8). Ephesians moves further than John, though, in tying the experience of enlightenment to the experience of baptism and thus to entry into a corporate *new human* (5:14, notes).

Fear

The difficulty in translating the term rendered literally as *fear (phobos)* is illustrated by a survey of several biblical instances. The stylistic device of parallelism in Hebrew poetry works in the beatitude of Psalm 112:1 to treat "fear" and "delight" as synonyms: "Happy is the one who *fears* the Lord, who *delights* in God's commandments." There are no overtones of terror in such an understanding. The "fear of the Lord" is thus often related to "wisdom" and "insight" into God's will (cf. Eph. 5:15-17, notes; e.g. Ps. 111:10; Prov. 2:5-6). Recall Sirach (Ecclus.) 1:16, cited above, where fearing the Lord is related to being "inebriated" by the fruit of wisdom (see Ecclus./Sirach 1–2). In particular, fidelity to the law is virtually synonymous with "fearing the Lord" (Balz: 9.201-8; 212-7).

In short, there are uses of the phrase "fear of the Lord" that are not so much laced with threat as they are with a deep sense of gratitude and at the same time a profound sense of awe. This is awe at both the transcendence and the "awe-full" nearness of God, whose name YHWH was rendered in the Greek OT (LXX) as "Lord *(kurios)*" out of precisely such "fear."

At the same time, the Bible frequently characterizes God as fearsome in his response to sin and disobedience (cf., e.g., Deut. 6:13-19; Isa. 2:10, 19-21; and many other texts relating "fear of the Lord" to judgment). God is not to be mocked or provoked, and God's grace is not to be presumed upon; this conviction is essential to the NT generally, finding expression in Ephesians 5:5-6 (cf. 4:25-26, notes). Notice, for example, that in 2 Corinthians 5:10-11 the "fear of the Lord" is related to "the judgment seat of Christ" (cf. also 1 Thess. 5:2-3; 2 Thess. 1:5-10). It is this conviction that underlies the surprising twist of grace in 2:4 (notes). God's generosity and resourcefulness at reconciliation are not blind to evil and sin.

' While God embraces the world with grace, he will not tolerate evil at home. In Romans 6:1-2, Paul asks rhetorically, "Should we continue in sin in order that grace may abound? By no means! How can we who died to sin go on living in it?" Believers are to remove themselves from the scene of wrath by no longer participating in that way of living (cf. 1 Thess. 5:4-5). One should be careful not to rule out such overtones in Ephesians 5:21.

Drunkenness as Alienation from God

Along with ignorance, sleep, and death, drunkenness is a common biblical characterization of life apart from God. *Drunkenness* is particularly well suited to depict those who live this way, not conscious of their true state of affairs. Through *debauchery* (Eph. 5:18, *dissipation,* NJB; cf. 4:19), they have drunk themselves into a moral and spiritual stupor.

A particularly striking example is Amos 6:3-6. This text combines many notes found in our text: the people deliberately turn their minds from "the evil day" (Amos 6:3; cf. Eph. 5:16); they sleep on beds of ivory (6:4; cf. Eph. 5:14); they sing idle songs, imitating David (6:5; cf. in contrast *psalming* in Eph 5:19); and they drink wine from bowls (6:6). In Isaiah 28, Judah's drunken leaders are like "the drunks of Ephraim" (28:1, 3); they have lost all ability to understand God's will (28:7-13). In Pauline writings, the connection between sleep and drunkenness and alienation from God is seen clearly in Romans 13:13 and 1 Thessalonians 5:7.

Destructive and Constructive Speech

The concern with both the beneficial and destructive effects of speech in Ephesians 5:4, 11-14, 19-20 finds an echo in James 3, which identifies the tongue as a powerful agent of destruction and grace. In Ephesians, as in James, words have power to shape reality—for good or ill (cf. Eph. 4:29). Words are thus *actions* that can communicate grace to those inside and outside the church. Words can bring destruction on both speaker and hearer alike (5:5-6). This accounts for the weight given in the notes on *naming* (cf. 3:14; 5:3, 11-12).

Hymnody

The presence of hymnody in this passage, both by example (5:14) and as a focus of exhortation (5:19-20), is a vivid reminder of an important feature in the piety of the early churches. Ephesians and other writings of the NT frequently quote the Psalms, thus indicating the practice among Jewish Jesus-believers of singing psalms. Such a practice would thereby have entered into the worship life of Gentile believers as well.

Ephesians 5:14 and 5:19b also speak of the rich tradition of hymns to Christ. Hymns are the cradle of Christology. We might think here of the hymns found in the Psalter or in Isaiah, for example, as the raw materials of Christology (e.g., Pss. 8; 110; Isa. 9; 11). Beyond Ephesians 2:14-16 and 5:14, and perhaps 1:3-14 and 1:19-23, we note John 1; Philippians 2:6-11; Colossians 1:15-20; and the many hymns in John's Revelation (e.g., chap. 5).

Hymnody serves *both* as a means of giving praise to God, to laud the glory and significance of Jesus as the Christ, *and* as a means of ethical exhortation. The last point is particularly relevant here. For example, Paul quotes one of the greatest of christological hymns, Philippians 2:6-11, to undergird his exhortation for radical, humble mutuality. Hymns are thus a repository of vision and guidance, a vision appropriated and honed in the act of worship. They are also, as this passage reminds us, a means by which believers receive the fullness of the Spirit.

THE TEXT IN THE LIFE OF THE CHURCH

This passage has many points of contact with issues faced by churches in the nonconformist stream of Christian tradition. A number of them have been explored at 2:1-10; 2:11-22; and 4:17—5:2.

The Nerve to Be Different

Perhaps the biggest challenge posed by this passage has to do with the nerve to be different. *Nonconformity* to *the world* (2:12) or *this age* (1:21) was a test of fidelity to Christ in the early church and has been since for many church traditions, especially for those who are heir to the Radical Reformation. Nonconformity's greatest vulnerability is rigidity and self-righteousness. Once nonconformity has become set into patterns of differentness, it is often nurtured and safeguarded by ethnic, socioeconomic, and cultural factors at least as much as by commitments to faithfulness. It has also often led to estrangement from the human family as a whole and thus to ignorance about "them" and "what they do."

In much of the church, however, nonconformity is increasingly a quaint relic of the past. Rural folk have moved to the city, and once ethnically and culturally distinct people have found a home in the broad mainstream of society. The harsh dualism of Ephesians—*light* and *darkness, children of light* and *sons of disobedience*—no longer strikes many Christians as true to their experience. Such dualism is increasingly identified as arrogant, dishonest, and finally self-deluding (Russell: 97, with a critique of dualism). "Embracing" texts such as Ephesians 1:10; 2:11-22; and 3:14 (notes) are more palatable.

As our study has shown, Ephesians is uncompromising with respect to nonconformity but places it strategically in the context of transformation. Ephesians sees nonconformity largely as part of the overall strategy of God to *gather up all things in Christ* (1:10). Heirs of the radical tradition of being church need to ask themselves whether greater friendship with "the world" is true friendliness toward those who live in it. To blunt the distinction of light and darkness softens the sometimes harsh glare of the light but does those sitting in darkness no favor. It breaks solidarity with them as fellow human beings. It no longer speaks truth to them about the true nature of darkness; it no longer "exposes" the works of darkness (5:11). More important, it also neglects to speak the truth about the gospel of transformation.

The absence of light means drowsiness and finally sleep also for those who are called to be light. They forget that *the days are evil* (5:16). Accommodation to "the world" is a betrayal of the vision of transformative nonconformity. So also is the closed, self-satisfied, and ethnically reinforced separatism to which elements in the believers church tradition have succumbed and to which others have justly reacted. Both miss the *hopeful* difference we see in Jesus, which Paul and his students were so concerned to instill in the church as his body.

Sex and Greed

In its morally numbing preoccupation with sex, Western culture is not particularly different from the first century. The present text shows great sensitivity to the seriousness of sexual preoccupation in word and deed (5:3, 5). Sexual license is an issue in and of itself, and in 5:2-21 it also is part of greed more generally. The church can help to develop new taboos against abuse and disrespect of persons in the area of sexual relations (TLC for 4:17—5:2). But the church needs to be equally sensitive to abuse and disrespect generated by all forms of greed, particularly when the (financial) market increasingly functions as the source of value and values.

At the same time, the church's disposition toward sex and all of God's material gifts needs to be shaped by gratitude and thanksgiving, by worship. Here too, the separatism and nonconformity of the church needs to be motivated by the desire not to flee the scene but to transform it into the creation that God once called and wishes again to call "*good*."

Culture Wars at Worship Time

When in our music God is glorified,
and adoration leaves no room for pride,
it is as though the whole creation cried
Alleluia! (*HWB,* 44)

Hymnody represents one of the central elements of worship. In many congregations, it has also become a source of the most intense conflicts. Music-making in the church has become a battleground for the clash of cultures. It is a clash between innovation and tradition, between music as evangelistic tool versus music as preserver of identity, between inherited treasure and inspired utterance, and between the extremes of elitism and the banalities of ephemeral popularity (Dawn, 1995:165-204, with excellent discussion).

Our text is a reminder that music-making is one of the church's most important acts (5:19-20). It is inextricably related to being filled with the Spirit. On one hand, it is the effect of having received from God the gift of the Spirit. On the other, it becomes communication directed outward from the singer(s). As such, it has three audiences: one is fellow believers or the congregation (5:19); the second is Christ (5:19); and the third is God the Father (5:20).

It is right to sing *to each other.* In this context, hymnody becomes a way of *speaking truth to the neighbor* (cf. 4:15, 25; 5:19, *laleō, speak*). This also means that the church's music must address brothers and sisters in a way that speaks to them and engages their experience. Communication thus becomes a crucial measure of appropriateness. This will *necessarily* result in a great variety of styles of music, which the church does well to anticipate and even celebrate.

An eighteenth-century hymn by Graf von Zinzendorf is a fitting example of hymnody as mutual encouragement and worshipful peace-making amid the tensions of a culturally diverse community of faith. It is called *Heart with Loving Heart United:*

May we all so love each other and all selfish claims deny,
so that each one for the other will not hesitate to die.
Even so our Lord has loved us, for our lives he gave his life.

Still he grieves and still he suffers, for our selfishness and strife.
(*HWB*, 420, stanza 2)

Concerns at the heart of Ephesians come to forceful expression in
the final stanza. It expresses the plea that God might give the church
"love's compassion so that everyone may see / in our fellowship the
promise of a *new humanity*" (italics added).

The second audience for the church's song is Christ. Hymnody is
one of the most important means by which the church reminds itself
of who its Lord is, what it means for him to have given himself for the
church (5:2), and what he calls members of his body to be and do in
the world. Hymnody is one way to *learn Christ* (4:20), from birth, to
ministry, to death, to resurrection, and finally to exaltation and lordship. Of the countless hymns that are sung to Christ, John Oxenham's
"In Christ There Is No East or West" captures the essence of worship
as envisioned by the author of Ephesians:

In Christ there is no East or West, in him no South or North,
but one great fellowship of love throughout the whole wide earth.

In him shall true hearts ev'rywhere their high communion find.
His service is the golden cord close binding humankind.
(*HWB*, 306, stanzas 1-2)

Finally, just as Psalm 22:3 speaks of God as "enthroned on the
praises of Israel," so the church, made up of Jews and Gentiles,
furnishes a home for God (2:21-22) with its ceaselessly performed
hymnody of thanksgiving.

Now thank we all our God with heart and hands and voices,
who wondrous things has done, in whom this world rejoices,
who, from our mothers' arms, has bless'd us on our way
with countless gifts of love, and still is ours today. (*HWB*, 86, stanza 1)

In this way the capacity to express praise, awe, respect, and love
becomes a further measure of the appropriateness of hymnody.
Clashes over style and aesthetics will always accompany the hymnic
worship of the church (Dawn, as above). This is so because "we are
all self-appointed experts in the field of liturgical and corporate praise"
(R. Martin, 1991:64). More important, there will be serious tensions
and conflicts *especially if the church is faithful*, if it is successful in
breaking down walls of division and widening the circle of the family
(TLC for 2:11-22).

In many churches, music has become one of the prime contexts
for strife and thus for peacemaking. It is thus particularly fitting for

Ephesians to have the call for *mutual subordination* follow right after the exhortation to sing hymns. Such central churchly tasks as giving Spirit-filled guidance to each other, on one hand, and "enthroning" God, on the other, cannot be allowed to fall prey to matters of taste, disrespect, and intransigence that tend to characterize all sides in the culture wars around worship.

Mutual Subordination

The issue of *subordination* in Ephesians 5:21 is as important as it is contentious for contemporary believers. It is enough here to note that *mutual subordination* is a manifestation of empowerment with and by the Spirit of God. This is one realm in which the church's redemptive difference should show itself most dramatically. It is also one realm in which the church's difference is waning in favor of different notions of power and sovereignty.

Do believers in the radical stream of the church understand *subordination* as wisdom born of the Spirit? Or do they see it as folly? Do they see subordination as light or as darkness? Do they see *mutual* subordination as the shape of sovereignty for those who have learned the truth that is in Jesus?

One must ask these questions sensitively since there are many in the church, especially women, who have not experienced subordination as mutual, nor as voluntary, least of all as an expression of *their own* empowerment. For many, subordination equals subjection—of women to men, poor to rich, black to white, uneducated to educated, laity to clergy, employee to supervisor. To appeal to the *fear of Christ* (5:21) is then viewed as only reinforcing such one-sided servitude (TLC for 5:21—6:9). This text is restoring, renewing, and empowering *only* if *all* in the church see *others* as greater than *themselves*. Only then will *all* experience themselves as beloved children of light, as Spirit-filled sages and singers.

Ephesians 5:21—6:9

The Household Code

PREVIEW

The Household Code in Ephesians looms large in the church's struggle for faithfulness in the relationship between women and men in home and church. "Household Code" roughly translates Luther's German *Haustafel* (table of house-rules), still the preferred label in more technical discussions (e.g., Best, 1998:519-21; cf. J. H. Yoder, 1994:162). Some prefer "Domestic Code" (E. Martin: 181) or "station codes" (Schroeder, 1976:546; R. Martin, 1991:73). Regardless of the label, our text is part of a larger tradition of formalized instructions for the household (TBC).

At the outset, notice several features of this text: First, the family in the Household Code includes the extended family and those who are economically related to that social unit—more the family business than just the nuclear family (Thurston: 138-9). In addition, given the emphasis on church as home and family in the earlier parts of Ephesians (e.g., 2:19-22; 3:14; 4:6, 16), these instructions should be read as applying by implication to the church family as a whole.

Second, comparison with 1 Peter shows that the instructions in Ephesians are directed more heavily to those in dominant social positions (slaves are a notable exception; TBC). This is important for appreciating the particular twist our author places on the tradition.

Third, Christ is both model and Lord throughout this passage. Does this tend to undergird hierarchical structures of authority in home and society, or to soften them, or even to undo them? Readers may want to read the TBC to familiarize themselves with the tradition of the Household Code and better appreciate the specific ways Ephesians takes up the tradition.

Structure of the Household Code (5:21—6:9)

Be filled with the spirit . . . (5:18)
by being subordinate to each other in fear of Christ. (5:21)
 WIVES to their own husbands as to the Lord,
  because a husband is head of the wife
   as Christ is head of the church,
    and Savior of the body.
   As the church is subordinate to Christ,
  so also the wives to their husbands. (5:22-24)
 HUSBANDS, love the wives
   as Christ loved the church
    and gave himself up for her
     in order to render her holy,
     in order to present the church to himself glorious,
     in order that she might be holy and blameless.
  So husbands ought to love their wives as their own bodies
   as also Christ the church,
    because we are members of his body.
    [becoming one flesh, Gen. 2:24]
   This is a great mystery of Christ and the church.
  So let each one of you love his own wife as himself,
 but the wife is to fear the husband. (5:25-33)

 CHILDREN, obey your parents,
  for this is just.
  [honoring parents, Exod. 20:12//Deut. 5:16]
 And FATHERS, do not provoke your children to anger,
  but nurture them with training and instruction. (6:1-4)

 SLAVES, obey those who are lords according to the flesh,
  with fear and singleness of heart,
   as slaves of Christ doing the will of God,
  knowing that each one who does good will be repaid by the Lord.
 And MASTERS, do these things toward them,
  knowing that both their and your Master is in heaven,
   and with him there is no respect of status. (6:5-9)

OUTLINE

Bridge or Heading? 5:21

Wives and Husbands, 5:22-33
 5:22-24, 33b Wives
 5:25-33   Husbands

Children and Parents, 6:1-4
    6:1-3   Children
    6:4   Fathers

Slaves and Masters, 6:5-9
    6:5-8   Slaves
    6:9   Masters

EXPLANATORY NOTES

Bridge or Heading? 5:21

As indicated in the discussion of 5:21 in the previous section, the call to *subordination* is grammatically dependent on the command to *be filled with the Spirit* (5:18). The imperative *to be subordinate* is not explicitly present in verse 22 in the most reliable Greek manuscripts (NIV, NRSV, and many other versions begin a new paragraph at 5:22 and repeat the call for subordination; Schematic Trans.). The call to subordination in 5:21, furthermore, is in direct continuity with what it means to *walk as the wise in evil days* (5:15-16). Thus, *mutual subordination* is the walk of the wise, a manner of life rooted in God's wisdom, empowered by the Spirit, and enlivened by worship.

Mutual subordination is nothing less than charismatic activity. Therefore, even though the Household Code is a tradition that predates Ephesians (TBC), it expands on one aspect of what it means to *be filled with the Spirit*, specifically, to *be subordinate to one another*. Verses 18 and 21 are the twin lenses through which readers of Ephesians are invited to view the familiar tradition of the Household Code.

Wives and Husbands 5:22-33

The first relationship addressed in the Household Code is that between wives and husbands: wives are to be *subordinate* to their husbands; husbands are to *love* their wives. Even a quick comparison of the Household Codes in Ephesians and Colossians shows that Ephesians expands considerably on these brief instructions, revealing the author's vision and special concerns (Chart 2, TBC, comparing this text with Col. 3:18-19).

It is most significant that Ephesians compares the relationship between wife and husband directly to that between church and Christ. The two marriages illuminate each other. They do so to such an extent, in fact, that in 5:32 the author must specify *which* marriage is being talked about. While the immediate concern is clearly to offer guidance to wives and husbands for their relationship to each other, there is the overarching concern to illumine the relationship of the church to "her" Lord and Savior.

5:22-24, 33b Wives

As in Colossians, wives are addressed first. They are to be sub-ordinate *to their own husbands as to the Lord*. As stated above, that command must be inferred from 5: 21 (Structure of 5:21—6:9; Schematic Trans.). While *hupotassō* can imply more negatively "blind obedience, docile servility, and unthinking subservience" (R. Martin, 1991:69), the term means quite literally "to order oneself under" (5:21, notes). I prefer to use this less-interpretive translation and allow the meaning to emerge.

The instructions to wives are brief. Instead of the clause in Colossians, "as is fitting in the Lord," we find the stronger *as to the Lord*. The phrase echoes the unusual *in fear of Christ* in 5:21 (5:3-21, notes on *fear*). *Fear (phobos,* also translated as *respect),* reappears in 5:33b in verb form *(phobeomai),* to identify the proper stance of wife to husband. These two occurrences thus form an *inclu-sio* (marking a section by repeating a beginning word or phrase at the end).

A wife's subordination to her husband is to correspond, first, to her own subordination to Christ (5:22) and second, to the church's subordination to Christ, who *is head of the church, himself Savior of the body* (5:23). The stance of the wife in relation to her husband is thus grounded in the relationship of the church to the church's Lord and Savior, Christ. That relationship is to illumine the quality of subordination of the wife to her husband.

Marriage is here combined with the image of *body* and *head*. *Body* as a metaphor for church is found earlier in Ephesians (1:23; 2:16; 3:6; 4:4, 12, 16) and is familiar from earlier Pauline letters, notably Romans 12 and 1 Corinthians 12. But to speak of Christ as *head of the body* appears elsewhere only in Ephesians 1:22 and 4:15, and earlier in Colossians 1:18 and 2:19.

What is the extent or limit of this subordination? On one hand, *in everything* (5:24, NIV, NRSV) sets no limits. On the other, such sub-ordination is qualified by the fact that it is voluntary, as is the church's subordination to "her" Lord. It is qualified, more significantly, by how Christ, and thus the husband, is *head*.

Like *subordination*, *head* can have several meanings *["Head"]*. It can imply superior status and authority, and it can mean "origin" (or "source"). As the essay on *"Head"* indicates, in Ephesians *head* carries the meaning of both authority and source. On one hand, God has made Christ *head over* all powers and every name for or through the church, which is his *body* (1:22, notes; headship is related to status, authority, and victory through reference to both Ps. 8:6 and 110:1). On the other hand, the church as an organism—as a *body*—grows into the *head*, which is at the same time the *source* of its growth (4:15-16; cf. 2:15).

Head thus expresses both the *status* of Christ as Savior and Lord over all (cf. Col. 1:18) and the *purpose* of Christ as *source* and *goal* of the church. The husband's relationship to his wife is thus given enormous significance, even if the husband's role can only emulate the cosmic or churchly headship of Christ very faintly.

Does the introduction of Christ and husbands as *heads* aid *mutuality* of subordination? Or does it render subordination all the more one-sided? The wording of the instructions to wives would appear to fall considerably short of the *mutuality* called for in 5:21. Wives, unlike husbands, are conspicuously *not* asked to love, but rather (in dependency on 5:21) to *subordinate themselves* out of *fear* (reemphasized in 5:33!). At best, the wifes' subordination to her husband suggests obedience, deference, respect, and discipleship, but hardly reciprocity, let alone being his peer.

Nothing is gained by obscuring the evident difficulties of this text. There truly is tension in this passage, regardless of one's interpretive stance, and it runs deep. It is not simply a tension between gospel and culture. On one hand, the author's primary concern is for the church to be faithful (*subordinate*) to "her" Lord. When applied to the wife-husband relationship, this suggests unqualified subordination of the wife to the husband. On the other hand, and entirely in keeping with the great Christ hymn in Philippians 2:6-11, nothing signifies a deeper, more unqualified subordination to the Christ presented in Ephesians than offering *mutual* subordination. This means being servants and slaves of *each other* and refusing to lord it over *each other* (notes on 1:15-23; 2:11-22; 3:1-21; 4:1-16; 6:10-20).

Given this last point, we should thus be on the lookout for features with the potential to loosen or even undo a notion of familial relationships based on a chain of command. Let me identify a few. The first one is the weakest, at least as it relates to women in the Household Code as found in Ephesian. It is sometimes pointed out that, in contrast to what one might have expected in a patriarchal list of household duties, wives are addressed first and also directly as moral agents in their own right (e.g., Best, 1998:532; E. Martin: 183, 188; Schroeder 1959:89; J. H. Yoder 1994:171). One should be careful not to overplay this point. Wives *are* directly addressed in Colossians and in 1 Peter, but not clearly so in Ephesians, as the translations indicate (GNB, NIV, NRSV, REB have a direct address; NAB, NJB do not). Indeed, Ephesians has no clear *direct* address to wives (esp. 5:33).

A more important counterweight to patriarchal reinforcement is the grammatical dependency of the instruction to wives on the **mutual** *subordination* of 5:21, a point consistently obscured by translators. If the author of Ephesians has adapted the Code found in Colossians, as most scholars rightly hold, then the summons to *subordination* has been lifted out of the command to women (cf. Col. 3:18; 1 Pet. 3:1) and made into the rubric for the whole Code (5:21). Barth makes the most of this: A "wife's subordination to her husband is commanded *only* within the frame of *mutual* subordination" (1974:610, italics added).

Note, however, that such a "frame" is provided *only* in the Ephesian version of the Household Code; it is *not* characteristic of the Household Code tradition as a whole. *Mutual (allēlōn)* is a frequent and crucial term in Pauline exhortation (cf., e.g., Rom. 12:10, 16; 13:8; 14:19; 15:7; 1 Cor. 11:33; 12:25; Phil. 2:2; 1 Thess. 3:12). It is not used lightly here or elsewhere in Ephesians (4:2, 25, 32). Thereby the author has deliberately injected the Pauline emphasis on reciprocity into household arrangements *not* typically characterized by such mutuality and reciprocity. Could this have been done lightly? Could it have passed unnoticed by superiors in domestic relations?

The third aspect that potentially destabilizes the patriarchal order is, ironically, the way the author employs the term *head*. In Ephesians, the two meanings of head as "authority" and "source" converge to the advantage of the church *["Head"]*. In 5:23, Christ as *head* is identified also as the body's *Savior*. That is surely a reference to his offering of his life (5:25; cf. 2:13, 16; 5:2) and also to his ongoing "saving" of the church (5:26; cf. 3:16-19). As 1:15-23 shows, the church is the prime beneficiary of the power that raised and exalted Christ—that *gave him to be head for the church* (or *through the church;* 1:15-23, notes). This is reinforced in 2:5-6, where those who were *once dead have been raised and seated with Christ in the heavenlies.*

Most explicitly, in 4:15-16 Christ is the *head* into which the *body*—the church—*grows*, and the body receives from Christ what it takes to grow (4:15-16, notes). In Ephesians the church does not so much exist for Christ as Christ exists for the church. The author of Ephesians wants these overtones to be part of the resonance *head* carries in the command to wives and, by implication, to husbands. The nature of Christ's headship is meant to set the terms within which *subordination* is given content. Headship means lordship, yes, but a lordship that is expressed most fully in liberating and exalting the subordinate one. That is the character of both Christology and ecclesiology in Ephesians.

No doubt the tension in these words to wives results in part from fusing the appeal to Christ with a Household Code tradition reflective of patriarchal assumptions. But as stated earlier, the ambiguity results also from the inherent paradox at the heart of discipleship: being subordinate to and imitating a Lord who is a slave (cf. Phil. 2:6-11). This fragile and unstable mixture prevents any easy inference as to what this text means concretely for the relationship of wives to their husbands. As we shall now see, this unstable chemistry also pervades the words directed to husbands.

5:25-33 Husbands

Husbands are given considerably more attention in Ephesians than in Colossians (esp. Chart 2, TBC; in Colossians, the greatest attention is given to slaves; in 1 Peter, to slaves and wives; Chart 1, TBC). Perhaps in the life setting in Ephesians, the church is more established and thus includes more settled and more complete families (Gnilka: 276; Best, 1997:189-203, and 1998:524-7, considers the Code as found in Ephesians and Colossians to be out of touch with the social realities of a church made up of mixed families of believers and unbelievers). In a patriarchal structure, the father/husband determines the ethos of the family. Addressing that role/station should therefore have a ripple effect on the whole family system (J. H. Yoder, 1994:177-8). This accounts for the extent of attention given to husbands.

Be that as it may, it hardly explains the disproportionate amount of space given to slaves in 6:5-9. More likely, the author is using the husband slot in the Code to explore the relationship between Christ and church, as also in the rest of the letter (esp. 1:22-23; 2:11-22; 4:1-16). The exhortation to husbands gives the author opportunity for two things: to provide a model for how husbands are to behave toward their wives as imitators of Christ, *and also* to reflect theologically and worshipfully on the relationship between Christ and the church. The latter objective has a tendency to crowd out the former, leading to the need for a clarifying comment in 5:32.

This section can be divided into two parts. A brief overview might be helpful here. In the first part (5:25-28a), husbands are asked *to love their wives as Christ loved the church* (5:25). This love is described as Christ *giving himself up* for the sake of his bride, the church, to present her to himself *glorious, holy, and unblemished, without spot or wrinkle* (5:26-27). The ambience of romantic love is mixed with that of self-sacrifice. Verse 28a reminds husbands that Christ's love for the church, his body, is the model for the love they are to have for their own wives, their own bodies.

Verse 28 concludes the first part and opens the second (5:28-33) by recalling the image of *the body* (seen earlier in the instructions to wives, 5:23) and by introducing the concept of self-love. Verse 29 follows the appeal to self-love with a proverb-like observation that no one hates his own *flesh*. This is related to Christ's *care and nurture* of his own body, the church (5:30).

Flesh and *body* interact here in unusual fashion. Normally in Pauline letters, *flesh (sarx)* opposes *spirit (pneuma;* cf. Rom. 8; Gal. 5; also Eph. 2:3, 11). Not so here. The reference to *flesh* may be invited by Ephesians 5:31 quoting Genesis 2:24: *A person will leave father and mother and be joined to his wife. And the two will become one **flesh***. This fleshly union and the process leading up to it are described as *a great mystery*, a term loaded in Ephesians with the full agenda of salvation (1:10; 3:3-9; 6:19). The *mystery* is not, however, the unity of husband and wife, but rather God's design for the unity of the cosmos as reflected in the "fleshly" union of Christ and church, as made clear in 5:31-32 (cf. 2:14-15).

After reflecting on Christ and the church, the author returns in 5:33 to husbands, exhorting them to love their wives as they do themselves. At the end of the verse, wives are asked indirectly and tersely to *fear their husbands*. The reintroduction of *fear* (or *respect;* cf. 5:21) signals the conclusion of this section of the Code and forms an *inclusio* (marking a section by repeating a beginning word or phrase at the end).

At first reading, the text appears to have as its chief objective to buttress the superior place of husbands over wives. First, the relationship of husbands to wives is analogous to that of the Lord and the church. In 5:21 believers are to *fear* Christ; in 5:33 wives are to *fear* their husbands. Even if *fear* is not to be understood as "fright" or "terror" (most versions prefer "respect"; 5:21, notes), it does suggest an inferior's awe-full respect for a superior. Second, wives are identified with the husbands' own *flesh* to such an extent that love of wife is love of self, as we see in 5:28b. The patriarchal prerogative of the husband thus appears to be given both christological and psychological legitimation.

But is it? As in the instructions to wives earlier, both the appeal to Christ and the appeal to self-love have the potential to destabilize patriarchal privilege. First, we must pay attention to *how* Christ is to be emulated by his fellow *heads* (husbands). Despite the explicit allusion to the Genesis creation account in 5:31, the husband is *not* invited to lord it over his wife (cf. Gen. 3:16) but to *love* her with the same love with which Christ loved the church. In Genesis 3, the husband lording it over the woman was a divine *curse* pronounced as a response to sin; in Ephesians, the husband's love emulates God's *blessing* of creation in Christ (cf. Eph. 1). The love of the husband is to emulate the love that desires the full re-creation and flowering of creation.

Whereas *fear* frames this passage (5:21, 33), there is, in fact, nothing in Christ's demeanor as described here that is remotely fearsome. Christ *loved* the church *and gave **himself** up for her*, a phrase that points to his death on the cross—already given prominence in the drama of peace, reconciliation, and new creation in 2:14-16. To imitate that headship may turn out to be truly fearsome, but for husbands, not wives! Here Christ's self-giving love intentionally echoes 5:2, where love and self-sacrifice are set forth as a model for how believers are to worship with their whole life (5:2, notes). This Pauline turn of phrase, *Christ . . . gave himself up* (5:25), is loaded with the full freight of Christ's work of salvation (cf. Gal. 2:20). To imitate such a Christ is the imitation of God (5:1) and radically self-giving.

Here such love is specifically demanded of *husbands*. They are to love *as Christ loved*. Their role is that of living and dying for the sake of the *other*, their spouse. A husband's love finds expression in the liberation, not of himself, but of his spouse. If such identification with Christ buttresses the status of the husband, it is, ironically, for the purpose of serving the interests of his spouse. Such love necessarily subordinates *self*-interest to the interests of the *other*.

The term employed for *love* here is *agapē,* a term often set over against the rather "cool" *philia,* friendship love, or the "hot" *eros,* sensual or sexual love. *Agapē,* in contrast, is characterized as not selfish or driven by emotion or attraction. These distinctions have been overplayed. *Agapē* is too quickly emptied of passion and desire, and understood largely as self-denial, directed wholly to the interests of the other (cf. 1 Cor. 13). To be sure, this *other*-directedness does characterize in large measure the love commended here, as we have just seen. Christ's love *is* deeply self-giving. But the analogy of marriage and the allusion to sexual union is intended to express also the passion and desire at the root of Christ's love for the church. We should thus not miss the element of passionate love in the following imagery of the bridal bath (5:26-27) and the consummation of marriage (5:31; contra Best, 1998:540).

Three purpose clauses in 5:26-27 elaborate on the self-giving of Christ's love (Structure of 5:21—6:9; Schematic Trans.). First, Christ is depicted as washing his bride *in order to make her holy*. The phrase *cleansing her by washing with the water in word* is rich in association. Baptism is the most immediate. *In word*, or *with the word*, is then usually taken to refer to a baptismal formula such as *in the name of Jesus* (Best, 1998:543-4; Gnilka: 281; Houlden: 334; Lincoln: 375; Schnackenburg: 250).

Though it would be difficult to deny some allusion to baptism, in Pauline circles baptism was more commonly connected to participation in Christ's death and resurrection (cf., e.g., Rom. 6). Moreover, though an allusion to baptism would stress past events in the believers' lives, Christ's sanctifying and cleansing love is here envisioned as ongoing. That is the basis for appealing to Christ's love as a model for husbands in their *ongoing* love for their wives. *Washing in word* (5:26) may thus suggest, in addition to baptism, the *ongoing* nurturing and sanctifying effect of the ministry of the word (cf. the emphasis on word-ministries in 4:11).

Our text also evokes the rich imagery of Ezekiel 16:8-14 (e.g., Barth, 1974:693; Best, 1998:543; Lincoln: 375). Yнwн, upon finding young Jerusalem naked and bloodied, bathes her and readies her for marriage. Such an allusion serves in Ephesians to place Christ's act of finding a bride and readying her for marriage in the larger context of salvation, described with quite different imagery in chapter 2. Ephesians 2 describes a liberation of *sons of disobedience* from the clutches of the evil power of the air (2:1-10), and then a great act of peacemaking *in the flesh* and the rebirth of a *new human* (2:11-22). The same event is here depicted as an act of washing and sanctifying a bride.

This image of *washing*, on one hand, depicts Christ as the maid readying the bride for the wedding or, as Best puts it, as the "beautician" (1998:546). On the other hand, Christ is depicted as the lover amorously engaged in the care of his beloved. Neither image is one of domination. Servanthood, desire, and pleasure combine to portray the self-giving and saving love of Christ.

The purpose of Christ's loving activity is to render his spouse *glorious, holy,* and *without spot or wrinkle* (5:27). We might object that this panders to (male?) fantasies of the perfect consort. However, the central intention is not to reinforce unrealistic and impossible expectations of one's wife, but to recall for readers the infinitely *gracious* work of salvation in and through Christ *on their behalf*. The *holiness* and *blamelessness* of the church is *Christ's* work, however much it engages all of the energies of its members. *Holiness* and *blamelessness* are an essential outcome of Christ's peacemaking (cf. 2:20-22; cf. 2:10; 4:24). So likewise are husbands to make the full and complete humanity of their wives their consuming passion.

This way of characterizing a husband's *love* in effect renders the subordination of the wife to such a husband **mutual** subordination. That is not to claim that such subordination is necessarily understood by the author to be equal in measure to that of wives. Patriarchal assumptions may well have prevented the author from fully drawing such an inference. That should not prevent *us*, however, from observing that the content of the love the husband is called to exercise is hardly distinguishable from the most severe expressions of subordination: washing, caring for, and dying for the sake of others.

But a surprise awaits us, at least at the outset. Up to this point, the central emphasis has been on *love-for-the-other*—Christ's love for the church (5:25-27). The second half of the words to husbands (5:28-33) now introduces *love of self* as the motivation for a man's love for his spouse.

At first sight, this exhortation seems to be appealing to a rather base instinct or to a rather self-evident truism: *no one ever hated his own flesh* (5:29). A closer reading, however, undermines such an understanding. First, Christ is described in 5:29 as *nourishing (ektrephō)* and *taking care of (thalpō)* the *church* just as a man cares for *his own flesh*. These terms are rare in the NT. *Ektrephō* appears only in Ephesians, here and in 6:4, where it describes the nurture and education of children (6:4, notes; 1 Thess. 2:7 has the related *trophos,* "nurse," or "nursing mother"). *Thalpō* appears elsewhere only in 1 Thessalonians 2:7, where Paul likens himself to a mother nursing her infants.

In other literature, these two verbs together sometimes stipulate the husband's duties in a marriage contract (Gnilka, 285; Perkins: 134). But here they depict the depth of care and concern the husband is to have for his wife. Such care is measured by the degree of love all have for their own *flesh* and, much more important, by Christ's care for his own *body,* the church.

Second, Ephesians 5:31 quotes Genesis 2:24 and gives it an important role. Some have even suggested that it is the center around which much of this passage takes shape (e.g., Tanzer: 339). *A man leaves his father and mother and "fuses" (proskollaomai) with his wife—and the two become one flesh. Proskollaomai* is variously translated as an active, such as "cling to" (NAB), "cleave to" (NASB), or "unite with" (GNB); and as a passive, such as "be united to" (NIV, REB), "become attached to" (NJB), or "be joined to" (NRSV). It means literally "to glue on" or "to" or "to be fastened to" (Liddell and Scott).

This citation from the creation narrative captures well the ambience of love and desire associated with the union of man and woman, and serves the present context well. Both separation from parents and conjugal union with one's spouse take on heightened meaning when read through the prism of Christ's relationship to the church. As 5:32 reminds us, that is the primary point of the citation (so also Miletic: 18-22).

With this playful interweaving of two marriages, Ephesians invites the full engagement of a biblically informed imagination. The Christology in Ephesians is much marked by Israel's wisdom tradition (notes for 1:3-14; 3:10). One of the Jewish traditions associated with Wisdom is that she left her heavenly home and found a home in Israel (cf. Ecclus./Sirach 24). Viewed in this way, Genesis 2:24 becomes an allusion to Christ's act of leaving his heavenly home and attaching himself to humanity.

Husbands are invited to reflect on their own relationship with their wives with an imagination thus awakened to their own experience of salvation in Christ. More than an image of sexual and marital union, the phrase *the two become one flesh* now evokes the great hymn of peace in 2:11-22. Through his death on the cross, Christ creates a *new human (anthrōpos)* out of *the two* (2:15) *in* or *through his flesh* (2:14). In 5:31, *the two* are, of course, Christ and the church, man and woman, not Jews and Gentiles. Even so, the unions of both sets of *twos* are part of the same impulse toward reconciliation, re-creation, and union that constitute the heart of the divine mystery, *to gather up all things in and through Christ* (1:10).

Genesis 2:24 thus retells in a highly concentrated fashion the story of liberation through Christ. At the same time, that liberation is related directly to the recovery of creation, a frequent theme in Ephesians (cf. 2:10; 4:24). At the heart of that liberation lies a passionate love so great that a man leaves his home to become one with his beloved. The love of man and woman in marriage provides the occasion to act out that drama of salvation on the domestic stage.

What gives this line of thought its coherence is the close affinity in this text between *flesh* and *body, sarx* and *sōma.* The prime image of the church in Ephesians is the *body* of Christ. As Christ's *body,* the church carries his *fullness* (1:23). Ironically, such *love of **self*** becomes a way of speaking of the *effects* of Christ's *love-of-the-**other***. Christ died for the sake of his *own* body (2:15-16). The result of that self-giving love is a *new human (anthrōpos),* the *body of Christ*, which includes healed humanity—the inclusion of the *other*—and also Christ himself. In 2:15, Christ reaches out to create the *new human* **in himself**; in 4:7-16, Christ as its head sees to it that the body grows *into himself.*

The reconciliation and union of Christ and the church is of such height, width, length, and depth (3:14-19) that for Christ to love the church is, in effect, to love himself. So *love of self* describes, not the *starting point* of the husband's engagement with his wife, but, via the analogy of Christ, the *consequence* of the *love for the other*—his wife, for whom he left his home and with whom he has become one flesh. The husband will gain his life by losing it.

This difficult and too easily misunderstood notion of *love of self* is informed by a further tradition. Every Jew, including the author of Ephesians, knew that at the heart of the law, and thus at the core of faithfulness to God, lies the double commandment. It is captured well in the Gospels:

> One of the scribes came near and heard them disputing with one another, and seeing that he answered them well, he asked him, "Which commandment is the first of all?" Jesus answered, "The first is, 'Hear, O Israel: the Lord our God, the Lord is one; you shall love the Lord your God with all your heart, and with all your soul, and with all your mind, and with all your strength.' The second is this, 'You shall love your neighbor as yourself.' There is no other commandment greater than these." (Mark 12:28-31; cf. Matt. 22:35-40; Luke 10:25-28; cf. Rom. 13:8-10; Gal. 5:13-14)

Everyone who has ever loved knows full well that to make the measure of love *for the other* the love one already has *for oneself* is in effect a summons to self-sacrifice. Notice that in Luke the double commandment ushers in the parable of the Good Samaritan (Luke 10:29-42; cf. John 15:12-17).

In the OT, *love for self* is not commanded so much as assumed. Love for self is not self-absorption so much as the primal and mostly unconscious need to protect and nurture oneself—to stay alive. To love the neighbor *as oneself* is the glue of social solidarity, of covenant. A community lives or dies by whether members are willing to relinquish their sense of privilege for the sake of the other, and thus for the sake of the community. The heart of the call to love the neighbor *as oneself* in Leviticus 19:18 (cf. 19:34) is *not* an appeal to *self*-interest. Instead, it is a most radical summons to make one's own already-existing interests the full measure of what one is prepared to seek *for the other*—in effect, to *subordinate* one's interests to those of the other.

When in Ephesians 5:33 husbands are asked to love their wives *as they do themselves,* such love is informed by realism about instincts of self-preservation and, more important, by the heart of covenant law. Husbands are being prodded by means of law (Lev. 19; Gen. 2) and example (Christ) to make their already deeply embedded sense of privilege the full measure of what they wish and do for their wives.

Imitating Christ in his love for his own body might suggest that wives are absorbed into the identity of their husbands, and that they find their worth solely in the identity of their husbands, however loving those husbands might be. The command in Leviticus 19:18 to love the neighbor, the *other* (cf. also the love for the "alien" in 19:34), reminds the husband that marital love is *covenant love.* In covenant love, the other is *not* absorbed into oneself, but that *one* **together with** *the other* constitutes *one flesh* (2:11-22, the reconciled new human *in the flesh* [2:14]).

Almost as an aside, the author returns with an abrupt jolt to the theme of *fear* (5:33b). Even if one translates *phobeomai* as *respect* or *awe,* not *fear,* the symmetry is missing. The verse makes a *direct* address to husbands, that each of them is to *love* his wife, then adds the *indirect* word to the wife, that she is to *fear* her husband. Perhaps the author's intent here is little more than to bring this section of text to a neat conclusion by means of this *inclusio* (cf. *fear* in 5:21). All the more surprising, then, that mutuality is missing (cf. again 5:21; so also Best, 1998:559-60).

Does what is asked of husbands in this passage live up to the summons in 5:21 to *be subordinate* **to each other**? Lincoln suggests love and subordination are "two sides of the same coin" (393; cf. Penner: 135-6, 142). But is the love described in Ephesians an expression of (self-)subordination? The discussion above suggests as much, even as it works *within* the cultural assumptions of male privilege. The import of these words depends, first, on how one views Christ. Second, it depends on whether it is possible for husbands to emulate in their actions and disposition the Christ whose lordship looks like slavery. This last point is crucial. Sarah Tanzer, for example, despairs at the possibility that this text is good news for wives, given the "limits of human behavior" (335). To state her concern differently, this exhortation *would be* liberating for women only if they could marry the Messiah! Tanzer is right. The hope in this text lies in whether in some measure they do marry the Messiah, whether in some significant way their husbands can *learn Christ* (4:20), whose lordship finds its fullest expression in servitude.

In this ambiguous mix, some signals appear to strengthen the foundations of male domination, and other signals have the potential to erode those same foundations. The text invites us to ask: Is it possible that in putting their own *Lord Christ* before *lords* (husbands, fathers, masters), the author of Ephesians is uttering a prophetic word more critical and potentially transformative of patriarchy than he can appreciate? Despite mixed signals, there is a basic direction in the argument: the *mystery* that the author of Ephesians is so eager to divulge is that God's work *in Christ* is one of liberation, reconciliation, restoration, and unification with each other and with God. The disposition of husbands toward their wives is essentially to mimic *that* work of Christ. They are to participate in the context of marriage in the mystery of *gathering up all things* (1:10).

It is true that in Ephesians this word is directed primarily toward husbands, to those who in a patriarchal context take their own superior station for granted. But it is addressed to them also as those who take their relationship to Christ with utmost seriousness. Their most natural point of identification is with the *head*—in this case, Christ. It becomes critically important, then, to know the Christ who is put before them as a model. Herein lies the trick in this passage: the *head is* given the *servant* as a model. In constructing the argument this way, the author of Ephesians engages in the same subversive activity as the author of that other washing text, where Jesus—*as Lord!*—washes the feet of his disciples (John 13:1-20).

In Ephesians, Christ's character and role as *head* are that of self-giving liberator, loving groom, and amorous servant. The other *heads* are given nothing else to imitate (cf. 4:32—5:2). This direction of the argument carries the challenge of this text to the first readers and brings its ongoing challenge to married couples today.

Children and Parents 6:1-4

The instructions to children and parents are brief and to the point. Even so, a comparison with Colossians shows that the author leaves his mark also on this brief part of the Household Code (Chart 2, TBC).

6:1-3 Children

Children are addressed directly: *Obey your parents in the Lord.* Many manuscripts do not contain *in the Lord*, and its presence here may be due to the influence of Colossians 3:20 on those copying the text (Chart 2, TBC). Even so, the phrase is consistent with the way the author grounds his exhortations and motivates his readers, especially if *Lord* is allusive both of God and of Christ. Many commentators take *in the Lord* to be part of the more original reading (e.g., Barth, 1974:654, n. 194; 755; Lincoln: 395; Schnackenburg: 261. Best, 1998:564, doubts its originality).

Such instruction would have enjoyed wide resonance in Greco-Roman society generally. But its Jewish rootage here is shown by the supporting arguments. First, children should obey their parents *because this is right(eous)* or *just*. This is surely code for behavior in keeping with God's will as expressed in the law (Schrenk, 1964:188). That is made explicit in the immediately following quotation of the fifth commandment, that children are to *honor father and mother* (close in wording to the LXX of Deut. 5:16 and esp. of Exod. 20:12; Lincoln: 397; Perkins: 137; quoted also in Matt. 15:4; 19:19; Mark 7:10; 10:19; Luke 18:20). *Obedience* is thus one expression of a larger *honoring* of parents. It is true that the law as a dividing wall has been broken down; yet as a guide for those who are *in the Lord,* it is still in force (Eph. 2:14-16, notes on the law).

It is striking that the *promise* for such fidelity to the law is the thoroughly material blessing of *long life on the earth*. At first glance, there is some tension between this "earthly" *promise* and the "heavenly" *inheritance* mentioned earlier in the letter (1:14, 18; 5:5). Some interpreters thus downplay the promise here as little more than a way to give the law gravity (e.g., Schnackenburg: 262). Others reinterpret this promise in light of a spiritual inheritance (e.g., Schlier, 1971:282). However, reckoning with both the open-ended eschatology of this letter (2:7, notes) and the comprehensiveness of its understanding of salvation (1:10, notes), a promise for *long life on the earth* should not surprise us (e.g., Best, 1998:568).

Indeed the author has widened the blessing to include the Gentiles by deleting the phrase "that the Lord your God is giving you," a reference to the Promised Land (cf. Exod. 20:12; Deut. 5:16). The presence of the Household Code in this letter is itself strong testimony to the attention the author pays to life *on the earth*. In Ephesians, salvation encompasses everyday social dimensions of life, including the most generative one, the family. The obedience expected of children is thus set into the context of *mutual subordination* (5:21) and also of respect for the duration of God's act of *gathering up all things in Christ* (1:10).

Children by itself defines a relationship more than it indicates age. Pheme Perkins cites a Qumran text to support her claim that not young so much as adult children are being asked to obey and care for their aging parents (4Q416, Frag. 2; 3.16-17; Perkins: 137). Though it would be foolish to limit the text's relevance to adult children, the Qumran text draws our attention to the likelihood that the Code here speaks to the relationship of children to their parents generally, regardless of age. The fact that children are being addressed directly is a significant indicator of the importance accorded them as moral agents in their own right; it may be a further indicator of the age spread the author and audience would have assumed (so also Best, 1993:57; 1998:563; Lincoln: 403).

As in the case of *subordination* in the first set (5:21-33), no explicit limit is here placed on *obedience* (6:1). It is, of course, typical of terse commandments to ignore mitigating circumstances. Tragically, such commands are still today used to force obedience to unjust and injurious parental orders and expectations. However, our text does set *implicit* limitations on obedience. First, the called-for obedience is *in the Lord*, meaning that the context of obedience to parents is the believing community (so also Lincoln: 403; Thurston: 142). The second limitation comes through the following words directed to fathers.

6:4 Fathers

The term *parents (goneis)* is now replaced by *fathers (pateres)*. While *pateres* can include parents of both genders (cf. Heb. 11:23), the explicit shift from the inclusive *goneis* to *pateres* likely reflects the patriarchal nature of family responsibilities. In the cultural context of the time, the *father* was ultimately responsible for the moral and religious education of the children (Best, 1998:563).

The potential for abuse of such authority is immediately signaled by the fact that the first order to fathers is that they not *provoke* their children *to anger*. As terse as this is, the word *provoke* covers all the types of abuse of power committed by people whose culture has given them unquestioned authority. The counsel given here echoes advice given fathers generally in Greco-Roman culture. It presupposes the virtually unlimited legal rights of a father over his children (on first-century parent-child relationships and the potential for, and reality of, abuse, see Lincoln: 398-402, 406).

That this means more than an injunction against irritating children is suggested by the use of the verb form of *provoking to anger (parorgizomai;* cf. Col. 3:21, "to irritate," *erethizō)*. In 4:26, believers are to be angry, but not to sin. "Not to sin" means addressing the *provocations to anger (parorgismoi)* before the sun sets (4:26, notes). In the present text, fathers are not to give their children reason to be angry. In light of 4:26, we should recognize that the specific choice of vocabulary means also that fathers are to do nothing that would leave *themselves* subject to *God's* wrath. The fathers are not to force their children into a position of having to deal with their father's violations or become complicit in their father's violations of God's will.

The wording thus hardly suggests an unqualified or unquestioning obedience of children to parents and fathers. This becomes all the more true when "children" are adults. In short, fathers are to behave toward their children as fellow members of a covenant community that is marked by *mutual subordination*, but also by mutual and joint accountability before God—a theme made explicit in the following instructions to slaves and masters.

A comparison of the instructions to fathers with the Colossian precedent shows the hand of the author of Ephesians clearly (Chart 2, TBC). As frequently in Ephesians, a negative prohibition is followed by a much more important and profound positive exhortation (cf. esp. 4:25-32; note structure of argumentation in 2:1-10 and 5:3-14). The alternative to the violation of the parent-child relationship is for fathers to *nurture* their children *in the training and instruction of the Lord*.

Nurturing (ektrephō) marks Christ's "feeding" (NIV) and "nourishing" (NRSV) of his church in 5:29 (notes). The care and nurture modeled by Christ is to mark the disposition of fathers to their children. While *ektrephō* can mean "rear" or "bring up," the note of nurture should not be underplayed. In describing his apostolic activity among the Thessalonians, Paul likens himself in the same breath to a nursing mother (*trophos thalpē,* 1 Thess. 2:7; cf. Eph. 5:29) and an exhorting and encouraging father (1 Thess. 2:11). In our present text, the roles of mother and father have been combined in what is expected of fathers.

The author now adds two further terms that overlap with *nurture* in meaning. Fathers are to nurture their children *in the training (paideia)* and *instruction (nouthesia) of the Lord.* Both terms relate to instruction, with *paideia* carrying overtones of discipline (cf. Heb. 12:5-11) and *nouthesia* connotations of warning (cf. 1 Cor. 10:11; Bertram, 1967; Lincoln: 407; Schnackenburg: 263). Both reflect the gravity of responsibility a parent carries for the moral and spiritual development of children.

The absolute use of the title *Lord* brings God into the picture, thus placing training, discipline, and instruction in the context of familiarizing children with the ways of God. *Of the Lord* may thus be a "genitive of quality" (Lincoln: 408), indicating that the instruction and training is "about the Lord." A Jewish father would have understood that to mean training children in the law. An example of such use of the law is seen in 6:3. On the other hand, in Pauline circles *Lord* also was a favorite way of referring specifically to Christ. The prime responsibility of *fathers* in relation to their children is thus to train them in the way of the Christ, to help them to *learn Christ*, meaning *the truth that is in Jesus* (4:20-21)—kindness, love, and servanthood (2:13-17; 5:2, 25-26). Fathers can only do that effectively by modeling the walk of Jesus themselves.

The genitive might also be a "subjective genitive," however, in which the instruction is the Lord's (Bertram, 1967:624; Best, 1998:570). In that case, we might think of God and/or Christ performing their saving mission through the instructions provided by fathers. Both meanings are permitted grammatically, and both fit well the flow of the presentation.

The gravity of responsibility given here to fathers requires that parental responsibility be fully respected. In the first century, Jew and Gentile alike would have assumed that. It is a point less obvious in our day. At the same time, rooting the exercise of authority in the imitation of the servant Lord Jesus again *necessarily* destabilizes hierarchical and abusive power structures in the family. The obedience of children to their parents in verse 1 is here mirrored in the call on fathers in effect "to turn their hearts to their children," in the words of Zechariah's hymnic celebration of the coming reign of God (Luke 1:17). Here such "turning" is expected of fathers who are part of the body of the Messiah who has come and who is present in the families of the church, not least in their children.

This section of the Code, as the previous one, is to be read through the lens of *mutual subordination* (5:21; so also Lincoln: 393, 402, 409).

Slaves and Masters 6:5-9

Unlike the pairings of wives and husbands, and children and parents (fathers), slavery is not part of the social reality of most readers of this commentary. Slavery was, however, a familiar and common institution for early readers of Ephesians, and the attention given to slaves both in our text and in other instances of the Code in the NT is witness to the reality of slavery in Pauline congregations (cf. 1 Cor. 7; Philem.).

Slavery was as pervasive and as entrenched an institution when Ephesians was written as are labor-management structures in today's modern economies. There were voices calling for humane treatment of slaves (e.g., Seneca; Epictetus), and self-interest dictated that for the most part slaves should be treated less brutally than the law permitted. Nevertheless, slaves had no rights, regardless of their education and their importance to their masters (on slavery, see Bartchy: 65-73; Best, 1998:572-4; Lincoln: 415-20).

As in Colossians, considerably more attention is paid in our text to slaves than to masters. This may reflect something of the social makeup of the congregations. It may also reflect something of the social stresses a gospel of freedom in step with Galatians 3:28 might have exercised on the growing churches at the end of the first century (so Schüssler Fiorenza, 1983:214-8; J. H. Yoder, 1994:175, 190). This latter point is disputed by those who believe slavery was so entrenched in the culture that it did not occur to people, including slaves, to do away with it, no matter how much the slaves yearned for freedom (cf. 1 Cor. 7:21; Balch, 1981:107; Lincoln: 418, but see 358; MacDonald: 112).

In any case, the Code is clear that slave-master relationships are to be brought under the lordship of Christ. Here too we see the vision of the author at work in shaping inherited material.

6:5-8 Slaves

As in Colossians 3:22-24, slaves are addressed first and directly (Chart 2, TBC). As in the case of children, this also reflects the social reality in the church in which they are seen and treated as moral agents in their own right (Lincoln: 419-20, 424; J. H. Yoder, 1994:171-2). Like children, the form their subordination takes is *obedience (hupakouō)*.

Two sets of comparisons shape the exhortation. One is the analogy between being slaves of *fleshly lords* and being *slaves of Christ*. The other is the contrast between "normal" servitude marked by hypocrisy and a desire to ingratiate oneself, and a servanthood marked by integrity and honesty—the kind of servitude one offers Christ.

The christological motivation present elsewhere in the Household Code is here sharpened. *As to the Lord* (cf. 5:22) or *in the Lord* (6:1) now becomes being *slaves of Christ* (6:6; cf. 1 Cor. 7:22). The obedience offered human masters is in essence faithful service to Christ himself. In a somewhat surprising combination, such service is marked on one hand by *fear and trembling* (cf. 5:21, 33). Even more, on the other hand, it is marked by *integrity of heart (haplotēs)*, by generosity, a good disposition, even enthusiasm—service with "heart and soul" (6:5-7, evoking the great commandment of Deut. 6:5; Best, 1998:578; Lincoln: 421).

The familiar pattern in Ephesians of following a negative prohibition with a much more important positive exhortation is present here as well (cf. 4:25-32; 6:4). It is most clearly shown in the *not/but rather* pattern in 6:6. Christian slaves are *not* to serve for appearance's sake, or to be motivated by the need to please their human masters. Such would be the greatest temptation for those whose welfare, even survival, depended on the good will of their masters. Their servitude is *rather* to be one marked by wholehearted service to Christ.

As in 4:28, where thievery is to be replaced by doing *the good* (cf. 2:10!), so here slavery *as to Christ* is *doing the will of God* (6:6), *doing good* (6:8). As indicated in the notes for 2:10 and 4:28, *doing the good* is heavily freighted vocabulary in Ephesians. It places faithful servitude into the context of God's overall designs for humanity (2:10, notes).

Further, such servitude is placed into the larger context of divine remuneration. God pays close attention to the good that is done and repays it, whether or not *fleshly* masters have paid attention (6:8). Left undefined is whether this refers to an eschatological reckoning or to the ongoing divine vigilance to see that both good and evil are repaid (cf. Rom. 13:3-5). Similar assurances are given to slaves in Colossians 3:24-25, where certainty of eschatological "reward" and "inheritance" is connected with a wisdom saying regarding divine repayment of both good and evil. In 1 Peter, where slaves suffer at the hands of unjust masters, they are reassured of God's vindication (cf. 2:23) and can look forward to the same fate as that of Christ, who also suffered injustice. Their endurance is placed in the context of imminent judgment and liberation (1 Pet. 4:7).

In contrast to 1 Peter, however, Ephesians assumes that *both* slaves *and* masters are *within* the church. Nothing is said here about suffering injustice, except in the warning to masters in 6:9 to desist from threatening their slaves. Instead, slaves are to render their service in light of Christ's lordship, as *mutual subordination* (5:21).

Are limits placed on such service? Being *slaves of Christ* suggests that there are none, as befits service to Christ. On the other hand, this premise inherently sets limits on what can be asked of slaves, especially *within* the body of Christ where *both* slaves *and* masters ultimately share one *master in heaven*. It may thus be quite deliberate that Ephesians omits the phrase found in Colossians, *in everything* (*kata panta,* Col. 3:22). A further qualification on the *obedience* of slaves is implied in the following words to masters.

6:9 *Masters*

The word to *masters* is brief—at least on the surface. Several
distinct features emerge in close comparison with Colossians 4:1
(Chart 2, TBC). The author replaces the call for justice and fairness in
Colossians with a specific injunction, *Desist from threatening* slaves!
But more important, he first adds a terse yet laden command, *Do the
same to them!* The injunction concludes with the assertion found at
the end of the words to slaves in Colossians, affirming that with God
there is no favoritism, no respect for status. In Colossians, that is a
word of reassurance spoken to slaves, that God will judge their masters without respect for their status. Here it warns masters that before
God they have no privileges, that they *together with their slaves* are
fellow-slaves of Christ.

At first glance, the demand in Colossians 4:1 for fairness and justice appears to be a stronger and richer admonition to masters than
that found in Ephesians. However, given the substantial content of the
exhortation to slaves in Ephesians, the command to masters to *do the
same* is striking and much less respectful of the "special" prerogatives
and responsibilities masters might think they have in relation to their
inferiors. With the command *Do the same to them,* the author is
applying the call to **mutual** subordination (5:21) to a social relationship of structural inequality.

Ephesians 6:9 reminds masters that they share the same Master in
heaven. The test of their fidelity to that Master is whether they emulate a faithful slave in their relationships to slaves. In short, masters
are to learn to be masters from a slave. As absurd as that might seem,
it is consistent with the Christ presented throughout the exhortation
(cf. 5:2, 25-26) and in keeping with the heart of Pauline admonition
generally (esp. Phil. 2:6-11). Indeed, the clause *Do the same to them*
is a functional equivalent to the call for being subordinate *to each
other* with which the Household Code began in 5:21 (contra Best,
1998:580), thereby supplying a fitting conclusion.

Though this is hardly a frontal attack on the institution of slavery,
the exhortation, if taken seriously, is profoundly destabilizing to relationships of structural inequality. Even apart from the insistence in 6:9
that with God status is of no account, an echo of the vision of unity
and equality in Galatians 3:28 may be heard in the phrase at the end
of 6:8, *whether slave or free* (cf. 1 Cor. 12:13; Col. 3:11). The fact
that masters are to begin imitating their faithful slaves *immediately*,
suggests that at least in the church, slaves should not have to wait
for judgment day for the good they do to be rewarded (6:8; so also
Lincoln: 424; contra Schüssler Fiorenza, 1983:268).

THE TEXT IN BIBLICAL CONTEXT

Origins of the Tradition of the Household Code

Beyond Ephesians 5–6, the tradition of the Household Code is also found in Colossians 3:18—4:1; 1 Peter 2:13—3:7; and in more highly adapted form in 1 Timothy 2:8-15; 5:1-2; 6:1-2; and Titus 2:1-10; 3:1. Sometimes Romans 13:1-7 is also considered to be part of this tradition (cf. 1 Pet. 2:13-17; Schroeder, 1976:546).

The historical context and origin of this tradition has been a matter of considerable debate and is too complex and involved to receive a full treatment here (e.g., extensive studies of the Household Code: Balch, 1981; 1992; Crouch; J. H. Elliott, 1981; Lührmann; Schüssler Fiorenza, 1983:251-84; Schrage; J. H. Yoder, 1994; BCBC treatments by E. Martin: 181-95; Waltner: 95-103, 180-3). A few matters should be highlighted, however.

The ancient household or family was organized in a pyramidal structure of authority, with the father at the top, followed by mother, children, then freed-persons (former slaves), and at the bottom the slaves. The actual social expression of this usual model varied from time to time and place to place. Women, for example, were sometimes heads of households, even when not widows (Wordelman: 392). Even so, the prevailing assumptions of the age were patriarchal, in both Jewish and Gentile society. The ordering and proper functioning of these relationships were thus of general concern. We should not be surprised to find letters of the NT addressing these concerns.

Most scholars today believe that the writers of the NT learned the tradition of the Household Code from the Hellenistic Jewish synagogue, but that the roots of the tradition were deep and varied. It owes much to the widespread and stereotypical Hellenistic instruction on household management (*peri oikonomias,* literally meaning "laws or rules of the house"; Lührmann: 85-90). The household, an essential building block of society, was viewed as a microcosm of that larger social whole.

Aristotle's widely cited comments on household management anticipate the structure of the Household Code in Colossians and Ephesians. In analyzing the component parts of the state, Aristotle proposes that

> the investigation of everything should begin with the smallest parts, and the primary and smallest parts of the household are master and slave, husband and wife, father and children; we ought therefore to examine the proper constitution and character of each of these three relationships. (*Politics* 1.1253b; quoted in Lincoln: 357; Schüssler Fiorenza, 1983:255)

Recognizing the relationship of the microcosm (family) to the macrocosm (society), we should take what is said about wives and husbands, children and parents, and slaves and masters, to set a tone for how people are to comport themselves in church and society generally.

Against majority opinion, David Schroeder, and following him Ernest Martin, Erland Waltner, and John Howard Yoder, have taken a different approach. Though they concede that in many ways the Household Code in the NT reflects broader Hellenistic culture, Jewish and Gentile, there are features that mark it as distinctly Christian. The following are of special importance: First, the described relationships have a reciprocal nature. Second, in each instance the NT texts accord unusual respect to the normally inferior "stations" by addressing them directly and first. Third, the use of the imperative owes more to OT law than to Hellenistic lists of domestic duties. Fourth, there is the distinctive appeal to Christ as motivator and model (Schroeder, 1959; 1976:547; E. Martin: 287; Waltner: 180; J. H. Yoder 1994:178-9, 187).

The first approach tends to devalue the references to Christ and love *(agapē)* as a thin Christianizing veneer over what remains a thoroughly patriarchal tradition and thus "in no sense revolutionary" (Best, 1993:85; cf. 1998:583). The second approach, taken by Schroeder and those who have followed his lead, highlights the references to Christ, interpreting the Code in light of the servant Jesus encountered in the Gospels and in hymns like Philippians 2:6-11. Tellingly, John H. Yoder calls his treatment of the Household Code "Revolutionary Subordination" (1994:163-92).

The Household Code in the New Testament

In my view, it is best to allow for multiple sources for this tradition (as Schroeder himself concedes, 1976:547; J. H. Yoder, 1994:189, n. 55). It is especially important to understand that a variety of life settings and theological and pastoral agendas have given varied shape to this tradition, as Charts 1 and 2 show (below). In Chart 1, note especially the differences in sequence, vocabulary, supporting arguments, and expansions. This invites us to pay attention to how and why the tradition is adapted in each case.

Chart 1
Skeleton of Household Code in Colossians, Ephesians, 1 Peter

Col. 3:18—4:1	*Eph. 5:21—6:9*	*1 Pet. 2:13—3:7*
		Be subordinate to *every human institution* on account of the Lord. (cf. Rom. 13:1-7)
		(instruction to slaves here; see below)
	. . . be(ing) mutually subordinate out of fear of Christ,	
Wives, be subordinate to your husbands.	*wives,* to their own husbands. (expansion on Christ and husbands as head)	*Wives,* be subordinate to your own husbands. (expansion on winning unbelieving husband by imitating the suffering Christ)
Husbands, love your wives.	*Husbands,* love your wives as Christ loved the church. (major expansion on Christ and church as husband and wife)	*Husbands,* show consideration to your wives as weaker, but also as fellow-heirs.
Children, obey your parents.	*Children,* obey your parents. (expansion with appeal to Law)	(no mention of children-parent pair)
Fathers, don't provoke your children.	*Fathers,* don't provoke your children to anger. (expansion on fathers as educators and nurturers)	
Slaves (douloi), obey your human masters *(kurioi).* (expansion on Christ as ultimate Master)	*Slaves (douloi),* obey your human masters *(kurioi)* as slaves of Christ. (major expansion on being slaves of Christ)	*Slaves (oiketai,* house-servants), be subordinate to your masters *(despotai)* (major expansion on serving and suffering as Christ suffered)
Masters, be just; you have a heavenly Master.	*Masters,* behave like your slaves; you have the same impartial Master in heaven.	(no word to human masters)

Chart 2
Comparison of Household Code in Ephesians and Colossians
(italics in Ephesians mark additions to the Colossian Code)

Ephesians 5:21—6:9	Colossians 3:18—4:1
5:21 . . . be[ing] **mutually subordinate** in fear of Christ,	
22 **wives,** to their own husbands as to the Lord, 23 *because a husband is head of the wife as also is Christ head of the church, himself savior of the body.* 24 *But just as the church is subordinate to Christ, so also the wives to their husbands in everything.*	3:18 **Wives,** be subordinate to the husbands, as is fitting in the Lord.
25 **Husbands**, love the wives, *just as Christ loved the church and gave himself for her;* 26 *in order to render her holy, by having cleansed her by the washing with the water in word,* 27 *in order to present the church to himself glorious, having no spot or wrinkle or any such thing, in order that she might be holy and blameless.* 28 *So ought the husbands to love their wives as their own bodies. The one who loves himself loves his own wife.* 29 *For no one ever hated his own flesh but nourishes and takes care of it, just as also Christ the church,* 30 *because we are members of his body.* 31 *"For this reason a person will leave his father and mother and be joined to his wife. And the two will become one flesh."* 32 *This is a great mystery (I am speaking of Christ and the church).* 33 *Even so, let each one of you love his own wife as himself; but the wife is to fear the husband.*	19 **Husbands,** love the wives and do not be bitter toward them.
6:1 **Children, obey your parents** in the Lord, for this is right. 2 *"Honor your father and mother"* —which is the first commandment with a promise— 3 *"so that it may be well with you and you may live long on the earth."*	20 **Children**, obey your parents in everything, for this is your acceptable duty in the Lord.

4 And **fathers**, do not provoke your children *to anger, but nurture them with the training and instruction of the Lord.*

5 **Slaves**, obey your human (fleshly) masters *with fear and trembling* in integrity of *your* heart as to Christ, 6 not for sake of appearance as do "pleasers," but *as slaves of Christ doing the will of God* from the heart (soul), 7 offering service *with enthusiasm* as to the Lord and not to humans, 8 knowing that *whatever good each one does,* he will *receive the same again from the Lord,* whether slave or free.

9 And **masters**, *do the same to them, desisting from threat,* knowing that both their and your Master is in heaven, *and with him* there is no favoritism.

21 **Fathers**, do not provoke your children, or they may lose heart.

22 **Slaves,** obey your human (fleshly) masters in everything, not for the sake of appearance as "pleasers," but in integrity of heart, fearing the Lord. 23 Whatever you do, work from the heart (soul) as to the Lord and not to humans, 24 knowing that from the Lord you will receive the reward of inheritance; you serve (are slaves of) the Lord Christ. For the one who does evil will be repaid for the evil; there is no favoritism.

4:1 **Masters**, treat your slaves justly and fairly, for you know that you also have a Master in heaven.

Subordination in Various Life Settings

Subordination as Putting Up with Injustice

Why did NT writers employ this tradition? First, it is often suggested that the church needed to place limits on the freedom invited by a gospel in which distinctions between Jews or Greeks, slaves and free, and male and female were no longer significant (cf. Gal. 3:28). As John H. Yoder puts it, "Don't overdo celebrating your liberation!" (1994:190; much earlier, Schroeder, 1959:151, speaks of those in subordinate stations being in danger of "overinterpreting" the gospel). But why?

Perhaps the call for good order in domestic relations was urged by the needs of evangelism and witness. In a society where a father determined the religious life of those in his charge, the conversion of a socially inferior member of the household, such as wife or slave, could easily be viewed as socially destabilizing insubordination (Russell, 1984:102; Schüssler Fiorenza, 1983:262-6). Hostility to the church as a socially disruptive liberation movement might imperil the church's efforts. Rather ironically, believers were asked to rein in their freedom for the sake of the gospel of freedom. The Household Code reassured society and instructed believers that Christians are not a threat to family, economy, or society. Stated more positively, a wife's *willing* and *chosen* subordination to her (unbelieving and possibly hostile) husband, or believers' subordination to (hostile) "human institutions," could be a witness intended to lead to the conversion of spouse and society.

In 1 Peter, the Code appears to fit this setting and purpose well (see esp. 3:1; cf. Titus 2:5, 8; Schertz, 1992a; Schroeder, 1990:48-58; Schüssler Fiorenza, 1983:260-6; J. H. Yoder, 1994:176, 185; Waltner's treatment of 1 Peter 2:11—3:12 is appropriately entitled "Christian Witness in Hostile Society"). In such a setting, the chief concern of the Code is *not* adapting to prevailing social mores, but rather the imitation of Christ in difficult and even hostile circumstances. Prevailing social patterns and structures are part of the *problem*, not the solution.

In a hostile society, *subordination* is therefore a form of Christliness in a situation of powerlessness and suffering, in imitation of a Christ who himself put up with a terrible situation—for the sake of its transformation, to be sure! *Subordination* is thus a mode of behavior motivated by the desire to see transformation. But it is also marked by a willingness to suffer injustice in light of the certainty of divine intervention and judgment (cf. 1 Pet. 4:12-19). Evangelism, eschatology, and the imitation of Christ as the righteous One who can count on divine vindication—these all undergird this stance of subordination.

Subordination as a Virtue in a Well-Ordered Society

In a different life setting, *subordination* is a *virtue*. In this case, subordination of those who are in socially inferior positions is not a *tactical* or *strategic retreat* from the radical freedom in Christ for the sake of the larger victory of the gospel—and thereby ironically an expression of such freedom. Nor is it the stance of those who really have little choice other than to suffer injustice. Instead, it is a *positive virtue* in the proper ordering of relationships *in* family and church. Subordination is not putting up with injustice, but undergirding right order.

As the church grew more conservative and more conventional—perhaps especially in circles where suffering was not as immediate a factor as in the case of 1 Peter—eschatological fervor subsided. Instead, institutional and organizational needs took on greater prominence (Gnilka: 276; Lincoln: 390). The church may also have had to take serious issue with those who disparaged family life (R. Martin, 1991:72; Schüssler Fiorenza, 1983:266-70). In such a life setting, attention has shifted from life at the often-troubled intersection of church and world (as in 1 Peter) to life wholly *within* the church. Interestingly, this conception of order and relationships within the church owes much to ideals present in the surrounding world.

A hierarchical and patriarchal social pattern requires subordination on the part of those in the inferior "stations" of wife, child, and slave. Nevertheless, the appeal to Christ in the NT Household Codes implies also a stance of love, care, and respect on the part of the dominant ones (often called "love-patriarchalism"; cf. Koontz: 204-5, "benevolent patriarchy"; Lincoln: 391; Schüssler Fiorenza, 1983:269-70; Schroeder, 1959:127). No doubt this constituted, then as now, a significant alternative to exploitation and abuse of privilege and dominance. Even so, unlike 1 Peter, this model principally presents Christ, not as a pattern for *sub*ordinates, but as a pattern for *super*ordinates—husbands, fathers, and masters.

Which Context Fits Ephesians?

Two arguments; two perspectives; two colorings of subordination; two appeals to Christ. In one case, Christ is a fellow-*sub*ordinate (suffering wife and slave), in the other a fellow-*super*ordinate (head, husband, master). These frames of reference reflect quite different primary audiences and different strategies. As indicated above, the first option fits the context of 1 Peter well. It should be quite apparent by now that the second alternative is much more reflective of the way the tradition is taken up in Colossians and Ephesians.

As in Colossians, the household envisioned in Ephesians is wholly *within* the church. There is little indication that troubled relations with the outside world occasioned the use of the Code in Ephesians, as it appears to have in the case of 1 Peter. Ernest Best is dubious that the way the Household Code of Ephesians pictures family life in the church reflects actual experience. He considers the assumption of Christian family life with no unbelieving members to be out of touch with first-century church reality, and thus ethically "inadequate" (1997:201) and "pastorally unrealistic" and "defective" (1998:526).

In my view, Best misunderstands the purpose and pastoral function of an ideal model. Even so, he is correct in observing that in Ephesians, as in Colossians, *believing* wives are to be subordinate to *believing* husbands, *believing* children are to be obedient to *believing* fathers, and *believing* slaves to *believing* masters. And all of this is enveloped by a repeated appeal to Christ as model, motivator, and ultimate authority figure—a model chiefly for those in the *super*ordinate position, to be sure.

Many interpreters consider these features to show that the author of Ephesians, writing later than the Paul of Galatians 3:28, no longer senses any tension between the subordination of *only* wives and the call to **mutual** subordination. In this reading, *mutual* for Ephesians simply means that everyone in the church and family should be subordinate to their superiors. As Letty Russell puts it, "We are *all subject*, but some are *more subject* than others!" (1984:101, her italics). Ephesians has reverted from Paul's Christ-centered egalitarianism to the social mores prevailing *outside* the church and has made them normative *within* the church (Johnson: 341).

This retreat from the radicalism of early Pauline teaching is viewed to be in tension also with the relativizing of family associated with Jesus in the Gospels (Mark 3:31-35 and par.; Matt. 10:34-37 and par.; 19:29; but see 15:4-6). In Ephesians, the family (even as conceived of in larger terms than a modern nuclear family) is viewed as part of God's ongoing blessing of humanity (note, e.g., the use of Law in the instructions to children, in 6:2-3).

Letty Russell calls this a return to "a modified plan of business as usual" (1984:100; cf. Johnson: 340-2; Perkins, 1997:140; Schüssler Fiorenza, 1983:270; Tanzer: 331). Hierarchical relations are viewed as being given christological legitimation and thus, fatefully, permanence. Some count the Household Code as so much out of step with the generous and embracing vision of Ephesians as a whole that they consider it to be a later and quite regrettable insertion into the body of Ephesians (e.g., Tanzer: 340-2; cf. Munro, 1983:27-37). The way this text has been put to use gives considerable weight to these criticisms.

A different reading of the Household Code is possible, however, with respect to both intended purpose and potential effect. First, there is no compelling reason to consider the Household Code as a foreign implant in Ephesians. It appears in exactly the same sequence of themes found in Colossians. Moreover, it is consistent with the gist of the letter as a whole. The household, and marriage especially, is viewed through the lens of Christ's self-giving lordship and the unity of body and head that marks Ephesians as a whole (esp. chaps. 2; 4; Houlden, 1977:329). Whether or not the Household Code was inserted in the letter at a later date is ultimately irrelevant since it arrives at our homes in the present canonical envelope. As those who read this text canonically, we neither have nor desire the luxury of "solving" by excision the problems this text raises.

Second, the author's depiction of Christ and his role in salvation must be considered part of the context of the Code as we find it in

Ephesians. Christ is seldom if ever the focus of attention in Ephesians *apart from* how he benefits the church—to such an extent that the church frequently takes the place of Christ (e.g., notes for 1:23; 3:19). No document in the NT pays greater and more respectful attention to the church than does Ephesians (Introduction).

Many do view the strong presence of Christology in the Household Code in Ephesians as a way to "cement" traditional hierarchical relationships in the family. But the role of Christ as described in the Code is entirely consistent with the way the rest of the letter presents him: Christ is God's self-giving agent to make peace with, exalt, and re-create humanity. It is *that* Christ who is the Lord and who appears in the Household Code as model and motivator.

Christ is not put forward in Ephesians' Household Code as a model for the vulnerable, as a fellow innocent sufferer at the hands of oppression and injustice—what we see in 1 Peter. In Ephesians, Christ is presented as a model for the strong and the dominant. And what are they shown? A passionate lover whose love finds expression most profoundly in a servanthood to the death. The Pauline themes of mutual servanthood and the imitation of Christ (cf. Phil. 2:6-11) inform the way the author adapts the tradition of the Household Code in Ephesians, even if these themes sit cheek to jowl—and with some discomfort, to be sure!—beside the patriarchalism that informs the Household Code tradition the author inherits (Hays: 65). One is unfaithful as an interpreter if one lifts this passage out of its setting either, on one hand, to dismiss it, or on the other, to isolate it as a law to be enforced without paying adequate attention to its internal dynamic and its larger context.

The Home as Public Witness

As stated earlier, the instructions for the household speak to relationships *within* the church. This has led to the charge that, unlike 1 Peter 3 or even 1 Corinthians 7, no interest is shown in the Christian life as it intersects with the world; or that many marital and economic relationships carried the burden of brokenness and hostility (e.g., Best, 1993:82-85, 96; 1998:524). However one should not expect of the Household Code in Ephesians what it does not set out to do. The author is not interested in dealing with immediate needs of pastoral care or evangelism so much as in grounding valued familial relationships in the overall project of God to *gather up all things in Christ* (1:10). Hence, Ephesians focuses on Christ and church.

Thereby, however, familial relationships *do* become public witness—a public that includes *the powers* (3:10; 6:12). The *children of light* are to confront the *works of darkness* in the interests of transforming darkness into light (5:3-15); believers are together to avail themselves of divine power to take on the powers (6:10-20). Just so, familial life is to be a public act of Spirit-filled worship (recall grammatical dependency of the Code on 5:18-21). It is for such a public witness that Ephesians puts forward a vision of family relationships being lived *as to Christ* (6:5).

THE TEXT IN THE LIFE OF THE CHURCH

An Embattled Text

Today the Household Code is highly controversial in the life of the church, especially as it relates to relationships between men and women. The Southern Baptist Convention in the United States has recently taken an explicit stand reasserting the importance of the headship of the husband in the home, citing Ephesians 5 as biblical support. Others view this text as a pernicious attack on women, and thus best left out of the operative canon of Christian women.

Between these two poles are those who hold a high view of Scripture but who nevertheless see the text being *mis*used as a weapon against women. They recognize that "headship" is misunderstood as authority, and that the cultural context of patriarchy is erroneously taken as normative (e.g., Grenz: 107-17; Scholer: 40-4; Swartley, 1983:256-69 ["Head"]).

Experience, individually and socially, and the "political" stance or location of the interpreter will have a great deal to do with how the text is read and interpreted. Many find in the text confirmation that the "old" (traditional) ways are best and most reflective of God's will for family and church. Others, coming to the text with a painful history of brokenness in familial and economic relationships, have experienced this text as either cover for the church's complicity in this brokenness, or even as a cudgel used against them. Especially if they also come to the text open to hearing the word of God, they experience great tension.

The interpreter needs to be as conscious as possible of her or his own interests, perspectives, hopes, and fears, and to be aware of, and pastorally sensitive to, the experiences of others. The ground interpreters stand on is holy because it is Scripture they are interpreting. It is also holy because experiences of women and men, children and parents, and slaves and masters render it so. These experiences are sometimes marked by courageous fidelity to a gospel of the new creation, but too often by oppression and dehumanization.

For example, I bring to the interpretation of this text the tools of a scholar and also my own experience as husband of a pastor with whom I share parenting and household duties. I celebrate the full participation and ministry of women in church, home, and workplace as consistent with the gospel and also as fruit of the gospel (Yoder Neufeld, 1990:289-99). However, as a privileged and educated male, I am less vulnerable than many women, children, and men who are powerless as they struggle to survive.

I worked on this text when I was on sabbatical leave in Central America and became acutely aware of such variant perspectives. Most of the women and men there are peasants, with little if any power and little if any land to call their own, people for whom economic slavery is an everyday reality. Women and children live a doubly vulnerable life, often subjected to abuse in their own homes.

In my own country, Canada, too many women and children know what it is to be subject to authoritarian and often abusive husbands and fathers. They know what it is to have such behavior tacitly if not explicitly sanctioned by appeal to texts such as the Household Code in Ephesians (Heggen; Melissa A. Miller; Thistlethwaite). Too many men know what it is to be unemployed or underemployed, and thus what it means to be subject to the whims of a cruel master, even if that master turns out to be the faceless market. Many, especially women, have experienced this text as "dangerous to their health" (Russell, 1985:141).

Interpreters of this text are today keenly conscious of their and others' experience. But they also listen attentively in and through the text for the voice of God. Such listening is not always easy. It is troubling, for example, how in this text little more than *fear* is commended to wives, even if interpreted as "respect" or "awe" (5:21, 33). Such *fear* is especially disturbing since the author intends to set forth a *positive* vision of family life as the context for the imitation of Christ. This text is hardly adequate *by itself* to provide a vision for the place and role of wives in a marriage relationship.

At the same time, to listen in this text for the word of God as a husband, father, and boss—surely the intended first row of the audience—brings considerable discomfort. He is invited to imitate one whose lordship and headship takes the form of passionate and self-sacrificing love. He will be troubled that, as father, he is singled out for an explicit warning not to be abusive. But he will also be heartened, if somewhat overwhelmed, by the exhortation to be his children's teacher in the school of Christ—learning and teaching them to be servants of others. Surely the many husbands and fathers who have *learned Christ* well

(4:20) are proof enough that to take up the challenge to love *as Christ loved* will fatally corrode the structures of support for male privilege. If something other was intended, then the writer made a great mistake by holding before the readers this model—the Christ we encounter in these and the other pages of the NT.

There remains the question of whether this text "cements" patriarchal relationships (e.g., Schüssler Fiorenza, 1983:270) or whether it subverts them. We cannot settle this argument apart from how real people read this text and live it out in the varying social configurations we call "family." Nor can it be settled apart from who the Christ is, the one who is encountered in the text and followed in life. The only convincing rebuttal to the charge that this text should be expunged from the operative canon of Christians is that husbands, fathers, and bosses practice servanthood in imitation of the *Lord* modeled for them in this text.

The power of conversion and transformation does not lie in the text or in the success of its argument, but in the Spirit of the servant Christ. The writer signals this by appending the Household Code grammatically to the command to be filled with the Spirit (5:18, notes; Schematic Trans.).

Are Husbands the Saviors of Wives?

Many women will insist that their salvation—their liberation—is not and should not be dependent on their husbands as the church's salvation depends on Christ. That is certainly correct, in that the analogy between Christ and husband is limited. The objection goes deeper, however. The analogy itself is viewed as deeply permeated with patriarchal assumptions that it will be the husband who will save the wife, and not vice versa. There is a measure of truth in this objection.

However, as careful as we must be with the analogy between Christ and husband, we must remember that in Ephesians the appeal for husbands to be concerned for the liberation/salvation of their wives is being made in a patriarchal cultural context. Indeed, the text presupposes such a social structure. It places before the socially *dominant* member of the marriage relationship the summons to pattern his behavior after the *Lord*.

Restating the Household Code today for *equal* partners in marriage would and *should* sound different (so also Jewett: 139-41; Lincoln: 393-4). However, now as then, instructions for a household would *with equal force* need to put before *anyone* who exercises responsibility, freedom, and authority in a relationship—husband *and* wife, father *and* mother—the call to imitate Christ. To do so is to mimic a *Lord* whose headship comes to fullest expression in the liberation of the *other*, in the empowerment of the *other*, and in loving and self-denying servanthood *for the sake of the other*. That remains a challenge deeply disturbing and destabilizing to all social arrangements, inside or outside the church.

Furthermore, such a reformulation will invite husbands and wives alike to participate in the mystery of Christ and the church (5:32), to render their marriage a drama of liberation, empowerment, peacemaking, reconciliation, and boundless love. Their marriage then becomes a place where the great ingathering of all things in Christ (1:10) is experienced and proclaimed. Therein lies the timeless and always radical component in the Household Code as we find it in Ephesians.

Revolutionary Subordination?

There is much in this analysis and interpretation of the Household Code that echoes the well-known and controversial treatment by the late John H. Yoder (1994:162-92, "Revolutionary Subordination"). I share his view that, regardless of the origin of this tradition, the appeal to Christ in the Household Code carries a germ of change more than of legitimation for prevailing social structures.

Nevertheless, on some points I diverge from Yoder. It is important to distinguish clearly, in a way Yoder does not, the argument underlying the use of the Code in 1 Peter from that in Ephesians (and in the earlier Colossians; TBC). In 1 Peter, the appeal to Christ serves to strengthen the resolve of those enduring injustice to suffer in light both of the evangelistic potential of suffering and the imminent judgment and liberation of God (so also Schertz, 1992a; Waltner: 82-118). The argument one might take up with 1 Peter is not whether or not patriarchy is a good thing, but whether it should be endured, and whether suffering under it makes sense.

If there is anything revolutionary about the subordination called for in the Code as found in 1 Peter, it resides in bringing about the conversion of the dominant partner through faithful subordination. Of crucial importance is understanding that such evangelistic suffering is inseparable from God's intervention as judge and liberator. That argument is not by nature any different from the one that pacifism or nonresistance must make in *all* situations of injustice. Much of Yoder's treatment of the Household Code relates to this sort of a historical and theological context (1994:185).

In Ephesians, as in Colossians, the Household Code is put forward as an essentially positive vision of social relations. Suffering is not a central issue. Christ is *not* presented as a reassuring fellow-sufferer.

He is instead put forward as a model for the *super*ordinated member
of the family. The Ephesian Code will thus be revolutionary only if
already-dominant partners in the relationship hear the summons to
mutual subordination as directed first and foremost to them, and if
the Christ they take as model is Lord in being a slave.

Yoder's construct of a church "tempted" to "impose" its vision of
liberty "*violently* upon the social order *beyond* the confines of the
church" (1994:185, italics added) hardly fits the situation of 1 Peter.
There the subordinates are in no position to rebel other than at great
cost to themselves. They are most certainly not in any position to
impose anything on anyone. Nor does it fit Ephesians, where the
light falls on relationships *within* the church, and only indirectly on
witness to the world at large. The chief (albeit not exclusive) audience
in Ephesians is made up of those in *dominant* social positions *within*
the church community.

The author of Ephesians is hardly arguing with males *too* eager
(J. H. Yoder, 1994:190) to overthrow patriarchy. Instead, Ephesians
plays on their existing sense of superior status and cajoles them to
redefine their already-existing dominance as servanthood in imitation
of Christ. This is nothing less than "revolution from above." But it is
revolutionary *only* if it goes beyond ameliorating an inherently unjust
structure and successfully subverts it in the interests of those in the
weaker social positions. Only then is it love as Christ loved; only then
does family life participate in the creation of *the new human* (2:15).

Such self-sacrificing love of the socially dominant is *not* a cur-
tailment of Christian liberty. It is the full and powerful exercise of
freedom! Yoder is correct in asserting that the church should not
"impose" its gospel of liberty on the world (1994:185). At the same
time, if the church is to be in a position to *inform the powers of the
multivaried wisdom of God* (3:10), members of "Wisdom's body"
must exercise that gospel *within* the church (as Yoder himself reminds
us; 1994:148; 1994a: 56, 61). For members of Christ's body, what is
expected of the church is more important than what can be expected
of society with regard to changes in structural relationships of inequity and injustice. Change should "begin with the household of God,"
to echo 1 Peter 4:17. That is a necessary implication of calling the
church the body of *Christ*.

The Household Code and Suffering

Anabaptist theology has typically had greater affinity with suffering
rather than with power and lordship. In that community, studies
of the Household Code have thus focused more on 1 Peter (e.g.,

Schertz, 1992a; Waltner: 82-118). Even when they have spoken generically to the Household Code, Anabaptist scholars have done so largely through the prism represented by the dynamics of 1 Peter (cf. Schroeder, 1959; 1990; J. H. Yoder, 1994:162-92). Thankfully, there is today heightened sensitivity to the suffering of women and children at the hands of husbands, fathers, and leaders. Thus in this present context, the challenge of 1 Peter's "pacifist" approach remains a troubling one for the church (e.g., essays by Gerber Koontz, Penner, and Schertz in Elizabeth Yoder, 1992).

Ephesians puts as great a challenge before those who find themselves in positions of power and privilege: can husbands, fathers, and bosses be converted? How and for whom will they exercise their power? Are they strong enough to relinquish power? Can they follow Jesus in such a way that social structures are humanized and also transformed into the image of the Christ? These are the kinds of questions Anabaptist men are less used to answering. But they are critically important for those increasingly at home in the world and its structures and habits of power.

> Gather us in—the rich and the haughty,
> gather us in—the proud and the strong.
> Give us a heart so meek and so lowly,
> give us the courage to enter the song. (*HWB:* 6, stanza 2)

Christ and the Church

On a different but crucial note, the relationship between Christ and the church is at least as important to the author as that between husband and wife, if not more so (5:31). The controversy in our day around the wife-husband relationship has made it difficult to appreciate what the present text offers. It invites us to recover a relationship with Christ that exults in the gracious intimacy believers can enjoy with the divine, individually and corporately. The search in our day for spiritual depth and immediacy in prayer and music is witness to a deep yearning among believers for recovery of "first love" (Rev. 2:4). Some are rediscovering the spirituality of medieval mystics; others have found a new breath of air in charismatic renewal.

Our text serves notice that such warm spirituality is best found and exercised at the center of everyday familial, social, and economic obligations. It is an insight close to the heart of Anabaptism that worship, spirituality, and ethics are not in tension with each other; they are to be found in the one and same place.

Ephesians 6:10-20

Waging Peace: Putting on the Armor of God

PREVIEW

With 6:10-20 we come to the climactic conclusion of Ephesians. The various strands of emphasis on power and fullness pervading the letter are finally pulled together. What emerges is a striking image of the church at the center of God's saving action. Since Ephesians would have been read aloud to audiences, this rousing call to battle performs the function of what students of ancient rhetoric call a "peroration." In a peroration, the author or speaker recapitulates the main themes of the letter or speech to motivate the audience to action (Lincoln: 432-3; Perkins: 141; Yoder Neufeld, 1997:110). The imitation of God (5:1) relates to forgiveness and kindness, but also to doing battle with the cosmic forces resisting the gathering up of all things in Christ (1:10).

The call to take up arms in a cosmic struggle comes somewhat as a surprise after the focus on the microcosm of the household in 5:21—6:9. *Cosmic* in no way excludes the arena of human relationships, however. Indeed, Ephesians aptly places the Household Code immediately *after* the call to nonconformity (5:3-21) and *before* the summons to take up God's armor. Thus the author challenges readers to understand that what they see as "only" everyday social relationships are actually an arena of struggle with the powers.

Ephesians 6:10-13 gives a summons to be empowered with God's own power. Believers are to put on God's own armor. The armor in verses 14-17 probably reminded first-century readers of soldiers they saw daily. More important, however, the author draws on the tradition of *God* putting on armor, as found specifically in Isaiah 59:17 (TBC). So the call to put on God's armor is a summons for readers to imitate the divine warrior. Not surprisingly, the enemy, in proportion to such an armor, is the devil and his forces. Verses 14-17 describe the warrior in God's armor as clad in truth, justice, faith, and salvation, ready to announce peace, and wielding the word of God.

Verses 18-20 bring the metaphor of battle to a close with a focus on prayer as struggle and as a stance of solidarity among saints "at war." Paul is presented one final time as a messenger bound, an *ambassador in chains*, illustrating how deeply ironic is the power and freedom of the gospel and its messengers.

Structure of 6:10-20

Henceforth, be empowered in the Lord!

Put on God's armor
    so that you might be able to resist the devil and the powers of evil!
Take up God's armor
    so that at the end of that evil day you will be standing!

Stand!
    • girded with truth
    • having put on justice
    • ready to announce the good news of peace
    • having taken up the shield of faith(fulness)
Grasp!
    • the helmet of salvation/liberation!
    • and the sword of God's word,
    • praying at all times
        for all the saints
        and also for me,
            for boldness to make known the gospel,
            for which I am an ambassador in chains.

The distinctive way Ephesians handles this material is noticeable in comparing Ephesians with Colossians. Notice that Colossians moves from the Household Code in 3:18—4:1 immediately to a call to prayer in 4:2-4. As in the case of the Household Code, Ephesians modifies Colossians by wedging the call to battle between the Household Code and the call to prayer. The call to vigilance and prayer is thereby welded both grammatically and conceptually to the call to arms.

A note of caution: most commentators like to envision the *individual* Christian in the armor (e.g., Best, 1998:586; Thurston: 145). Support for an individualistic interpretation grows if the passage is read in light of Cynic-Stoic views of life as battle (e.g., Malherbe, 143-74; Lincoln: 437-8, with survey). However, this limits what kind of struggle is imagined and misses the biblical allusions to God as the divine warrior. It is much more in keeping with the gist of Ephesians to see this summons to battle directed to the church *as a whole*, to the *body of Christ* acting as a unified divine force (so also Barth, 1974:791; Schnackenburg: 285; cf. Yoder Neufeld, 1997:111).

OUTLINE

Summons to Divine Warfare, 6:10-13

The Divine Armor, 6:14-17
6:14a	Truth
6:14b	Righteousness/Justice
6:15	Peace
6:16	Faith(fulness)
6:17a	Salvation/Liberation
6:17b	Spirit/Word of God

Prayer as Struggle and Solidarity, 6:18-20
6:18	Vigilant and Alert Prayer in the Spirit
6:19-20	Praying for Paul

EXPLANATORY NOTES

Summons to Divine Warfare 6:10-13

Henceforth readers are to take up God's power (6:10). *Finally* (NIV, NRSV) does not show quite as clearly as does *henceforth* (both possible translations of *tou loipou*) that this is the climax of the exhortation of chapters 4–6 and thus the reason for the previous buildup around power and identification with Christ (e.g., 1:19-23; 3:20). *Henceforth* may reflect as well the context of a baptismal challenge (6:11, notes about "putting on"; cf. 4:22, 24-25, notes).

The imperative *Be empowered!* is striking, for the Bible rarely uses the imperative in relation to *divine* empowerment, no doubt because it is God alone who empowers (cf. Rom. 4:20; Phil. 4:13; 1 Tim. 1:12). But we have repeatedly observed in Ephesians how much the church is invested with status and initiative. So, while it may strike us as presumptuous, we should read this as "Seize power! Fill yourselves with God's power!"

This reminds us of the ancient battle calls found in the OT, where God is called to rise up and make war against his enemies on behalf of his people (Exod. 15:3; Num. 10:35; Ps. 35:1-3, 22-28; Isa. 42:13; Judg. 5:12, where the people are to rise to do battle). Three words for power are strung together in verse 10. *Be empowered with the strength of the Lord's might!* On the surface, this is typical of an author who often likes to use as many words as possible (Schnackenburg: 271). We might also hear a faint echo of Paul's exhortation in 1 Corinthians 16:13: "Keep alert, stand firm in your faith, be courageous, be strong!" (NRSV). Or we might identify *Lord* with Christ and recall Ephesians 3:16-17, where the indwelling Christ strengthens believers.

Here, however, the use of a chain of power terms indicates something more. Stringing together power terms is a way to characterize the greatness of *God's* power. Already in 1:19 we find a chain of synonyms illustrating how overwhelming is the power of God that raised Christ from the dead and made him victorious over all powers. Colossians 1:11, which lurks in the background, also heaps up synonyms to depict God's power.

Both Colossians and Ephesians imitate Isaiah 40: "He who sits above the circle of the earth . . . is great in *strength, mighty* in *power*" (40:22, 26, italics added). Closer in time to Ephesians, such language also appears in Qumran's famous War Scroll as a way to ascribe ultimate victory and power to God, even though much of the scroll is taken up with orders for God's troops, the "sons of light" (1QM 11.4-5). The wording of the summons in Ephesians 6:10 becomes thus a measure of the breathtakingly lofty status the writer of Ephesians accords the saints (Yoder Neufeld, 1997:116).

Ephesians goes one step further. The church is called on to *put on God's whole armor* (*panoplia,* lit., "whole or complete armor"). This is sometimes interpreted to mean that God provides the necessary protection for the struggles of life. This armor is not what God is wearing but what God provides the believer. However, by drawing explicitly from Isaiah 59 for several items of armor, the author makes sure readers see that it is God's own armor that the community is to don (TBC).

The stress is on the communal body of believers inhabiting the armor of the divine warrior, rather than on the individual believer donning the metaphorical armor of the Roman soldier, as too often claimed (R. Martin, 1991:75; Thurston: 147-8). It is *God's* battle the church is called to wage (so also Schnackenburg: 272). To *put on* recalls the putting on of *the new human,* who is none other than the Messiah (4:24; cf. 2:15-16; cf. Rom. 13:12, 14). To *put on* is therefore also an allusion to baptism (cf. 4:22-24, notes).

Everything about the origin of this motif in the tradition of the divine warrior tells us that this is not a defensive struggle (contra Berkhof: 52; Best, 1993:60; 1998:588; Klassen, 1984:128). Nor is it only a mop-up after the victory has been won (contra Thurston: 145; Lincoln: 442-3). Yes, the resurrection of Christ implies the defeat of the powers (1:19-23, notes). Yes, final victory is assured. But such assurance always and necessarily *precedes* divine warfare in the Bible; it in no way underplays the gravity of the struggle that is about to ensue (e.g., Josh. 6:2; Judg. 7:9; 1 Sam. 24:4; von Rad: 42-4).

In Ephesians, the celebration of power and fullness is not meant to downplay the present and future struggle for the salvation of the world, but as in ancient warfare, to give courage for that struggle. The battle is real, even if the outcome is assured. The enemy is real, even if not *blood and flesh*. The armor and the weapons are real, even if they are "only" the persistent and prayerful exercise of truth, peace, justice, and the word of God.

Paul anticipates "nonfleshly" warfare in 2 Corinthians 10:3-6, where his "weapons of war" are pointed at the disobedient Corinthians. More closely related, the specific choice of imagery shows that the church's struggle is an essential component of the battle described in 1 Corinthians 15:24-25. Paul there describes Christ's reign or kingdom as successful warfare against the powers of evil. The summons to battle in Ephesians means that Christ's body—those who have been raised to life and seated with him in the heavenlies (2:6; cf. 1:20-23)—is also participating in Christ's reign (so also Barth, 1974:804). This is the eschatological battle; this is the *evil day* (6:13), however many *evil days* (5:16) that *day* might entail. The church lives in the eschatological moment, *buying out the time* (5:16, notes), which, as it turns out, implies taking the struggle to heal the cosmos to its very edges (so also Schnackenburg: 275-6).

To be sure, the church does not displace God. After all, for the church to be the body of God's Messiah (1:23), for it to possess the fullness of God (1:23; 3:19), for believers to be raised and seated in the heavenlies with the Messiah (2:5-6)—all this is the result of God's grace (2:8-10). Human pride and accomplishment are excluded (2:9). But that should not obscure the encouraging and sobering nature of this summons to put on God's armor. It is encouraging because the "size" of the armor banishes all thought of fear in the face of the enemy. It is sobering because it implies an arena of battle that pits the church against God's enemies.

The call to *stand* in the phrase *so that you may be able to stand against the strategies of the devil* increases the force of the summons. Such *standing against* is not a passive or even just a defensive stance. In Exodus 14:13, "standing" is admittedly the proper stance of the people in face of God's warring on their behalf. In the present passage, however, God's people are themselves summoned to inhabit the role of that divine warrior. "Standing" has thus taken on a decidedly different coloring. The power and armor of God enable believers to *stand against*, to resist and finally undo the *strategies* (lit., *crafty methods*) of the devil. A resilient, courageous, and ultimately victorious *standing* is one of the most important motifs in this passage (cf. 6:13-14; Arnold, 1989:120; Yoder Neufeld, 1997:129-31).

Verse 11 identifies the enemy as *the devil* (*diabolos;* lit., "slanderer, one who throws into confusion" *[Powers]*). While this is the same *evil one* we meet in 2:2 (cf. 6:16), the term *devil* appears also in 4:27 but is rare in the letters bearing Paul's name (1 Tim. 3:6-7). Verse 12 stipulates that the struggle is *not with blood and flesh.* Why does that need to be said? Perhaps some believers were experiencing firsthand the hostility of authorities or rival religious groups, even if this letter gives no specific evidence of that. They might have been tempted to see such hostile persons as the actual enemy.

Further, we have noted earlier the frequent points of contact between Ephesians and the thought and language of the community at Qumran, by the Dead Sea. Thus the scroll called *War of the Sons of Light Against the Sons of Darkness* makes it explicit that the final battle against the forces of evil will be most immediately against its "blood and flesh" representatives (e.g., 1QM 12.11-12; 15.13; 19.4; cf. CD 1.2). Perhaps some readers of Ephesians would have entertained such thoughts. The explicit rejection of warfare against *human* enemies in this letter is consistent with the strong peace emphasis in 2:14-16, echoed here in 6:15.

The need to explicitly reject warfare against *blood and flesh* was no doubt prompted also by the author's use of the tradition of the armor of God as found in Isaiah 59, Wisdom of Solomon 5, and 1 Thessalonians 5 (TBC). The history of this motif shows that most often in the Bible, "blood and flesh" is what becomes the object of divine warfare. In Isaiah and Wisdom of Solomon, it is fleshly human society gone bad that God wars against as judge and executioner (TBC). Even 1 Thessalonians 5, where the image of the divine warrior has undergone radical transformation (5:8), identifies human beings sitting in darkness (5:4) as the object of the divine warrior's intervention (5:2-3).

In Ephesians, we can observe a rather significant transformation of the tradition at this point. *Blood and flesh* are *not* the enemy. *Blood and flesh* are under the control of the enemy (2:2, notes). The church must struggle against that enemy, not against the victims of that enemy.

Markus Barth misses this point by suggesting that the author's choice of the rare term *palē (struggle)* over *polemos* (war) or *machē* (fight) reflects pacifist tendencies (1974:764). Most often in ancient literature, *palē* does refer to athletic "wrestling," but it can also refer to conflict and warfare generally (Greeven: 721). More important, however deeply concerned about peace, the author of Ephesians has absolutely no interest in playing down the gravity of the warfare here described. Indeed, the call to *divine* empowerment and the summons to put on the *divine* armor suggests quite the opposite. To state it ironically, pacifism is *real* warfare against enmity (cf. 2:11-22, esp. 2:6, notes).

The list of the powers in 6:12 is impressive: *rulers (archai), authorities (exousiai), cosmic potentates (kosmokratores) of this darkness, spiritual aspects (pneumatika; lit., spiritualities) of evil in the heavenlies. Rulers* and *authorities* are familiar from 1:21; the others are found only here. Some of the terms are drawn from the political realm *(rulers, authorities)*; others may have had astrological connotation *(cosmic potentates;* Arnold, 1989:65-8; Best, 1998:593-4). Whatever the origins of these terms, they are intended to be shorthand for the myriad of powers, great and small, personal and impersonal, individual and systemic, that resist the saving activity of God among humanity (Lincoln: 445; Yoder Neufeld, 1997:122-4 [Powers]).

The translation of the concluding item on the list, *pneumatika,* illustrates this comprehensiveness. *Pneumatika* is a neuter plural of the adjective "spiritual," literally translated as "spiritualities" or "spiritual things" or "matters." NIV and NRSV have *spiritual forces.* But in 1 Corinthians 2:13, NRSV translates that same term as "spiritual things" and NIV as "spiritual truths." So "the spiritual dimensions or aspects of evil" might be a better translation than "spiritual forces." This widens the sense of what the church is called upon to struggle against.

To further specify that these *spiritualities* are *in the heavenlies* is not a reference to things or places above and beyond the plane of human experience. Such language indicates status more than place. After all, believers are already *in the heavenlies* (cf. 2:6). *In the heavenlies* means that these evil potencies have the status of overlords over human affairs (cf. 2:2). But the power and armor of God, worn by those who *in and with Christ* are also *in the heavenlies*, make the church more than a match for them.

By means of the stress on comprehensiveness in the list of evil powers, the author indicates that the church is to take up the struggle with *all* the powers resisting God's saving designs for the cosmos. Any restrictive definition of the powers undervalues the victory of Christ and thereby defeats the central argument in Ephesians. We recall 1:21, where Christ has been given victory over *all principalities, powers, dominions, authorities*, and *every name*. The allusive list of powers in 6:12 is therefore suggestive of the full range of evil into which the *authority of the air* lures the *sons of disobedience* (2:1-3; notes on "culture of darkness," 5:11-14; "Light and Darkness," TBC for 5:3-21 [*Powers*]).

As a bridge to the description of the armor itself, the author reiterates in 6:13 the call to *take up the whole armor of God*. In 6:11 the saints were asked to *put on* the armor, suggesting protective gear; now in 6:13 the language suggests taking up weapons. This is to be done so that the saints may be able (lit.) *to resist on the evil day*. NRSV's *withstand* (NIV, *stand your ground*) has a defensive connotation that does not fit the imagery the author has chosen here. *Resist* in the sense of "to oppose" captures the sense of "standing against" much better.

The reference to *the evil day* in 6:13 is puzzling. We might take *evil day* to refer to the time of the final eschatological battle, when God and his holy ones overcome the devil and his evil forces. However, Ephesians generally gives little attention to traditional apocalyptic eschatology [*Apocalypticism*]. Perhaps, then, *the evil day* refers to any of the days of battle, with all the struggle, pain, and sacrifice they bring with them, without intending any particular eschatological scenario (note the plural *evil days* in 5:16).

As often, a solution might lie in combining the two notions. Since we recognize the important ties between 1 Corinthians 15:24-27 and Ephesians 6:10-20 (cf. 1:19-23, notes), we can be sure that the author wants "those who belong to Christ" (1 Cor. 15:23) to see the present struggle as part of a final decisive messianic battle to the finish. This is true however long that battle might last, no matter how many *days* (5:16) such a *day* might contain (cf. Arnold, 1989:113-5; Barth, 1974:804; Best, 1998:597; Schnackenburg: 275-6). "Final" and "decisive" does not imply "the end of history" (contra Lincoln: 446), but the day(s) before all things are fully and completely gathered up in the peace that is Christ. Then history, *the coming ages* (2:7), can finally ensue, with *God* being *all in all* (4:6; cf. 1 Cor. 15:28).

Verse 13 presents the translator with one more puzzle. NIV and NRSV translate *katergazomai* as *having done everything*. True, the term usually carries the sense of "doing" or "producing" in the Pauline literature (e.g., Rom. 2:9; 4:15; 7:15; 15:18; 1 Cor. 5:3; 2 Cor. 4:17; 5:5; Phil. 2:12). But *what* are believers to have *done*? The most immediate answer might be putting on the armor. After all, the command to *stand* is repeated in Ephesians 6:14. Believers are to stand, having put on (past tense!) the *belt*, the *breastplate*, and the *shoes*. But the term *katergazomai* can also mean "to defeat" or "to destroy," which would appear to fit the present context of struggle and battle just as well or better (*BAGD*: 421; Bertram, 1965:634-5; Yoder Neufeld, 1997:128-9).

Hence, the sentence reads, *And having conquered completely, to be standing*. In ancient warfare, the soldiers standing at the end of battle are showing themselves to be victorious. *Standing* is a sign of strength in battle, a stance of victory found all over the biblical and related literature (e.g., Ps. 18:33-34; Wisd. of Sol. 18:16, 21-23; 1QM 14.4-8).

The Divine Armor   6:14-17

The armor in which the church is to take its stand is elaborated in verses 14-17. As stated above, the tradition from which the author draws this image is chiefly Isaiah 59:17-19 and its dependent texts rather than the familiar armor of the Roman soldier (cf. texts and items of armor, in "Isaiah 59 and Its Offspring," TBC).

We begin with some general observations. First, the armor is both metaphorical and real. The armor works as a metaphor only because in reality *truth, justice, peace, faith(fulness)*, the *word of God*, and *prayer* are the effective means by which the powers are overcome. Those who interpret this passage in a more restrictedly "exorcistic" way must keep this in mind. The powers are vanquished through the exercise of truth, justice, peace, and liberation, just as they are through the exercise of the word and prayer. The emphasis in this metaphor falls on those virtues and actions, and not on the elements of armor that are the vehicle of the metaphor (*belt, shoes,* etc.). The specific items of armor and weaponry are to some extent interchangeable (TBC, on diverse ways this image is appropriated).

Second, by reaching behind 1 Thessalonians 5 to Isaiah 59, the author of Ephesians makes clear that the armor is *God's*. This has important implications for how one reads the metaphor of the armed warrior as a whole. The pedigree of the motif shows that the metaphor is intrinsically more offensive than it is defensive (contra Berkhof: 47-50).

Third, although vengeance and wrath are part of God's warring in Isaiah and Wisdom of Solomon and set the context for the image in 1 Thessalonians 5, however ironically (Elias: 206-9; Yoder Neufeld, 1997:84-93), they are not stressed in Ephesians (even if present; 5:5-7, notes). The battle against the powers is nevertheless real, and their defeat is certain. Vengeance and wrath are not explicitly present likely because of their association with divine warfare *against blood and flesh*. And that is *not* the nature of this struggle.

The whole armor of God depicted in the following verses is meant to show that the faithful community is called to *stand* (cf. 6:11, 13). They are also to *do* God's work, to *act* as the Messiah's body through the exercise of the same virtues and actions that have marked God's saving intervention in the past. These virtues and actions are *truth, justice, peace, faithfulness/solidarity, salvation/liberation,* the *word,* and *prayer.*

6:14a Truth

Truth (alētheia) is at the head of the list of armor, identified with the girding of the loins. The pride of place given to *truth* should not surprise us since the author has already greatly stressed *truth* throughout the letter (1:13; 4:15, 21, 24-25; 5:9). Significantly, *truth* marks both the nature of God's presence in the world in Jesus (4:21, 24) and the way those who have *put on Christ* are to behave toward each other (4:15, 25). Its presence here is particularly reminiscent of the Greek (LXX) version of Isaiah 11:5, where God's anointed one will gird himself with truth.

That *truth* is here included in the *armor* shows that for the author the exercise of *truth* is more than a matter of being honest, as much as integrity and "trustworthiness" (Houlden: 339) are essential components of readiness for a struggle with the powers. *Truth* is an active dimension of the church's life. It is a way in which God intervenes in a world whose culture is best characterized as *the lie* (4:25-27, notes). It means upholding standards of gracious integrity *within* the community of *the new human* (4:15, 25). It means speaking the "truth-full" good news to those still under the sway of evil (e.g., 2:2, 17; there is no good reason to exclude this dimension from its meaning, as do Lincoln: 448; Schnackenburg: 277, n. 29).

Exercising *truth* also means speaking to the powers the *truth* that is in Jesus (4:21), *the multivaried wisdom of God* (3:10; Berkhof: 50-1). The exercise of *truth* in word and deed will often be highly conflictual. *Truth* is experienced often as an attack and is therefore often vigorously and sometimes violently resisted. The *truth* is armor against the deceitful strategies of powers resisting the truth (6:11; cf. 4:14). It is also a weapon with which to undo *the lie*.

6:14b Righteousness/Justice

The next piece of armor is the *breastplate of righteousness/ justice*. *Righteousness* and *justice* both translate the one Greek word *dikaiosunē*. For purposes of hearing the full range of meaning, I have placed both terms together in this discussion. Along with *truth*, *righteousness/justice* has already been identified as the *fruit of light* in 5:9, and as the means through which *the new human* is created (with *the holiness of truth*, 4:24). To relate *righteousness* to "justification" is of little help in this case (contra Barth, 1974:795-7). It may even be a hindrance because it stresses that righteousness is what God imputes to the believer on the basis of faith, and not by works (2:8-10, notes).

A quite different understanding is at work here: the point is *doing* the *right* thing. Notice in Isaiah 59:17 that God puts on *righteousness/justice* as, the *breastplate*. God does so because there is no one who practices *justice*, no one to intervene on behalf of those who are being killed and tortured in the public square (59:7, 14). The armor signals the nature of God's intervention as judge and liberator. *Righteousness* is what God *does* as warrior—it is *justice* at work. We should not think of the *breastplate of righteousness/justice* in Ephesians as the safe cocoon of impunity (as many understand "justification"). Instead, it is the active participation in the divine battle against the powers on behalf of their victims.

As in the case of God in Isaiah 59, *justice* is what the saints put on; *justice* is what saints practice (cf. Isa. 11:5). In Isaiah 59, God could find no one to intervene. In Ephesians 6, the church wears justice on its breast, so that now there *is* someone to intervene.

6:15 Peace

Ephesians introduces a novel element to the divine armor in verse 15. Believers are to have *feet shod in readiness (hetoimasia) to announce the good news of peace*. Interpreting the passage in essentially defensive terms, Best opts for translating *hetoimasia* as *firmness*, having firm footwear so as to (with)stand the onslaughts of the enemies (Best, 1998:599-600). As valuable as is firm footwear, *readiness* communicates the holy impatience to get the good news of peace out. *Peace* is, after all, a central concern of Ephesians, as we see in 2:11-22, most beautifully expressed in the hymn of 2:14-16.

The presence of *peace* in this passage on armor has been called a "lofty paradox" (Harnack, 1963:13; cf. Schnackenburg: 278). There is a paradox if the gospel of peace is a part of the "arsenal" of the divine warrior. It is a paradox of sorts also if the gospel of peace makes one ready to do battle (Lincoln: 449). The author already hints at the paradox in 2:16, where the one who himself is peace *murders* enmity through his own death.

Compelling as such observations are, another interpretation may be more persuasive. There is no paradox in the readiness of a warrior to announce peace once hostile powers have been defeated (Yoder Neufeld, 1997:137-9). In the background is the image of the messenger of peace in Isaiah 52:7, who comes announcing peace, the cessation of conflict (cf. Isa. 57:19, used in Eph. 2:17; cf. Rom. 10:15; contra Best, 1998:600). Indeed, to speak here of *readiness to announce peace* means that peace is not yet fully present, however much Christ has already made peace between Jews and Gentiles (2:11-22). The *gathering up of all things in Christ* (1:10) remains an ongoing conflictual process in which the church is to play an essential role. Such a struggle is in actual experience the practice of suffering love in imitation of the ultimate announcer of peace, Christ; yet it is also an assault on the powers.

6:16 Faith(fulness)

Another novel item of armor is the *shield of faith (pistis)* with which *to quench the flaming darts of the evil one*. This image of the shield of faith is almost universally interpreted as defensive. The shield is needed to fend off the fiery darts of the attacking evil one. But to identify the shield as defensive does not tell us whether the one wearing the shield is on the defensive or the offensive in a battle. Ancient depictions of siege warfare in both word and picture show that shields were carried by the forces putting a city under siege, fending off the fiery arrows of the defenders (Yoder Neufeld, 1997:139-40; Perkins: 146-7, acknowledging this, does not draw the conclusion).

A shield *is*, of course, by its very nature defensive. *Trust* or *confidence* in God's power *is* a critical part of the armor in this passage. Throughout the Psalms, God is called a "shield" (e.g., Pss. 3:3; 5:12; 7:10; 18:2, 30, 35; 35:1-3; 59:11; 76:3; 115:9-11; 119:114; 144:2). The last phrase of Psalm 91:4 is highly reminiscent of the Ephesians text:

He will cover you with his pinions,
   and under his wings you will find refuge;
his faithfulness is a shield and buckler.

Psalm 28:7 also anticipates Ephesians' stress on divine power in relation to the armor:

The LORD is my strength and my shield;
   in him my heart trusts;
so I am helped, and my heart exults,
   and with my song I give thanks to him.

But a defensive interpretation of this image does not capture the
thought of Ephesians. In 6:16, the readers are not depicted as dependent on the protection of the divine warrior, as true as that dependency is in the lives of those who have *faith*. The bracing nature of
the present summons emerges because such dependency is taken for
granted. In this instance, the believers themselves are the warrior!

As the discussion of the Pauline phrase "saved by faith" in 2:8
showed, *pistis* can mean "trust," in this case in God's power to save
(Lincoln: 449). With the article it is often translated as "the faith,"
referring to the content of "Christian faith" (as Best, 1998:601, interprets it here). But *pistis* can also mean *faith**fulness*** (cf. notes on
1:1 and 3:12; Bultmann and Weiser; Yoder Neufeld, 1997:139, n.
140). It is through Christ's *faithfulness* toward us that we have been
granted boldness and confidence. So putting on the *shield of pistis* is
another way of participating in messianic *faithfulness*.

God's faithful action in Christ provides the undergirding for the
community engaged in mortal combat with the powers. To the same
abundant extent, the exercise of this armor means that the saints can
be counted on to *keep faith* with *blood and flesh*, to intervene on
their behalf. *Faith**fulness*** means "solidarity," here with God and
with humanity.

The image of the shield of *faithfulness* is thus every bit as offensive as it is defensive. The church is called to put the powers under
siege. The shield is part of the arsenal of intervention, as Psalm 35:1-3
illustrates forcefully, where God is asked to take up shield and buckler,
spear and javelin, and to intervene on behalf of the afflicted.

6:17a Salvation/Liberation

Ephesians now returns to a specific element of God's armor in
Isaiah 59:17, *the helmet of salvation* or, to use an entirely fitting
synonym, *liberation*. Its presence in the list is highlighted by the fact

that whereas the putting on of previous items of armor was grammatically related to the command to stand in 6:14, a new imperative is sounded here: *Take up the helmet!* In Isaiah 59, *God is the one who puts on the helmet of salvation.* This background means that one will want to be careful not to interpret the phrase of Ephesians 6:17 as the protection God offers the saints by assuring them of their own salvation (against many commentators who read it as "receive the helmet," as in Best, 1998:602; Lincoln: 450).

True, the salvation of the believers is already assured (2:8). That is, after all, the gist of the whole first half of the letter. In the context of putting on the armor, however, the image of *grasping the helmet of salvation* is meant to place on the church the task of bringing liberation to those in bondage by imitating the God of Isaiah 59. Close attention to the vocabulary will support such an interpretation: Ephesians 6:17 uses the term for *salvation* found in the Greek of Isaiah 59:17 (LXX), *sōtērion*, rather than the more frequent *sōtēria* (Eph. 1:13; Paul in 1 Thess. 5:8). This indicates a deliberate connection to Isaiah 59 (Yoder Neufeld, 1997:87-9, 141-2, on Eph. 6:17; Isa. 59; 1 Thess. 5).

6:17b Spirit/Word of God

The saints are to take the *helmet of liberation* and *the sword of the Spirit*, the *word of God*. It is sometimes noted that the word for sword is *machaira*, which in Greco-Roman times referred to a dagger or small sword rather than the large sword called *xiphos* or *rhomphaia*. Sometimes interpreters draw the conclusion that the author wants to play down the militancy or aggressiveness of the text (e.g., Berkhof: 52; similarly Klassen, 1984:128; J. H. Yoder, 1994:203). However, the Greek Bible (LXX) early Christians used most frequently employs *machaira* to translate the Hebrew *ḥereb,* the term for "sword" used in such important divine warfare texts as Deuteronomy 32:41-42, Jeremiah 25:30-38 (32:30-38, LXX), and except for 66:16, always in Isaiah (e.g., 27:1; 34:5-6; 65:12).

Furthermore, the author of Ephesians is consciously using a *scriptural* metaphor, employing *scriptural* language, and is heavily dependent on Isaiah. Hence, the choice of *machaira* draws comparison with God as the divine warrior, not with the Roman soldier.

The rest of the image supports this interpretation. This sword is the *sword* of the *pneuma,* both *Spirit* and *wind* (2:1-2, notes). In both Isaiah 59:19 and Wisdom of Solomon 5:23, "wind" is part of the arsenal of the divine warrior. The overtones of power and force are not derived only from there, however. In Pauline churches,

"Spirit" signified the powerful presence of God, the divine force of the eschatological future already "blowing" among believers (e.g., Rom. 8; Gal. 5; 1 Cor. 12; 2 Cor. 3). In Ephesians 6, *the sword of the Spirit (pneuma)* is set against *the spiritual aspects (pneumatika) of evil in the heavenlies.*

This sword is *the word of God.* In Ephesians the term *word of God* has not yet come into use as a synonym for Scripture. Instead, it refers to the whole variety of divine revelation and intervention. Though *word* here translates *rhēma,* that term is more or less synonymous with *logos* in 6:19 (Yoder Neufeld, 1997:144). The range of allusions is great (see, e.g., the *word* as means of *washing,* 5:26). Of interest to us here are particularly texts that show the *word* within contexts of divine warfare.

Notable in these divine warfare texts is the *logos* in Wisdom of Solomon 18, both as the name given to the avenging angel carrying the sword of judgment (18:14-16), and as the weapon by which the defender of the people wards off the angel of death (18:22). Compare also Isaiah 11:4, LXX, where the divinely chosen king smites the world with "the word of his mouth" ("word," *logos* in Greek; in place of the Hebrew *shebet,* "rod"). Immediately following is the parallel phrase "breath *(pneuma)* of his lips" (Isa. 11:4, LXX). Strikingly similar to our text is Hebrews 4:12, where the "word *(logos)* of God" is like a "two-edged sword *(machaira)."* Revelation 1:16 and 2:12 illustrate the interchangeability of terms: the "two-edged sword" coming from the "mouth" of the exalted Christ is the *rhomphaia* (cf. 2:16; 19:15). Note also the close proximity of "the word of truth" and "the weapons of justice" in 2 Corinthians 6:7 (TRYN).

Again, we see that the author has chosen a symbol *(sword)* laden with overtones of divine intervention and power, even if he is not dependent on any one particular text.

The content of *the word* is left undefined. Some commentators are sure it can mean only "the gospel" (e.g., Arnold, 1989:111; Fee, 1987:729; Schnackenburg: 280). That identification is no doubt in large measure valid, all the more so if "gospel" is understood as rich and comprehensive "good news," as multivaried in its scope and expression as is the wisdom of God (3:10). Others think it might refer to a slogan or formula intended to fend off the evil powers (Best, 1998:604; this is interpreted "exorcistically" by many of the so-called third wave [Powers]).

In this case it is important that the church understand the call to make *the word of God* effective. It is less important that specific content be given to the term *the word of God.* For the church to "wield" the *word of God* (as a *sword*) means that it must find ways of making sure that *word* does not "return . . . empty" (Isa. 55:11). In his treatment of this text, Arthur Cochrane (128) appropriately points to Martin Luther's famous hymn "A Mighty Fortress."

> And though this world, with devils filled,
> Should threaten to undo us;
> We will not fear, for God hath willed
> His truth to triumph through us:
> The prince of darkness grim,
> We tremble not for him;
> His rage we can endure;
> For lo! his doom is sure;
> One little *word* shall fell him. (trans. F. H. Hedge, italics added)

Prayer as Struggle and Solidarity 6:18-20

Translators typically treat this section as a discrete passage. Nevertheless, these three verses are grammatically dependent on the imperative in verse 17 calling on saints to *take up* the helmet and the sword (so also Fee, 1987:730) or, as some suggest, on the main imperative to *stand* in verse 14 (e.g., Arnold: 112; Barth, 1974:777; Lincoln: 451). In Greek, participles can function as imperatives, but it is best here to see these verses as grammatically connected to the rest of the armor. Prayer plays a central role in the struggle of the communal divine warrior. Prayer is battle. Prayer is also, however, a way to keep alert. It is a form of vigilance, of keeping the senses honed to danger and to opportunities for victory.

The importance Ephesians gives to prayer as part of the church's struggle with the powers is shown by comparison with Colossians 4:2-4, likely the source for these verses. Colossians makes no connection between wakefulness, prayer, and battle. It does not picture Christian life as battle. The powers have been defeated and have already been paraded in a victory procession (Col. 2:15; cf. E. Martin: 116). In Ephesians, prayer is "militarized" and drawn into the struggle with the powers. In doing so, Ephesians echoes the close connection of vigilance and alertness to divine warfare in Paul (e.g., Rom. 13:11-14; 1 Thess. 5:6, 8; cf. Arnold, 1989:112, exploring prayer as a means of struggling with the powers; Wink, 1992:308-14).

6:18 Vigilant and Alert Prayer in the Spirit

The critical importance given to prayer is indicated by the fact that it is to take place, literally, *in every time* (*kairos,* "loaded time"; 1:10, notes). Praying at every important moment becomes equivalent to *exploiting every opportune moment* (*kairos;* 5:16, notes). Hence the need for alertness. Again, we should not interpret this in a defensive sense. This is the corporate divine warrior on the lookout for opportunities to transform darkness into light.

The relationship of prayer to battle is further indicated by the fact that it is *in [the] Spirit ["In"]*. One might understand this as a reference to praying in tongues as prayer empowered *by the Spirit* (cf. Rom. 8:26-27; 1 Cor. 14:14-15; Fee, 1987:730-1). If such is intended, then this form of worship must be understood as combat with the powers, much as worship inspired by the filling of the Spirit is an act of courageous nonconformity and transformation (Eph. 5:18-21). In verse 17 *Spirit* is associated with *sword* and *word*. In this case we might think of praying *with the Spirit,* "wielding" the Spirit in prayer, unleashing the power of God. Neither interpretation should be excluded. It is clear that prayer is effective power-filled engagement in the struggle for the cosmos (on prayer as combat: Ellul, 1973:139-78, esp. 150-3; McClain: 69-73, 104-15; Wink, 1992:297-317).

But prayer is also the exercise of solidarity with fellow strugglers. *Pleading for all the saints* is a way in which members of the divine warrior participate in meeting each other's needs. In the Bible the divine warrior is the one who *responds* to the prayers of the needy (cf. Ps. 35:1-3). Hence, the implication is present that those who do the praying are themselves necessarily drawn into the response to that prayer (cf. Ellul, 1973:160-78).

6:19-20 Praying for Paul

After prayer has been offered *for all the saints,* it is also to be offered for Paul, that he *be given openness of mouth to boldly speak the word, the mystery of the good news*. In keeping with the way Ephesians places Paul behind the saints, at the end of the line, (3:8, notes), the request that Paul be prayerfully remembered *follows* the command to pray for all the saints. The saints find themselves in the armor and role of the divine warrior, but Paul is a prisoner, a divine emissary in chains (cf. 3:1; 4:1; for the image of *ambassador,* 6:20, see 2 Cor. 5:20; Philem. 9, NRSV note).

There is great irony in the image of an emissary in chains. A bound ambassador is a contradiction in terms—except from a Pauline perspective. Imprisonment brought great suffering to Paul (note esp. Philippians), but it only deepened his qualifications to be an ambassador of the one who went to the cross. In Paul's day, the cross stood for shameful torture and execution, and yet it became the central expression of God's power and wisdom (1 Cor. 1:18-25). Hence, Paul's own imprisonment could hardly thwart his commission to let the secret out of the bag, to get out the good news of God's reconciliation in Christ (cf. Eph. 3).

The message to the readers is clear: their own vulnerability likewise does not disqualify them from inhabiting the armor of God and the task it implies. In doing so, they imitate their great apostle Paul, who amid great suffering and calamities nevertheless wielded the "weapons of righteousness" with endurance and love for his churches (2 Cor. 6:1-13).

In 6:20 we thus see one more instance of the profound irony that informed Paul's apostolic ministry, here expressed in the image of the bound messenger, the *ambassador in chains*. The heroic status of Paul, as observed in chapter 3, is exploited for all its motivational force, in a way highly reminiscent of Paul himself, who time and again was prepared to place himself in a subservient position in relation to his churches. Notice, for example, how often he asks for prayer in his letters (e.g., Rom. 15:30-32; Phil. 1:19; 1 Thess. 5:25). Here in Ephesians, while Paul is in chains, the saints are in the armor of the divine warrior. Their prayers are a plea for God to embolden the chained ambassador, to free his mouth even as his body is in chains. The prayers are also a way of coming to Paul's aid. One might even say that the act of writing in his name is a way of answering that prayer.

The image of the armed struggle against the powers thus ends on a strong note of mutuality: Paul serves as a model who puts the welfare of *all the saints* before his own. Deference to the needs of others and respect for *all* the saints are two of the strange weapons wielded in imitation of God and his Messiah. Strange warfare, indeed! However, it is lethal from the vantage point of *the powers*, who find nothing as threatening as a prayerful community exercising truth, justice, peace, and a courageous speaking of the word of God, thus announcing the good news that enmity is dead!

THE TEXT IN BIBLICAL CONTEXT

The Divine Warrior

Ephesians 6:10-20 is one of many texts in the Bible that deal with divine warfare (e.g., Exod. 14–15; Deut. 32–33; Pss. 18; 68; Isa. 59; 63; Hab. 3; among Mennonite writers, cf. Ted Hiebert; Waldemar Janzen; Millard Lind; Ben Ollenburger; Devon Wiens; Yoder Neufeld). The image of God as warrior is one of the primal metaphors in the Bible, in the OT and the NT.

One of the oldest songs recorded in biblical literature, the song of Miriam and Moses in Exodus 15, celebrates the LORD as a mighty warrior who has driven horse and chariot into the sea (15:1, 21). This image of God underwent some radical changes over the centuries. The most dramatic was the prophetic insight that the people of Israel could not count on God's warring on their behalf against their enemies unless they lived true to their covenant with God. Instead, God could be expected to go to war against them (e.g., Isa. 29:3-10; Jer. 21:3-9; 29:16-19). The warrior became judge and executioner of Israel's enemies (e.g., Isa. 13) and also of Israel.

God could use natural disasters to fight his enemies (e.g., Exod. 15; Deut. 32; 2 Sam. 22.9-16//Ps. 18:8-15; Ps. 77:16-18). God could surround himself with allies such as the tribes of Israel, the hated Assyrians or Babylonians, and the armies of heaven or, as they are frequently called, the "heavenly hosts." Typical of apocalyptic literature generally, the Revelation of John illustrates dramatically how this imagery lent itself to picturing God as judge and liberator on a cosmic scale.

At the root of this tradition lies the conviction that ultimately God alone is the warrior. Victory is God's and God's alone. One important way this finds expression is in the command for the people to stand and watch the LORD act on their behalf, as at the Red Sea in Exodus 14:13-14. Even when the people come "to the help of the LORD" ("YHWH," Judg. 5:23), as is more commonly the case, the battle and the victory are always God's.

Isaiah 59 and Its Offspring

The specific tradition of the divine warrior that the author takes up begins with Isaiah 59 and continues through the Wisdom of Solomon 5 and 1 Thessalonians 5. It shows the prophetic transformation of the motif, but also the more radical changes Paul has introduced.

Isaiah 59 pictures God as infuriated at the violence and oppression that marks Israelite existence. There is no one to see that justice is done, so God puts on the divine armor and brings judgment on the violators of the covenant and liberation for the faithful. The armor is thus a symbol of judgment as much or more than it is of liberation. Wisdom of Solomon 5 takes up the Isaianic motif and interprets it from within the same frame of thinking. God puts on the armor to vindicate the just by bringing down their oppressors.

Wisdom of Solomon may have been written as late as the time of Paul's ministry. This only increases our wonder at Paul's radical reinterpretation of Isaiah 59 in his first letter to the Thessalonians.

Into a world marked by darkness, drunkenness, sleep, and a fatefully mistaken sense of security, the "day of the Lord" comes like "a thief in the night" (1 Thess. 5:2). The images are threatening and are intended to be so. But a surprise awaits. Who is in the divine armor? Weak and suffering believers! And what are they wielding in their struggle? Faith, love, and the hope of salvation!

To be sure, Paul does not for a moment abandon the conviction that God will judge the cosmos and all its inhabitants, as 1 Thessalonians 1:10 and 2:14 clearly show. Yet, at the heart of Paul's gospel is also the conviction that the God before whose holiness and justice we all "fall short" (Rom. 3:23), the same God, surprises the world with grace. Indeed, the desire to surprise with grace is the fullest expression of God's justice (cf. Rom. 5).

First Thessalonians 5:1-11 is an instance of that good news. Like a thief in the night, the divine warrior surprises those sitting in darkness, but the warrior is in the form of a community that practices faith, hope, and love (5:8). The *day of the Lord* becomes once again a day of *salvation*. Amos' terrible irony of day becoming night (5:18, 20) has been reversed: night has turned into day (Elias: 197-9; Yoder Neufeld, 1997:73-93).

Ephesians builds on that transformation. Notice, for example, the act of turning darkness into light through exposing the darkness for what it is (Eph. 5:11). At the same time, Ephesians 6:10-20 does not simply imitate 1 Thessalonians 5, even if both texts express the conviction that the community of believers has been drawn into the activity of the divine warrior. In Ephesians, the adversary has changed. In effect, the church as Christ's body is now implicated in Christ's reign, marked by warfare with the powers (cf. 1 Cor. 15:24-28).

We can more fully appreciate the distinctive way Ephesians treats the tradition of God's armor by placing the contents of the armor in these related texts side by side.

The Armor of God

Isa. 59:17	*Wisd. of Sol. 5:17-20a*	*1 Thess. 5:8*	*Eph. 6:14-17*
	panoply or whole armor		panoply or whole armor
			girdle of truth
breastplate of righteousness/ justice	breastplate of righteousness/ justice	breastplate of faith and love	breastplate of righteousness/ justice

The Armor of God (continued)

Isa. 59:17	Wisd. of Sol. 5:17-20a	1 Thess. 5:8	Eph. 6:14-17
			shoes of the runner of peace
			shield of faith or faithfulness
helmet of salvation	helmet of impartial justice	helmet the hope of salvation	helmet of salvation
	sword of stern wrath		sword of the Spirit, the word of God
clothed with the garments of vengeance and wrath			
(next, in 59:19, natural phenomena: wind, river)	(next, in 5:20b-23, creation as ally in warfare: lightning, hail, sea, rivers, wind)		

In comparing the elements of armor, we observe a great deal of both continuity and creativity in how the biblical writers adapt the motif. *Helmet* and *breastplate* are the most consistent elements. Wisdom of Solomon compares *righteousness/justice* to a breastplate, and a close parallel, *impartial justice,* to a helmet. In 1 Thessalonians 5, Paul overlays the helmet and breastplate with his favorite triad of virtues: *faith, love,* and *hope.* It may be that he sees faith and love as another way of expressing God's righteousness/justice (cf. Rom. 5:8, 18). Ephesians returns to the Isaianic original with *the breastplate of righteousness/ justice* and *the helmet of salvation.* At the same time, we are struck by the creativity with which the author expands the image.

We must keep this long tradition in view so we can appreciate the shock early readers and hearers of this letter would have experienced at the summons for them to put on *God's* armor. Ephesians calls them to enter the battle against the spiritual powers of darkness in the heavenlies. It is true that this is *God's* battle and *God's* victory; it is also true that the *saints* are drawn into the struggle of God for the sake of the cosmos.

Are the Powers All Bad?

The depiction of the powers in 6:12 is sharply negative. The over-arching image of warfare leads of course to seeing them as such. But in the NT, the powers are not uniformly evil [Powers]. Colossians 1:16 credits Christ with having created them! At present, however, they are clearly viewed in Ephesians as hostile (cf. 2:2), even if 2:7 and 3:10 might allow for the future reconciliation of the powers in some sense, perhaps as part of the *ingathering of all things* (1:10). For the most part, the depiction is decidedly negative.

The writer of Ephesians was specifically concerned to impress on readers the gravity of the struggle toward pacification of the cosmos. That objective alone governs the depiction of the powers. Within the frame of the argument in Ephesians, the anticipated fate of the powers is defeat (cf. 1:20-22). Ephesians is silent on whether that means their elimination or whether there is to be restoration beyond defeat.

Baptism and Putting On the Armor of God

In Pauline letters, "taking off" and "putting on" are favorite ways to represent the transformation of believers in baptism (e.g., Rom. 13:12, 14; Gal. 3:27; Col. 3:8-12). It is widely thought that this language reflects the actual ritual of baptism, where those to be baptized took off their old clothes, were baptized, and then received new clothes reflecting the new life in Christ (Meeks: 150-7). We have already noted that according to 4:22-24 believers were taught to *take off . . . the old human*, and *put on* the *new human* (cf. Col. 3:5-11; E. Martin: 147-65).

The identity of the *new human* has already been established in 2:15 as Christ himself, albeit in the form of reconciled humanity. In baptism, believers are incorporated into that body and person of Christ (Gal. 3:27). They "put on" the Lord Jesus Christ, as Romans 13:14 states it.

Romans 13:12-14, however, also draws a close connection between putting on Christ in baptism and putting on armor: "Take off the works of darkness and put on the weapons of light, since the night is far gone and the day is at hand" (v. 12, TRYN). This is highly remi-niscent of 1 Thessalonians 5:1-11, but also of baptism as prepared-ness for battle in Romans 6:1-14. There the baptized are exhorted not to present their members to sin as "weapons of injustice," but rather to present their members to God as "weapons of justice" (6:13, TRYN; NIV and NRSV translate rather weakly "instruments of wick-edness" and "instruments of righteousness").

Ephesians 6:10-20 draws heavily on this connection (so also, e.g., Gnilka: 310). Putting on *the new human*, the *body* of Christ, is identification with the task of Christ. That means putting on the armor of God and entering the fray of messianic battle with the powers, exercising truth, justice, peace, faithfulness, liberation, and the word of God with prayerful vigilance and discipline. Baptism is a ritual of enlistment as much as it is identification with the death and resurrection of Christ—or better, because of this identification.

THE TEXT IN THE LIFE OF THE CHURCH

The Language of Violence

These verses are clearly meant to challenge and encourage the church to courageous engagement with the powers that resist God's peace. They have provided great encouragement and motivation for peacemakers (as illustrated repeatedly by e-mail dispatches from Christian Peacemaker Teams [CPT]). Sadly, they have also provided encouragement for a crusade mentality that has left countless victims in its wake. The certainty of being right and of doing the work of God, when fused with a view of the other as enemy, has led to arrogance and blindness, often to great violence (Volf: 57-98, with insightful discussion of "exclusion").

Questions are increasingly raised, especially among Christians dedicated to peacemaking, about the acceptability of militaristic language, even when it is highly metaphorical and even when it is derived from the Bible (e.g., Russell, 1984:122). Some who have been close to war feel deep revulsion at the vocabulary of violence, especially when employed as a positive metaphor.

In addition to the issue of glorifying violence, does such language paint reality too much as parties/dimensions "over against" each other and thereby crowd out other paradigms of change? Does it create and nourish a mentality that sees violent struggle, however spiritually redefined, as the only way to salvation?

While acknowledging the importance of these questions, we need to recall that the author of Ephesians uses other even more powerful ways to reflect on God's great program of making peace with the cosmos and its inhabitants (e.g., gathering, 1:10; re-creating, 2:10, 15; dying *for* 2:15-16; 5:2). This particular text forces the church to deal with whether there is something in the very way *the powers* relate to human life (cf. 2:2; 6:11) that requires vigilance, empowerment, and struggle, expressed here in the language of battle and warfare.

The interpretation of Ephesians offered in this commentary sees militarism, indeed enmity itself (cf. 2:16), as one of the powers that must be resisted and overcome. Warfare language then becomes both fitting and highly ironic. The persistence of organized, culturally nurtured enmity, oppression, and alienation is so strong in our world that it becomes necessary to conceive of the struggle against these as battle with *the powers.* This battle requires all of the divine empowerment and armor that God places at the church's disposal. Our critical and *essential* task is to maintain the irony in such warfare, however, and to remain deeply conscious that this is always a battle *for* blood and *flesh* and *never* **against** *blood and flesh.* The history of the church tells us that this is just as difficult as it is urgent.

We might add that the words in Ephesians 6:10-20 sound one way when spoken with resilient hope and even spiritual bravado by a tiny and outnumbered minority, perhaps oppressed and seemingly powerless. The same words sound quite different when wielded by a church wedded to institutions and systems of power and control. In such a context, the irony cannot help but disappear and give way to literal warfare—religious, psychological, and/or physical. Then the mystery of the gospel is not revealed (6:19; cf. 3:10) but is fatally obscured. The gospel of peace is stifled, not proclaimed (6:15). The heart of the gospel is betrayed, the Spirit is grieved (4:30).

For this text and its imagery to be good news for us and our world, it matters absolutely who we are as readers and what our allegiances are. We must ask, for example, whether this metaphor of God's armor, however truthful, is appropriate for a "Christian" imagination that has been deeply militarized and is thus incapable of seeing its irony. The writer of Ephesians would no doubt bless any attempt to find more-fitting metaphors than those of warfare, but only if they could nurture the alertness, resilience, confidence, and identification with God as well as this metaphor did in its day (cf. Bergant: 102).

Are the Powers "Real"?

Does the language of *the powers* mesh with how Christians view reality today? Remarkably it does, if for very different reasons. Many, not only beyond the shores of the highly secularized and "demystified" West, have a lively sense of evil or demonic forces wreaking havoc in the lives of people. For them "spiritual warfare" is an experiential reality for which this text supplies profound encouragement *[Powers].* Such Christians know prayer as battle (e.g., Warner, 1991:133-43).

Sadly, Christians with this perspective of spiritual warfare are often remarkably indifferent or even hostile to dealing with issues of systemic, structural, social, political, and cultural evil such as economic

disparities and exploitation, nationalism, militarism, racism, and sexism. In many cases, they may even ally themselves with those very
powers of oppression. This passage challenges such believers to see
spiritual warfare as an often painstakingly ordinary, everyday struggle
for peace, justice, truth, and liberation in human relationships, small
and great.

Others view human life as affected much more devastatingly by
social, political, and economic forces. Ephesians 6 offers support for
their concerns as well. Since the view of salvation in Ephesians is as
comprehensive as the cosmos and *all things* within it (1:10), then the
view of the powers should encompass the full dimensions of opposition to that salvation *[Powers]*.

As stated above, the view of demonic forces affecting persons
is vulnerable to underestimating broad-ranging opposition to God's
efforts at peacemaking. Likewise, however, a view of the demonic
restricted to influences on institutions in society is just as vulnerable
to underestimating how individual persons may be bound (e.g., Luke
13:16). Our text challenges Christians to recognize the "spiritual" factors at the root of militarism, racism, and sexism. It tells us that believers require divine empowerment in the costly struggle for justice and
peace. *The powers* will never be fully understood let alone overcome
by human beings left to their own devices. That is why the struggle
against them must be accompanied and sustained by the vigilant exercise of prayer for power, courage, and insight (Ellul; McClain; Wink
[Powers]).

In the end, whatever the metaphors, whatever the imagery, and
whatever the contexts of struggle, it is *God's* power at work in the
community of saints that enables them to participate in the *gathering
up of all things in Christ* (1:10).

Resistance or Nonresistance?

The tradition of the divine warrior influencing this text presents an
important challenge to churches with a commitment to nonresistance
and nonviolence. As mentioned earlier, a strand in the Bible stresses
quite strongly that *God* is the one who sees to it that justice is assured
and evil defeated (e.g., Rom. 12:19). In line with this, the only appropriate stance of human beings is one of patient and quiet dependency
on God—*non*resistance (cf. the paradigmatic role of Exod. 14:13-14 in
Lind's work; Matt. 5:39, "Do not resist an evildoer," has led to the
term *nonresistance*).

This is an important strand, and peace churches have mined this
lode well. Such a "quiet" stance can itself, of course, be a form of

resistance to the powers (Berkhof: 50-2; J. H. Yoder, 1994:147-53).
Yet it must be acknowledged that along with fostering great courage
in the face of overwhelming hostility, nonresistance has also often led
to disengagement from the world.

As we have seen, the understanding of the church in Ephesians,
even if taken by itself, leaves little room for disengagement. The
church is one flesh with the Christ through whom God is reconciling
the world to himself (2:14-17; 5:29-32; 2 Cor. 5:19). In other words,
believers are not so much *dependents* as *participants* in the messianic task. If the powers are to be vanquished, it is not enough for
the church simply *to be* a church keeping to itself. The church's true
existence consists of the active and bold actualization of gospel truth,
justice, peace, and liberation in human relationships (cf. 3:10; 5:11;
6:20; Berkhof: 51-2; J. H. Yoder, 1994:147-9; yet Berkhof and
Yoder downplay the offensive nature of the church's struggle much
more than does Ephesians). Here at the end of the letter, Ephesians
draws the church into the role of the one who intervenes—the divine
warrior.

This passage and, indeed, the letter as a whole provide the basis
for a courageous engagement with all the powers—spiritual, personal,
impersonal, political, social, cultural, and economic—that resist the
reconciliation of *all people* and *all things* to God. Indeed, it makes
such engagement the litmus test of being *in Christ*. It is absolutely
important that those who are so engaged do so as members of the
Christ whose own engagement took the form of dying *for* his enemies
and of creating a new humanity out of those enemies (2:11-22). Such
radical self-giving *kills* the enmity (2:15); that peaceableness represents a frontal assault on the powers. The double implication in the
image of the divine armor of protection and summons to struggle is
captured well in the 1708 *Prayer Book for Earnest Christians*, read
widely in Amish and Mennonite circles:

> Clothe us now, O Father! with the armor of your divine strength, so we
> may withstand the deceitful advances of the evil enemy, who fights against
> truth. Give us the shield of true faith, to maintain victory over all that may
> hinder us from experiencing your righteousness. Place on our heads the
> helmet of your salvation, that we need not fear any human being, who
> withers like the grass. Instead, may we fear you, O Lord, since you search
> out human hearts and test our inner being.
>
> So now place into our hearts the sword of your Holy Spirit, which is
> your holy Word and Spirit. Thus may we stand firmly for your holy name
> and fight for the truth up to the time of our blessed end. (Gross: 55-6)

Baptism as Enlistment

The relationship of putting on the armor and baptism is of great relevance to the understanding and practice of baptism in the believers church. In that tradition, baptism ideally follows a mature decision to follow Christ and to take on the responsibilities of membership in the church. At the same time, in many such churches, baptism has become a rite of *conformity* to the expectations of the immediate culture—family and congregation.

Insofar as the summons to *put on the armor of God* is parallel to the call to *put on the new human* (4:24), none other than the "Lord Jesus Christ" (Rom. 13:12, 14), our text is a forceful reminder that baptism is a rite of enlistment into the messianic community. It is at the same time a ritual of empowerment for the messianic task.

Even though he was writing in a context of suffering and oppression (cf. "The Cross of the Saints" [1554], Menno: 599-600), Menno Simons knew that baptism necessarily implicates believers in active struggle against *the powers:*

> Against [those who have put on Christ in baptism,] the devil and his accomplices, such as the world and the flesh, being very envious, have declared war and have become their deadly enemies. The regenerate in turn have now become enemies of sin and the devil and have taken the field against all their enemies with the Author and finisher of their faith, under the banner of the crimson cross, armed with the armor of God, surrounded with angels of the Lord, and always watching with great solicitude lest they be overcome by their enemies who never slumber, but go about like roaring lions, seeking whom they many devour, hurt, and harm. ("The Spiritual Resurrection" [1536], Menno: 56-7; italics added; cf. 1 Pet. 5:8, "like a roaring lion")

> Let me say it once more. Do battle! The crown of glory is prepared for you! Shrink not, neither draw back! ("The Cross of the Saints," Menno: 622; cf. 1 Pet. 5:4, "crown of glory")

Ephesians 6:10-20 is therefore one more reminder, along with Romans 6 and 13:11-14, of how important it is that baptism be undertaken by those who can appreciate the task and count the cost of being Christian.

Ephesians 6:21-24

Closing Comments and Benediction

PREVIEW

The letter to the Ephesians ends on a personal note and a forceful benediction laden to overflowing with theological freight. This post-script conforms generally to other letters in the Pauline correspondence [Pauline Letter Structure] and, indeed, to general letter-writing etiquette in the first century. It contains mention of circumstances, persons, and delivery of correspondence, but also a concluding benediction. Close affinity with Colossians 4:7-8 hints at the strong possibility that the "personal" tone may be more literary than relational.

Tychicus is identified as the bearer of the letter. In addition to delivering the letter, it is his task to strengthen the link between Paul and the recipients of the letter. He is commended as a reliable letter carrier, who can be trusted to give an accurate picture of Paul's circumstances. In addition, he can take news to Paul about the readers' state of affairs and, equally important, strengthen and encourage the recipients of the letter. In effect, Tychicus can act in Paul's stead. The letter concludes with a benediction or blessing of *peace* and *grace* that echoes the greeting of *grace* and *peace* at the beginning of the letter (1:2).

The presence of *peace* and *grace* at the beginning and at the end of this letter is a fitting frame for the sustained and profound consideration of the peacemaking grace of God that constitutes the heart of this letter.

OUTLINE

The Mission of Tychicus, 6:21-22

Closing Benediction, 6:23-24

EXPLANATORY NOTES

The Mission of Tychicus 6:21-22

Verses 21-22 highlight the role of Tychicus in bearing this letter to the recipients. Formally, this is a note of recommendation for the letter carrier. In addition, Tychicus can be trusted to give a full account of Paul's circumstances, presumably also about his imprisonment (3:1; 4:1; 6:20). Paul also trusts him to gather information from the believers, to encourage their hearts, and to strengthen them in their daunting task. In short, the mission of Tychicus is part of the long reach of Paul's apostolic activity—both Paul's use of apostolic letters and of emissaries.

We know little about Tychicus. He was from Asia (Acts 20:4), he was part of the circle around Paul (Col. 4:7; 2 Tim. 4:12; Titus 3:12), and he had some connection with Ephesus (Acts 20:4; 2 Tim. 4:12; this may account for the association of this letter with Ephesus; 1:1-2, notes). We should thus think of Tychicus as one of Paul's trusted inner circle of co-workers, a *beloved brother and faithful servant (diako-nos) in the Lord.*

Several questions emerge, however, in a careful reading of these verses. The wording is virtually identical to Colossians 4:7-8, making literary dependency of Ephesians on Colossians virtually certain (Introduction). In particular, compare Ephesians 6:21-22 with Colossians 4:7-8 (here rendered very literally to make comparison easier; italics show wording unique to each letter).

Ephesians 6:21-22	Colossians 4:7-8
In order that you yourselves also may know about me, *what I am doing*—everything will make known to you Tychicus, beloved brother and faithful servant in the Lord, whom I sent to you for this very purpose, so that you might know things concerning us, and that he might encourage your hearts.	Everything about me will make known to you Tychicus, beloved brother and faithful servant *and fellow slave* in the Lord, whom I sent to you for this very purpose, so that you may know about us, and that he might encourage your hearts.

The fact that the wording in Ephesians is for all practical purposes identical to Colossians 4:7-8 suggests close literary dependence on that earlier letter (Introduction).

Second, if Paul is the author, the absence of greetings as we find them in the Colossians parallel is puzzling, especially since Paul worked in Ephesus for several years. As much as any verses in Ephesians, these two raise the strong possibility that this letter was written by one of Paul's followers (so most commentators, including Lincoln: 462; R. Martin, 1991:78; Perkins: 151; Schnackenburg: 286-7; in contrast, see Barth, 1974:810; Best, 1998:612-4 agrees that the author was not Paul but thinks it more likely that the author of Colossians borrowed from Ephesians).

Somewhat fancifully and ingeniously, it has been proposed that Tychicus tips his hand as the actual author of this letter by borrowing Paul's commendation of him from Colossians and retaining the first person plural in Ephesians 6:22. Thereby he would include himself in a letter that hitherto has focused solely on Paul (e.g., Mitton, 1951:268).

In my view, the evidence does point to the authorship of someone other than Paul. What is striking, even so, is that despite the fact that Paul has become the central revered apostolic figure for the community out of which the letter emerged and for which it was intended, a true reflection of the great apostle must acknowledge that he did not work alone. Other *faithful servants* extended the reach of his apostolic mission. They did so during his lifetime; observe the multiple authorship of his letters as well as the extensive greetings at the conclusion of his letters (e.g., 1 Thess. 1:1; Rom. 16). And, if I and many other scholars are correct about the pseudepigraphical nature of this letter, faithful co-workers extended Paul's ministry even after his death.

Regardless of whether Tychicus carried Paul's letter to Ephesus, or whether "Tychicus" carried "Paul's" letter to various churches, the indisputable result has indeed been that countless *hearts* have been *encouraged* by it toward greater faithfulness.

Closing Benediction 6:23-24

Three things strike a careful reader of the two concluding verses. One is that Ephesians stands alone among Pauline letters in offering the closing benediction in the third person rather than in the customary second person plural. The second is the rich and luminous verbosity we have come to expect of this author. Third is the both tantalizing and puzzling final stress on incorruptibility.

First, the personal tone of 6:21-22 gives way to the indirect and thus less personal blessing of *the brothers and sisters* and *all who love our Lord Jesus Christ*. *Brothers* (NIV) by itself does not capture the inclusiveness intended by the Greek *adelphoi*. While this is the only place where the familial *brothers and sisters* is used in Ephesians, it is not used as a form of direct address as is usual in Paul's writings. Might this be an indication that the letter was meant from the outset to be read by a wider circle of churches? (so, e.g., Lincoln: 465; Perkins: 151). Whether or not this benediction is more "aloof" (Barth, 1974:815), addressing the readers as *brothers and sisters* is in keeping with the weight given the motif of *family* in this letter (see esp. 2:11-22; 3:14; NRSV's *whole community*, while intending to be inclusive, obscures this connection).

Further, the offer of *grace* to those who *love our Lord Jesus Christ* mirrors perfectly the essential structure of the letter. The first half of Ephesians is a rich tableau of God's grace at work. It is followed by an equally profound exploration of what responsive love looks like in the community of believers. God's grace and human love and faithfulness are indissoluble (cf. Rom. 5–6).

Second, this concluding blessing distinguishes itself by the richness of its vocabulary. The offer of *peace* here is unique in the Pauline correspondence, indicating the importance placed on peace in this letter (esp. 2:11-22). In the closing comments of other Pauline letters, *peace* is either related specifically to "the God of peace" (Rom. 15:33; 1 Thess. 5:23; 2 Thess. 3:16), referred to less directly (2 Cor. 13:11; Gal. 6:16), or missing (1 Cor., Phil., Col., 1 and 2 Tim., Titus, Philem.). Here the double benediction of *peace* and *grace* deliberately echoes the opening greeting in 1:2. It is no doubt intended to frame the letter as a whole. As our exploration throughout this commentary has shown, Ephesians is one long extended consideration of God's gracious peacemaking in Christ and the life of faithfulness that this peaceable grace has made possible.

Consistent with this emphasis on *peace*, the author adds *love with faith* (NIV, NRSV) to his wish list for the readers. Both *love (agapē)* and *faith (pistis)* have been given great depth in the letter; they also appear together in 1:15 and 3:17. *Love* motivates God's gracious actions toward the human community (1:4; 2:4; 3:17, 19). But *love* also marks the stance and behavior of those who have been saved by that divine love (esp. 4:2, 15-16; 5:2, 25; and not least, 6:24). I have repeatedly explored the importance of understanding *faith* both as *trust* and as *faithfulness*, as "love in action" (notes on 2:8; 3:12; 6:16).

The distinctive phrase *love with faith(fulness)* reminds us of the terse assertion in James that *faith without works is dead* (2:17, 26). By alerting readers to this connection in the context of the benediction, the author reasserts an essential Pauline insight that comes to expression in 2:10: human *love* and *faithfulness—good works*—are nothing other than a gift of God (so also Barth, 1974:811).

The second part of the benediction in verse 24 reflects the insight that just as *love* and *faith(fulness)* are an essential part of God's offer of *peace* (6:23), *grace* too is inseparable from deliberate acts of *love* on the part of those who have been graced. *Grace is with those who love our Lord Jesus Christ.* This benediction has a negative counterpart in 1 Corinthians 16:22: "Let anyone be accursed who has no love for the Lord" (NRSV). We also recall that immediately after the invitation in Ephesians 5:2 to love as Christ loved, we find a sharp reminder that those who do not so *walk* will not enjoy any inheritance in the *kingdom of Christ and of God* (5:5). Even so, however much we sense an implicit warning in this offer of grace, what is stressed is that God's *peace* and *grace* precede and undergird human exercise of *love* and *faith(fulness)*.

Finally, we consider the last phrase, *in incorruptibility (en aphtharsia)*. *Aphtharsia* means "imperishable," "incorruptible," or "immortal." In Pauline writings it usually refers to the resurrection life (e.g., Rom. 2:7; esp. 1 Cor. 15:42, 50-54). But what does it qualify in this sentence? Is God's *grace* without end or limit (e.g., Gnilka: 325)? Is our *love* for Christ to be "unending" (so NIV, NRSV, NASB, REB; Best, 1998:620)? Does *Christ* live "eternally in the heavenlies" (R. Martin, 1991:79)?

In my view, it is wrong to make a choice. As so often in the analysis of this letter, we are tempted to resolve grammatical ambiguities rather than respect and relish the multiplicity of interpretive possibilities such ambiguity invites. *In incorruptibility* is a "rhetorical flourish" (Lincoln: 466) intended to place the *whole* of God's interaction with redeemed humanity into the context of hope and permanence—a fitting benediction indeed:

Imperishable grace be with all whose love for the immortal Lord knows no end! AMEN!

Outline of Ephesians

Schematic Translation of Ephesians

The following translation is based as closely as possible on the Greek text and grammar and reflects the organization of the original sentences. The translation is schematically organized to allow readers to see repeated patterns of words and phrases. Italics indicate Greek words behind the English, the presence of hymnic material, or Scripture quotations by the writer of Ephesians.

1:1-2 Address and Opening Greeting

Sender: 1 Paul, an apostle of Christ Jesus by the will of God,
Addressee: to the holy ones who are [in Ephesus] and/also [. . .,]
                faithful in Christ Jesus:
Greeting: 2 Grace to you and peace from God our Father and [the]
                Lord Jesus Christ.

1:3-14 Opening Worship: The Blessing of God

3 Blessed be the God and Father of our Lord Jesus Christ
    who blessed us with every spiritual blessing in the heavenlies in
    Christ
          4 just as he chose us in him before the foundation of the cosmos
                to be holy and blameless before him in love,*

* In love can be read with the next verse: predestined us in love.

326

5 who predestined us for adoption (sonship) through Jesus Christ
for him[self]
>> according to the pleasure of his will,
>>> 6 to the praise of his glorious grace
>> which he gave to us in the Beloved,
> 7 in whom we have redemption through his blood, the
forgiveness of sins
>> according to the wealth of his grace
>>> 8 which he lavished on us in all wisdom and
>> understanding,*
9 who made known to us the secret (mystery) of his will
>> according to his good pleasure
>> which he established beforehand in him
>>> 10 for the administration of the fullness of times,
>>> [namely,] to gather up all things in the Christ
>>>> —things on the heavens and things on the
>>>> earth in him—
11 in whom we, the predestined, have been allotted [as] an
inheritance
>> according to the plan of the one who energizes all things
>> according to the resoluteness of his will
>>> 12 so that we might exist for the praise of his glory
>>> who first hoped in the Christ
13 in whom also you having heard the word of truth
>>> the good news of your salvation
>> having also believed in him
> were sealed with the Holy Spirit of promise
>>> 14 which is the guarantee of our inheritance
>>> toward redemption of the [God's?] possession
> to [the] praise of his glory.

1:15-23 Thanksgiving and Intercession

15 For this reason also I,
> since (once) I heard of your faith in the Lord Jesus
>> and love toward all the saints,
16 do not cease to give thanks for you,
> remembering you in my prayers,
>> 17 that the God of our Lord Jesus Christ, the Father of glory
> might give you a spirit of wisdom
>> and revelation
>> in (through) knowledge of him,

---

* *In all wisdom and understanding* can be read with the next verse: *made
known to us in all wisdom. . . .*

 [18] having the eyes of your heart enlightened,
so that you might know what is
the hope of his calling,
the wealth of the glory of his inheritance in (with) the saints,
 [19] the surpassing greatness of his power for us who
believed,
according to the energy of the strength of his might
 [20] which he exercised in the Christ,
having raised him from the dead,
and having seated him at (in) his right [cf. Ps. 110:1]
in the heavenlies,
 [21] far above every rule and authority and power
and lordship and every name that is named, not
 [22] and only in this age but in the one to come,
he put all things under his feet [Ps. 8:7],
and he gave him to be head over all through
(for, in) the church
 [23] which is his body,
the fullness of the one who fills all things
in every way.

2:1-10 From Death to Life Together with Christ

1 And you
dead in your trespasses and sins
 [2] in which you once walked
according to the aeon of this world
according to the ruler of the authority of the air
the spirit now at work among the sons [and daughters] of
disobedience
 [3] among whom also we all once walked in the desires of
our flesh
performing the wishes of the flesh and of the mind
and we were by nature children of wrath as all the rest,

 [4] BUT GOD
being rich in mercy
because of his great love with which he loved us
 [5] and we being dead in trespasses
made us alive together with (through) Christ
 [6] —*by grace you have been saved*—
and raised us together
and seated us together in the heavenlies in (with) Christ
 [7] in order to show in (to) coming ages the overwhelming

wealth of his grace in (through) kindness toward us in Christ
Jesus.

8 For *by grace you have been saved* through faith
and this not from yourselves
it is a gift of God
9 not of works
lest anyone boast.

10 For we are his product (or work of art)
created in Christ Jesus for good works
which God prepared beforehand
so that we might walk in them.

2:11-22 Christ Is *Our* Peace

11 For this reason
remember that once you Gentiles in flesh,
called "the uncircumcision" by those called "the circumcision"
made by hand in flesh,
12 that* you were at that time
without Christ,
alienated from the commonwealth of Israel
and strangers to the covenants of promise,
having no hope
and without God in the world.

13 BUT NOW
in (through) Christ Jesus
you who once were *far* off
have been brought *near* [Isa. 57:19] in (through, by) the blood
of Christ.

14 *For HE IS OUR PEACE*
who made both (ta amphotera) into one
and [who] broke down the dividing wall of the fence
—the enmity—in his flesh
15 *having abolished the law of commandments in regulations*
(or dogmas),
in order that he might create the two in him[self] into one
new human,
making peace,

---

* NIV and NRSV repeat *remember*, whereas the Greek begins the clause with
that (hoti), assuming *remember* from verse 11.

16 *and might reconcile both (hoi amphoteroi) in one body to
God through the cross,*
    having killed the enmity in (through) it (or in him[self]).
17 And when he came, he proclaimed the good news of *peace*
[Isa. 52:7] to you *the far*
                    and *peace to the near* [Isa. 57:19];
18 for through him we have access—both *(hoi amphoteroi)* in
one Spirit—to the Father.

19 So then
    you are no longer strangers and aliens;
    you are, rather, co-citizens with the saints
        and members of the household of God,
    20 built on the foundation of the apostles and prophets,
Christ Jesus himself being the head—or cornerstone
[Isa. 28:16],
        21 in [through] whom the whole structure joined together
            grows into a holy temple in the Lord,
        22 in [through] whom you also are built together
            into a dwelling place for God in (by) [the] Spirit.

Chiastic Structure in Ephesians 2:11-22

A Once strangers and aliens—without God		2:11-12
B Christ has brought near the far off		2:13
C Christ is peace		2:14-16
B¹ Christ proclaimed peace to the far and the near		2:17-18
A¹ No longer strangers and aliens—God's dwelling		2:19-22

3:1-13 The Secret Revealed

1 For this reason I, Paul, the prisoner of Christ [Jesus] for [the] sake
of you Gentiles—

    2 assuming you heard of the administration of the grace of God
given to me for you,
        3 the mystery (or secret) made known to me according to
revelation,
                (as I wrote earlier in brief, 4 so that by reading
                you might come to understand my insight into the
                mystery of Christ,)
        5 which in other generations was not made known to
        humanity (sons of humans),
            as has now been revealed to his holy apostles and prophets
            in spirit (or by the Spirit),

6 [namely,] that the Gentiles are fellow heirs and members of the same body and sharers of the promise in Christ Jesus through the gospel,

7 of which I became a servant according to the gift of the grace of God given to me according to the energy of his power.

8 To me, the least of all the saints, this grace was given, [namely,] to announce to the Gentiles the good news of the unsearchable wealth of Christ

9 and to bring to light the plan of the mystery which was hidden from the ages in the God who created all things,

10 in order that now the multivaried wisdom of God be made known to the rulers and authorities in the heavenlies through the church,

11 according to the plan of the ages which he made in Christ Jesus our Lord,

12 in whom we have boldness and access with confidence through his faith[fulness] (or through faith in him).

13 Therefore I ask not to lose heart in my sufferings for you, which is your glory.

3:14-21 An Apostolic Prayer

14 For this reason I bow my knees before the Father

15 from whom every family in heaven and on earth takes its name,

16 that (hina) according to the wealth of his glory he might give to you

to be strengthened with power through his Spirit into the inner human (or person),

17 that through the faith Christ might dwell in your hearts, as you are being rooted and established in love,

18 that (hina) you might be strong enough to grasp with all the saints

what is the width and length and height and depth,

19 and to know the love of Christ, which exceeds knowledge, that (hina) you might be filled into the whole fullness of God.

20 To the one who, in keeping with the power energizing us, is able to do infinitely more than all we can ask or think,

21 to him be the glory in the church and in Christ Jesus for all generations for ever,
AMEN.

4:1-16 Growing Together into Christ

1 I therefore beg you, I, the prisoner in the Lord
    to walk worthy of the calling to which you were called:
        • 2 with all humility
        • and gentleness,
        • with patience,
        • holding each other up in love,
        • 3 eager to keep the unity of the Spirit in the bond of peace:
            • 4 one body
            • and one Spirit,
            • as also you were called in one hope of your calling;
            • 5 one Lord
            • one faith
            • one baptism
            • 6 one God and Father of all,
            who is upon all and through all and in all.

7 But to each one of us was given the grace according to the measure of the gift of Christ.
    8 Therefore it says:
        When he ascended he took captivity captive,
        he gave gifts to people [Ps. 68:18].
            9 But what does it mean to say "*he ascended*" other than
        that he also descended into the lower [parts] of the earth?
        10 He who descended is the same one who also
            "*ascended*" over and above all the heavens in order that
            he might fill all things.
11 And he himself gave
        • the apostles,
        • and the prophets,
        • and the evangelists,
        • and the pastors
        • and teachers,
    12 for *(pros)* the equipment of the saints
        for *(eis)* the work of service
        for *(eis)* the building up of the body of Christ

13 until we all arrive
> at *(eis)* the unity of the faith
> > and of the knowledge of the Son of God,
> at *(eis)* the perfect man,
> at *(eis)* the measure of the stature of the fullness of
> Christ,

14 so that we might no longer be infants,
> tossed to and fro and blown about by every wind of doctrine
> > through *(en)* human trickery,
> > through *(en)* cunning for the purpose of deception,

15 but rather that, being truthful in love, we might in every way
grow up into *(eis)* him who is the head—Christ,
> 16 out of *(ex)* whom the whole body,
> > joined together *(sun-)* and
> > knit together *(sun-)* through every supporting ligament,˙
> > > according to the energy appropriate to each part,
> effects the growth of the body for the purpose *(eis)* of building
> itself up in love.˙˙

4:17—5:2 The Old and the New Human: Two Ways of Walking

17 For this reason I therefore declare and testify in the Lord—
You are no longer to walk as do the Gentiles
> in the futility of their minds,
> 18 darkened in their thinking,
> alienated from the life of God by the ignorance that is in them,
> > through the hardness of their heart,
> > 19 having become callous, they greedily handed themselves
> > over to every unclean work through debauchery.

20 But you did not so learn Christ
> 21 if indeed you heard and were taught in him
> > since truth is in Jesus
> 22 [namely,] that you are to have put off the old human
> *(anthrōpos)*
> > characterizing *(kata)* the former way of life
> > corrupted by *(kata)* the desires of deception
> 23 to be renewed in the spirit [Spirit] of your mind

˙ Or: *connected and fit together through every supporting joint* . . .
˙˙ Or: *of the body into (eis) his dwelling in love.*

²⁴ and to have put on the new human *(anthōpos)*
     created "in the image of" *(kata)* God in (with) righteousness
     and the holiness of truth.

²⁵ Therefore, having put off the lie—
   speak truth each with his neighbor [Zech. 8:16]
          since we are members of each other!
     ²⁶ *Be angry but do not sin!* [Ps. 4:5, LXX; 4:4, NRSV]
          Do not let the sun set on that which provokes you (or your
          provocations) to anger,
          ²⁷ and do not give a place to the devil.
     ²⁸ Let the one who steals no longer steal,
          rather let him labor by working the good with [his own] hands,
               in order to have something to share with the one who
               has need.
     ²⁹ Let no rotten word come out of your mouth,
          rather, if [you speak, then] something good
               for the building up of that which is lacking (the need),
               so that it might give grace to those who hear.
     ³⁰ And do not grieve the Holy Spirit of God,
          in whom you were sealed for *(eis)* the day of redemption.
     ³¹ Let all . . .
          • bitterness and
          • rage and
          • wrath and
          • angry yelling and
          • slander along with
          • every (other) evil
          . . . be removed from you
     ³² Rather to each other be
          • kind,
          • compassionate,
          • forgiving each other
          • just as God in Christ forgave you (us).

⁵:¹ Therefore, as loved children,
     be imitators of God
     ² and walk in love,
          just as also Christ loved us (you) and gave himself up for us
          (you) as an offering and sacrifice to God for a pleasing odor.

5:3-21 "Walk as Children of Light!"—
Transforming Nonconformity

3 But in no way let . . .
- sexual sin and
- every uncleanness or
- greed be named among you,
        as is fitting for holy people,
4 as also . . .
- base behavior [talk?] and
- silly talk or
- coarse joking,
        which [also] do not fit,
much rather [offer] thanksgiving!

5 For know this for certain!
Every fornicator or unclean person or one who is greedy (which
is idolatry)
        has no inheritance in the kingdom of Christ and of God.
6 Let no one deceive you with empty words;
        because of all this the wrath of God comes upon the sons
        [and daughters] of disobedience!
7 Do not become their co-participants *(sun-)!*
8 For you were once darkness, but now [you are] light in the
Lord.
Walk as children of light
9 —for the fruit of light [is found] in all goodness and
righteousness and truth—
10 testing what is pleasing to the Lord!
11 And do not co-participate *(sun-)* in the unclean works of
darkness,
        much rather expose [them]!
12 For the things that are done in secret by them are shameful
even to put into words.
13 But all things that are exposed by the light are revealed,
14 for everything that is revealed is light.
        Therefore it says:
        Arise, sleeper,
        and rise from the dead,
        and the Christ will shine on you! [cf. Isa. 60:1]

15 Watch, therefore, how carefully you walk,
        not as the unwise but rather as sages,

^{16} buying out the time *(kairos)*,
  because the days are evil!
^{17} For this reason do not be fools,
  rather know what is the will of the Lord!

^{18} Do not be drunk with wine,
  in which lies debauchery,
  but rather be filled in [with the] Spirit,
  • ^{19} speaking to each other with psalms and hymns and
  spiritual songs,
  • singing and "psalming" to the Lord in your hearts,
  • ^{20} giving thanks always for all things to the God and
  Father in the name of our Lord Jesus Christ,
  • ^{21} being subordinate to each other in the fear of Christ!

5:21—6:9 The Household Code

^{21} [Be filled with the Spirit (5:18)] . . .by being (or so that you might
be) subordinate to each other in fear of Christ,

  ^{22} WIVES to their own husbands as to the Lord
    ^{23} because a husband is head of the wife
    as also is Christ head of the church,
    himself Savior of the body.
  ^{24} So just as the church is subordinate to Christ,
so also the wives to their husbands in everything.

  ^{25} HUSBANDS, love the wives
  as also [the] Christ loved the church
  and gave himself for her
    ^{26} in order to render her holy,
      having cleansed her by the washing with the water in
      word,
    ^{27} in order himself to present the church to himself glorious,
      having no spot or wrinkle or any such thing,
    in order rather that she might be holy and blameless.
  ^{28} So ought the husbands to love their own wives as their own
bodies.
    The one who loves himself loves his own wife.
    ^{29} For no one ever hated his own flesh but nourishes and
    takes care of it,
  just as also Christ the church,
    ^{30} because we are members of his body.

³¹ *For this reason a person will leave father and mother and be joined to his wife. And the two will become one flesh* [Gen. 2:24].

³² This is a great mystery (I am speaking of Christ and the church).

³³ Even so, every one of you, let each one love his wife as himself, but the wife is to fear the husband.

^{6:1} CHILDREN, obey your parents in the Lord,
   for this is right.
 ² *Honor your father and mother—*
   which is the first commandment with a promise—
 ³ *so that it may be well with you and you may live long on the earth* [Exod. 20:12].

⁴ And FATHERS, do not provoke your children to anger,
   but nurture them with the training and instruction of the Lord.

⁵ SLAVES, obey your human *(fleshly)* masters
   with fear and trembling in integrity of your heart as to Christ
   ⁶ not for sake of appearance as do "pleasers,"
   but as slaves of Christ doing the will of God from the heart (soul),
   ⁷ offering service with enthusiasm as to the Lord and not to humans,
   ⁸ knowing that whatever good each one does,
   he will receive the same again from the Lord,
   whether slave or free.

⁹ And MASTERS, do the same to them,
   desisting from the threat,
   knowing that both their and your Master is in heaven,
      and with him there is no favoritism (lit., respect of person).

6:10-20 Waging Peace: Putting on the Armor of God

¹⁰ Henceforth, be empowered in the Lord and in the strength of his might!

¹¹ Put on the whole armor of God
   so that you might be able to stand against the strategies of the devil!
   ¹² Because with us the struggle is not against blood and flesh
   but against the rulers, against the authorities, against the cosmic potentates of this darkness, against the spiritual aspects (or forces) of evil in the heavenlies.

13 For this reason take up the whole armor of God,
  so that you might be able to resist on the evil day,
    and having conquered completely, to be standing!

14 Stand therefore
      having girded your waist with truth
      and having put on the breastplate of righteousness/justice
      15 and having put on your feet what makes you ready to
      announce the good news of peace,
      16 in every circumstance having taken up the shield of
      faith(fulness)
          with which you will be able to quench all of the fiery darts of
          the evil one;
  17 and grasp the helmet of salvation/liberation
  and the sword of the Spirit,
        which is the word of God,
      18 through all prayer and entreaty, praying at all times in [the]
      Spirit,
      staying alert for this purpose in all perseverance and prayer for
      all the saints
        19 and also for me,
            that a word might be given me in openness of my mouth
              in boldness to make known the mystery of the gospel,
                20 for the sake of which I am an ambassador in
                chains
            that in this I might be emboldened to speak as is
            necessary.

6:21-24 Closing Comments and Benediction

21 In order that you yourselves also may know my circumstances—
what I am doing—
    Tychicus, beloved brother and faithful servant in the Lord, will
    make known to you everything,
        22 whom I sent to you for this very purpose,
          so that you might know how we are,
          and that he might encourage your hearts.

23 Peace to the brothers [and sisters] and love with faith(fulness)
    from God the Father
    and the Lord Jesus Christ.
24 Grace [be] with all who love our Lord Jesus Christ in incorruptibility.

Essays

APOCALYPTICISM The term derives from the Greek *apocalupsis,* which means "disclosure" or "revelation." It refers to both a kind of literature and an eschatological perspective or ideology. The literature takes its name from the last book of the Bible, the Revelation or Apocalypse of John. Not surprisingly, given its severely conflictual vision of the future and the highly mythological and symbolic nature of the final events of the age, the term *apocalyptic* has become synonymous with a threatening future, cataclysmic natural disasters, cosmic conflict, and final all-encompassing judgment.

Well-known examples in the Bible of apocalyptic literature are Daniel (chaps. 7–11) and Revelation. Ezekiel, parts of Isaiah (chaps. 24–27), Zechariah (chaps. 1–6) and sections of the Gospels (Mark 13 and Matt. 24) can also be counted. The list of apocalyptic writings in the Apocrypha and pseudepigrapha of both OT and NT is extensive. Apocalypses are attributed to visionaries from every stage of sacred history, such as Adam, Enoch, Abraham, Elijah, Ezra, and NT figures such as John, Peter, Paul, and Thomas (Charlesworth, 1983; Hennecke).

These writings are quite diverse, but they share some important elements. First, they are visionary: they all rehearse what was given to the writer in a dream or a vision. Second, the content of the vision is typically what God will do at a God-determined time to either restore the fortunes of Israel, or sometimes more radically, to restore the universe as a whole. Divine intervention is usually depicted as larger than life, often as a cosmic battle in which the world as we know it will be forced to give way to a new heaven and a new earth.

The authors' view of the present world is typically quite pessimistic. These writings are born in a context of suffering and oppression, when all indications point to the absence of a wise and sovereign God, not to the orderly unfolding of God's will. The chaos brought about by sin and the rebellion of hostile spiritual realities *[Powers]* is of such seriousness that only a cataclysmic divine intervention will bring change. Only revelation can reveal that the apparent anarchy of the moment is but one chapter in God's plan. When God finally will intervene, this present evil age will come to an end, and so will death.

This way of perceiving the working of God in history reflects a highly "dualistic" view of reality. The dualism is between the faithful few and the rest of humanity, between light and darkness, between this age and the next, between the reign of God and the ruler of this world, and between God and Satan.

No one doubts that many or most of these writings are pseudepigraphical *[Pseudepigraphy]*. This is most obviously the case where the purported author lived in the far-distant past, such as an Adam or an Enoch. An important claim lies at the basis of such pseudonymity: the present suffering and chaos must not be taken as evidence of the absence or weakness of God. It is part of a future already foretold at the very beginnings of the story. In short, God's providence is at work even in the turmoil of the present. More, the present agony is evidence that the time of God's saving intervention is soon! The greater the turmoil, the closer the day of salvation.

An important exception to this general characteristic of apocalyptic writing is the Apocalypse of John. The author of the book of Revelation is not given a pseudonym. We may not know who John of Patmos was, but we do know his name and that he was writing to churches he knew. The absence of pseudonymity in the case of the Revelation of John may reflect the general conviction of Jesus' followers that the great cosmic change predicted in the ancient visions had begun to come true in the resurrection of Jesus.

Many Jews and Christians in the first century were greatly influenced by such thinking. Recent times of crisis such as the Maccabean wars or the struggles with Rome were fertile ground for apocalyptic thought and writing. The extensive library of the apocalyptically oriented community at Qumran, on the shores of the Dead Sea close to Jericho, is of special interest. Perhaps not many of the NT writings are apocalyptic in terms of literary genre. But most pages of the NT are deeply shaped by, or at least affected by, apocalyptic ideas, notions, and thought patterns. We need think only of such central themes as the kingdom of God, resurrection, judgment, the return of Christ, and, of course, the importance of revelation.

The conviction that God had raised Jesus to life following his crucifixion was interpreted in the framework of apocalyptic expectation. Easter was perceived as the "first fruits" of a general resurrection that would encompass the whole of humanity, resurrection for some to judgment, for those "in Christ" to everlasting life (cf. in the Pauline writings esp. 1 Thess. 4:13—5:11; 2 Thess. 1; 1 Cor. 15; Rom. 8).

The letter to the Ephesians has presented interpreters with some special challenges with respect to its eschatology. As to genre, it is not apocalyptic. But many apocalyptic ideas are reflected in it. The author speaks dualistically about *this present darkness* (6:12; cf. 5:8, 11), of the *sons of disobedience* being under the evil *authority of the air* (2:2-3), of the present *evil days* (5:15; cf. 6:13), and finally of the struggle with the *principalities* and *powers* (6:10-20, KJV). We might add to that the repeated theme of the disclosure of the *mystery* (1:9; 3:3, 9), and the central importance of Easter (1:19-23; 2:4-7). Many of these themes are quite at home within the apocalyptic tradition. Tracing apocalyptic ideas, various scholars have identified many points of contact between Ephesians and the thought of Qumran (e.g., Gnilka, Kuhn, Perkins).

At the same time, while there is mention of *the day of redemption* (4:30; cf. 1:14), Ephesians has no explicit mention of the return of Christ and only a fleeting mention of judgment (5:5). Furthermore, resurrection is celebrated as a present reality, for Christ and also for those who are *in Christ* (2:5-6). Moreover, salvation, when not spoken of in the past tense (2:5, 8), is envisioned as a process of transformation and growth, a gathering into a divine unity of *all things* (1:10; cf. 4:13-16). These stresses can stand in some tension with apocalyptic crisis thinking. As the commentary shows, they also imply an ethic that is quite different from one of waiting and enduring until God acts.

In short, dualism and unity, crisis and growth, separation and transformation coexist in Ephesians. In this commentary I take the view that the author deliberately engages apocalyptic thinking in a way that differs from Paul's approach in some other letters (e.g., the Thessalonian correspondence), but in a way that faithfully develops directions in which Paul's thinking can be taken (Yoder Neufeld, 1993).

For a discussion of these tensions and the way the author of Ephesians engages them, see the Introduction (above). For fuller discussion of apocalypticism, see, among the many resources, Brown: 774-80; Collins, Hanson, Yarbro Collins, and the extensive literature cited in those sources. For another BCBC essay on apocalyptic, see J. Daryl Charles's commentary on Jude (in *1-2 Peter, Jude:* 330-3); for apocalyptic in Paul, see Jacob Elias's essays on apocalyptic and eschatology in his BCBC commentary, *1 and 2 Thessalonians* (354-7).

AUTHORSHIP   As indicated in the Introduction, the authorship of Ephesians presents an enigma. Numerous views have been advanced, which I outline here, then describe and assess in some detail. Since the historical context of Ephesians is intertwined with the authorship issue, I recommend that you read again, after perusing this essay, the "Historical Context" portion in the Introduction, as well as the section on Ephesians' relation to Colossians. Here I describe the various proposed solutions to the enigma presented in the Introduction.

Option 1: Paul Wrote an Unusual Letter
One way of approaching the puzzling features that mark Ephesians (see Introduction) is to consider them to be within the range of what we might expect from a creative and contextual theologian (cf. 1 Cor. 9:19-23). Paul's letters are by no means alike in tone, structure, or emphasis. 1 Corinthians, for example, is taken up mostly with responses to specific problems of ethics and worship. Galatians and 2 Corinthians show Paul defending the integrity of his commission and message in quite different ways, sometimes to the point of rudeness (see also Phil. 3). Romans is a carefully reasoned presentation of Paul's convictions to a congregation he had not yet met. Why should it come as a surprise that Paul, perhaps toward the end of his life, with time on his hands while sitting in prison, would have penned a letter such as this, celebrating in the grandest possible manner the grace of God expressed in Christ?

> Though Paul was capable of writing or dictating letters in boiling wrath, with cynical irony, or in the midst of streaming tears, his occasional outbursts of temperament did not oblige him to explode all the time. (Barth, 1974:50; cf. Schlier, 1971)

Since such a letter would have been written to be read publicly in the context of gathered worship, we should not be surprised that it reads and sounds more like a sermon than a letter intended to respond to a specific situation. In contrast to Paul's usual practice, Ephesians provides few if any clues of an occasion or immediate problem to which it responds. The letterlike features at the beginning and the end are more like an envelope into which a treatise or sermon has been inserted. The letter to the Hebrews is another example of a sermon with the barest features of a letter.

In this explanatory option, Paul restates in Ephesians some of his favorite themes: God's call of both Jews and Gentiles to find their identity in Christ, the lordship of Christ over the powers, the church as Christ's body, and holy and blameless living as an expression of newness of life in Christ. As to the noticeable differences in emphasis regarding church, salvation, and eschatology, Paul's thinking could have undergone some significant changes over the years. This would not have been the first nor would it be the last time the views of a pioneer would undergo significant development. New contexts and new questions demand such flexibility.

As one example, perhaps reflecting a later stage in the life of Paul and his churches, the sense of immediate expectancy that marked Paul's earliest letters had given way to a perspective more adapted to "the long haul." Perhaps Paul intended such a letter to be read in all the churches in and around Ephesus. That would explain the more generalized way of speaking of the church, but also the absence of a specific address in many of the manuscripts (see the issue of "Address" at 1:1, notes).

Some have seen in the absence of an address at 1:1 in the usually most reliable manuscripts a clue to the purpose of such a letter. Many years ago Goodspeed (1-75) proposed that Ephesians is a cover letter for an early collection of Paul's letters. It provides a summary of the major emphases of Paul's teaching and preaching. Ephesians was not intended to replace so much as to accompany and illumine Paul's letters that were being circulated. (For the argument that Paul himself initiated the collecting and circulating of his letters, see Trobisch).

Others have similarly suggested that the absence of an address indicates that Ephesians was a circular letter or encyclical intended for a network of Pauline congregations in Asia Minor (e.g., R. P. Martin, 1991:4-6). One version of this hypothesis has it that the original manuscript(s) contained a blank space into which the next address in the circle could be inserted (see 1:1-2, notes). Some early manuscripts record the last name on the list of congregations and thus associate the letter with Ephesus. The chief problem with this suggestion, as attractive as it is, is that in the ancient world, there are few if any instances of such a practice of filling in blanks. Much of this remains shrouded in mystery.

Another factor possibly contributing to the differences in style and tone is that they may be due to Paul employing a scribe or secretary who penned the letter on his behalf—like Tertius in Romans 16:22. Such a secretary (amanuensis) was sometimes granted considerable freedom, like a modern speechwriter. Paul remains in essence the author, even if the formulation of the ideas is affected by scribal assistance. The explicit multiple authorship of many of Paul's letters is a reminder that his writing may have been much more collaborative than is often assumed. His co-workers may have affected the tone and style of his letters considerably.

In short, many believe the differences between Ephesians and the rest of the Pauline writings are not important enough to undermine confidence in Paul's authorship or in the integrity of Ephesians as a letter (e.g., Barth: 36-50; Foulkes: 25-48; van Roon).

Option 2: Someone Other Than Paul Wrote an Unusual Letter
Presently a majority of scholars view this letter's peculiar characteristics described in the Introduction as pointing to a writer other than Paul. They consider Ephesians to be pseudepigraphical or pseudonymous *[Pseudepigraphy,* with part on *Ephesians].* Such an author might have accompanied Paul, imbibed his teaching, and perhaps aided him in the formulation of his correspondence (Paul's letters usually carry the names of more than one author; see discussion of the *amanuensis,* above; Meeks: 81-4). He would then also have carried on this task after Paul's death. He may have been part of what is sometimes called a "school," an association, however informal, of persons engaged in protecting and developing Paul's apostolic legacy (Beker: 68-72; Best, 1998:36-40; Lincoln: lxx). This could account for the reflective, even at times ponderous, style and tone, as well as for the theological emphasis on the church universal. It could also explain one of the most noticeable features of Ephesians, the strong similarity between Ephesians and Colossians. See Introduction.

The possibility that such developments took place in the mind of one and the same author of both of these letters, Paul himself, cannot be precluded with any finality. Authors do undergo change and development in their thinking. Furthermore, as any teacher or preacher knows, new contexts and new pastoral challenges will affect the reworking of a favorite lecture or sermon. While *possible,* in my view it is more *probable* that these features point to an author other than Paul, to one thoroughly steeped in Paul's thought and writings and deeply concerned that Paul's apostolic voice continue to be heard. (On the possible and the probable with respect to authorship, see Lincoln: lxviii-lxix). The inclusion of Ephesians in the NT canon witnesses to the fact that it is that voice the church heard as the letter was read.

Writers such as the author of Ephesians, whether Paul or a Pauline school of disciples, were not conscious of writing Scripture. Christians, with all Jews, knew the Scriptures as the Law, the Prophets, and the Writings. Many years would pass before letters of Paul were recognized as possessing such status. So when we propose that the author of Ephesians borrowed from, altered, and reacted to Colossians or other letters of Paul, we should not think of this as tampering with Scripture. It is one of the great and wonderful mysteries of grace that God chose to use correspondence collected and edited in the turbulent first century of the church as a guide for believers in centuries and millennia to follow. We do not betray that divine decision when we attend to the full humanness and historicity of these writings. The treasure that is carried in a clay jar is a priceless treasure all the same (2 Cor. 4:7).

Treasuring Ephesians
It needs to be stressed that the appreciation of Ephesians or of this commentary does not require a particular view of authorship. From the beginning the church correctly recognized Ephesians as expressing the apostolic message in a most forceful way. I share that conviction. But to say that a particular view on authorship is not required does not mean that the issue is of no theological or pastoral consequence. For example, one can be convinced that Paul wrote Ephesians. But one will then have to struggle with the evident differences between Ephesians and other Pauline letters. That may be

as troublesome as proposing an author other than Paul. At the same time, such a solution will remain an irritant, especially for readers for whom it has never before been proposed, and for whom the question of integrity goes to the heart of the trustworthiness of revelation—as it should. As often as possible, this commentary allows readers to judge the evidence themselves, while pointing out the implications of the question of authorship for interpretation.

COSMOLOGY OF EPHESIANS The author of Ephesians would have shared with his contemporaries a cosmology quite different from our modern one (Perkins: 37-8). For example, up is better than down; God is in the heavens, or even above the heavens; and between God and human beings are both good and bad spiritual realities and powers. Many speculated on what was in the heavens, often with detailed classifications of those spiritual realities. In Ephesians we see no such speculation. We have to derive our picture from the few hints and suggestions the author makes in the process of discussing God's actions in and for Christ, the effect of evil on human life, and the status and task of believers. The data can be summarized as follows:

- God, Christ, believers, and evil powers all reside in the heavenlies (1:3; 2:6; 3:10; 6:12).
- God, Christ, and those who are raised and exalted with him (1:20; 2:6) are located above all powers (1:21).
- Christ descended to the lower parts of the earth (4:9).
- Christ ascended far above all the heavens (4:10).
- the prince of the power of the air controls the disobedient (2:2; the air appears to be synonymous with the heavenlies in 6:12).

In chart form it might look like this:

The Cosmology of Ephesians

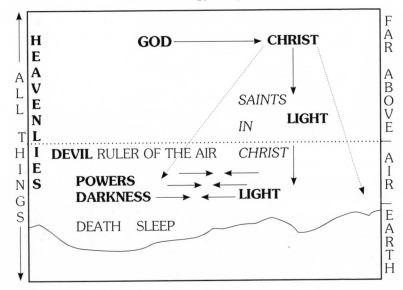

We observe, first, that the *heavenlies* encompass virtually all of reality. Nothing indicates that the *heavenlies* refers to a future realm distinct from the present, in the sense that spiritual blessings (1:3) are awaiting the believers in the future. The future is intimated in 1:14 with references to *seal* and *guarantee* with the *Spirit of promise*, in 2:7 with the *ages to come*, in 4:30 with *the day of redemption*, and possibly, with *the kingdom of Christ and of God* in 5:5.

Second, the chart locates the saints everywhere in the cosmos. On one hand, they are very much on the earth, engaged in the normal sphere of human relationships, as the second half of Ephesians presupposes (see esp. the Household Code in 5:21—6:9). On the other, they are *in the Christ* who has already been raised and seated *in the heavenlies, far above all powers* (1:20-21). Ephesians 2:6 makes it explicit that they have been raised and seated *with Christ*. So *in the heavenlies* is where both Christ and the saints are to be found. At the same time, they are not as yet removed from what we might call the "lower" heavenlies, from the arena where *the ruler of the power of the air* still holds sway over the disobedient (2:2). It becomes abundantly clear in 6:10-13 that saints are in the "space" in which encounter with the devil and his rebellious powers is unavoidable and also sought after. For that encounter, they need the Spirit and power of God (5:18-22; 6:10-13).

This ambiguity of location is quite intentional and fruitful for the agenda underlying Ephesians. For the saints to be *in the heavenlies* means that they are *in Christ* as sons and daughters of God, and that they enjoy all the blessings such an association brings with it. They are thus also fully participants in the task of reconciling the cosmos to God. They can do so only in possession of *every spiritual blessing* (1:3). Empowerment with the very "energy" of God (see my "Schematic Translation" of 1:11)—God's Holy Spirit—is a precondition of such engagement (5:18-21).

GNOSTICISM *Gnosticism* derives from *gnōsis,* Greek for "knowledge." Gnostics prized knowledge as salvation, liberation from the numbing sleep of materiality, and a return to divine origin in the realm of spirit. *Gnosticism* refers to the specific movements of the second century that were widely prevalent, especially in the eastern Mediterranean. Their writings and beliefs have been variously preserved. We learn of these groups and their leaders from church leaders who preserve their writings as they attempt to expose and oppose them. We learn about them most dramatically from the rich Gnostic library found at Nag Hammadi in the Egyptian desert in 1945, roughly the same time as the Dead Sea scrolls *[Apocalypticism].* Because it postdates Ephesians considerably, this literature is of interest mostly as evidence of the way in which some could read Ephesians in the decades and centuries that followed its writing.

The origins of Gnosticism are highly debated. Early church fathers blamed it on Simon Magus (Acts 8:9-24). Today scholars look for its roots in Hellenism, or in Iranian religion, or in the kind of Judaism that has affinities to apocalypticism and speculative wisdom. The latter option presently finds the greatest number of supporters.

Gnosticism, as also the adjective *gnostic,* can then be taken to refer to the "systems" that developed in the second century and also to a less institutionally defined movement or worldview present already during Paul's mission. Paul, his students, and the writer of the Gospel of John sometimes wrote in ways that would make them popular with Gnostics later on. At other times they engaged these ideas very critically. For example, compare 2 Corinthians

3:17-18, a text a Gnostic might appreciate, with Paul's insistence on the physicality of "fleshly" faithfulness in 2 Corinthians 5:6-10 (cf. Gal. 6:7-10). The claim in the Gospel of John that to know God is to have eternal life (17:3) would have been welcomed by Gnostics, but the well-known phrase "the word became flesh" (John 1:14; cf. 1 John 1:1) would no doubt have put them off.

At the price of oversimplification, we can summarize the essential ideas or motifs of Gnostic thinking as follows:

1. Gnosticism is marked by a radical dualism. In the case of apocalypticism, the dualism relates to right and wrong, between this present evil age and the age to come, and between God and Satan [Apocalypticism]. In Gnosticism, the dualism is more radical: the material created world versus the realm of the spirit.

2. The material world is not created by God, who is transcendent, but by a lesser foolish power; creation of the world was, in fact, an act of rebellion.

3. The divine spark still resides in (some) humans, whose true essence as spirit or soul is imprisoned in material physical existence and needs to be awakened. Persons thus awakened receive knowledge (gnōsis) about the true nature of reality, about their true identity, and about their restoration to God. Enlightenment is salvation in the sense that through the raising of consciousness the fetters of this material world are shown to be illusory. The goal of enlightenment is arrival in the light, in the divine fullness (plērōma).

4. In Christian Gnosticism, Christ is the Savior because he is the revealer, the raiser of consciousness, and the one who awakens those who are asleep. He is not the Savior because he dies or because he overcomes the powers through cross and resurrection.

5. Morality finds expression in either asceticism (the denial or subjugation of the physical body) or, less certainly, in libertinism (if the body is evil then what it does is of no consequence for the spirit). We know of the latter only from those who fought Gnosticism in the church; accusations of libertinism usually go hand in hand with accusations of heresy.

For a full survey of the primary and secondary literature on this material, and for an excellent introduction to the ideas referred to as "Gnostic," see, e.g., Koester, 1982:381-8; Rudolf, 1983; 1992. For collections of Gnostic writings, see Foerster; Layton; Robinson.

Students of Ephesians have long identified a number of features that, if they are not Gnostic, are at least highly resonant with Gnostic vocabulary and ideas. For example, we notice how easily the author speaks of readers of the letter as already raised and seated in the heavenly places (2:6-7). Has a future eschatology given way to a Gnostic spiritualizing and dehistoricizing of resurrection? Does the repeated reference to the fullness (plērōma, in 1:10, 23; 3:19) anticipate the use in second-century Gnosticism of that term to refer to the sphere of perfection surrounding the transcendent God? Is Christ to be identified with Gnosticism's "primal man" (the new anthrōpos/human of 2:15 or the perfect man of 4:13)? The brief hymnic "wake-up call" in 5:14 has sometimes been interpreted as Gnostic. Does the holy marriage between Christ and the church in 5:25-33 anticipate the ritual of the "bridal chamber" in second-century Gnosticism? Might one read the struggle with the powers

in chapter 6 as the soul's victory over hostile heavenly powers while on its way back to God? (For these and other examples of Gnostic resonance, see, e.g., Barth, 1974:12-8; Best, 1998:87-9; Koester, 1982a:269-70; Pokorny; Schlier, 1965; 1971).
Along with most scholars, I do not view Ephesians as a Gnostic document. I do see evidence, however, for an appreciative and critical engagement with notions that in subsequent decades developed in directions the church wisely came to reject. It is not difficult to see why Gnostics would mine this vein vigorously. Ephesians is best read in close relationship to the rest of the Pauline letter corpus. In that reading, the distinctive voice of the author emerges, a voice clearly at odds with world-negating Gnosticism.

"HEAD" *Head (kephalē)* most immediately refers anatomically to the top part of a person's body. It can also refer to the top of just about anything else, such as a mountain or a wall ("headstone"; cf. Ps. 118:22, LXX, quoted in Matt. 21:42 and parallels). "Top" is probably as succinct a rendering of the meaning of *kephalē* as one might hope for. A related meaning of *head* is "source," as in the word *headwaters*. In English, as in Greek, *head* also functions metaphorically, denoting "what is first, supreme, or extreme" (Schlier, 1965:673). Not surprisingly, in the Septuagint *kephalē* occasionally translates the Hebrew *ro'š* (head) in contexts where it refers to one who bears authority and responsibility (e.g., Judg. 10:18; 11:11; 2 Sam. 22:44; Isa. 7: 8-9). But this is *not* normally the case (Scholer: 42). Other Greek words, such as *archōn,* are used. We should expect the term as used in the NT to be shaped by biblical as well as conventional usage.
There is an ongoing and vigorous debate, fueled by the contemporary differences over relationships of men and women in home, church, and society, over whether the primary metaphorical meaning of *head* is "authority" (e.g., Fitzmyer; Grudem) or "source" (e.g., Bedale; Fee, 1987:502-5, with a vigorous critique of Grudem on 502, n. 42; Kroeger, 1987). The debate is not subsiding, partly because of the volatile intersection of biblical authority and social change. To quote R. T. France, "This, as they say, could run and run!" (44, n. 16). Since both sides can muster examples for their preferred reading, is it not likely that both metaphorical meanings would have suggested themselves to the readers of writings like Ephesians (so also, interestingly, e.g., Bedale; France: 38-41; Lincoln: 368-70)?
The metaphorical significance of *head* in Ephesians obviously encompasses both (for more extensive discussions and related literature, see also Barth, 1974:183-92; Best, 1998:193-6; Lincoln: 67-70, 368-70; Miletic: 67-87; Schlier, 1965:673-82). Whereas each of the following texts from Ephesians is discussed in the commentary, their relation to the motif of *head* is summarized here.

1. In Ephesians 1:21-22, God is said to have raised and exalted Christ over the whole cosmos, including all powers and authorities, literally *giving him to be head over all.* As this text illustrates, being *head* means being first, superior, preeminent, in authority, and in control (for fuller discussion, see 1:15-23, notes). Status, not source, is the primary meaning in this passage. Nowhere is this clearer than in the great christological hymn in Colossians 1:15-20, even if there both status and source inform the meaning of Christ being "head" (cf., e.g., E. D. Martin, 1993:59-77; Schweizer, 1982:55-88).

Christ is the "firstborn *(prōtotokos)*" of both creation (Col. 1:15) and resurrection or re-creation (1:18). He is "before *(pro)* all things" (1:17), "preeminent in everything *(prōteuōn)*" (1:18), the one in whom the fullness of God
dwells (1:19; cf. 2:9); in short, Christ is the head of the body (1:18; cf. 2:10).
Whereas the body is more clearly specified to be the church in 1:18, it is
commonly recognized that *body* is derived from a tradition that metaphorically viewed the cosmos as a whole as a body. Both Colossians and Ephesians
understand the headship of Christ to extend to the church (Col. 1:18; Eph.
4:15-16), but just as important, to the whole of the universe. We might add
that, whereas Ephesians 1:10 does not use the term *head* so much as *heading* (1:10, notes), the reference to "all things" being gathered up (lit., "being
brought under one heading") in and through Christ clearly carries overtones
of cosmic headship.

2. In Ephesians 4:15, Christ is said to be the *head* into which *we* are to
grow, and from whom *we* derive what it takes to grow (4:1-16, notes). As
head, Christ is both source and goal *of the whole body*—the church, both
first and last. He is *the perfect man* (4:13), and in that sense at the top—the
goal toward which the church is *building* (4:12). At the same time, Christ
is the gift-giving supplier (4:7-11) of what the church needs to grow into
Christ, of what the body needs to grow into the head. We are reminded that
Colossians 1:15-20 similarly views Christ as one who "created all things" in
the cosmos (1:16), the one who "holds all things together" (1:17; cf. Eph.
4:16). "Status" and "source" quite naturally converge as meanings for *head*.
To speak of Christ as *head* is to speak of his priority in *every* sense.

3. Before going on to the last of the Ephesian "head" texts, it is important to draw attention to 1 Corinthians 11:2-16. There is no need here to
enter the ongoing debate about hair, veiling, or what it means for a woman
prophet to wear an "authority" on her head (see, e.g., Fee, 1987:491-
530; Grenz: 108-17; Murphy-O'Connor: 104-109; Schüssler Fiorenza,
1983: 226-230). It is relevant to notice the way the word *head* is used
metaphorically to depict a chain of authority or origin—or more likely, both:
God→Christ→man→woman (1 Cor. 11:3). Some notion of the order of
creation seems to be operative in the attempt to regulate life in Corinth. On
the other hand, in 11:11-12, Paul appears to offer an alternative way of
understanding the implied relationship between men and women by stating
that "in the Lord" men and women have a mutuality of origin. The tension in
the argument is palpable. Paul either intends to trump a notion of social order
based on a certain understanding of creation with the new order in Christ,
or he is struggling to remain true both to his inherited sense of the "order
of creation" and to the "order of the new creation." Interpreters continue to
debate this passage vigorously (for sample of the interpretive scope, see, e.g.,
Swartley, 1983:166-74). In the argument the word *head* appears to carry
some metaphorical freight that we can no longer track with complete confidence. However, it is clear that Paul has no intention whatsoever of curtailing
the authority of women to exercise the gift Paul saw as the highest gift the
Spirit bestows on the church (1 Cor. 14:1; 11:5).

4. In Ephesians 5:23 the motif of *head* is used to draw an analogy
between the relationship of husband and wife and that of Christ and the

church: a husband is head of the wife as Christ is head of the church, himself Savior of the body (5:23). The metaphorical force of *head* is here at least initially more one of "status" and "authority" than of "source" (so also France: 40; Lincoln: 368; contra Miletic: 103; Patzia, 1990:268). Notice that *head* is placed in direct relationship to the subordination of wives to their husbands as to the Lord (5:22). Notice also that Christ is identified as Savior of the body, the church. While we see in 2:15 that creation is very much a part of salvation (2:15, notes), the emphatic *himself* in 5:23 appears to highlight his status as liberator. Last, we should note that, whereas men are to love their wives as they do themselves, wives are to *fear* their husbands (5:33). On the surface, at least, the text appears to support patriarchy, the superior position of husbands over wives.

However, a number of factors play havoc with any easy inference that husbands are at the top in marriage relationships:
1. Christology in Ephesians focuses on the status of Christ as cosmic Lord and the expression of his lordship in re-creating humanity: the Lord is the Savior; the boss is the liberator. The meaning and content of Christ's headship is peacemaking, re-creation, and self-offering for the benefit of a restored humanity. The *head* is *our peace* (2:14).
2. Christ's headship finds its fullest expression in Christ's giving up his life for the sake of the life of humanity (2:11-22, notes). This is explicitly echoed in 5:2 and in 5:25.
3. The writer of Ephesians introduces the Household Code with a summons to *mutual* subordination, empowered for such servitude by the Spirit. In effect, the sons and daughters of God are to recognize *each other* as heads (5:21; for this and other points above, see fuller discussion at 5:21—6:9, notes).

At the present time, headship is a highly charged issue (in addition to authors listed above, see survey of interpretive poles in Swartley, 1983:256-69). It divides traditionalists and complementarians from egalitarians. These divisions run between conservative and critical traditions of interpretation, and within evangelical interpretive circles (cf., e.g., Fee; France; Grudem; Grenz and Kjesbo; Kroeger; Patzia; and Scholer). The arguments typically center on the status to be given to cultural setting and its effect on what is normative, and on the lexical question as to whether *head* means chiefly "source" or "authority" (see above; for summary discussions of the issues and participants within the evangelical context, see, e.g., Grenz; Scholer).
These issues will not be dealt with in a life-giving way by finding a lexical loophole or by placing cultural-contextual parentheses around the text. The approach taken in this commentary has been to take seriously both the lexical and cultural-contextual questions. In my view, *head* does contain overtones of superiority and authority. The context in which the writer of Ephesians was writing was indeed one in which patriarchy was taken as a given. It is thus all the more important to ask what kind of a *head* Christ is and what effect such headship might have on entrenched structures of unequal power and authority.
The contention argued in the commentary is that the Christ who is offered to those in superior social positions—whatever those might be in any given time and place!—is one whose headship fundamentally undermines privilege

and status. Yes, Christ *is* the cosmic emperor, the *head* of the universe. But when we look closely, the emperor's new clothes are those of a slave. It is, after all, at the name of "Jesus"—the humble and poor man from Galilee—that "*every* knee shall bow" (Phil. 2:11). The slave will, however, have a hold on husbands, fathers, and bosses—or anyone else, regardless of gender, who in our day wields power and authority—only if he is also *head*. To miss seeing *that* Christ, present throughout Ephesians, is to misread the Household Code as a summons to one-sided subordination rather than to permanent revolution—the revolution of the gathering up of all things under one "heading"—Christ.

"IN"   The little word *in* (*en*) is as elastic as it is important. Simply stated, *en* can be translated in spatial, causal, and temporal senses. I offer here only a brief survey of the options. (For full discussion and numerous textual examples, see, e.g., BAGD; Blass: 117-8; Oepke; Smyth.)

1. *Place*
   • It can mean quite literally "in" ("in the heavens," "in the city"). Relatedly, it can mean "on" ("on the way"), "at," or "near" ("to sit at God's right hand").
   • In terms of personal relations, it can mean "among," "with," or "in the presence of" (e.g., "among the saints," "in Christ").
   • More metaphorically, but still dependent on this spatial or local sense, *en* can refer to a state of being ("in chains," "in immortality").
   • It can also refer to the influence of one on another ("in the Spirit").

2. *Instrumentality*
   • In such instances *en* has a causal sense; "in" as "by means of" or "through" (e.g., "justified by the blood," "redeemed through Christ").
   • Sometimes this can function adverbially: "in power" as "powerfully."

3. *Time*
   • Sometimes *en* clearly has a temporal meaning, as in "in the course of" or "during" ("in the day" as "during the day").
   • It can also anticipate a time "when" ("in the day" as "when the day comes").

All three meanings of *in* (*en*) fit well the thought of Ephesians. In terms of "place," the chosen are *with* Christ *in the heavenlies* (2:5-6). Further, Christ is an inclusive personal reality, *in whom* the saints experience the blessings of God (1:3, 7, 11, 13). This is captured most clearly in the image of *the body of Christ* (1:23; 2:16; 4:4, 12, 16; 5:30; cf. Rom. 12:4-8; 1 Cor. 12:12-27; Col. 1:18, 24; 2:19). Christ is the "space" in which God and the saints meet. It needs to be emphasized, however, that in Ephesians the "circumference" of Christ extends beyond reconciled humanity. Ultimately the size of Christ's body is cosmic; it extends to the very edges of creation, embracing *things in heaven and things on earth* (1:10). Such a conception is clearly a view of personhood quite different from our concept of the modern individual. While metaphor clearly plays a role, there is also present a notion of corporate personality that allows the author of Ephesians or the Gospel of John to speak of believers participating in Christ and to know that they will be understood.

The instrumental sense of *en* is also often present in Ephesians, notably as it relates to Christ. In some respects the instrumental sense is implicit in the designation *Christ*, which is Greek for *Messiah*. Jesus is God's anointed one, his agent of liberation. Christ is the agent of God's creation (1:4; 2:10, 15). Christ Jesus died on the cross, thereby bringing redemption (1:7) and making peace (2:16). As such, he is the *means* by which, or the *agent* by whom, God acts. By means of Christ's death and resurrection, God makes peace, reconciles with humanity, and re-creates it in God's image (2:4-7, 10, 14-18; 4:24). It is obvious that the spatial and causal senses of *en* come together *in Christ*. Christ is both means and goal of God's saving of creation. The crucially important phrase in 1:10 must be translated both as *gathering up all things* **in** *Christ and* **through** *Christ*. Likewise, those who are *in Christ* are at the very center of that great movement toward unity in God and are implicated in its realization (1:22; 3:21; 4:13; 6:10-20).

Finally, the temporal sense of *en* comes to expression in 2:7, where the grace of God will be shown *in the coming aeons*, that is, *during* future ages. It can also be seen in the phrase *in/on the evil day* in 6:13.

PAULINE LETTER STRUCTURE   In keeping with ancient letter-writing conventions, letters in the NT share a basic structure (Aune: 158-225; Bailey and Vander Broek: 23-31; Brown: 409-21; Doty; Koester, 1979; 1982a:54-6; Roetzel, 1998:51-66; Stowers, 1986; 1992):

1. Opening formula
   • Sender(s)
   • Recipient(s)
   • Greeting
2. Thanksgiving
3. Body
4. Concluding formula

The opening identifies the sender and the recipient. This is followed by a greeting. Greek letters begin with "Greetings!" *(chairein)*, whereas Jewish letters begin with "Peace!" *(shalom* in Hebrew; *eirēnē* in Greek). The greeting is often combined with a positive remembrance of the addressees or a recollection of circumstances that have led to the writing of the letter. Following the opening is an expression of gratitude to God or the gods for such gifts as friendship and health.

Only after such preliminaries is the substance—the "body"—of the letter introduced, often with a phrase such as "I want you to know," "I appeal to you," or "Please." In informal personal letters such a body may be quite brief, and in more formal letters essay-like. This section is concluded with some statement of motivation, recapitulation, or reminder. A letter typically concludes with a wish for health, a farewell, and concluding greetings.

The ancient world knew various types of letters (Aune, Stowers, above). Most frequent were personal letters of friendship. But there were also letters from philosophers and teachers to their followers and adherents, exhorting them to live appropriately. Not surprisingly, their followers often wrote letters such as these in honor of such teachers after they died [*Pseudepigraphy*].

Paul's letters typically share this basic structure, even if there is considerable variation among the letters. Scholars do not always agree about how they should be analyzed structurally, but they agree on some important features (see works cited above, the numerous introductions to Pauline literature, as well as the essay "Epistolary Analysis" in Elias: 348-50).

Schema of Paul's Letters

1. Opening formula
   - Sender(s)
   - Recipient(s)
   - Greeting/blessing
2. Thanksgiving
3. Body
   - Specific concerns
4. Exhortation (paraenesis; sometimes seen as part of the body)
   - Eschatological comments
5. Concluding formula
   - Greetings/benediction/doxology

With respect to the opening, we discover that Paul fused Jewish and Greek letter-writing conventions. Paul's letters begin with "Grace and peace." "Peace" corresponds to the Jewish greeting of *Shalom,* and "grace" *(charis)* is both a profound greeting, indeed a blessing, and a pun on the Greek "Greetings!" *(chairein).* Paul's simple but profound modification of convention gives witness to the remarkable fusion of Jewish and Gentile realities that marked early Christianity. We note further that in all the letters it is, strictly speaking, not Paul and his coauthors who greet, but "God the Father and the Lord Jesus Christ," the God who, as Ephesians reminds us repeatedly, has in and through Christ brought about this fusion.

Sometimes the writer(s) of the letter is introduced in such a way as to give notice of the tone and the agenda of the letter (see, e.g., Gal. 1:1, where Paul is clearly in a combative mood). The addressees are typically identified as "brothers [and sisters] in Christ," or as "holy ones/saints." The opening and the thanksgiving that immediately follows set the tone, strengthen bonds, and nurture the shared identity of being *in Christ.* These features are so much a part of Paul's mode of communication that when, for example, the thanksgiving is missing, as in Galatians, it would immediately have been perceived as an expression of intense displeasure, and rightly so.

There is some ambiguity about the body of the letter in Paul. Each letter is given shape, of course, by the diverse circumstances to which the letter is responding. The body of the letter to the Romans, a congregation Paul had never visited, reads much like an essay on God's grace. In contrast, 1 Corinthians has Paul responding to a laundry list of problems to which he was alerted both by word of mouth and by letter (1:11; 7:1). The matter is complicated by the fact that several of Paul's letters may be composites of several letter fragments (e.g., 2 Corinthians; Philippians).

It is characteristic of Pauline letters that the exhortation, the paraenesis, comes either at the end of the body or immediately following it (scholars differ in their schematization). It is typically introduced with the phrase: "I exhort you, therefore." "Therefore" is premised on what has preceded, as Romans 12:1 illustrates most clearly. The exhortation to live a certain way is always *a response to God's prior grace.* As a way of providing further motive for a life of faithfulness, as well as giving warning or encouragement, the paraenesis often includes or is followed by some eschatologically oriented comments (see, e.g., 1 Thess. 4:13—5:11).

Finally, sometimes the Pauline letter concludes with personal information regarding Paul's travel or inability to do so (e.g., 1 Cor. 16:15-18), greetings to specific persons in the addressed congregation and/or from the writers (see, e.g., Rom. 16; 1 Cor. 16:19-20; Phil. 4:21-22), and a closing benediction or doxology (e.g., Rom. 16:25-27; 2 Cor. 13:13).

Paul's apostolic letter served as "official" apostolic communication, but in ambience and style was much more like a personal letter (Koester, 1979). This expressed Paul's understanding of himself as apostle: he was a brother and a servant of the congregations to which he was writing; he was also apostolically responsible for them. This mix of authority, peership, and servanthood went to the very heart of Paul's apostleship; it also frequently gave Paul grief, as especially 2 Corinthians shows throughout.

POWERS

The "Powers" in Ephesians and the Bible: A Brief Overview

The *powers* (also called "principalities and powers") are often taken to refer to the whole gamut of forces opposing God, from Satan or the devil to demons possessing and tormenting individuals. Others view the powers more specifically as God-ordained yet fallen structures of reality that undergird but also undermine human life.

In the NT Ephesians offers one of the largest inventories of terms for such powers. *Devil (diabolos)* rather than Satan is the designation for the chief evil power (4:27; 6:11; cf. also 2:2, where three terms for this power are listed: *the aeon of this world; the ruler of the authority of the air; the spirit now at work among the sons of disobedience).* The list of the other *rulers and authorities* (3:10) is rather exhaustive. It includes *every rule and authority and power and lordship and every name that is named, not only in this age but also in the one to come* (1:21). Ephesians 6:12 lists *the rulers, the authorities, the cosmic potentates of this darkness, the spiritual aspects* (or *forces;* lit., *spiritualities) of evil in the heavenlies.* One might conceivably add to this list *coming ages (approaching or attacking aeons,* 2:7), *darkness* (5:11), and less likely *the width and length and height and depth* (3:18).

The interest in the powers is not unique to Ephesians. Prime examples are the Gospels, especially Jesus' conflict with Satan and his acts of expelling demons, and of course, the Revelation of John. Of immediate interest for this study are the Pauline writings, where the powers are depicted variously. On one hand, Paul views them as evil: *the rulers of this age* are responsible for the crucifixion of Christ (1 Cor. 2:6-8). They try but ultimately fail to come between believers and God (Rom. 8:38), since they have been defeated by the cross (Col. 2:15) and will be vanquished completely at the final victory of Christ (1 Cor. 15:24). But even if the powers are experienced presently as hostile, they were originally created by Christ (Col. 1:16) and are to be shown due respect and deference (Rom. 13:3; Titus 3:1; for full discussion of the whole range of powers, see, e.g., Grundmann, 1964; Schlier, 1961; esp. Wink, 1984).

Several questions are raised immediately. Are these texts reflecting the same view of the powers, or are there various powers? Are they always spiritual or angelic, or might they sometimes be human and/or structural? In other words, are they always personal beings, or are they sometimes spiritual forces most easily but nevertheless only metaphorically spoken of in personalistic terms? Are they always evil, or do they sometimes do God's bidding?

The search for clarity is encumbered by this ambiguity in the scriptural data. The matter is compounded by significant shifts in understanding over the centuries, shifts that have left their mark on the biblical record. Early on it appears that "the satan" could refer to a human "adversary" (e.g., 2 Sam. 19:22; 1 Kings 11:14; Ps. 109:6) or to a heavenly "accuser" (cf. Job 1–2; Zech. 3:1-2; in Num. 22:22, 32, "the satan" is a divine messenger). In short, he is not always depicted as unmitigated personified evil. Only in the few centuries leading up to the time of Christ did an elaborate demonology develop in Judaism. Perhaps under the influence of a Persian dualism, evil angelic powers were understood to be at war with good angelic powers (for specific literature, see Finger and Swartley: 10-2; Hamilton: 987-8; Kuemmerlin-McLean: 138-40; Reese: 140-2). "Satan" became a proper name for God's evil competitor (e.g., Jubilees 23:29; Assump. Moses 10.1; other names: "the devil," "Beliar," "Beelzebub," "Mastema," and so on).

By whatever name, the devil was understood to be the "ringleader" (Hamilton) of a hierarchy of demonic angels. NT writers reflect some of this diversity of views. Throughout the NT the "chief adversary" is variously called "Satan," "devil," "prince of this world," "god of this world," "Beelzebul" the ruler of demons, or "Belial." Demons, most often noted in the synoptic Gospels, are mentioned throughout the NT.

How does this relate to the powers? As indicated above, it is not always clear whether "rulers and authorities" refers to demonic forces or to "structures" that, however much fallen, undergird human social existence. For the most part, NT writers shared with the larger Jewish community a view of Satan or the devil as the chief commandant of the evil forces wreaking havoc in the affairs of humanity. At the same time, they did not draw clear lines between personal and impersonal forces, celestial powers, and earthly rulers (e.g., 1 Cor 2:6-8), or demonic forces and divinely created if "fallen" structures of human life (Cullmann: 95-114; Wink, 1984; 1986; Yoder, 1994:136-8).

This possible double reference is illustrated in the way the Greek term *stoicheia* (Gal. 4:3, 9; Col. 2:8, 20; Heb. 5:12; 2 Pet. 3:10, 12) is variously translated as, e.g., "elements," "ruling spirits," "ABCs," and "elementary truths." The NRSV alone translates the same term as "elementary spirits" in Galatians 4, as "basic elements" in Hebrews 5, and as "elements" in 2 Peter 3. No doubt some of this ambiguity comes about because ancients, Jews and Gentiles alike, saw much of reality as deeply affected by "spirit" or "spirits," both good and evil. Human life was believed to take place, individually and corporately, in a highly charged spiritual force field or "atmosphere."

The approach taken in this commentary intends to respect this ambiguity and implicit comprehensiveness. Ephesians well reflects such comprehensiveness. I noted above that in the NT, Ephesians has the largest number of terms for the powers. This conforms, on one hand, to the ornate style of Ephesians (Introduction), and we should thus be careful not to see this as an inventory of the powers. At the same time, such abundance of terms is surely intended to leave out nothing. Just as God is *gathering up **all things** in*

Christ (1:10), so the body of that Christ is to engage *all* powers—*all* forces resisting God's saving initiative, whether personal or impersonal, structural, systemic, or spiritual. The pointed demand in 5:3—6:9 for an alternative culture in both society and home, leading up to the summons to battle with the powers in 6:10, makes it crystal clear: though *blood and flesh* are not the enemy (6:12) the struggle takes place in the everyday material contexts of faithful living.

A Variety of Interpretations

Contemporary interpretations of the powers and thus also of Ephesians can be placed on a continuum or spectrum reflecting the diversity of signals in the Scriptures. At the one end is the view of the church's mission as "spiritual warfare" with personal demonic forces. Evangelism and exorcism are the means. At the other end of the spectrum is the view of the powers as primarily impersonal social and cultural forces, structures, and institutions that bring war, violence, and oppression. Public witness, prophetic critique, and political activism are the means of struggle. Most Christians likely find themselves somewhere between these poles. In believers church circles, a majority likely tends to the second pole, given the emphasis in recent years on active peacemaking and restorative justice. But a significant segment also believes the mission of the church includes vigorous spiritual warfare against Satan and his demonic hordes. The texts relating to powers are read largely through the lenses of these perspectives.

One can illustrate this diversity among scholars in the believers church tradition. Clinton Arnold, a scholar with Mennonite Brethren roots who has made important contributions to the study of Ephesians and of the powers, defines the "principalities and powers" as "angelic beings, both good and evil, but most commonly in reference to the realm of Satan" (1992a:467). His scholarly work on Ephesians reflects this understanding of the powers as personal beings (1989; 1992; see also Best, 1998:178-9; Lincoln: 444), as does his more popular work on spiritual warfare (1997). This approach is consistent with that taken by the so-called Third Wave movement in mission, dubbed so by one of its leading proponents, C. Peter Wagner (1988; he distinguishes this movement from earlier Pentecostalism and Charismatic renewals). The Third Wave is perhaps best known for its stress on spiritual warfare against "territorial spirits." (For fuller discussions with an exorcistic view of the church's mission in dealing with the powers, see, e.g., Arnold, 1992; 1997; Boyd; Page; Wagner, 1991; Warner, 1988; 1991).

Another representative of the believers church tradition, John H. Yoder, offers a quite different interpretation, one just as intentionally biblical. Building on the work of Hendrikus Berkhof's *Christ and the Powers*, which he translated from the Dutch in 1962, Yoder views the powers mentioned in the NT as an "overwhelmingly broad totality,"

> religious structures (especially the religious undergirdings of stable ancient and primitive societies), intellectual structures (-ologies, and -isms), moral structures (codes and customs), political structures (the tyrant, the market, the school, the courts, race, and nation). (J. H. Yoder, 1994:142-3; 1964:8-14)

Berkhof and Yoder are echoed more recently in the influential writings of Walter Wink, who defines the powers as

> legitimations, seats of authority, hierarchical systems, ideological justifications, and punitive sanctions which their human incumbents exercise and which transcend these incumbents in both time and power. (Wink, 1984:85)

> In the biblical view, they are both visible and invisible, earthly and heavenly, spiritual and institutional. The powers possess an outer, physical manifestation (buildings, portfolios, personnel, trucks, fax machines) and an inner spirituality, corporate culture, or collective personality (Wink, 1992:3; see also 1998; 1998a).

> They are linked together in a bewilderingly complex network, in what we can call the Domination System (Wink, 1998:36).

Similarly, speaking out of the experience of the war in former Yugoslavia, Miroslav Volf calls the powers

> all-pervasive low-intensity evil . . ., the interiority of warped institutions, structures, and systems . . . under which many suffer but for which no one is responsible and about which all complain but no one can target. (87)

Such an interpretation draws attention to how pervasive and insidious these powers are. As social, political, and economic realities, the powers are diffused throughout the culture. Their demonic character rests more in their capacity to control the imaginations and behavior of human beings, individually and communally, than on their transcendent nature or personal agency. Unlike the earlier interpretation, this one rests heavily on Colossians 1:16, where Christ is declared the creator of the powers. Yoder draws the inference succinctly: given that the powers are "in their general essence . . . parts of a good creation, . . . we cannot live without them." In their fallen state, and in the absolute claims they place on individuals and society, "we cannot live with them" (1994:143). As Wink puts it repeatedly, "The Powers are good; the Powers are fallen; the Powers will be redeemed" (1992:65; 1998:51; cf. Yoder, 1985:114). It is clear that judgment and transformation are more appropriate categories of response to such powers than exorcism. To be sure, judgment and transformation are also understood as spiritual undertakings. (McClain: 38-47, 89-136, e.g., employs the vocabulary of exorcism for such critical engagement with the powers so conceived. For similar interpretation of the powers, see, e.g., Cochrane; Eller, 1987; Ellul, 1976:151-60; McGill: 47-52, 86-93; Macgregor; Mott: 3-21; Mouw: 85-116; Schlier, 1961; re Ephesians in particular, see, e.g., Barth: 800-3; Russell: 119-21; Schlier, 1971:291; Schnackenburg: 272.)

It is obvious that both "worldview" (cf. Wink, 1992:3-10; 1988:13-56) and rootage in various Christian traditions (McAlpine: 3-6) affect both the reading of the Bible and its interpretation in relation to the present task and mission of the church. Thomas McAlpine has identified these with the following typology as reflected in his chapter headings:

- Transformation by Osmosis: The Reformed Tradition
- Over Against: The Anabaptist Tradition
- Expect a Miracle: The Third Wave Tradition
- Sociological Bible: The Social Science Tradition

His typology is helpful in identifying the variety of stances, but his nomenclature is less helpful. For example, present-day Anabaptists find themselves in every one of these categories (as his discussion of scholarship shows; see his extensive bibliography, including among "Anabaptist" types several leading Catholic scholars, thus raising further doubts about his categories). Clearly Christians are at quite different points in their view of the powers and in the task that implies for the church. Often the whole gamut of perspectives is found in one congregation. Worldviews coexist in traditions, indeed, even as unreconciled perspectives within one person. Sometimes these differences are defined as those between what we might call supernaturalists and materialists, the former typically the ones claiming to be biblical. McAlpine remarks somewhat whimsically but insightfully,

> Appeals to simply "believe the Bible" are not very helpful here. For example, Genesis 1 speaks both of a solid firmament which keeps the rainwater in place and in which the stars are placed and of the beasts of the field. Our [present-day] pictures of the world contain the beasts of the field, but include the firmament only with major adjustments. Are the principalities and powers more like the firmament, or the beasts of the field? There is hard theological work to be done on the area. (78)

McAlpine argues that common ground is the best place to do such work. He suggests that to find common ground is itself a struggle against the powers, and for that reason it is critically important to the mission of the church (86). Gayle Gerber Koontz, in reflecting on the divisiveness the strong differences in perspective have often introduced into the church, makes much the same point:

> Should we not rather pray that God would form us *together* into one body whose head is Christ, a body not weakened by divisions resulting from carelessly narrow theological definitions, but one which can stand *together* strong in faith, hope and love in the face of demonic powers? (1988:93; emphasis added)

> Contemporary experience of the demonic in *all* its forms *and formlessness* points us—*all* of us—to this need for extraordinary faith and courage (1988:99; emphasis added).

Whereas McAlpine and Gerber Koontz are speaking to the church's mission today, they reflect a core concern in Ephesians. Any restrictive definition of the powers undervalues and thereby defeats the central argument in Ephesians, that God's design is to gather up *all things*. A full appreciation and a faithful translation for our day of what the author of Ephesians has in mind requires that we not force an exclusive choice between an exorcistic and a prophetic view of evil and the church's response to it.

Early readers would have related their understanding of the powers to the practices of astrology or magic, in which the rulers of evil and darkness were conjured up to work their power (so Arnold and Best, correctly). But they would also have understood the powers as referring to realities we today quite rightly identify as cultural, social, and political dimensions of dehumanization and oppression (so Volf, Wink, and Yoder, correctly). The task is to remain alert to the demonic features of these dimensions of human individual and social life and to see the struggle against them as fundamentally spiritual. Strugglers with the powers must guard against downplaying or underestimating the spiritual oppression of individuals and families. They must guard just as vigilantly against underestimating the spiritual nature of the –anities, -alities, -ologies, -isms, -doms, and –hoods (cf. Yoder, 1964:8, n.1).

Ephesians assumes that a variety of gifts will dictate how this struggle is undertaken. The author shows little interest in the mechanics of either how the powers affect human life or how they are to be combated. Ephesians does show, however, a very marked interest in wisdom (1:8, 17-23; 3:10, 14-19; 5:15-17), in nonconformity (4:17—5:17), in worship (1:3-14; 3:14-21; 5:18-21), and in standing against (6:10-20). The letter stresses the practical and communal exercise of truth, justice, peace, and the word of God, and finally prayer. These enable believers to preach the good news (6:14-20), which in Ephesians is most centrally the overcoming of enmity within the human community and with God (as in Eph. 2–3!).

In Ephesians, the greatest evidence of the demonic lies in the existence of disobedience to God's will for humanity (2:1-10), in the hostile and exclusionary divisions in the human community (2:11-22; 3:1-13), and in the darkness of a culture blind to the gravity of license, greed, and falsity (4:17—5:21). We know, as does the author of Ephesians, that the larger culturally experienced forces are the chief culprits in nurturing such hostilities. That is why the alternative cultural forces of truth, justice, and peace are so important. When these are wielded by a community that is in Christ—that has put on the new human—then its very life is exorcistic, casting out evil.

PSEUDEPIGRAPHY The word *pseudepigraphy* derives from two Greek terms: *pseud-* ("false") and *epigrapha* ("inscriptions/superscriptions"). Many prefer the closely related "pseudonymity." Both refer to writing under a false name, a pen name.

Pseudepigraphy was widespread in biblical times, both inside and outside Jewish and Christian circles. In the two or three centuries before and after the time of Christ, for example, many Jewish documents were produced in the names of famous persons or revered teachers, collected in the so-called Apocrypha and Pseudepigrapha. Apocalypses, testaments, psalms, prayers, and legends were attributed to famous biblical personalities, some from the very beginnings of the biblical story (e.g., Ezra, Solomon, the twelve patriarchs, Moses, Abraham, Enoch, and even Adam; see Charlesworth, 1983-85; 1992). The so-called NT Apocrypha include gospels, acts, letters, and apocalypses attributed to the important disciples of Jesus, Jesus' brothers, even his mother, as well as to the great apostles Peter and Paul (Charlesworth, 1992; Hennecke).

The pseudonymity of documents is not particularly troubling when they are not part of Scripture. Pseudepigraphy and noncanonical status might be regarded as mutually reinforcing. The question of whether one finds pseudepigraphy in the canon of Scripture is more troubling. Many Christians find such a possibility theologically unacceptable, threatening the integrity of the Bible as revelation (see, e.g., Guthrie, 1990:1011-28). Most scholars, including many evangelical scholars, consider it more than likely, however, that some documents bear the names of those who did not write them. It has, for example, become common to question whether David composed the psalms, or whether the eighth-century prophet Isaiah composed chapters 40–66. There is a virtual consensus that 2 Peter and the pastoral letters are pseud-epigraphical (J. Daryl Charles's BCBC commentary on 2 Peter and Jude goes against the acknowledged current; in *1–2 Peter, Jude:* 260-3). For most scholars, the list is considerably longer (see introductions to the Bible, recently again R. Brown: 585-9).

Inspiration or canonical status is, of course, not dependent on modern judgments regarding authorship (so, e.g., Barth, 1974:50, who defends Paul's authorship of Ephesians; Lincoln: lxxiii; R. P. Martin, 1991:1-3; Meade: 153-7, 215-6; Metzger: 21-2; Patzia, 1990:121-41; 1995:76-8). Even so, the phenomenon of pseudepigraphy continues to be controversial in circles where the Bible is held in high regard.

While the ethics of authorship in biblical times no doubt differed from those in our day, the practice of writing in someone else's name was sometimes controversial. For example, 2 Thessalonians 2:2 warns of letters being written in Paul's name claiming that the day of the Lord had already arrived. It is not clear whether in that case the problem is first and foremost pseudepigraphy or errant eschatology. Late in the second century, Tertullian was swift in his condemnation of the presbyter who admitted to having penned the Acts of Paul and Thecla, even if out of love and respect for Paul. Again, the problem may be more that Paul is depicted as allowing a woman to preach and baptize than the act of impersonating Paul (for this and other examples, see Metzger: 14).

We should, even so, be careful not to apply to biblical times the modern ethics of authorial integrity as it relates to plagiarism or forgery (Best, 1998:12; Brown: 585-9; Lincoln: lxxi; Metzger; Patzia, 1990:122). In Jewish circles in the two or three centuries before and after the turn of the era, pseudepigraphy "was the norm in biblically inspired groups" (Charlesworth, 1992:541). We might expect something similar for circles devoted to central figures such as Peter, Paul, James, John, and Thomas.

What might have been the motivations for writing under the names of famous persons? First, it was a sign of respect, even "kinship" (Metzger: 21; for a full survey of motivations, see 5-12). Unlike most modern writers who are concerned that they themselves get full credit for the ideas they publish (hence the hallowed academic convention of crediting sources properly), many pseudonymous writers were quite happy to disappear behind the person inspiring their words. They would have viewed their work as a form of giving credit where credit is due.

Second, pseudepigraphy shows dependency on the revelatory tradition associated with the named author. There is an intense concern to make sure the "deposit" of "sound teaching," as the Paul of the pastorals puts it (1 Tim. 6:20; 2 Tim. 1:12, 14), is both protected and rendered current. Pseudepigraphy is, in Dunn's words, "a means of affirming the continuity of God's purpose between the circumstances of the named author and the circumstances of the actual author" (68). Brown wonders whether we might not make a distinction between "writer" and "author" (585). In this case the one writing in the name of a James or a Peter, for example, recognizes that person as the true "author," the real source of the content of the writing.

Third, heated controversy over the correct understanding of a revered figure's teachings sometimes led to writing in his name. The pastoral letters and 2 Thessalonians are often taken to be examples in the biblical canon (see Elias: 374-7); beyond the canon, the list is long.

Fourth, finding acceptance for one's writing would no doubt often have been a motivation for pseudepigraphy. No doubt the mantle of a respected person might aid in the acceptance of an author's ideas. In the case of the canonical writings, the judgment of the church was that the accepted writings indeed conformed to the "foundation of the apostles and prophets" (Eph. 2:20), and in particular, to the legacy of the stated author.

Should we assume that pseudonymous writers fooled readers, even if for noble reasons? No doubt there were numerous cases of intentional and successful deception (hence the warning in 2 Thess. 2:2; see extensive discussion in Metzger; also Brown: 587-8). Even so, a number of scholars have suggested that pseudepigraphy was so accepted that it was often quite "transparent," especially if the writing was associated with a school or circle of writers and teachers associated with a particular person. "Both writer *and original readers* would have been *knowing participants* in this particular mode of communication" (Lincoln: lxxii; emphasis added; cf. Dunn: 84). Both writer and readers would thus have felt no tension, for example, between the repeated stress in Ephesians on *truth* (4:15, 25; 6:14) and the strong possibility that a student and collaborator of Paul wrote this great letter after his death (see below).

Ephesians

With respect to whether Ephesians was written by Paul or by someone else in his name, a significant majority of scholars believe several factors point in their cumulative weight to an author other than Paul (on the cumulative nature of such an argument, see Best, 1998:35-6; Lincoln: 1xviii-lxix; Patzia, 1990. For a different conclusion on the basis of the same data, see Barth, 1974:49). Evangelical scholars also increasingly opt for an author other than Paul (e.g., R. P. Martin, 1991:4; Lincoln: lxi-lxxiii, and literature cited; Patzia is apparently unwilling to commit himself, but believes the issue should not be theologically divisive; 1990:121-41; 1995:76-8).

The data are rehearsed in great detail in several recent commentaries (e.g., Best; Lincoln; Schnackenburg; and virtually all NT introductions, recently in Brown: 626-33). The data taken into account can be summarized as follows:

1. In contrast to letters Paul undoubtedly wrote, Ephesians is very general, giving little explicit indication of specific issues, audience, or location.

2. With the exception of 2 Thessalonians and the pastoral letters, Ephesians appears to show familiarity with all Pauline letters, especially with Colossians, on which it may be directly dependent.

3. The language and style of Ephesians is quite distinct and very different from the undisputed letters of Paul.

4. The theological emphases are distinct and are best understood as a development of Pauline themes:
   • The church takes on unprecedented prominence. Moreover, the church is consistently thought of as a universal catholic reality.

- Resurrection and exaltation become more prominent than the cross.
- The eschatology of Ephesians is characterized by a stress on the present more than on the future. When the future does come into view, it is apt to be characterized by growth. There is no mention of the return or appearing of Christ.
- Salvation is not related to a future judgment but to the *gathering up of all things*, and as part of that cosmic process, the reconciliation and re-creation of humanity in and through Christ.

Though these themes are all rooted in Paul's apostolic teaching, their treatment in Ephesians suggests further development and critical engagement with others in the Pauline school with respect to how Paul's legacy should be understood in light of the ongoing life of churches within the orbit of his mission. That does not mean that the deletions, additions, or shifts of emphasis are always a *conscious* correcting or updating of Paul. Over time, congregations, preachers, and teachers have time to forget and remember, to recall and often quite unconsciously to recast what they intend to *preserve*. Tradition is never dead. As is often observed, the pastoral letters are explicitly concerned with "guarding the deposit" (1 Tim. 6:20; 2 Tim. 1:14); they are also most distant in tone, style, and content from the letters Paul undoubtedly wrote.

If we combine the observation that Ephesians betrays evidence of a great deal of reworking of Paul's own teaching and writing with the suggestion that the letter emerged from a "school", then perhaps we should not think in terms of a solitary author (Acts 19:9-10 shows Paul passing on a legacy to his disciples). Ephesians becomes very much a collaborative effort, even if penned by one no doubt brilliant author, a collaboration that includes Paul, even if only through the letters and teaching he left behind as a *foundation* (2:20). For convenience' sake, and because only one author is named at the beginning of the letter, I refer to "the author" in the singular throughout the commentary.

If Paul was not the brilliant writer (Barth says this brilliance can point only to Paul; 1974:50; 1984:23), we can look tentatively to the co-writers at the beginning of Paul's letters or to those who send greetings at the ends of those letters, persons closely associated with Paul who survived him. Mitton guesses it was the only one from such a circle who is named in this document, Tychicus (6:21; Mitton: 230). Other candidates have also been proposed: Onesimus (Goodspeed) and Luke (R. P. Martin, 1968). In the end we should respect the pseudepigrapher's desire to hide behind the one whose apostolic mission this great letter is intended to further *[Authorship]*.

WISDOM *Wisdom (sophia)* refers to a tradition or set of traditions that in the Bible comes to clearest expression in Proverbs, Job, Ecclesiastes (*Qohelet*), and many psalms (e.g., Pss. 1, 19, 37, 49, 73, 112, 119, 127-128, 133). The apocryphal books of Baruch, Ecclesiasticus (Sirach/Wisdom of Jesus son of Sirah), and Wisdom of Solomon, which are part of the Catholic canon, are also important wisdom writings (note the frequent references to Wisdom of Solomon throughout this commentary). Solomon is identified as the source of much of this wisdom, and a good part of it may have ancient roots (see esp. Prov. 10–31), but most scholars believe the bulk of this literature in its present form is postexilic.

This literature, especially Proverbs, contains a great deal of proverbial wisdom, aphorisms of wisdom distilled from experience in light of the divine source of creation. The sages believed that the Creator brought into being an orderly creation, in which human life takes place according to divinely ordained rules. Hence, the presence of mundane instructions on table manners (Prov. 23:1-3; Sirach 31:12-31) as well as the lofty celebration of Torah as the distillation of wisdom (Ps. 119; Baruch 4:1; Ecclus./Sirach 24:23).

The wisdom tradition thus shows us the reflective side of Jewish piety. Given that God is Creator of the whole world and all peoples, the wisdom tradition represents an open window to the wisdom of other peoples (note the presence of Egyptian wisdom in Proverbs, and of Hellenism in Wisdom of Solomon). It was the assumption of a good creation at the hands of a benevolent deity that gave the troubling reflections in Job and Ecclesiastes their sharp edge. Note the debate among the sages about justice, God, and creation, reflected in the arguments between Job and his friends, or the world-weary opening cry of the Preacher/Teacher of Ecclesiastes to the effect that "all is vanity" (1:2).

Unlike in prophecy, where the utterances are imbued with the ambience of proclaiming the words of Yahweh directed at specific circumstances, in wisdom those words and the day-to-day experiences of the people become the object of probing reflection. The ways of God are visible in creation and law, but they are beyond knowing without the help of revelation. The sages were endlessly curious about the way God and God's creation work, and deeply impressed by the limits of wisdom, by the mystery of God (compare the words of Job's friends in Job 11:1-8 and 36:22-26 with Paul's wonderful pastiche of wisdom aphorisms in Rom. 11:33-36).

In Jewish wisdom the acknowledged need for revelation in no way closed the door on intellectual activity, and vice versa. Such a conviction also informed the growth of prophetic traditions over many decades, such as those attributed to Isaiah. Apocalyptic literature such as Daniel insisted that *only* revelation (the meaning of the Greek *apocalypsis [Apocalyptic]*) could offer insight into the real state of the world and into the mystery of God's designs for it, but these writings too were the product of self-consciously intellectual circles of visionaries. A careful study of the Revelation of John, for example, shows how meticulously even a recitation of visions and dreams was rehearsed in literary form (cf. also Millard Lind's BCBC vol., *Ezekiel* (BCBC), esp. pages 18-19).

Wisdom literature contains poetic celebrations of Wisdom as the personified daughter of God and companion of faithful people (e.g., Job 28:12-28, which should be read as a poem about personified Wisdom, as correctly presented by NJB; Prov. 1; 3:13-20; 8-9; Baruch 3:9—4:4; Sirach 6:18-31; 14:20—15:8; 24; 51:13-22; Wisd. of Sol. 6-9). Creation and law are personified in the figure of an intensely attractive woman who is identified with *God's* activity as Creator and Lawgiver and with the *human* activity of faithfulness and "scientific" inquisitiveness. "Solomon" has Wisdom as a science and theology tutor (Wisd. of Sol. 7, esp. 7:15-28), but he also desires her as a lover and wife (8:2), a desire the wisdom literature intended to instill into all the faithful (e.g., Prov. 8:2-5; 9:1-6; Baruch 3:36—4:4; Sirach 4:11-13; 14:20-27).

This rich tradition is relevant to the NT in various important ways. Jesus' ethical and parabolic teachings are deeply rooted in wisdom and would have been recognized as such by his contemporaries. Further, early believers made the connection between personified Wisdom and the Christ (explicitly in 1 Cor. 1:24-30; Matt. 11:18-19, 28-30; James 3:13-18 also hints at it). Most dramatic are the hymns that celebrate Christ in the language and categories of personified Wisdom. Colossians 1:15-20 identifies Jesus Christ as the image of God (cf. Wisd. of Sol. 7:25-26) who created all things (cf. Prov. 8:30; Wisd. of Sol. 7:22). The poem on the "Word" *(logos)* in John 1:1-18 appears to owe much to this tradition, as the following passage from the Wisdom of Solomon illustrates:

> For [Wisdom] is a reflection of eternal light,
> a spotless mirror of the working of God,
> and an image of his goodness.
> Although she is but one, she can do all things,
> and while remaining in herself, she renews all things;
> in every generation she passes into holy souls
> and makes them friends of God, and prophets. (Wisd. of Sol. 7:26-27)

These words help to show us why early followers of Jesus would have drawn from this rich well.

The radical implications of identifying the crucified teacher from Galilee with Wisdom herself (Matt. 11:18-19; 1 Cor. 1) are particularly noteworthy. The self-giving Messiah is identified with the Wisdom that created the world, who gives guidance to humanity on how to order its existence and fashion its behavior. Hence Colossians 1:16 can claim that Christ is the one who has created and is Lord and disciplinarian of the principalities and powers (cf. 2:15 *[Powers]*); the Creator is also the one who makes peace through his own death on the cross (1:20). In making the identification of Jesus with the Wisdom of God, his early followers make the radical claim that he represents God's solution to both human sinfulness and human history and is the key to understanding created reality in all its manifestations and dimensions.

The NT thus contains the good news of Jesus' death and resurrection and the promise of salvation, but also a rich storehouse of proverbial and parabolic wisdom about how to comport oneself in daily life. To give but one example, the love of enemies (Matt. 5:43-48), most dramatically expressed in the death of Christ (Rom. 5), is to be exercised in light of the meticulous care the divine Creator offers even the birds and the flowers of the field (Matt. 6:25-34). Salvation and creation emerge from the one God, and are part of the same loving impulse (Yoder Neufeld, 1999:174-91).

Ephesians reflects the wisdom tradition in a number of ways. As much as any writing in the NT, it values wisdom and insight, most dramatically in 1:8, 17-18; and 3:14-19. It also values wise and righteous living (5:3-21).

Second, its view of salvation is repeatedly depicted as re-creation (cf. 2:4-10, 15; 4:24). Surely the characteristic emphasis on Christ gathering up *all things* (1:9-10) is a generosity of vision informed by the comprehensive horizon of wisdom.

Third, Ephesians owes much to a Christology rooted in wisdom literature. Much like personified Wisdom, Christ is the one in whom God and reconciled humanity meet. He is the agent of *God's* reconciliation and re-creation of humanity (e.g., 1:9-10; 2:14-18). He is also as the one who provides humanity with its identity as *the new human* (2:15; 4:24). He is the *head of the body* (1:23; 2:15-16; 4:11-16; 5:23). Just as Wisdom "enters holy souls and makes them friends of God and prophets" (Wisd. of Sol. 7:27), so in Ephesians Christ is the one who lives within so as to enable believers to be filled with the fullness of God (3:16, 19). The often romantically described intimacy between the righteous and Lady Wisdom is evoked in the relation of Christ and the church as his bride in 5:25-32, only now the genders are reversed. Though much of this in Ephesians is a development of what we find in Paul's letters generally, the debt to the rich wisdom tradition is clear.

Ephesians reflects the wisdom tradition in yet another way. In its dependency on and creative restatement of Paul's teaching, at greater distance from the specific circumstances that usually precipitated Paul's letters, Ephesians stands firmly in the wisdom tradition of "revelatory reflection," if I may coin a phrase. What is often observed to be an "overworked" style of writing in Ephesians may, in addition to having the feel of worship about it, be evidence of the highly processed nature of reflective wisdom. The author quite consciously reformulates and restates the apostolic "deposit," all the while probing its implications.

Such reflection is undertaken with the full conviction that God is intimately present in and through Christ and the Holy Spirit, inspiring the apostle, his co-workers and students, and his congregations (see notes for 1:17-18; 2:20). Such wisdom participates just as fully in the ongoing disclosure of God's manifold wisdom (2:7; 3:10; 6:19). This observation might shed light on how Ephesians can contain so many echoes of other letters in the Pauline collection, most especially Colossians, while at the same time make so rich and distinctive a contribution to Pauline theology *[Pseudepigraphy]*.

For a more extensive survey of the highly varied wisdom tradition and the extensive secondary literature, see R. E. Murphy.

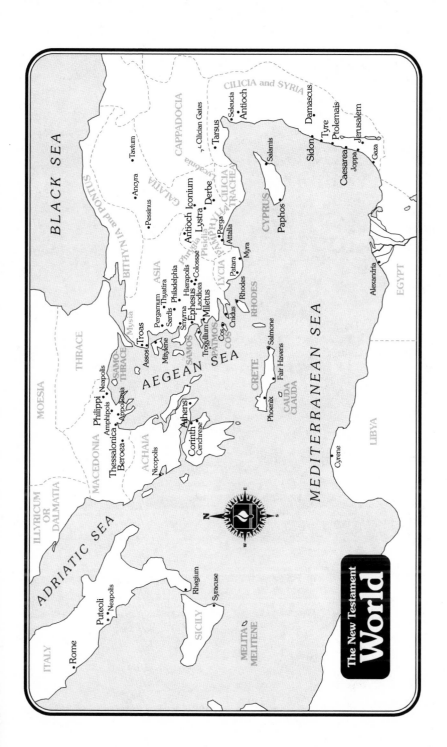

The New Testament World

Bibliography

ABD   David Noel Freedman et al., eds.
   1992   *The Anchor Bible Dictionary.* 6 vols. New York: Doubleday.
Arnold, Clinton E.
   1987   "The 'Exorcism' of Ephesians 6.12 in Recent Research: A
          Critique of Wesley Carr's View of the Role of Evil Powers in
          First-Century A.D. Belief." *Journal for the Study of the New
          Testament* 30:71-87.
   1989   *Ephesians: Power and Magic: The Concept of Power in
          Ephesians in Light of Its Historical Setting.* SNTS MS, 63.
          Cambridge: Cambridge Univ. Press.
   1992   *Powers of Darkness: Principalities and Powers in Paul's
          Letters.* Downers Grove, Ill.: InterVarsity Press.
   1992a "Principalities and Powers." *ABD,* 5:467.
   1997   *3 Crucial Questions About Spiritual Warfare.* Grand Rapids,
          Mich.: Baker Books.
Augsburger, David W.
   1980   *Caring Enough to Confront: The Love-Fight.* Scottdale, Pa.:
          Herald Press.
Aune, David E.
   1987   *The New Testament in Its Literary Environment.* Library of
          Early Christianity, 8. Philadelphia: Westminster.
BAGD   Bauer, Walter, W. R. Arndt, F. W. Gingrich, and F. W. Danker
   1979   *A Greek-English Lexicon of the New Testament and Other
          Early Christian Literature.* 2d rev., augmented ed. Chicago/
          London: Univ. of Chicago Press.
Bailey, James L., Lyle D. Vander Broek
   1992   *Literary Forms in the New Testament: A Handbook.* Louisville:
          Westminster John Knox.
Bailey, Kenneth E.
   1976   *Poet and Peasant.* Grand Rapids, Mich.: Eerdmans.

Balch, David J.
   1981   *Let Wives Be Submissive: The Domestic Code in 1 Peter.*
          SBLMS, 26; Chico, Calif.: Scholars Press, 1981.
   1992   "Household Code." *ABD,* 3:318-20.
Balz, Horst, and Günther Wanke
   1974   *"Phobeō." TDNT,* 9:189-219.
Banks, Robert J.
   1980   *Paul's Idea of Community: The Early House Churches in Their
          Historical Setting.* Grand Rapids: Eerdmans.
Bartchy, S. Scott
   1992   "Slavery (Greco-Roman)." *ABD,* 6:65-72.
Barth, Markus
   1974   *Ephesians.* 2 vols. Garden City, N.Y.: Doubleday.
   1984   "Traditions in Ephesians." *New Testament Studies* 30:3-25.
Bauman, Harold E.
   1982   *Congregations and Their Servant Leaders: Some Aids
          for Faithful Congregational Relationships.* Scottdale, Pa.:
          Mennonite Publishing House.
BDB   Brown, Francis, S. R. Driver, and Charles Briggs
   1907   *A Hebrew and English Lexicon of the Old Testament.*
          Clarendon: Oxford.
Bedale, Stephen
   1954   "The Meaning of *Kephalē* in the Pauline Epistles." *Journal of
          Theological Studies* 5:211-15.
Beker, J. Christiaan
   1991   *Heirs of Paul: Paul's Legacy in the New Testament and in the
          Church Today.* Minneapolis: Fortress.
Bergant, Dianne
   1994   "Yahweh: A Warrior God?" In *The Church's Peace Witness,* ed.
          Marlin E. Miller and Barbara Nelson Gingerich, 89-103. Grand
          Rapids: Eerdmans.
Berkhof, Hendrik
   1977   *Christ and the Powers.* Trans. John Howard Yoder. Scottdale,
          Pa.: Herald Press.
Bertram, Georg
   1964   *"Ergon . . ." TDNT,* 2:635-55.
   1965   *"Katergazomai." TDNT,* 3:634-35.
   1967   *"Paideuō . . ." TDNT,* 5:596-625.
Best, Ernest
   1993   *Ephesians.* New Testament Guides. Sheffield, U.K.: JSOT.
   1997   *Essays on Ephesians.* Edinburgh: T & T Clark.
   1998   *Ephesians.* International Critical Commentary. Edinburgh: T & T
          Clark.
Beyer, Hermann W.
   1964   *"Eulogeō . . ." TDNT,* 2:754-65.
Blass, Friedrich, and Albert Debrunner
   1961   *A Greek Grammar of the New Testament and Other Early
          Christian Literature.* Trans. and rev. Robert W. Funk. Chicago:
          Univ. of Chicago Press.

Block, Bill
    1997   "The Pure Church Ideal and Real Membership." In *Naming the Sheep: Understanding Church Membership: Voices in Dialogue,* ed. Resources Commission, Conference of Mennonites in Canada, 46-54. Winnipeg: Resources Commission, Conference of Mennonites in Canada.

Bornkamm, Günther
    1967   "*Mustērion.*" *TDNT,* 4:802-27.

Bowe, Barbara
    1996   *A Key to the Letter to the Ephesians.* Quezon City, Philippines: Claretian Publications.

Boyd, Gregory A.
    1997   *God at War: The Bible and Spiritual Conflict.* Downers Grove, Ill.: InterVarsity Press.

Breck, John
    1994   *The Shape of Biblical Language: Chiasmus in the Scriptures and Beyond.* Crestwood, N.Y.: St. Vladimir's Seminary Press.

Brown, Raymond E.
    1997   *An Introduction to the New Testament.* New York: Doubleday.

Bruce, F. F.
    1976   "Election, NT." *IDB Suppl.*: 258-59.
    1984   *The Epistles to the Colossians, to Philemon, and to the Ephesians.* Grand Rapids: Eerdmans.

Büchsel, Friedrich
    1964   "*Elegchō. . . .*" *TDNT,* 2:473-75.
    1964a "*Exagorazō.*" *TDNT,* 1:126-28.

Bultmann, Rudolf
    1964   "*Ginōskō. . . .*" *TDNT* 1:689-719.

Bultmann, Rudolf, and Artur Weiser
    1968   "*Pistis. . . .*" *TDNT,* 6:174-228.

Caird, G. B.
    1956   *Principalities and Powers: A Study in Pauline Theology.* Oxford: Clarendon.

Carr, Wesley
    1981   *Angels and Principalities: The Background, Meaning, and Development of the Pauline Phrase hai archai kai hai exousiai.* SNTS, 42. Cambridge: Cambridge Univ. Press.

Carrington, Philip
    1940   *The Primitive Christian Catechism.* Cambridge: Cambridge Univ. Press.

Charles, J. Daryl
    1999   "2 Peter, Jude." In *1-2 Peter, Jude,* by Erland Waltner and J. Daryl Charles. Believers Church Bible Commentary. Scottdale, Pa.: Herald Press.

Charlesworth, James H.
    1985a "Pseudepigrapha." *HBD:* 836-40.
    1992   "Pseudonymity and Pseudepigraphy." *ABD,* 5:540-41.

Charlesworth, James H., ed.
    1983-85 *The Old Testament Pseudepigrapha.* Vol. 1: *Apocalyptic Literature and Testaments.* Vol. 2: *Expansions of the "Old Testament" and Legends, Wisdom and Philosophical*

Literature, Prayers, Psalms, and Odes, Fragments of Lost Judeo-Hellenistic Works. Garden City, N.Y.: Doubleday.

Clark Kroeger, Catherine, and James R. Beck, eds.
1996 *Women, Abuse, and the Bible: How Scripture Can Be Used to Hurt or to Heal*. Grand Rapids: Baker Books.

Cochrane, Arthur C.
1986 *The Mystery of Peace*. Elgin, Ill.: Brethren.

Collins, John J.
1987 *The Apocalyptic Imagination*. New York: Crossroad.
1992 "Apocalypses and Apocalypticism: Early Jewish Apocalypticism." *ABD*, 1:282-88.

Crouch, James E.
1971 *The Origin and Intention of the Colossian Haustafel*. FRLANT, 109. Göttingen: Vandenhoeck & Ruprecht.

Cullmann, Oscar
1956 *The State in the New Testament*. New York: Charles Scribner's Sons.

Dawn, Marva J.
1995 *Reaching Out Without Dumbing Down: A Theology of Worship for the Turn-of-the-Century Culture*. Grand Rapids: Eerdmans.
1997 *Sources and Trajectories: Eight Early Articles by Jacques Ellul That Set the Stage*. Grand Rapids: Eerdmans.
1999 "The Biblical Concept of 'the Principalities and Powers': John Yoder Points to Jacques Ellul." In *The Wisdom of the Cross: Essays in Honor of John Howard Yoder*, ed. Stanley Hauerwas, Chris K. Huebner, Harry J. Huebner, Mark Thiessen Nation, 168-86. Grand Rapids: Eerdmans.

Delling, Gerhard
1964 "Hēmera." *TDNT*, 2:943-53.
1972 "Hupotassō." *TDNT*, 8:39-46.

Dinkler, Erich
1992 "Eirēnē—The Early Christian Concept of Peace." In *The Meaning of Peace: Biblical Studies*, ed. Perry B. Yoder and Willard M. Swartley, 164-212. Louisville: Westminster John Knox.

Dintaman, Stephen F.
1992 "The Spiritual Poverty of the Anabaptist Vision." *Conrad Grebel Review* 10/2:205-8.

Doty, William G.
1973 *Letters in Primitive Christianity*. Guides to Biblical Scholarship, New Testament Series. Philadelphia: Fortress.

Douglass, James W.
1972 *Resistance and Contemplation: the Way of Liberation*. Garden City, N.Y.: Doubleday.

Dunn, James D. G.
1987 "The Problem of Pseudonymity." In *The Living Word*, by James D. G. Dunn, 65-85. London: SCM.

Edwards, Mark J., ed.
1999 *Galatians, Ephesians, Philippians*. Ancient Christian Commentary on Scripture. New Testament, 8. Downers Grove, Ill.: InterVarsity.

Elias, Jacob W.
  1995   *1 and 2 Thessalonians*. Believers Church Bible Commentary.
         Scottdale, Pa.: Herald Press.
Eller, David B., ed.
  1990   *Servants of the Word: Ministry in the Believers' Church*. Elgin,
         Ill.: Brethren Press.
Eller, Vernard
  1987   *Christian Anarchy: Jesus' Primacy over the Powers*. Grand
         Rapids: Eerdmans.
Elliott, John H.
  1981   *A Home for the Homeless: A Sociological Exegesis of 1 Peter,
         Its Situation and Strategy*. Philadelphia: Fortress.
Elliot, Neil
  1994   *Liberating Paul: The Justice of God and the Politics of the
         Apostle*. Maryknoll, N.Y.: Orbis.
Ellul, Jacques
  1973   *Prayer and Modern Man*. Trans. C. Edward Hopkin. New York:
         Seabury.
  1976   *The Ethics of Freedom*. Trans. Geoffrey W. Bromiley. Grand
         Rapids: Eerdmans.
Emonds, Hilarius
  1938   "Geistlicher Kriegsdienst: Der Topos der militia spiritualis in
         der antiken Philosphie." In *Heilige Überlieferung: Ausschnitte
         aus der Geschichte des Mönchtums und des heiligen Kultes*,
         21-50. Münster: Aschendorffsche Verlagsbuchhandlung. Repr. in
         *Militia Christi: Die christliche Religion und der Soldatenstand
         in den ersten drei Jahrhunderten*, ed. Adolf von Harnack, 133-
         62. Tübingen: Mohr, 1905; and Darmstadt: Wissenschaftliche
         Buchgesellschaft, 1963.
Esau, John A.
  1995   "Recovering, Rethinking, and Re-imagining: Issues in a Mennonite
         Theology for Christian Ministry." In *Understanding Ministerial
         Leadership: Essays Contributing to a Developing Theology of
         Ministry*, ed. John A. Esau, 1-27. Text Reader Series, 6. Elkhart,
         Ind.: Institute of Mennonite Studies.
Esau, John A., ed.
  1995   *Understanding Ministerial Leadership: Essays Contributing
         to a Developing Theology of Ministry*. Text Reader Series, 6.
         Elkhart, Ind.: Institute of Mennonite Studies.
Fee, Gordon D.
  1987   *The First Epistle to the Corinthians*. Grand Rapids: Eerdmans.
  1994   *God's Empowering Presence: The Holy Spirit in the Letters of
         Paul*. Peabody, Mass.: Hendrickson.
Finger, Thomas N.
  1985   *Christian Theology: An Eschatological Approach*. Vol. 1.
         Nashville: Thomas Nelson; Scottdale, Pa.: Herald Press, 1987.
  1989   *Christian Theology: An Eschatological Approach*. Vol. 2.
         Scottdale, Pa.: Herald Press.
Finger, Thomas, and Willard M. Swartley
  1988   "Bondage and Deliverance: Biblical and Theological Perspectives."
         In *Essays on Spiritual Bondage and Deliverance*, ed. Willard

M. Swartley, 10-38. Occasional Papers, No. 11. Elkhart, Ind.: Institute of Mennonite Studies.

Fischer, Karl-Martin
1973 *Tendenz und Absicht des Epheserbriefs.* FRLANT, 3. Göttingen: Vandenhoeck & Ruprecht.

Fitzmyer, Joseph A.
1989 "Another Look at *Kephalē* in 1 Corinthians 11:3." *New Testament Studies* 35/4:503-11.

Foerster, Werner
1964 "*Eirēnē,* . . . *Eirēnopoios.*" *TDNT,* 2:400-20.
1972-74 *Gnosis.* 2 vols. Oxford: Clarendon.

Foulkes, Francis
1989 *Ephesians.* Rev. ed. Tyndale New Testament Commentaries. Grand Rapids: Eerdmans; Leister, England: Inter-Varsity.

France, R. T.
1995 *Women in the Church's Ministry: A Test Case for Biblical Interpretation.* Grand Rapids: Eerdmans.

Gallardo, José
1984 "Ethics and Mission." In *Anabaptism and Mission,* ed. Wilbert R. Shenk, 137-57. Institute of Mennonite Studies; Missionary Studies, 10. Scottdale, Pa.: Herald Press.

Geddert, Timothy J.
2000 *Mark.* Believers Church Bible Commentary. Scottdale, Pa.: Herald Press.

Gnilka, Joachim
1971 *Der Epheserbrief.* Freiburg: Herder.

Goodspeed, E. J.
1933 *The Meaning of Ephesians.* Chicago: Univ. of Chicago Press. Repr., 1956.

Greeven, Heinrich
1967 "*Palē.*" *TDNT,* 5:721.

Grenz, Stanley J., with Denise Muir Kjesbo
1995 *Women in the Church: A Biblical Theology of Women in Ministry.* Downers Grove, Ill.: InterVarsity.

Grimsrud, Ted, and Loren L. Johns, eds.
1999 *Peace and Justice Shall Embrace: Power and Theopolitics in the Bible.* Festschrift for Millard Lind; Telford, Pa.: Pandora Press U.S.; Scottdale, Pa.: Herald Press.

Gross, Leonard, translator and editor
1997 *Prayer Book for Earnest Christians.* Scottdale, Pa.: Herald Press.

Grudem, Wayne
1985 "Does *Kephalē* ('Head') Mean 'Source' or 'Authority over' in Greek Literature? A Survey of 2,336 Examples." *Trinity Journal* 6:38-59.

Grundmann, Walter
1964 "*Dunamai.* . . ." *TDNT,* 2:284-317.
1965 "*Ischuō.* . . ." *TDNT,* 3:397-402.
1971 "*Stēkō, Histēmi.*" *TDNT,* 7:636-53.
1972 "*Tapeinos.* . . ." *TDNT,* 8:1-29.

Guthrie, Donald
    1990 *New Testament Introduction.* Rev. ed. Downers Grove, Ill.: InterVarsity.

Gwyn, Douglas, George Hunsinger, Eugene F. Roop, and John H. Yoder
    1991 *A Declaration on Peace: In God's People the World's Renewal Has Begun.* Scottdale, Pa.: Herald Press.

Hamilton, Victor P.
    1992 "Satan." *ABD,* 5:985-89.

Hanson, Paul D.
    1975 *The Dawn of Apocalyptic.* Philadelphia: Fortress.
    1992 "Apocalypses and Apocalypticism: *The Genre* and *Introductory Overview.*" *ABD,* 1:279-82.

Harnack, Adolf von
    1963 *Militia Christi: Die christliche Religion und der Soldatenstand in den ersten drei Jahrhunderten.* Tübingen: Mohr. 1905. Repr., Darmstadt: Wissenschaftliche Buchgesellschaft.

Hauerwas, Stanley, Chris K. Huebner, Harry J. Huebner, and Mark Thiessen Nation, eds.
    1999 *The Wisdom of the Cross: Essays in Honor of John Howard Yoder.* Grand Rapids: Eerdmans.

Hay, David M.
    1973 *Glory at the Right Hand: Psalm 110 in Early Christianity.* SBLMS, 18. Nashville: Abingdon.

Hays, Richard B.
    1996 *The Moral Vision of the New Testament: Community, Cross, New Creation: A Contemporary Introduction to New Testament Ethics.* San Francisco: HarperSanFrancisco.

HBD   Paul J. Achtemeier et al., eds.
    1985 *Harper's Bible Dictionary.* San Francisco: Harper & Row.

Heggen, Carolyn Holderread
    1993 *Sexual Abuse in Christian Homes and Churches.* Scottdale, Pa.: Herald Press.
    1996 "Religious Beliefs and Abuse." In *Women, Abuse, and the Bible: How Scripture Can Be Used to Hurt or to Heal,* ed. Catherine Clark Kroeger and James R. Beck, 15-27. Grand Rapids: Baker Books.

Hendrix, Holland
    1988 "On the Form and Ethos of Ephesians." *Union Seminary Quarterly Review* 42:3-15.

Hennecke, Edgar
    1964 *New Testament Apocrypha.* Vol. 2: *Writings Relative to the Apostles; Apocalypses and Related Subjects.* Ed. Wilhelm Schneemelcher. English trans. ed. R. McL. Wilson, 1965. Philadelphia: Westminster.

Hiebert, Theodore
    1986 *God of My Victory: The Ancient Hymn in Habakkuk 3.* HSM, 38. Atlanta: Scholars Press.
    1992 "Warrior, Divine." *ABD,* 6:876-80.

Holmes, Michael W., ed., rev.
1999 *The Apostolic Fathers: Greek Texts and English Translations.*
Updated ed. Grand Rapids: Baker Books.
Houlden, J. L.
1977 *Paul's Letters from Prison: Philippians, Colossians, Philemon,
and Ephesians.* Westminster Pelican Commentaries. Philadelphia:
Westminster.
Huebner, Harry
1997 "Church Discipline: Is It Still Possible?" In *Naming the Sheep:
Understanding Church Membership: Voices in Dialogue,* ed.
Resources Commission, Conference of Mennonites in Canada,
89-94. Winnipeg: Resources Commission, Conference of
Mennonites in Canada.
Huebner, Harry, and David Schroeder
1993 *Church as Parable: Whatever Happened to Ethics?* Winnipeg:
CMBC Publications.
HWB
1992 *Hymnal: A Worship Book.* Prepared by Churches in the
Believers Church Tradition. Elgin, Ill.: Brethren Press; Newton,
Kan.: Faith & Life Press; Scottdale, Pa.: Mennonite Publishing
House.
IDB
1962 *The Interpreter's Dictionary of the Bible.* Ed. George A.
Buttrick. 4 vols. Nashville: Abingdon.
IDB Suppl.
1976 *The Interpreter's Dictionary of the Bible.* Supplementary vol-
ume. Ed. Keith Grim. Nashville: Abingdon.
Janzen, Waldemar
1982 *Still in the Image: Essays in Biblical Theology and Anthropology.*
Institute of Mennonite Studies Series, 6. Newton, Kan.: Faith &
Life Press; Winnipeg: CMBC Publications.
Jeremias, Joachim
1964 "Akrogōniaios." *TDNT,* 1:792.
1967 "Lithos . . . ." *TDNT,* 4:268-80.
Jeschke, Marlin
1983 *Believers Baptism for Children of the Church.* Scottdale, Pa.:
Herald Press.
Jewett, Paul K.
1975 *Man as Male and Female: A Study in Sexual Relationships
from a Theological Point of View.* Grand Rapids: Eerdmans.
Johnson, Elizabeth E.
1992 "Ephesians." In *The Women's Bible Commentary,* ed. Carol A.
Newsom and Sharon H. Ringe, 338-42. Louisville: Westminster
John Knox.
Käsemann, Ernst
1961 "Das Interpretationsproblem des Epheserbriefes." *Theologische
Literaturzeitung* 86:1-8.
Kennedy, George A.
1984 *New Testament Interpretation Through Rhetorical Criticism.*
Chapel Hill: Univ. of North Carolina Press.

Kimel, Alvin F., ed.
1992   *Speaking the Christian God: The Holy Trinity and the Challenge of Feminism*. Grand Rapids: Eerdmans.

Kirby, J. C.
1968   *Ephesians, Baptism and Pentecost: An Inquiry into the Structure and Purpose of the Epistle to the Ephesians*. London: SPCK.

Kitchen, Martin
1994   *Ephesians*. New York: Routledge.

Klassen, William
1984   *Love of Enemies: The Way to Peace*. Philadelphia: Fortress.
1992   "Peace: New Testament." *ABD*, 5:207-12.
1992a "War in the NT." *ABD*, 6:867-75.

Koester, Helmut
1979   "1 Thessalonians—Experiment in Christian Writing." *In Continuity and Discontinuity in Church History: Essay Presented to George Hunston Williams*, ed. F. Forrester Church and Timothy George, 33-44. Leiden: Brill.
1982   *Introduction to the New Testament*. Vol. 1: *History, Culture, and Religion of the Hellenistic Age*. Philadelphia: Fortress.
1982a *Introduction to the New Testament*. Vol. 2: *History and Literature of Early Christianity*. Philadelphia: Fortress.

Koontz, Gayle Gerber
1987   "The Trajectory of Feminist Conviction." *Conrad Grebel Review* 5:201-20. Repr. in *Essays on Peace Theology and Witness*, ed. Willard M. Swartley, 1988:154-78. Occasional Papers, 12. Elkhart, Ind.: Institute of Mennonite Studies.
1988   "Response to Timothy M. Warner." In *Essays on Spiritual Bondage and Deliverance*, ed. Willard M. Swartley, 89-99. Occasional Papers, 11. Elkhart, Ind.: Institute of Mennonite Studies.
1992   "Redemptive Resistance to Violation of Women: Christian Power, Justice, and Self-Giving Love." In *Peace Theology and Violence Against Women*, ed. Elizabeth G. Yoder, 27-47. Occasional Papers, 16. Elkhart, Ind.: Institute of Mennonite Studies.

Kreider, Alan
1999   *The Change of Conversion and the Origin of Christendom*. Harrisburg, Pa.: Trinity Press International.

Kroeger, Catherine Clark
1987   "The Classical Concept of Head as 'Source.'" In *Equal to Serve: Women and Men in the Church and Home*, ed. Gretchen Gaebelin Hull, 267-83. Old Tappan, N.J.: Revell.

Kroeger, Catherine Clark, and James R. Beck, eds.
1996   *Women, Abuse, and the Bible: How Scripture Can Be Used to Hurt or to Heal*. Grand Rapids: Baker Books.

Kuemmerlin-McLean, Joanne K.
1992   "Demons: Old Testament." *ABD*, 2:138-40.

Kuhn, Karl Georg
1968   "The Epistle to the Ephesians in the Light of the Qumran Texts." In *Paul and Qumran: Studies in New Testament Exegesis*, ed. J. Murphy-O'Connor, 111-8. Chicago: Priory Press.

Layton, Bentley
    1987 *The Gnostic Scriptures.* Garden City, N.Y.: Doubleday.
Lebold, Ralph
    1986 *Learning and Growing in Ministry: A Handbook for Congregational Leaders.* Scottdale, Pa.: Mennonite Publishing House.
Liddell and Scott Henry George Liddell and Robert Scott
    1940 *A Greek-English Lexicon.* 9th ed. Oxford: Clarendon Press.
Lincoln, Andrew T.
    1990 *Ephesians.* Word Biblical Commentary. Dallas: Word Books.
Lind, Millard C.
    1980 *Yahweh Is a Warrior: The Theology of Warfare in Ancient Israel.* Scottdale, Pa.: Herald Press.
Lindemann, Andreas
    1975 *Die Aufhebung der Zeit: Geschichtsverständnis und Eschatologie im Epheserbrief.* Gütersloh: Gerd Mohn.
    1985 *Der Epheserbrief.* Zürcher Bibelkommentare NT, 8. Zurich: Theologischer Verlag.
Loewen, Howard John
    1994 "An Analysis of the Use of Scripture in the Churches' Documents on Peace." In *The Church's Peace Witness,* ed. Marlin E. Miller and Barbara Nelson Gingerich, 15-69. Grand Rapids: Eerdmans.
Lührmann, Dieter
    1980 "Neutestamentliche Haustafeln und antike Ökonomie." *New Testament Studies* 27:83-97.
Lund, Nils Wilhelm
    1942 *Chiasmus in the New Testament: A Study in Formgeschichte.* Chapel Hill, N.C.: Univ. of North Carolina Press.
McAlpine, Thomas H.
    1991 *Facing the Powers: What Are the Options?* Monrovia, Calif.: MARC.
McClain, George D.
    1998 *Claiming All Things for God: Prayer, Discernment, and Ritual for Social Change.* Nashville: Abingdon.
McClendon, James Wm., Jr.
    1986 *Systematic Theology,* Vol. 1: *Ethics.* Nashville: Abingdon.
    1994 *Systematic Theology.* Vol. 2: *Doctrine.* Nashville: Abingdon.
MacDonald, Margaret
    1988 *The Pauline Churches.* Cambridge: Cambridge Univ. Press.
McGill, Arthur C.
    1982 *Suffering: A Test of Theological Method.* 1968. Repr., Philadelphia: Westminster.
Macgregor, G. H. C.
    1954 "Principalities and Powers: The Cosmic Background of Saint Paul's Thought." *New Testament Studies* 1:17-28.
Malherbe, Abraham J.
    1983 "Antisthenes and Odysseus, and Paul at War." *Harvard Theological Review* 76:143-73.
Martin, Ernest D.
    1993 *Colossians, Philemon.* Believers Church Bible Commentary. Scottdale, Pa.: Herald Press.

Martin, Ralph P.
  1968 "An Epistle in Search of a Life-Setting." *Expository Times* 79:296-302.
  1991 *Ephesians, Colossians, and Philemon.* Interpretation. Atlanta: John Knox.
Mauser, Ulrich
  1992 *The Gospel of Peace: A Scriptural Message for Today's World.* Studies in Peace and Scripture (IMS), 1. Louisville: Westminster John Knox.
Meade, David
  1986 *Pseudonymity and Canon.* Grand Rapids: Eerdmans.
Meeks, Wayne A.
  1983 *The First Urban Christians: The Social World of the Apostle Paul.* New Haven: Yale Univ. Press.
Mendenhall, George E.
  1962 "Election." *IDB,* 2:76-82.
  1962b "Predestination." *IDB,* 3:869.
Menno Simons
  1956 *The Complete Writings of Menno Simons.* Trans. Leonard Verduin. Ed. J. C. Wenger. Scottdale, Pa.: Herald Press.
Metzger, Bruce M.
  1972 "Literary Forgeries and Canonical Pseudepigrapha." *Journal of Biblical Literature* 91:3-24.
Michaelis, Wilhelm
  1965 "*Kratos. . . .*" *TDNT,* 3:905-15.
  1967 "*Machaira.*" *TDNT,* 4:524-27.
  1967 "*Methodeia.*" *TDNT,* 5:102-3.
Michel, Otto
  1967 "*Oikos. . . .*" *TDNT,* 5:119-59.
Miletic, Stephen Francis
  1988 "*One Flesh*": Eph. 5.22-24, 5.31: Marriage and the New Creation.* Analecta Biblica, 115. Rome: Editrice Pontificio Istituto Biblico.
Miller, John W.
  1989 *Biblical Faith and Fathering: Why We Call God "Father."* New York: Paulist.
  1999 *Calling God "Father": Essays on the Bible, Fatherhood, and Culture.* Rev. ed. of 1989 vol. New York: Paulist.
Miller, Marlin E.
  1979 "The Gospel of Peace." In *Mission and the Peace Witness,* ed. Robert L. Ramseyer, 9-23. Scottdale, Pa.: Herald Press.
Miller, Marlin E., and Barbara Nelson Gingerich, eds.
  1994 *The Church's Peace Witness.* Grand Rapids: Eerdmans.
Miller, Melissa A.
  1994 *Family Violence: The Compassionate Church Responds.* Waterloo, Ont.: Herald Press.
Mitton, C. L.
  1951 *The Epistle to the Ephesians: Its Authorship, Origin and Purpose.* Oxford: Clarendon.

Munro, Winsome
    1983   *Authority in Paul and Peter: The Identification of a Pastoral Stratum in the Pauline Corpus and 1 Peter.* Cambridge: Cambridge Univ. Press.

Murphy, Nancey, Brad J. Kallenberg, and Mark Thiessen Nation, eds.
    1997   *Virtues and Practices in the Christian Tradition: Christian Ethics After MacIntyre.* Harrisburg, Pa.: Trinity Press International.

Murphy, Roland E.
    1992   "Wisdom in the OT." *ABD,* 6:920-31.

Murphy-O'Connor, Jerome
    1979   *1 Corinthians.* Wilmington, Del.: Michael Glazier.

Mussner, Franz
    1955   *Christus, das All und die Kirche.* Trier: Paulus.

Myers, Ched
    1981   "Armed with the Gospel of Peace: The Vision of Ephesians." *Theology, News and Notes* 28:17-24.

Nickelsburg, George W. E.
    1972   *Resurrection, Immortality, and Eternal Life in Intertestamental Judaism.* HTS, 26. Cambridge: Harvard Univ. Press.

Oepke, Albrecht
    1964   "*En.*" *TDNT,* 2:537-44.

Oepke, Albrecht, and Karl Georg Kuhn
    1967   "*Hoplon . . .*" *TDNT,* 5:292-315.

Ollenburger, Ben C.
    1987   *Zion, the City of the Great King: A Theological Symbol of the Jerusalem Cult.* JSOTSup, 41. Sheffield, U.K.: JSOT.
    1988   "The Concept of 'Warrior God' in Peace Theology." In *Essays on Peace Theology and Witness,* ed. Willard M. Swartley, 112-27. Occasional Papers, 12. Elkhart, Ind.: Institute of Mennonite Studies.
    1994   "Peace and God's Action Against Chaos in the Old Testament." In *The Church's Peace Witness,* ed. Marlin E. Miller and Barbara Nelson Gingerich, 70-88. Grand Rapids: Eerdmans.

Page, Sydney H. T.
    1995   *Powers of Evil: A Biblical Study of Satan and Demons.* Grand Rapids: Baker Books.

Patrick, Dale
    1992   "Election: Old Testament." *ABD,* 2:434-41.

Patzia, Arthur G.
    1990   *Ephesians, Colossians, Philemon.* New International Biblical Commentary. Peabody, Mass.: Hendrickson Publishers.
    1995   *The Making of the New Testament: Origin, Collection, Text and Canon.* Downers Grove, Ill.: InterVarsity.

Penner, Carol
    1992   "Content to Suffer: An Exploration of Mennonite Theology from the Context of Violence Against Women." In *Peace Theology and Violence Against Women,* ed. Elizabeth G. Yoder, 99-111. Occasional Papers, 16. Elkhart, Ind.: Institute of Mennonite Studies.

Penner, Erwin
    1990   *The Power of God in a Broken World: Studies in Ephesians.* Luminaire Studies. Winnipeg: Kindred.

Perkins, Pheme
    1997   *Ephesians.* ANTC. Nashville: Abingdon.
Pfammatter, Josef
    1987   *Epheserbrief/Kolosserbrief.* Die Neue Echterbibel: Neues Testament. Würzburg: Echter.
Pfitzner, Victor G.
    1967   *Paul and the Agon Motif: Traditional Athletic Imagery in the Pauline Literature.* NovTSuppl., 16. Leiden: Brill.
Pokorny, Petr
    1965   *Der Epheserbrief und die Gnosis: Die Bedeutung des Haupt-Gliedergedankens in der entstehenden Kirche.* Berlin: Evangelische Verlagsanstalt.
Quell, Gottfried
    1967   "Eklegomai. . . ." *TDNT,* 4:145-68.
Rad, Gerhard von
    1991   *Holy War in Ancient Israel.* Trans. Marva J. Dawn. Grand Rapids: Eerdmans.
Ramseyer, Robert L.
    1979   "Mennonite Missions and the Christian Peace Witness." In *Mission and the Peace Witness,* ed. Robert L. Ramseyer, 114-34. Scottdale, Pa.: Herald Press.
    1984   "The 'Great *Century'* Reconsidered." In *Anabaptism and Mission,* ed. Wilbert R. Shenk, 178-87. Institute of Mennonite Studies, Missionary Studies, 10. Scottdale, Pa.: Herald Press.
Ramseyer, Robert L., editor
    1979   *Mission and the Peace Witness.* Scottdale, Pa.: Herald Press.
Reese, David George
    1992   "Demons: *New Testament." ABD,* 2:140-42.
Resources Commission, Conference of Mennonites in Canada, ed.
    1997   *Naming the Sheep: Understanding Church Membership: Voices in Dialogue.* Winnipeg: Resources Commission, Conference of Mennonites in Canada.
Richards, Kent Harold
    1992   "Bless/Blessing." *ABD,* 1:753-55.
Roetzel, Calvin J.
    1983   "Jewish Christian-Gentile Christian Relations: A Discussion of Ephesians 2, 15a." *Zeitschrift für neutestamentliche Wissenschaft* 4:81-89.
    1998   *The Letters of Paul: Conversations in Context.* 4th ed. Louisville: Westminster John Knox.
Robinson, James M., director
    1988   *The Nag Hammadi Library in English.* 3d ed. Trans. members of the Coptic Gnostic Library Project of the Institute for Antiquity and Christianity. New York: Harper & Row.
Roon, A. van
    1974   *The Authenticity of Ephesians.* Leiden: Brill.
Rubinkiewicz, Richard
    1975   "Ps LXVIII 19 (=Eph IV 8). Another Textual Tradition or Targum?" *Novum Testamentum* 17:219-24.

Rudolph, Kurt
1983   *Gnosis: The Nature and History of Gnosticism.* Trans. Robert McLachlan Wilson. San Francisco: Harper & Row.
1992   "Gnosticism." *ABD,* 2:1033-40.
Russell, Letty M.
1984   *Imitators of God: A Study Book on Ephesians.* New York: Mission Education and Cultivation Program Dept., General Board of Global Ministries.
1985   "Authority and the Challenge of Feminist Interpretation." In *Feminist Interpretation of the Bible,* ed. Letty M. Russell, 137-46. Philadelphia: Westminster.
Sanders, Jack T.
1971   *The New Testament Christological Hymns: Their Historical and Religious Background.* SNTSMS, 15. Cambridge: Cambridge Univ. Press.
Sawatsky, Rodney J.
1995   "Ministerial Status and the Theology of Ministry." In *Understanding Ministerial Leadership: Essays Contributing to a Developing Theology of Ministry,* ed. John A. Esau, 40-6. Text Reader Series, 6. Elkhart, Ind.: Institute of Mennonite Studies.
Sawatsky, Rodney J., and Scott Holland, eds.
1993   *The Limits of Perfection: A Conversation with J. Lawrence Burkholder.* Kitchener, Ont.: Pandora.
Schertz, Mary H.
1992   "Creating Justice in the Space Around Us: Toward a Biblical Theology of Peace Between Women and Men." In *Peace Theology and Violence Against Women,* ed. Elizabeth G. Yoder, 5-24. Occasional Papers, 16. Elkhart, Ind.: Institute of Mennonite Studies.
1992a   "Nonretaliation and the Haustafeln in 1 Peter." In *The Love of Enemy and Nonretaliation in the New Testament,* ed. Willard M. Swartley, 258-86. Studies in Peace and Scripture (IMS), 3. Louisville: Westminster John Knox.
Schlier, Heinrich
1961   *Principalities and Powers in the New Testament.* Trans. from German. Freiburg: Herder; London: Nelson.
1965   "Kephalē...." *TDNT,* 3:673-82.
1971   *Der Brief an die Epheser: Ein Kommentar.* 7th ed. Düsseldorf: Patmos.
Schmidt, Karl Ludwig
1965   "Kaleō...." *TDNT,* 3:487-536.
Schmitz, Otto
1967   "Parakaleō and Paraklēsis in the NT." *TDNT,* 5:793-99.
Schnackenburg, Rudolf
1991   *Ephesians: A Commentary.* Trans. Helen Heron. Edinburgh: T & T Clark.
Schneider, Johannes
1964   "Erchomai...." *TDNT,* 2:666-75.

Scholer, David M.
   1996   "The Evangelical Debate over Biblical 'Headship.'" In *Women, Abuse, and the Bible: How Scripture Can Be Used to Hurt or to Heal,* ed. Catherine Clark Kroeger and James R. Beck, 28-57. Grand Rapids: Baker Books.

Schrage, Wolfgang
   1974/75 "Zur Ethik der neutestamentlichen Haustafeln." *New Testament Studies* 21:1-22.

Schrenk, Gottlob
   1964   "*Dikē. . . .*" *TDNT,* 2:178-225.
   1967   "*Eklegomai. . . .*" *TDNT,* 4:168-192.

Schroeder, David
   1959   "Die Haustafeln des Neuen Testaments: Ihre Herkunft und ihr theologischer Sinn." D.Theol. diss., Hamburg Univ.
   1976   "Lists, Ethical." *IDB Suppl.,* 546-47.
   1990   "Once Your Were No People. . . ." In *The Church as Theological Community: Essays in Honour of David Schroeder,* ed. Harry Huebner, 37-65. Winnipeg: CMBC Publications.
   1993   "Binding and Loosing: Church and World." In *Church as Parable: Whatever Happened to Ethics?* by Harry Huebner and David Schroeder. Winnipeg: CMBC Publications.

Schüssler Fiorenza, Elisabeth
   1983   *In Memory of Her: A Feminist Theological Reconstruction of Christian Origins.* New York: Crossroad.

Schüssler Fiorenza, Elisabeth, ed.
   1994   *Searching the Scriptures.* Vol. 2: *A Feminist Commentary.* New York: Crossroad.

Schweizer, Eduard
   1961   "Die Kirche als Leib Christi in den paulinischen Antilegomena." *Theologische Literaturzeitung* 86:241-56.
   1972   "*Huios, Huithesia.*" *TDND,* 8:334-99.
   1982   *The Letter to the Colossians: A Commentary.* Trans. Andrew Chester. Minneapolis: Augsburg.

Shenk, Wilbert R., ed.
   1983   *Exploring Church Growth.* Grand Rapids: Eerdmans.
   1984   *Anabaptism and Mission.* Institute of Mennonite Studies, Missionary Studies, 10. Scottdale, Pa.: Herald Press.

Shillington, George V.
   1998   *2 Corinthians.* Believers Church Bible Commentary. Waterloo, Ont.: Herald Press.

Shogren, Gary S.
   1992   "Election: *New Testament.*" *ABD,* 2:441-44.

Sider, Ronald J.
   1993   *One-Sided Christianity? Uniting the Church to Heal a Lost and Broken World.* Grand Rapids: Zondervan.

Simons   *See* Menno

Smith, Derwood C.
   1973   "The Two Made One: Some Observations on Eph. 2:14-18." *Ohio Journal of Religious Studies* 1:34-54.

Smyth, Herbert Weir
1956   *Greek Grammar.* Ed. Gordon M. Messing. Cambridge: Harvard
        Univ. Press.
Snyder, C. Arnold
1992   "An Anabaptist Vision for Peace: Spirituality and Peace in Pilgram
        Marpeck." *Conrad Grebel Review* 10/2:187-203.
Steinmetz, Franz-Joseph
1969   *Protologische Heilszuversicht: Die Strukturen des soteri-
        ologischen und christologischen Denkens im Kolosser- und
        Epheserbrief.* FTS, 2. Frankfurt: Josef Knecht.
Stowers, Stanley K.
1986   *Letter Writing in Greco-Roman Antiquity.* Library of Early
        Christianity, 5. Philadelphia: Westminster.
1992   "Letters: *Greek and Latin Letters.*" *ABD*, 4:290-93.
Stuhlmacher, Peter
1981   "'Er ist unser Friede' (Eph 2,14). Zur Exegese und Bedeutung
        von Eph 2,14-18." In *Versöhnung, Gesetz und Gerechtigkeit:
        Aufsätze zur biblischen Theologie,* ed. Peter Stuhlmacher.
        Göttingen: Vandenhoeck & Ruprecht.
Swain, Lionel
1980   *Ephesians.* New Testament Message, 13; Wilmington, Del.:
        Michael Glazier.
Swartley, Willard M.
1983   *Slavery, Sabbath, War, and Women: Case Issues in Biblical
        Interpretation.* Scottdale, Pa.: Herald Press.
1990   "God as Father: Patriarchy or Paternity?" *Daughters of Sarah,*
        Nov.-Dec.: 12-14.
1994   *Israel's Scripture Traditions and the Synoptic Gospels: Story
        Shaping Story.* Peabody, Mass.: Hendrickson Publishers.
1996   "War and Peace in the New Testament." *Aufstieg und Niedergang
        der römischen Welt,* II.26.3:2298-408.
2000   "Discipleship and Imitation of Jesus/Suffering Servant: The
        Mimesis of New Creation." In *Violence Renounced: René
        Girard, Biblical Studies, and Peacemaking,* ed. Willard M.
        Swartley, 218-45. Studies in Peace and Scripture (IMS), 4.
        Telford, Pa.: Pandora Press U.S.; Scottdale, Pa.: Herald Press.
Swartley, Willard M., ed.
1988   *Essays on Spiritual Bondage and Deliverance.* Occasional
        Papers, 11. Elkhart, Ind.: Institute of Mennonite Studies.
1988a   *Essays on Peace Theology and Witness.* Occasional Papers, 12.
        Elkhart, Ind.: Institute of Mennonite Studies.
1992   *The Love of Enemy and Nonretaliation in the New Testament.*
        Studies in Peace and Scripture (IMS), 3. Louisville: Westminster
        John Knox.
Tanzer, Sarah J.
1994   "Ephesians." In *Searching the Scripture.* Vol. 2: *A Feminist
        Commentary,* ed. Elizabeth Schüssler Fiorenza, 325-48. New
        York: Crossroad.
TDNT   Ed. G. Kittel et al.
1964-76   *Theological Dictionary of the New Testament.* 9 vols. Trans.
          and ed. G. W. Bromiley. Grand Rapids: Eerdmans.

Thistlethwaite, Susan Brooks
  1985   "EveryTwoMinutes: BatteredWomenandFeminist Interpretation."
          In *Feminist Interpretation of the Bible,* ed. Letty M. Russell,
          96-107. Philadelphia: Westminster.
Thomson, Ian H.
  1995   *Chiasmus in the Pauline Letters.* JSNTSS, 111. Sheffield, U.K.:
          Sheffield Academic Press.
Thurston, Bonnie
  1995   *Reading Colossians, Ephesians, and 2 Thessalonians: A
          Literary and Theological Commentary.* New York: Crossroad.
Toews, J. B.
  1993   *A Pilgrimage of Faith: The Mennonite Brethren Church in
          Russia and North America 1860-1990.* Winnipeg: Kindred.
Trobisch, David
  1994   *Paul's Letter Collection: Tracing the Origins.* Minneapolis:
          Fortress.
Urbrock, William J.
  1992   "Blessings and Curses." *ABD,* 1:755-61.
Verner, D. C.
  1993   *The Household of God: The Social World of the Pastoral
          Epistles.* Chico, Calif.: Scholars Press.
Volf, Miroslav
  1996   *Exclusion and Embrace: A Theological Exploration of Identity,
          Otherness, and Reconciliation.* Nashville: Abingdon.
Von Rad   *See* Rad
Wagner, C. Peter
  1988   *The Third Wave of the Holy Spirit.* Ann Arbor, Mich.: Vine
          Books.
Wagner, C. Peter, ed.
  1991   *Engaging the Enemy: How to Fight and Defeat Territorial
          Spirits.* Ventura, Calif.: Regal Books.
Waltner, Erland
  1999   "1 Peter." In *1-2 Peter, Jude,* by Erland Waltner and J. Daryl
          Charles. Believers Church Bible Commentary. Scottdale, Pa.:
          Herald Press.
Warner, Timothy M.
  1988   "An Evangelical Position on Bondage and Exorcism." In *Essays
          on Spiritual Bondage and Deliverance,* ed. Willard M. Swartley,
          77-88. Occasional Papers, 11. Elkhart, Ind.: Institute of Mennonite
          Studies.
  1991   *Spiritual Warfare: Victory over the Powers of This Dark World.*
          Wheaton, Ill.: Crossway Books.
Weiser, Artur
  1968   "Pisteuō. . . ." *TDNT,* 6:174-228.
Wenger, J. C.
  1954   *Introduction to Theology: A Brief Introduction to the Doctrinal
          Content of Scripture Written in the Anabaptist-Mennonite
          Tradition.* Scottdale, Pa.: Herald Press.
Wengst, Klaus
  1987   *Pax Romana and the Peace of Jesus Christ.* Philadelphia:
          Fortress.

Westermann, Claus
    1992 "Peace (Shalom) in the Old Testament." In *The Meaning of Peace: Biblical Studies,* ed. Perry B. Yoder and Willard M. Swartley, 16-48. Louisville: Westminster John Knox.

Wiens, Devon
    1967 "Holy War Theology in the New Testament and Its Relationship to the Eschatological Day of the Lord Tradition." Ph.D. diss., Univ. of Southern California.

Wild, Robert A.
    1984 "The Warrior and the Prisoner: Some Reflections on Ephesians 6:10-20." *Catholic Biblical Quarterly* 46:284-98.
    1985 "'Be Imitators of God': Discipleship in the Letter to the Ephesians." In *Discipleship in the New Testament,* ed. Fernando F. Segovia, 127-43. Philadelphia: Fortress.

Windisch, Hans
    1925 "Friedensbringer—Gottessöhne." *Zeitschrift für die neutestamentliche Wissenschaft* 24:240-60.

Wink, Walter
    1984 *Naming the Powers: The Language of Power in the New Testament.* The Powers, 1. Philadelphia: Fortress.
    1986 *Unmasking the Powers: The Invisible Forces That Determine Human Existence.* The Powers, 2. Philadelphia: Fortress.
    1992 *Engaging the Powers: Discernment and Resistance in a World of Domination.* The Powers, 3. Minneapolis: Fortress.
    1998 *The Powers That Be: Theology for a New Millennium.* New York: Doubleday.
    1998a *When the Powers Fall: Reconciliation in the Healing of Nations.* Minneapolis: Fortress.

Wordelman, Amy L.
    1992 "Everyday Life: Women in the Period of the New Testament." In *The Women's Bible Commentary,* ed. Carol A. Newsom and Sharon H. Ringe, 390-6. Louisville: Westminster John Knox.

Yarbro Collins, Adela
    1992 "Apocalypses and Apocalypticism: Early Christian." *ABD,* 1:288-92.

Yoder, Elizabeth G., ed.
    1992 *Peace Theology and Violence Against Women.* Occasional Papers, 16. Elkhart, Ind.: Institute of Mennonite Studies.

Yoder, John Howard
    1964 *The Christian Witness to the State.* Newton, Kan.: Faith & Life. Repr., Eugene, Ore.: Wipf and Stock, 1997.
    1972 *The Legacy of Michael Sattler.* Scottdale, Pa.: Herald Press.
    1979 "The Contemporary Evangelical Revival and the Peace Churches." In *Mission and the Peace Witness,* ed. Robert L. Ramseyer, 68-103. Scottdale, Pa.: Herald Press.
    1983 "The Social Shape of the Gospel." In *Exploring Church Growth,* ed. Wilbert R. Shenk, 277-84. Grand Rapids: Eerdmans.
    1985 *He Came Preaching Peace.* Scottdale, Pa.: Herald Press.
    1987 *The Fullness of Christ: Paul's Vision of Universal Ministry.* Elgin, Ill.: Brethren Press.

1990   "The One or the Many? The Pauline Vision and the Rest of the Reformation." In *Servants of the Word: Ministry in the Believers' Church,* ed. David B. Eller, 51-64, with responses by Gerald T. Sheppard and Luke L. Keefer Jr. Elgin, Ill.: Brethren Press.

1992   *Body Politics: Five Practices of the Christian Community Before the Watching World.* Nashville: Discipleship Resources. Repr., Scottdale, Pa.: Herald Press, 2001.

1994   *The Politics of Jesus.* 2nd ed. Grand Rapids: Eerdmans.

1994a   *The Royal Priesthood: Essays Ecclesiological and Ecumenical.* Grand Rapids: Eerdmans. Repr., Scottdale, Pa.: Herald Press, 1998.

1997   "Practicing the Rule of Christ." In *Virtues and Practices in the Christian Tradition: Christian Ethics After MacIntyre,* ed. Nancey Murphy, Brad J. Kallenberg, and Mark Thiessen Nation. Harrisburg, Pa.: Trinity Press International.

1997a   *For the Nations: Essays Evangelical and Public.* Grand Rapids: Eerdmans.

Yoder, Perry B.

1986   *Shalom: The Bible's Word for Salvation, Justice, and Peace.* Newton, Kan.: Faith & Life.

Yoder, Perry B., and Willard M. Swartley, eds.

1992   *The Meaning of Peace: Biblical Studies.* Studies in Peace and Scripture (IMS), 2. Louisville: Westminster John Knox. Rev. ed. with changed pagination, Elkhart, Ind.; Institute of Mennonite Studies, 2001.

Yoder Neufeld, Thomas R.

1989   "Christian Counter Culture: Ecclesia and Establishment." *Mennonite Quarterly Review* 63/2:193-209.

1990   "Paul, Women, and Ministry in the Church." *Conrad Grebel Review* 8:289-99.

1993   "'Bound by Peace' (Ephesians 4:3): The Reconciliation of Divergent Traditions in Ephesians." *Conrad Grebel Review* 11/3:211-32.

1997   *"Put On the Armour of God": The Divine Warrior from Isaiah to Ephesians.* JSNTSS, 140; Sheffield, U.K.: Sheffield Academic Press.

1999   "Power, Love, and Creation: The Mercy of the Divine Warrior in the Wisdom of Solomon." In *Peace and Justice Shall Embrace: Power and Theopolitics in the Bible,* ed. Ted Grimsrud and Loren L. Johns, 174-91. Festschrift for Millard Lind. Telford, Pa.: Pandora Press U.S.; Scottdale, Pa.: Herald Press.

1999a   "Natural Church Development and the New Testament: Comparison and Assessment." *Mission Focus: Annual Review* 7:69-82 (issue has further articles on an "Anabaptist Look at Natural Church Development," by Ronald W. Waters and Lois Barrett).

2000   "Anastatic Anabaptists: Made Alive and Empowered to Preach Peace." *Vision: A Journal for Church and Theology* 1/1:57-65.

Zerbe, Gordon

1994   Response to Yoder Neufeld's "Bound by Peace" (see under Yoder Neufeld). *Conrad Grebel Review* 12/1:89-95.

Selected Resources

General Resources

Brown, Raymond E. *An Introduction to the New Testament.* New York: Doubleday, 1997. Excellent on Ephesians and related topics.

Patzia, Arthur G. *The Making of the New Testament: Origin, Collection, Text and Canon.* Downers Grove, Ill.: InterVarsity, 1995. An evangelical scholar's excellent introduction to critical issues on the origin of NT documents, including Ephesians.

Guthrie, Donald. *New Testament Introduction.* Rev. ed. Downers Grove, Ill.: InterVarsity, 1990. A conservative scholar who doubts that pseudepigraphy is found in the NT.

Focused Studies

Arnold, Clinton E. *Ephesians: Power and Magic: The Concept of Power in Ephesians in Light of Its Historical Setting.* SNTS MS, 63. Cambridge Univ. Press, 1989. Grand Rapids: Baker Book House, 1997. Evangelical scholar treats issues of spiritual power/s. Also wrote *Powers of Darkness: Principalities and Powers in Paul's Letters.* Downers Grove, Ill.: InterVarsity Press, 1992.

Fee, Gordon D. *God's Empowering Presence: The Holy Spirit in the Letters of Paul.* Peabody, Mass.: Hendrickson 1994. An eminent evangelical Pentecostal scholar exegetes passages relevant to the Holy Spirit in Paul's letters, including Ephesians.

Grenz, Stanley J., with Denise Muir Kjesbo. *Women in the Church: A Biblical Theology of Women in Ministry.* Downers Grove, Ill.:

InterVarsity, 1995. From an evangelical biblical perspective, forceful defense of women's role in the ministry of the church.

McAlpine, Thomas H. *Facing the Powers: What Are the Options?* Monrovia, Calif.: MARC, 1991. Incisive analysis of interpretations of the powers; calls for holistic reading of Bible.

Schüssler Fiorenza, Elisabeth. *In Memory of Her: A Feminist Theological Reconstruction of Christian Origin.* New York: Crossroad, 1983. A classic feminist interpretation of NT; influential discussion of the Household Code as a retreat from the radicalism of Jesus and early church.

Yoder, John Howard. *The Politics of Jesus.* 2d ed. Grand Rapids: Eerdmans, 1994. A milestone in Mennonite theology, ethics, and biblical studies; relevant on the powers and subordination.

Commentaries

Barth, Markus. *Ephesians.* 2 vols. Garden City, N.Y.: Doubleday, 1974. A mine of information and theologically informed opinion; still widely used. Insists Paul is author of Ephesians.

Best, Ernest. *Ephesians.* ICC. Edinburgh: T & T Clark, 1998. Cf. *Essays on Ephesians.* Edinburgh: T & T Clark, 1997. Sees Ephesians shifting focus from world mission to inner-directed concerns for church preservation and order—differing from interpretation given in this commentary.

Lincoln, Andrew T. *Ephesians.* WBC. Dallas: Word Books, 1990. Still the best commentary on Ephesians. Represents critical and evangelical sensibilities; technically and theologically satisfying.

Martin, Ralph P. *Ephesians, Colossians, and Philemon.* Interpretation. Atlanta: John Knox, 1991. Lively, engaging, for preachers-teachers, by a leading evangelical biblical scholar.

Penner, Erwin. *The Power of God in a Broken World: Studies in Ephesians.* Luminaire Studies. Winnipeg: Kindred, 1990. A pastorally perceptive commentary by a Mennonite Brethren Scholar.

Perkins, Pheme *Ephesians.* ANTC. Nashville: Abingdon, 1997. Concise, lucid, and particularly useful in identifying links between Ephesians and the Dead Sea Scrolls.

Russell, Letty M. *Imitators of God: A Study Book on Ephesians.* New York: Mission Education and Cultivation Program Dept., General Bd. of Global Ministries, 1984. A leading feminist scholar connects scholarship to the real life of believers.

Schnackenburg, Rudolf. *Ephesians.* Trans. Helen Heron. Edinburgh: T & T Clark, 1991. With the best of European Catholic scholarship, treats the history of interpretation over the millennia.

Index of Ancient Sources

The Author

Tom Yoder Neufeld was born in Winnipeg, Manitoba, and grew up in German-speaking Europe, where his parents spent many years in church ministry. After Yoder Neufeld returned to North America in 1964, he attended Mennonite Brethren colleges in California and Manitoba, then in 1970 graduated from the University of Manitoba with a B.A. Hon. in History. He studied at Harvard Divinity School on a Rockefeller Fellowship and earned an M.Div. there in 1973.

In following years, Yoder Neufeld was involved in ministry with Native Canadians in Winnipeg's inner city, in prison and hospital chaplaincy, and with pastoring a Mennonite congregation in the northern mining town of Thompson, Manitoba. Then he spent an intense year of study at Associated Mennonite Biblical Seminary, Elkhart, Indiana, where he met his wife-to-be, Rebecca Yoder.

He returned to graduate studies at Harvard Divinity School in 1980 and in 1983 began teaching New Testament and Peace Studies at Conrad Grebel College, affiliated with the University of Waterloo in Ontario. He and Rebecca were married in 1983. He finished his Th.D. program at Harvard in 1989. In 1997, Sheffield Academic Press published his dissertation on Ephesians 6 and its biblical background: *'Put On the Armour of God!' The Divine Warrior from Isaiah to Ephesians.*

Yoder Neufeld's work on this commentary began in earnest during a sabbatical year of 1990-91 in Jerusalem and Elkhart. Because of teaching and administrative duties, work on the commentary awaited further brief leaves in Waterloo and Guatemala City.

Tom Yoder Neufeld is director of Graduate Theological Studies at

Conrad Grebel College. His first love remains teaching and preaching. Singing and watercolor painting are rare but treasured pleasures. Tom, Rebecca, and their children, Miriam and David, are part of First Mennonite Church, Kitchener, Ontario, where Rebecca was until recently pastor to Hispanic members.